Michael T.

African Systems of Thought

General Editors
Charles S. Bird
Ivan Karp

Contributing Editors
James Fernandez
Luc de Heusch
John Middleton
Victor Turner
Roy Willis

ALLEGORIES
of the
WILDERNESS

*Ethics and Ambiguity
in Kuranko Narratives*

Michael Jackson

INDIANA UNIVERSITY PRESS
Bloomington

Manufactured in the United States of America

Library of Congress Cataloging in Publication Data

Jackson, Michael, 1940–
  Allegories of the wilderness

  (African systems of thought)
  Bibliography: p.
  Includes index.
  1. Kuranko (African people)—Folklore. 2. Tales—
Sierra Leone—History and criticism. 3. Kuranko (African
people) 4. Story-telling—Sierra Leone. I. Title.
II. Series
GR352.32.K87J3   398.2'0966'4   81-47772
                        AACR2

1 2 3 4 5 86 85 84 83 82

ISBN 0-253-30471-7

We now find that mythology also conceals an ethical system, but one which, unfortunately, is far more remote from our ethic than its logic is from our logic.

—CLAUDE LÉVI-STRAUSS (1978:507)

. . . ambiguity is of the essence of human existence, and everything we live or think has always several meanings.

—MAURICE MERLEAU-PONTY
(1962:169)

The allegorization of myth is hampered by the assumption that the explanation 'is' what the myth 'means'. A myth being a centripetal structure of meaning, it can be made to mean an indefinite number of things, and it is more fruitful to study what in fact myths have been made to mean.

—NORTHROP FRYE (1966:341)

Contents

Preface

The research which culminates in the publication of a book is always linked to a hidden biography in which chronology is irrelevant, and to a unique society which appears on no map and has no single language. During the years it takes for a book to be researched and written, and out of all the conversations, journeys, and observations necessary for the realization of such a project, this biography and this society are being made. The biography includes moments from the lives of many people whose paths cross fortuitously and whose contacts with one another often remain indirect. The society is a true kindred, for it has reality only through the individual who occasions its emergence, and he too in turn is a part of an infinity of encounters and reflections. These tangential worlds which emerge in the process of creating domains of knowledge are neither utterly incidental nor completely insignificant, for long after a book is written or an interpretation decided upon, they remain, on the verge of articulation, as memories whose strenth derives perhaps from the fact that they have never been hammered into shape or brought forward for general scrutiny. These fields of knowledge, created in passing as it were, might provide the raw material for other books and interpretations, and so create in their turn further subsidiary domains lying beyond what is immediately understood. But we choose to retain some aspects of these inchoate areas, and so prevent the regression of absurdities which occurs when meaning seeks to prevail over that which suggests its possibility.

These glimpses . . .

A night in Kabala in February 1972. I am lying in the darkness of my room, thinking of home. Gbongbon, like myself a stranger to the house, keeps me awake for hours and distracts me from my melancholy as she regales a score of children in the adjoining room with stories about Hare and Hyena. Her voice seems to fill the space under the tin roof and drift through the walls of the house. The next night I persuade her to tell more stories. A crowd from the neighborhood gathers on the porch under a full moon. Gbongbon's vivacity and gaiety belie the domestic unhappiness which has made her decide to leave her home village for a while and seek refuge among us. Singing the narrative songs, dancing about in order to excite the enthusiasm of the children, hitching her sleeping child up in the *lapa* which enfolds it on her back, breaking into another story as soon as one is finished, beaming and giggling as she relates the hilarious adventures of Hare and Hyena, she entertains us for the entire evening and leaves me with one of the most vivid and lasting memories of that time.

Another night now. I am in Kondembaia on one of my frequent visits to Keti Ferenke Koroma. As indefatigable as ever, he challenges me to stay all night and listen to his stories. The room is filled with people of all ages. Years later I will recall the suffocating musty odor of the closed room, the crumbling mud plaster of the walls, the guttering candle and the steady half-moon flame of the Coleman lamp, a child coughing, the laughter and eager comments, and Keti Ferenke's wry expression and occasional chuckle as he spellbinds us with one of his remarkable yarns.

And the mellifluence and poignancy of Kenya Fina as she relates the story of Na Nyale; the somber passion of Kumba Doron, whose flute trilled and warbled to summon the djinn from the blind bush . . .

I wonder were they right, these narrators, when they disclaimed any part in the authorship of the tales they told? For in doing so might not they be respecting the curious bond and sense of fellowship which art creates in people whose cultural backgrounds are diverse and whose languages are mutually unintelligible? Like Valéry, Rimbaud, and Shelley, who also disowned the importance of individual authorship and of particular cultural and historical settings, these Kuranko artists intimate the profound kinship of all poets. And there is, in these observations, a way in which I too have been able to think about the strong sense of identification which I feel toward the Kuranko storytellers and their works. Sinkari Yegbe once remarked to me, "The stories are for everyone, for adults and children alike." In my view it is the universality of these narratives, both within Kuranko culture and within the wider world, which it is our task to fathom.

If this book reflects a hidden biography and an anonymous kindred, then it is to this milieu that the book properly belongs. But in seeming to disclaim authorship of a work which bears my name, I simply wish to acknowledge the people and events which inspired it and made its realization possible. I wish to record here the names of Keti Ferenke Koroma, Kenya Fina Marah, Konde Karifa Koroma, Sulimani Koroma, Kumba Doron Sise, Sinkari Yegbe Sise, Denka Marah, Kanku Pore Kargbo, Abdul Marah, Saran Salia Sano, Bundo Mansare, Duwa Marah, Morowa Marah, Fore Kargbo, the late chief Pore Kargbo of Kamadugu Sukurela, the late Alpha Kargbo II, and chief Sewa Marah of Barawa section, to signify my gratitude for having had the opportunity to explore their world in such hospitable circumstances. My wife, my daughter, and myself owe a great deal to the Honorable Sewa B. Marah, Minister of Energy and Power, for his generous help during all our visits to Sierra Leone. I also wish to acknowledge my profound debt to Noah Bokari Marah, my field assistant, teacher, and friend throughout the period of my fieldwork.

The first period of my fieldwork (1969–70) was funded by the Nuffield Foundation. Further work was made possible by a travel grant from the British Universities Travel Association and by a Henry Ling Roth Fellowship awarded by the Faculty of Archaeology and Anthropology at the University of Cambridge (1972). Fieldwork in 1979 was carried out during sabbatical leave from Massey University, New Zealand. I would like to record my gratitude to Professor Derek Freeman and members of the Department of Anthropology at the Australian National University; tenure of a visting fellowship at the A.N.U. in the summer of 1977–78 enabled me to complete a first draft of this book under very convivial conditions. Thanks are also due to Ivan Karp and Charles Bird for invaluable advice and suggestions while I was preparing the manuscript for publication.

A NOTE ON ORTHOGRAPHY

I have not used diacritical marks or phonetic orthography in this book. As a general rule, 'u', 'i', and 'a' have continental values; 'o' is usually open (ɔ) but 'e', which is usually open (ɛ) is closed (é) at the end of words (e.g. *fɛlé* = fetish; *dɛmbaiyé* = family). Among the consonants, 'g' is hard except after open 'o' and 'or' where it has the phonetic value 'ɣ' (e.g. *morɣo* = person; *numorɣo* = joking partner). Elision of vowels to facilitate fluency is common in Kuranko speech. I have sometimes recognized such elisions, particularly in songs, by using an apostrophe. Plural is formed with the suffix *nu*, but in some instances it has seemed less cumbersome to pluralize by using Roman 's' (e.g. *jelibas*; *finabas*).

1 *Introduction*

This book is an interpretative study of 230 Kuranko narratives which I recorded during the course of anthropological fieldwork in northern Sierra Leone, 1969–70, 1972, 1979. The publication of these narratives was anticipated in an earlier volume which presents a general ethnographical account of Kuranko society (Jackson, 1977b). The orientation of that work was structuralist in method and existentialist in design. I sought to bring into relief that Kuranko world view, and I endeavored to show how the Kuranko address themselves to and resolve quotidian problems. There as elsewhere my aim has been to understand how people decide and make their own destinies within a social and historical context which has already been made by others at other times and demands only eternal recapitulation. The present work is a continuation of that project.

This is first of all a study of the ways in which Kuranko oral narratives facilitate the resolution of various ethical problems which arise in everyday life. Obviously these ethical problems emerge in particular social and personal situations. Yet it is remarkable how the resolution of these problems frequently entails a treatment of issues of choice, judgment, and values which leads us to consider matters far removed from the immediate domains of Kuranko experience and concern. We will be led to explore Kuranko concepts of morality and notions of the person, as well as the relationship between orthodox and fictional images of the world. We will thus proceed through the analysis of a corpus of Kuranko texts to examine the ways in which literature is a mode of moral inquiry. I hope to show that at least one genre of fiction—the folktale—can be understood as a technique for investigating problems of correct action and moral discernment. It is not merely a naive vehicle for advancing orthodox moral attitudes. My argument is that literature calls into question beliefs and values which are ordinarily taken for granted. Literature transfigures the commonplace and inspires the lis-

I

tener or reader to take a decisive attitude toward existence. But to encourage this kind of engagement, narratives of all kinds must use techniques which hold orthodox meanings in abeyance and secure the imaginative participation of the listener or reader. I will show that a key technique is contrived ambiguity.[1]

Kuranko narratives establish an initial situation which is ambiguous. The boundaries which ordinarily define significant social categories or groups are blurred. Distinctions are annulled. Symbols that are usually kept apart are merged. This deliberate and systematic obfuscation generates ethical dissonance; it heightens affect, increases anxiety, promotes ambivalent attitudes, and inspires the listeners to reduce the ambiguity. I take the view that Kuranko narratives initiate a dialectic of doubt and certainty. The narratives dramatize uncertainty, promote ambivalence, and exploit ambiguity as ways of stimulating the listeners to resolve problems of choice by arriving at judgments which, finally, everyone can agree on. Ethologists have shown that rituals are elaborate programs for the reduction of ambiguity (Cullen, 1966:363–374; Erikson, 1966:339; Rappaport, 1971:27), and I maintain that literature has the same implicit design.

This work is informed by an existentialist approach to literature. I have endeavored to break away from the formalist approaches which have lately dominated the anthropological study of myth, and I have eschewed narrowly textual and ethnographical analysis. It is my view that the creative and ethical domains of human social existence demand our attention, and this book is an attempt to explore those domains. I share Sartre's view that "through literature the collectivity turns to reflection and mediation; it acquires an unhappy consciousness, an unstable image of itself which it seeks to modify and improve" (Sartre, 1949:316). The storyteller, like the writer, reveals people to themselves and to their possibilities. Hazel Barnes has noted that for Sartre "literature is preoccupied with the relation between what man *is* and what he is choosing to make of himself within the historical perspective. Man cannot choose his age, but he must choose himself within it" (Barnes, 1961:13). Through their oral narratives the Kuranko reflect upon customs and values which are ordinarily not brought into discussion. They do not choose to change these customs or revise these values, but they choose the manner in which they realize them and the meaning they make of them. It is this interplay between givenness and possibility which is one of my main themes. The narratives mediate a change in experience, so that people actually participate in interpreting and constructing their social milieu, or in recognizing themselves and their own lives within the fixed forms of things and of laws. Like rituals, which overthrow the ordinary world only in order to reconstruct it, the narratives are the theatrical setting in which the Kuranko make and remake their world, not through passive consent or violent domination but through shared endeavor. In storytelling sessions each person makes the world over to himself.

The organization of the book is as follows. First, I present an ethnographical outline of Kuranko society and a survey of Kuranko morality and concepts of the person. Second, I discuss aspects of form, context, and authorship. I have drawn extensively on many studies in the ethnography of speaking, partly because I think it imperative that we avoid any inadvertent domination of the world of preliterate sensibilities by the modes of abstract analysis developed in literate cultures. Third, the narratives are presented in major sets in order to facilitate discussion of the themes and issues with which they are concerned. Each chapter thus contains a set of narratives, prefaced by an introductory essay and followed by an analytical commentary. It will become clear that each set of narratives announces a major ethical theme: problems of mutuality and of justice (chapters 3 and 4), the ethical ambiguity of extraordinary talents (chapters 4 and 6), the conflict between the generations (chapter 5), reciprocity and the ethics of friendship (chapters 5 and 6), problems of fidelity, trust, love, and marriage (chapters 7 and 8). While the thematic aspects of the study are summarized in chapter 8, a concluding chapter explores some of the more general implications of the work, notably the relationships between forms of thought and patterns of social life.

Of the 230 narratives recorded in the field, only 38 are published here. Space precluded a more extensive collection of texts, and it was found that many narratives could be adequately summarized or referred to in passing. The selection of narratives does not, therefore, imply a distorted view of the corpus, since I have made sure that every narrative is faithfully represented in the interpretative portions of the book.

Methods of Collection and Translation

When I began my research among the Kuranko in December 1969 I set myself the task of recording a substantial number of their oral nar-

ratives. This project reflected my long-standing interest in oral literature. But I quickly discovered that the narratives were invaluable aids
to learning the language and broadening my knowledge of its idioms. I
also used narratives as springboards for discussion on the topics and
problems raised by them. I came to realize that the stories could be
used, as the Kuranko themselves appeared to use them, as means of
opening up discussion on moral issues. The narratives provided a kind
of respite from conventional formulations. They became, therefore, not
only a subject of study; they were part of a method of study, an essential element of my fieldwork practice.

Most Kuranko people, old and young alike, have a great enthusiasm
for listening to stories. Storytelling is the most vital of all Kuranko arts.
I am sure that there are many hundred more narratives in the Kuranko
corpus than I was able to record. Keti Ferenke Koroma used to chal-
lenge me that he could tell more stories than I could record, and he
would enjoy ribbing me that I would not be able to stay awake long
enough to hear the stories he had to tell in a single night. In a storytelling session, the narrator does not cease until his audience has drifted
away or fallen asleep, and one has the impression, at least when a
skilled narrator is in charge, that the repertoire is infinite and inexhaust-
ible. Considerable prestige attaches to a narrator who can continue telling stories without pause, and at times, especially when young men get
together to tell stories, a competitive element prevails and quantity becomes more important than quality. Even so, it is clear from the collection I made that stories are sometimes repeated. It could also be argued
that many narratives are variations on the same theme, and that if all
Kuranko narratives were reduced to their basic plots the imaginative
resourcefulness of the literature would seem illusory. However, I hope
to show that variation and elaboration are just as significant as underlying structures and recurring schemas. Creative variation enables a narrator to retain at all times an element of surprise and suspense, even
though, from an objective point of view, the same story is being repeated. Individual elaboration also affords each narrator an opportunity
for assuming command over the tale he tells, even though he must not
appear to be projecting private meanings into it. In recording variants
and repetitions of stories, I have tried to throw light on this relative
semiotic freedom of the narratives and to show how they always remain
open to interpretation.

The trinary structure of episodes, for example, is not merely a device for maximizing information transfer by increasing redundancy. This structure is not a way of putting across a preordained set of meanings. It consists of a sequence of crises and surprises, not of tautologies, and although the trinary schema recurs in innumerable stories, the significance of actual episodes reflects changes in the underlying context of the story. Perhaps the most important context is the context of narration. This consists of a unique interaction between the storyteller and his audience, and the meaning of the story emerges from this interaction. It is not inherent in the story itself. It is because no two audiences are ever the same, and because each narrator brings his own style to the stories he tells, that it can be said that no tale is ever told twice. Any narrative is thus both familiar and unique. It is the original element in the storytelling sessions which explains why people never tire of hearing the same stories over and over again.

I restricted the number of stories I collected, not because I believed it possible to gather a "representative sample," nor because I found any redundancy in the meanings which emerged during storytelling sessions or in conversations with informants. The limited number of narratives in my collection reflects choices I made to balance my time and energies between different research projects, as well as various technical considerations. For instance, the labor of translating and recording commentaries on stories led me to restrict the number of stories I actually taped. Again, in publishing narratives one must make a selection from a corpus which is already a selection. My collection of stories betrays the interests of those who told them, the preferences of those who gathered to listen to them, my own intellectual interests, problems encountered in translation, and the circumstances of my fieldwork. The collection thus affords us insight not into *the* Kuranko world, but into *a* Kuranko world. Just as each narrative is a version of a world which is always part imagined, part real, so too my account of the narratives must be judged provisional and partly conjectural.

The Kuranko have a passionate interest in storytelling, and I was never at a loss for stories to record and talk about. I could suggest a venue for a storytelling session and there would always be a crowd eager to attend. Indeed, so enthusiastic and boisterous were some of the crowds that tape-recording became impossible. I found it best to record stories in sessions set up by a narrator in his own house, or in sessions arranged on the spur of the moment. My cassette tape recorder (a Philips portable) was at first an object of curiosity, but people soon got used to it and it could be concealed in the gloomy corner of a room or house veranda. My own presence was also made less obtrusive by the dim ambience of hurricane lanterns, smoke, candles, or moonlight. Moreover, once a narrator had captured the attention of his audience, such distractions of the night as a crying child, a coughing infant, or a domestic altercation would not break the spell he had created.

I tape-recorded eleven complete storytelling sessions. All these sessions were occasioned by my presence in the community and my interest in recording stories. Yet none were inauthentic or regarded by local people as artifical. In addition to these sessions, I taped several narratives which Denka Marah told during two visits to our house in Kabala. When Keti Ferenke Koroma visited us in Kabala in July 1970 he also recorded several stories. On these occasions there was no audience and the recording was done, contrary to convention, in the daytime. My field assistant, Noah Marah, related a few stories to me in English, and I recorded the occasional story as it arose out of conversations with villagers. Of the total number of narratives collected, thirteen were written by Kuranko pupils from the Kabala Secondary School after I had expressed an interest in receiving written folktales.

When we had recorded a number of stories, my field assitant and I began the task of translating them. We worked in the evenings, by the light of a hurricane lamp, when it was cool and quiet. Noah would play back a 5- to 8-second snatch of a story and we would then discuss ways of rendering it simply and accurately into English. I would write down a provisional translation, with marginal annotations, and then we would repeat the procedure with another snatch of the narrative. Occasionally we would make a complete transcription in Kuranko. (In order that the reader may evaluate the relationship between the English translation and the vernacular, I have included one of these transcribed texts as an Appendix.)

We were determined to retain as much of the Kuranko imagery and figurative language as possible, and we avoided English idioms and metaphors if they had no exact Kuranko equivalents. We also tried to preserve the rapid, exclamatory style of Kuranko narration, and we resisted the temptation to use English adjectives to qualify such habitual sentence beginnings as "He said" or "They said." As a result, the narrator's verbal dramatizations and tone of voice tend to be lost in translation. We also decided not to use paraphrasing or alter the actual sequence of narration in order to make better sense of or improve upon a narrator's actual delivery. One way of giving verisimilitude to our translations was to keep the sung portions of the stories in the vernacular and to use Kuranko ideophones wherever they occurred.

Anthropology is itself a science of translation which brings into sharp relief the indeterminate character of the relationship between observer and observed. In translating the narratives, Noah and I were keenly aware that we were also interpreters. Moreover, when we examined the remarks and commentaries given by storytellers and by those who had listened to the stories we recorded, it became clear that the narratives could not be understood apart from the interpretative acts of others. We were mindful, therefore, that there were no determinate meanings to be isolated and decoded. For the same reason, we decided that a published collection of the stories without any commentary would be totally unacceptable.

In our editorial work we made a distinction between focal and subsidiary meanings. Focal meanings are readily given to a story by the narrator or by informants, whereas subsidiary meanings are far more idiosyncratic and less easily spelled out. We have not ignored focal meanings or omitted exegetical asides when these occur in the course of a narrative. As for subsidiary meanings, these tend to arise out of the unique relationship between the anthropologist and the people he lives with. As such, these meanings are a synthesis of quite different traditions of thought. They constitute a form of guesswork, an appraisal of observations, comments, and intuitions. It goes without saying that Kuranko storytelling exists outside this domain of meaning, though it is inseparable from the focal meanings found within Kuranko discourse.

There is one class of narratives which is not well represented in this book, namely those narratives which Kuranko call *kuma kore* ("old talk" or "venerable speech") or *bimba kumenu* ("ancestral words"). *Kuma kore* includes oral histories of clanship and settlement, legends about heroes, and mythological accounts of the beginning of the world. These narratives are "charter myths" in the Malinowskian sense of the term (1963:249–250). They "justify by precedent" and supply a "retrospective pattern of moral values, sociological order, and magical belief" (Malinowski, 1974:146). I hope to publish a collection and study of these narratives at another time.

Another kind of narrative which I have largely excluded from this collection is the simple etiological or moral fable. These stories are invariably brief and make some moral point without equivocation. They provide pat answers to naive questions about the causes of various observed phenomena:

Why people blow their noses
Why herbivores avoid carnivores
How fishing began
Why the soldier ants are so called
Why the *fole* fish is hard to catch
Why fishing expeditions are not announced publicly
Why mosquitoes bother people
Why the swallow flies as it does
Why the chameleon moves as it does
Why cockroaches fear chickens
Why mice fear cats
Why baboons fear dogs
Why old women do not go fishing

Fables of this kind are comparable to, and may originate in, the illustrative examples which people use in everyday conversation when stressing some point. Parents use such stories to satisfy a child's curiosity, not to initiate further inquiry. The stories assign rather whimsical causes and tend to quash or trivialize deeper concern about the meaning of things.

Kuranko Social Organization: An Outline

The Kuranko are a Mande-speaking people who occupy the foothills and margins of the western and northwestern Guinea Highlands. The Kuranko population is widely distributed throughout Upper Guinea and, in Sierra Leone, is concentrated in the Koinadugu district in the northeast. Kuranko culture is heterogeneous and represents the merging of different "nuclear Mande" groups who settled or conquered the present areas of Kuranko hegemony from as long ago as the late seventeenth century. Much of the variability of contemporary traditions attests to these diverse origins.

Most Kuranko acknowledge and know something of their Mande heritage. The vicissitudes of their history are, moreover, reflected in clan narratives and chiefly traditions. The names of heroes and rulers of Mande, such as Mari Yata (Sunjata), Sumunguru, and Mansa Muse, are sometimes alluded to in narratives as well as in genealogies and praise songs recited by bards. The impact of Islam is shown in the narratives by occasional references to God (*Ala* or *Altala*), by a tendency to equate Mande with Eden, and by episodes which relate Islamic figures to Mande heroes. But the kind of record left to posterity by scholars such as Ibn Battuta is never found in the Kuranko chronicles; rather, we find an idealized and systematized version of the past, including real as well as conjectured events, made to meet the needs of the present rather than any standard of verisimilitude.

Kuranko livelihood is based upon the shifting cultivation of upland rice. Secondary crops such as cassava, millet, sweet potatoes, cocoyams, okra, sesame, groundnuts, maize, and tomatoes are intercultivated or grown in gardens around the villages. The upland rice farms are sited up to five miles from a village, on steep slopes cleared from dense bush. Farming is labor-intensive and bush-clearing, hoeing, and harvesting are done by cooperative groups known as *kerenu.* Recruitment to a *kere* is not based on kinship. Friendship and neighborhood ties determine the composition of the group. Each farm supports one family. The household head (*bontigi:* "house owner") supervises and plans the farmwork, chooses the varieties of rice to be planted, and manages the distribution, storage, and consumption of the rice. Rice is the staple crop. It is synonymous with food, and is respected above all other foodstuffs. The division of labor between the sexes is based upon an association of rice with men, subsidiary crops with women. Furthermore, the words *kore* and *kine* (uncooked and cooked rice respectively) also mean "elder" and "senior" in social contexts.

Because many farms are several miles from a village, individual families often build and live in a farmhouse during the growing season. Children keep vigil by day to keep birds from the maturing grain. Weeding, trap-making, fence-building, and gardening occupy much of the adults' time. The alternating pattern of wet and dry seasons imposes significant contrasts upon Kuranko social life. The hard work, isolation, and hunger associated with the growing season (particularly the period toward the end of the rains) are contrasted with the leisure, festivity, and abundance of food that characterize the dry season. A complex of physical, climatic, social, and emotional contrasts, drawn from ecological circumstances, underlies the organization of Kuranko rituals and narratives, providing their key images and settings.

One of the most visible and fundamental of these contrasts is that between town (*sue*) and bush (*fira*). Kuranko towns and villages are typically compact and populous (between 500 and 1,000 people). Each community is surrounded by a landscape of elephant grassland and orchard bush, interrupted by lines of low hills, lateritic tablelands, and granite inselbergs. In the more mountainous parts of the interior of Koinadugu, villages tend to be smaller. Paths through the dense forest debouch into a clearing where one finds a hamlet of ten or twelve farmhouses. The bush into which hunters venture and into which farmers must go each year is a domain of uncertainty and danger. Inhabited by wild animals, such as leopards, elephants, buffaloes, and snakes, and by capricious spirits (*nyenne*), the bush is nevertheless the source of one's livelihood. The bush farms yield food, and the forests provide game, as well as herbs for medicinal and culinary use. The bush is regarded ambivalently. Persons, objects, and settings which stand on the borderline between town and bush occur frequently in the narratives. They signify the point at which unruly natural power (*suwaga*) encounters secular power (*noe*), and where solitary endeavor departs from the constraints of communal enterprise. The force of these contrasts is also felt in the ritual of initiation (*biriye*). The transformation of irresponsible, amoral children into responsible moral adults is accomplished during a perod of sequestration in a "bush house," the *fafei*. The return of the neophytes to town signals the completion of this process, and the *fafei* is burned to the ground.

The Kuranko area is often referred to as the *ferensola* (lit. "town of twins"), signifying the theme of unity in difference. The *ferensola* is divided into several chiefdoms, many of which were amalgamated by the British in the 1920s. Each chiefdom is ruled by a paramount chief. Within the chiefdom different towns and hamlets are governed by town chiefs, most of whom belong to the same clan as the paramount. Politico-jural control within the community is in the hands of the chief and his council of elders (or "big men"). The elders represent every clan and and major subclan (*kebile*) in the community.

The community lacks any overall cohesiveness in terms of descent. There is no corporate lineage system, and the various clans in any village have diverse origins, traditions, customs, and religious affiliations. While some clans are staunchly Muslim, others remain free from Islam. While some clans belong to the ruling estate, others are commoners or are classed as *nyemakale*. The *nyemakale* estate includes the *jeli* clans (*jeliba*s are xylophonists and praise-singers to the chiefs) and the *fina*s (who are the bards, genealogists, and orators for ruling families). The integration of the local community is founded on factors other than kinship and descent: neighborhood and friendship networks, often organized as work cooperatives, play an important part in economic life; many craft specializations, such as weaving, blacksmithing, carpentry, leatherworking, and hunting, are learned through apprenticeships and are nonhereditary; cult associations based on sex and age distinctions cut across descent and estate boundaries; rites of passage, the settlement of disputes, and sacrifices all engage the interest and participation of the whole community.

The ethic of kinship amity is expressed through symbols which allow the fusing of kinship and neighborhood ties. For example, there is a general tendency for the same totemic usages to be respected by different clans resident in the same village. Furthermore, interclan joking partnerships or alliances tend to arise among the various clans resident in the same village. Both totemic usages and interclan joking alliances are said to have originated, long ago, in certain altruistic acts. The recollection of these ancestral, and apocryphal, events, and the adoption of the symbol of another clan's identity, are marks of respect, indications that the other is to be regarded as if he were a kinsman.

These approaches to the problem of establishing communitas, of transcending differences which exist given at the levels of kinship, descent, and estate, are, however, transitory and artificial. As for the integrative effects of intermarriage, these are offset by divorces and by recurring misunderstandings between affines. Inescapable distinctions exist between rulers and commoners, between kinsmen and neighbors, between villagers and strangers, between countrymen and enemies. And the social order depends upon the systematic elaboration of other distinctions too: between agnatic and uterine kin, between close and distant kin, between the old and the young, and between men and women. I have elsewhere described the oscillations between these various polarizations (some abstract, some particular) as a "dialectic of identification" (Jackson, 1977b:238).

A Kuranko village comprises several compound or ward areas known as *luiye*s.[2] A *luiye* consists of five to fifteen houses grouped in a semicircle around a courtyard. Each house faces the *luiye*; the back of the house opens onto an enclosed yard called the *sundu kunye ma*. In this area are the cooking hearths, outhouses, and rubbish heaps. While the *luiye*-side of the house, including the front rooms, is associated with men, the *sundu kunye ma* and the *sundu konkonu* (back room) are associated with women. A strict sexual division of labor is maintained within the household, and a strict division exists between "male" and "female" areas of the house. Although children generally have a free run of the house, men and women neither eat together nor sit together in public.

This distinction between male and female domains (*ke dugu* and *musu dugu* respectively) pervades every sector of Kuranko social life. The village stream is divided into "male" and "female" stretches; a woman is separated from men during sickness or confinement; cult sacra, meeting places, and performances are taboo to members of the opposite sex; sexual intercourse at the wrong time or in the wrong place is subject to both secular and supernatural punishments. Paternal and maternal roles in child-rearing are different and complementary: the paternal role connotes jural authority, discipline, provision of food, and social identifications; the maternal role connotes emotional attachment, personal care, and nurturance. In the Kuranko view, the identity of the child is determined, biologically and jurally, by the father. The mother is simply the passive vessel in which the male seed develops after implantation, and from which the child is born. Nevertheless, the destiny and personality of the child are influenced by the ways in which the mother raises it and by her behavior toward her husband. This is because the blessings of the child's agnatic forebears, upon which its destiny largely depends, are mediated by the mother. If a woman dishonors her husband or fails in her marital and conjugal duties, then the "path" of these blessings becomes "blocked" and the child suffers.

Each *luiye* in the village ideally comprises close agnates. In reality, actual sons and brothers of the *lutigi* (*luiye* headman) seldom reside together; most *luiye*s are made up of classificatory agnates, their wives and children, matrikin, and, perhaps, strangers. The residential pattern reflects the Kuranko emphasis on goodwill and cooperation among *luiye* members. Tensions between men and their adult sons may be relieved when the sons leave home, take up residence in another *luiye*, and gain a measure of self-sufficiency by making their own farms. Residential separation also tends to mitigate the tensions that sometimes develop between brothers. Similar factors underlie the pattern of household composition. Most households comprise a man, his wife (or wives), and their unmarried dependent children. Other people attached to the household, either temporarily or semipermanently, include fostered classificatory sons and daughters, dependent classificatory brothers and sisters, visiting kin, and perhaps an elderly widowed mother or grandmother.

The considerable variability of Kuranko residence patterns reflects the extent to which Kuranko men can choose where and with whom they wish to live. This freedom of choice can be related to several factors (apart from the emphasis placed upon amity among *luiye* and household members): land is not owned by the kinship group and, since land is nonhereditable, property and inheritance considerations do not make a man beholden to his senior agnates; land for farming is readily available if a man does not mind cutting himself off from his community in order to establish a farm hamlet in the bush; bridewealth can be amassed by seeking the help of a maternal uncle or by working abroad for wages. Residential separations also tend to reflect the tensions and rivalries that characterize the relationship between half brothers and between ortho-cousins. The distinction between uterine siblings (*na keli meenu*, lit. "mother one persons") and nonuterine siblings (*fa keli meenu*, lit. "father one persons") is of profound importance. It indicates the contrast between the emotional unity of siblings who have the same mother and the merely formal identifications denoted by common agnatic descent. The latent hostility and competitiveness of *fadenye* (the relationship between nonuterine siblings) are usually explained by reference to the latent hostility and competitiveness of co-wives. These tensions among co-wives in turn reflect inequalities of position and advantage within the household, or jealousies arising from the husband's favoritism.

Kuranko marriage preferences and strategies are regarded as ways of extending and affirming amity. Thus, sororal polygyny is said to prevent co-wife conflicts; sisters are more inclined to help each other than erstwhile strangers are. The prevailing pattern of village endogamy means that marriages follow from and reinforce neighborhood and friendship ties. Kinship marriages (avunculate and matrilateral cross-cousin marriages are the most frequent) are based upon the strength of the bond between brother and sister in the previous generation. The bond of amity between brother and sister derives in turn from bridewealth-linking: a man marries with bridewealth received from his sister's marriage; he is beholden to her and must safeguard her interests.

Marriages are, however, frequently not harmonious. Over 18 percent end in divorce, usually during the first two years. For technical reasons, a divorce must be followed by immediate remarriage so that the woman's brothers receive bridewealth from their sister's new husband to replace the bridewealth they have to refund to her previous husband. It is significant that the term for divorce, *sumburi*, also means "elopement." Although adultery does not make divorce inevitable (adultery cases are often settled out of court in order to avoid scandal), most divorces follow from love affairs. But pressures from kinsmen and the problem of refunding bridewealth still make divorces difficult. Conjugal and marital disharmony arise out of many factors: difficulties which the new wife faces in adjusting to her husband's household, particularly if she is a junior wife and her husband is much older than she is (most marriages are based on infant betrothal and there is usually a great age difference between a man and his junior wives); a husband favoring one wife at the expense of another; a wife who is barren; domestic recalcitrance; a wife who spends long periods staying with her kinspeople; a wife who loses several children in childbirth or early infancy. It is generally the woman who is blamed, and assumes the blame, when troubles arise in the family. The conflict between maternal or domestic duty and personal desire is a recurring theme in the narratives.

Jurally, descent is agnatic. Inheritance is leviratic and succession follows the principle of primogeniture. The crucial principle determining all significant social relationships is birth-order position. The suffixes *dogoma, dogo, dogone* and the suffix *koro* denote "younger/junior/smaller" and "elder/senior/bigger" respectively. The suffixes are widely used to indicate the relative age of a classificatory father or sibling, and to address a person as *n'koro* ("my senior") is to signify respect for someone superordinate to oneself. Relative seniority in status is expressed by the concept of *fisa mantiye*. The concept connotes relative seniority in birth-order position, superiority of male over female, superiority of wife-receivers, superiority of the agnatic over the uterine line of descent, and, in the context of clanship, superordination of ruling clans and precedence in terms of the historical migrations of various clan groups into the *ferensola*. It is said that the elder "owns" or "is the master *(tigi)* of" the younger. "Ownership" implies a duty to provide for the welfare and protection of dependents: juniors, wives, and children. Reciprocally, dependents must respect the authority of an elder and do his bidding. This reciprocity obtains in the politico-jural domain as much as within the field of kinship. A chief is obliged to protect his subjects and to provide for their welfare; in return, his subjects pay him respect through tithe, loyalty, and conformity to the laws of the land.

The Kuranko Concept of the Person

Let us first consider Kuranko notions of the person from a very general point of view. The body is known as *fere* ("flesh") or *fere bonke* (lit. "body earth"). At death the body is returned to the earth. It is buried at the edge of the village, between the world of human beings and the wilderness. The term *nie* is complementary to *fere*. *Nie* is the life-force which animates the body. In the case of witches, the *nie* may leave the body at night and enter and animate the body of an animal familiar. This life-force is associated with breathing (*ki nie'l fe*: "to life breathe"). A living person may be described by the phrase *a nie a ro* ("he/she life is in"), and death is sometimes announced by the phrase *a nie ara ta* ("his/her life has gone away"). A person's shadow is called *ninne* (possibly meaning "little life"), and it is said that a dead person has no shadow. At death the *nie* is first transformed into a shade (*yiyei*), which can in some circumstances haunt the bereaved. But finally the *nie* becomes an ancestral spirit which has no bodily form.

In Kuranko the word *morgo* denotes the living person. In this sense *morgo* refers to the particular man, the empirical subject of speech, thought, and will, which is recognized in all societies (c.f. Dumont, 1965:15). When we consider another Kuranko word, *morgoye*, or "personhood," we are on less familiar ground. *Morgoye* is quite unlike the English word *personality*, which connotes personal identity, a "distinctive individual character expecially when of a marked kind" (OED). *Morgoye* refers to moral qualities which ideally characterize social relationships. While *personality* implies an individual who stands out against his or her social background, *morgoye* connotes abstract qualities of social relations. In particular, *morgoye* denotes altruism and magnanimity, virtues which the Kuranko set at the foundation of the social order. Of a generous person, mindful of others, who gives without ulterior motive, it is said *ke morgo* ("this is a person"). If a person behaves in some exemplary way, people may comment *morgo le kela* ("this is a true person"), and a magnanimous person will deserve the remark *ke l morgoye ti fo* ("this one's personhood is beyond the telling"). A true person thus does more than merely conform to social rules; he realizes or exemplifies social ideals. The Kuranko words *lembe* and *ghiliye* mean "respect," but they imply more than a slavish or automatic regard for convention. Respect means mindfulness of others, a surpassing of self in the interests of community. A gift thus signifies respect, and the recipient of a gift may express his gratitude by saying *ara m'fa* ("it has fed me") or *lembe morgo fa le* (lit. "respect person has fed me").

Sociability is expressed through giving and sharing. One who enjoys the company of others is a "sweet person" (*morgo di keye*). An unsociable person is considered to be "not a person" (*morgo ma kela*), or is called a "bush person" (*fira morgo*). A mean person is known as a "broken down person" (*morgo kore*) on an analogy with a dilapidated house, a broken calabash, worn-out clothes, an abandoned farm, and other such "useless" objects. Sometimes the phrase *morgo kende ma* ("a sick person") is used to describe someone who sets himself apart from others. The term *kende* may mean healthy in the physical sense or proper in the sense of well-behaved. Thus antisocial behavior may call out the response *kende ma kela* ("this is not proper/healthy"), and a socially maladroit or ungenerous person may be spoken of as "unwell" (*ke morgo kende ma*). Indeed, social misconduct is often regarded as a cause of illness, an indication of the way in which Kuranko regard the body politic and the individual's body as aspects of an underlying unity.

The most fundamental postulate in the Kuranko world view is that persons exist only in relation to one another. The notion of *morgoye* reflects the ontological priority of social relationships, not of personal identity. One of the recurring images in Kuranko descriptions of community is the image of the path. For instance, the saying *nyendan bin to kile a wa ta an segi* refers to the way in which a particular species of grass (used for thatching) bends one way as you pass through it and then bends back the other way as you return through it. Thus, when you explain your reason for giving a gift, especially to an affine, you customarily say *kile ka na faga* ("so that the path does not die"). If relations between people become strained, it is often said that "the path is not good between" (*kile nyuma san tema*), and if a person disappoints a friend then people may comment *a ma kile nyuma tama a bo ma* ("he did not walk on the good path with his friend"). The interdependence of members of the community or of a family may be expressed in terms of the network of ropes which are tied over the rice farms when the crop is nearing maturity. One end of the rope is always tied to the foot of the bird-scaring platform where the children sit with slingshots and keep birds from scavenging the rice. When this main rope is tugged, all the tributary ropes shake. This scares away birds. It is sometimes said that "one's birth is like the bird-scaring rope" (*soron i le ko yagbayile*), or "one's birth is like a chain" (*soron i la ko yolke*) because one's fate is always inextricably tied to the fate of others. In the case of the family group it is said that the main rope is like the father where it is secured to the bird-scaring platform, and like the mother at the free end; the children are the tributary strands.

These images, borrowed from the fields of farming and gift-exchange, at once indicate that Kuranko ideology reflects a mode of production, distribution, and exchange in which community relationships are central. For instance, the Kuranko say that one of the functions of the *kere* system is to create networks of mutual obligation and interdependence throughout the village. If labor recruitment for farming were based solely on lineage ties then there would be fewer bonds among neighbors. Bonds of amity are created among villagers by less formal means: visiting and sharing food, eating kola or drinking palm wine together, giving sympathy gifts to the bereaved, attending and participating in village festivals and rituals, greeting and talking to people during the business of day-to-day life, assisting friends and neighbors with labor, money, or food. Individual self-sufficiency is as absurd a notion to the Kuranko as is the notion of the individual as essentially the proprietor of his own person or capacities, owing nothing to society for them. "One's head is in the hands of others," say the Kuranko.

The ontological priority of the group as a network of interdependent parts, and the absence of the idea of the individual as an autonomous moral being, help us understand several aspects of Kuranko thought which at first glance might seem bizarre. From the Kuranko point of view the field of social relationships may include totemic animals, ancestors, bush spirits, a divine creator, fetishes, as well as man. In other words, Being is not necessarily limited to human being. *Morgoye* may be found in relations between man and ancestor, man and totemic animal, man and God, and so on. Indeed, the clan myths referred to in chapter 3 make it clear that totemic animals actually exemplify the moral ideal of *morgoye*. A corollary of this conception of Being is the view that relations among various beings are dynamic. Since personhood is distributed into the natural world rather than concentrated and fixed, it is readily conceivable that an animal can be a kind of ancestor, that God can become a person, that a fetish can speak, and that a man can change into an animal. As we shall see, such metamorphoses are commonplace occurrences in Kuranko narratives. In a sense, the narratives realize imaginatively many of the possibilities given in the Kuranko world view which are by their very nature rarely experienced in everyday life. It is not every day that one meets a shape-shifter or a person who has seen a bush spirit, but such people abound in the world of hearsay.

From this dynamic view it follows that relations among various beings are uncertain and problematical. Alliances with bush spirits may yield great benefit or bring great disaster. The blessings of one's ancestors give long life and prosperity, but if these blessings are withheld calamity may befall an entire family. One must be mindful of other beings at all times, particularly those, such as ancestors, whose influence has the most direct bearing upon one's welfare. Man is a governor in the cybernetic sense, adjusting and harmonizing relations not merely within the community but throughout a wide field of Being. Although the Kuranko place little value on individuality, they regard the individual person as responsible for the harmony of the world.

Let us consider the concepts of *baraka* and *fuguriye* in the light of the foregoing remarks. *Baraka* connotes a condition of blessedness or good fortune—food in abundance, long life, prosperity, harmony within the family—resulting from *duwenu* (blessings) which come from God and the ancestors. The curse (*danka*) is the opposite of *duwe*. It results in *fuguriye*—hunger, poverty, sickness, weakness, misfortune, disharmony. Some people aver that *baraka* and *fuguriye* can be inherited in a family. Thus the fortunes of one person are shared by all. Both *baraka* and *fuguriye* are, moreover, contingent upon a person's relations with others (including God and the ancestors). A person's worth is not, therefore, judged independently of the social context of his existence. If a man prospers it is often his lineage which is praised, not him. *Baraka* and *fuguriye* can only be properly understood in terms of the social matrix of personal activity. For example, gift-giving bestows *baraka* on the *relationship* between donor and recipient. In this sense *baraka* connotes mutual respect among all those associated with or identified in the exchange. Just as the gift is given symbolically from and to a category of persons, so blessings and curses implicate an individual's entire lineage. This is why a person's family or lineage must symbolically share in the offering of a piacular sacrifice, and why an entire lineage may suffer misfortune if any one of their number is cursed. The essence of moral responsibility among the Kuranko springs from the view that a person's actions affect and implicate all those who are related to him (those who are "one blood"). Any behavior which is based on an assumption of individual moral autonomy is censured as well as doomed.

Many Kuranko speak of *sabu* (moral agency, cause, reason) when explaining the ways in which each person's actions resonate through a wide field of relations. It is often said that there is no happening without a reason. In Kuranko thought the natural world is not inert, nor is it a domain of amoral forces. Reason, like Being, is distributed into the natural world, and the Kuranko do not acknowledge hard and fast distinctions between culture and nature, or between natural and supernatural processes. The fortunes of the individual are inextricably bound up with relations with kinsmen, friends, mentors, neighbors, strangers, ancestors, God, and other beings. *Sabu* refers to the dynamic interactions within this field of relations. The word is often explained in terms of gift-giving. For instance, if a person gives a voluntary gift to someone else, the gift improves the fortunes of the receiver and makes the donor his *sabu nyuma* ("good cause"), the reason for his good fortune. Or, if a person introduces someone to a friend who is the means by which the friend finds good fortune, then that someone will be known as *sabu nyuma*. Any agency of misfortune is known as a bad cause (*sabu yuge*). Although people often speak of divine will and ancestral influence in terms of implacable fate (*sawura*), it is always human choice which, in practice, determines the exact course of a person's destiny. In other words, it is considered unlikely that divine or ancestral wrath will be visited upon a person unless he or she has first transgressed the moral code. Nothing occurs without some reason, and the *sabu* or reason is a direct reflection of the moral quality of a person's relationships with other beings, both human and extrahuman.

It is admitted, nonetheless, that some transgressions are accidental and unintentional. In such cases a person might plead "I did not start upon it: it lay on my hand" (*ma l wuli a ma; a sa ra m'bolo ma le*), and he would not be held culpable. The "reason" would be attributed to God and an expiatory sacrifice would be offered. In all cases where a cause cannot be divined satisfactorily, people tend to put things down to God's will, which is held to be the ultimate cause of everything.

The World Personified

It is tempting to regard the Kuranko notion of a personified cosmos as a projection of concrete social relations. It is possible, for instance, to relate the various categories of extrahuman being to actual social categories. Thus, the altruism of the totemic animal symbolizes the ideal of amity among kinsmen. Ancestors designate descent groupings.

Alliances and contracts with bush spirits suggest the capricious domain of affinal relations. Neighborhood and community are defined by reference to God, a figure that transcends the narrower identifications of kinship and descent. It is also possible to show that various metamorphoses (man into totemic animal, bush spirit into person, etc.) correspond to certain transformations in the social field. Thus, sacrifice usually follows from some negligence or wrongdoing. It is a kind of moral counterpart to legal redress. Its aim is to reincorporate the deviant within the moral community. This is accomplished on two fronts simultaneously. An offering of raw rice flour is first made to the ancestors. This makes "pure" relations between the sacrificer and his ancestors *and* between the sacrificer and his lineage. Next, an animal is consecrated to God. The meat is distributed among all the lineages and groups represented in the village. This restores relations between the sacrificer and his community. The transformation in social identification from lineage to community is mediated by a shift in symbolic focus from ancestors to God (Jackson, 1977a). It could be argued that this dialectic of identification is the concrete basis on which ideas of metamorphosis within the field of the extrahuman are developed.

According to this view the fabulous is a kind of re-presentation of the mundane, an allegorization which enables people to think more objectively about immediate social concerns. Considered in this way, narratives about fabulous beings and events are really imaginative accounts of social relations. This view contains a great deal of truth, but it leads quickly into error if it fails to accommodate the ways in which allegorization inspires a richer expanse of meanings than is ordinarily suggested by the bland conventional descriptions of social reality. In brief, the meanings to which allegorical narratives give rise cannot be reduced to the social matrix even though they owe their origins to it. Let us consider one allegorical motif from this point of view.

Many of the narratives involve alliances between a person and a bush spirit. In every case the alliance is forged in uncertainty and its moral character remains ambiguous for most of the narrative. No doubt it is possible to show that this motif pertains to the ambiguity that arises in relations among distant kin or between affines. But there is far more to it than this. The hero who ventures alone into the wilderness and dares to make such alliances with capricious spirits is the focus of deeper ethical and intellectual concerns. The creation of community depends not merely on people behaving well. It is not the outcome of a slavish application of rules or a passive adherence to routine. The creation of a viable community depends upon vital forces which are "wild" or random and which must be fetched from outside the domain of rules and roles. Some of these vital forces are regarded as natural gifts, such as intelligence, strength, bravery, and the like. Others are embodied in medicines (*besenu*), or in musical instruments. But all are ethically ambiguous: they are potentially as destructive as they are regenerative. As we shall see in chapter 6, heroic journeys into the wilderness and pacts with bush spirits are elements of allegory whose moral resonances carry far beyond the world of concrete social relations.

The Constitution of Self

Selfhood, or *nyere morgoye,* is influenced by many given conditions: sex and birth-order position, clan and subclan identifications, place of origin, father's religious affiliation, and certain inborn factors. The self (*nyere*) can first be defined in terms of behavior and temperament. For some reason the word *so'on* means both behavior and lungs. People say of a well-behaved person "his lungs are good" (*so'on a kin*), and refer to an ill-behaved person as having "bad lungs." The word *yuse* means both heart and temperament, as in the phrase *ke yuse kin* ("good heart," i.e. even-tempered). Like many Kuranko words for emotions, reference is made to various internal organs which are allegedly the loci of different feelings. Annoyance and bitterness are related to the heart or spleen, respect to the liver, thought to the brain, language to the neck, life to the breath, and so on. An adult is normally held responsible for his or her behavior and is supposed to be able to control his or her feelings. This is so even when some behavioral trait exists which has proved resistant to correction from early childhood. Of an incorrigible person (*morgo koron*) it is sometimes said *a ka tala, a soron ta la bole* ("he is blameless, he was born with it"), or *a danye le wo la* ("that is how he is made").

Behavior and temperament reflect an interaction between acquired moral knowledge and innate dispositions. According to the Kuranko view a person is not born with any knowledge; it must be acquired from the elders. Everyone, however, is born with certain dispositions. One innate factor is *yugi* (habit, disposition, proclivity). *Yugi* may incline a person toward either exemplary or evil conduct. It exerts its influence despite a person's will and is an abstract, intangible force. If a person is luckless enough to have bad *yugi* (*yugi ma kin*), then he or she will be prone to lie, steal, cheat, and abuse others. Of an unselfish, considerate person, however, one might say *a yugi kin* ("his/her *yugi* is good").

Another important concept is *miran*. In its mundane usage *miran* refers to any personal property as well as any kind of container. Anything which a person can regard as an extension of himself could be called his *miran*. Thus, one's protective charms and ointments, one's clothing and personal belongings are all *mirannu*. One is incomplete without them. The more abstract meanings of *miran* cannot be conveyed by any one English word. In different contexts *miran* may suggest dignity, presence, bearing, oratorical prowess, charisma, self-esteem, confidence, and self-possession. But underlying all these usages is the idea that *miran* is a psychic "property" which is closely related to certain material possessions. Like the *mana* of the Polynesians, it can be increased or diminished by manipulating magical objects or as a result of one's social comportment. Enemies may employ magical means to diminish one's *miran* and so strike at one's self-confidence. It is for these reasons that self-protection (*nyere kandan*) necessitates the use of medicines and fetishes. Protection implies enclosure or containment. Just as personhood cannot be defined apart from a wide field of social relations, so self cannot be defined apart from the magical properties which amplify and contain it.

Many Kuranko parents use threat and force to intimidate their children, in the belief that obedience and respect go together. Of such autocratic parents it might be said that they have "taken the child's *miran* away" (*an dan miran bo a ma*). Similarly, if a person is intimidated or accosted by someone who possesses great *miran* he may declare *a ayene miran bo ra ma* ("when I saw him my *miran* went out of me"). Informants have described to me the sudden dread and panic that may overtake a person walking at night alone on some bush path in an area said to be inhabited by bush spirits. At such times it is felt that the *miran* of the bush spirit oppresses one and undermines one's self-confidence (*a miran diginta ma,* "its *miran* pressed down on me"). All these examples show that *miran* fluctuates. Although acknowledged to be an inborn trait, a child's *miran* can be diminished by hard discipline just as an adult's *miran* can be bolstered by medicines.

Another innate and nonheritable factor is *hankilimaiye*: cleverness, ingenuity, common sense, understanding. Unlike many Western concepts of intelligence, *hankilimaiye* cannot be assessed except in contexts of social activity (c.f. Wober, 1974). A clever person is socially competent and socially responsible. Accordingly, *hankilimaiye* signifies *communis sententia:* common sense. It carries the connotations of respect, prudence, filial piety, and knowledge of custom. A person who sets himself apart from the moral community is regarded as a fool (*yuwe*), someone "without salt in his head" (*kor' sa kunye ma*) and "without brains" (*kun' por' sa*). A socially responsible person has "good thoughts in his head" (*miria nyime a kunye ro*); his "head is full." Although the Kuranko concept of intelligence emphasizes social gumption rather than abstract intellectual skills, *hankilimaiye* sometimes defines idiosyncratic abilities such as cunning, guile, and extraordinary perspicacity. As the narratives in chapter 4 make clear, *hankilimaiye* is ethically ambiguous: a person may use his intelligence for the social good, or he may use it for selfish gain.

Faculties like *yugi, miran,* and *hankilimaiye* are not determinative in an absolute sense, which is why they may be alluded to in explaining behavior but not in justifying it. A mature person, which is to say an initiated person, is expected to be able to control his feelings and to use his natural talents for social ends. Moral excellence lies in accommodating oneself to a given moral order. It does not come from transcending or changing that order. Thus, the hero in Kuranko narratives does not seek to realize some inner imperative against the grain of social circumstance; his moral compass is the world of ancestral and time-honored values, and his worth is measured by his extraordinary ability to realize common ideals.

At first glance many Kuranko views seem fatalistic. If you ask a person what shapes his destiny (*sawura*), he will usually reply that *sawura* is decided by God, before birth, and cannot be changed. Yet Kuranko people do not *live* fatalistically. This is partly because you can never know your destiny in advance, and partly because you acquire moral understanding from elders which enables you to determine the manner in which you actually live your fate. For instance, Keti Ferenke Koroma says that his wisdom and talent for storytelling are God-given gifts. It is his destiny to compose and relate stories. But he once told me with great amusement, "I could never stop thinking of stories, yet I could stop myself telling them. If I am asked to tell a story, I cannot stop myself thinking of one to tell, but I can stop myself telling it." In short, a person is expected to show restraint. Restraint in turn depends upon "understanding" (*hankilimaiye*) and mindfulness of others.

Initiation rites indicate very clearly the way in which the creation of moral persons is a matter of human praxis and not left to chance. Even biological events like birth and death are brought symbolically under human control. Initiations are the high point of the social year as well as the turning point in each person's life. Initiation involves secret rites and public festivities: respectively, the transformation of amoral children into responsible adults, and the reconstitution of the community after the dispersals and estrangements of the rainy season (Jackson, 1977b:201–214). Since personhood expresses social values, it is understandable that the creation of personhood and of community should occur at the same time.

Through initiation a person acquires "new understanding" (*hankili kura*) and so becomes a "new person" (*morgo kura*). These changes depend upon learning to control one's feelings. In Kuranko parlance the neophytes are "tamed" (*kan kolo*). Their disorderly and diffuse natures are brought under control and systematized. They become "ripe." Indeed, people sometimes pun on the words "ripe" (*moi*) and "person" (*morgo*), as in the phrase *a ma mor' we, a gberan lon:* "he is not ripe/ person yet, he is still raw." The neophyte is expected to "control his mouth," to curb his impetuosity, and to avoid immoderation (*meeye*). He is introduced to cult sacra (*sumafannu*) and acquires through them an abstract attitude, a skill in thinking in oblique symbolic terms rather than through his feelings. He learns to defer immediate gratifications and to break his emotional ties with his mother. All this promotes *yiri:* steadiness of mind and body.

Great stress is also placed on the control of thought. An initiate must think carefully and clearly before he acts or speaks. Certain adages bring home the importance of cultivating consonance between intention and action:

> *morge kume mir' la i konto i wo l fo la*
> (whatever word a person thinks of, that will he speak; i.e. think before you speak lest you blurt out stupid ideas)

> *i mir' la koe mi ma, i wo l ke la*
> (you thought of that, you do that; i.e. think before you act lest your actions belie your intentions)

A neophyte is expected to show bravery and fearlessness. He must have a "strong heart" (*yuse gbele*) in the face of the physical operation and the ordeals he must undergo. Bravery implies fortitude and moral fiber. But self-control is never vaunted as an individual accomplishment as it is in many Western sports and similar displays of individual excellence. Self-control is always regarded as an aspect of social order, not as a means of self-aggrandizement. There is a close link, therefore, between mastery of self and upholding the laws of the group. This is why many men argue that women are never "law owners" (*tontiginu*). Women lack the fortitude of men. They are easily cowed.

Distributive Morality and the Ambiguity of Action

In Kuranko thought a person's moral commitments to others are apportioned differentially. The individual is not set apart from his social milieu and given an intrinsic moral value which is shared by all mankind. There is no notion that all men are equal in the sight of God. According to this form of "distributive morality" (Read, 1955), it is the relative social position of an individual which decides the manner in which his actions will be evaluated. Moral propriety is a matter of living up to the expectations of a role, rather than honoring an abstract, metacultural relationship with God.

We have already remarked the relative moral inequality between men and women, and mentioned the way in which legal and political inequalities are alleged to follow from those moral differences. The distributive nature of Kuranko morality is also shown by their ideas about children. Before a person is initiated he is not a complete moral person. He is a jural minor, outside the law, whose character is unformed and metaphorically "dirty." In the words of Saran Salia Sano:

> We never take seriously the deeds of an uninitiated boy. A boy is just as he was when he was born; he knows nothing, he has no understanding. A boy can swear and steal with impunity. He may even piss and shit on the protective things [*kandan le fannu*] around the gardens. None of this is taken seriously. People say "they are ignorant" and never take them to court. However, on the day of his initiation a boy's misdeeds are forgotten. After this he will be forgiven nothing. If he comes out of the initiation lodge with bad habits, those bad habits will never leave him.

This conception of a determinate relationship between social position and moral character gives rise to serious contradictions. It is often the case that a young boy has more sense than his elders, or a woman has greater courage and perseverance than a man. As we shall see, Kuranko narratives employ various figurative devices in order to resolve such contradictions, thereby making Kuranko ethics more viable than it really is.

The distributive character of Kuranko ethics is also shown by the effects of sociospatial distance on relationships. As a rule, the greater the genealogical and geographical distance between individuals, the less bound they will be by the principles of mutuality and reciprocity upon which the moral order rests. The alienation of the lands and property of nontribesmen by conquering war-chiefs, the killing of captured enemies, and the withholding of aid from strangers all indicate that *morgoye* was a relative thing. If all kinsmen lived together and all nonkinsmen lived apart, then the reckoning of moral obligations would be fairly unambiguous. But close kin are often estranged, and strangers may live together as kinsmen. In such circumstances, when the "close" kin demand help on the grounds that kinsmen should sustain one another, the help may be withheld or given only on condition that it be repaid. In real life, ethical judgments have to be revised according to the particularities of the situation at hand. Indeed, it is because moral obligations are contingent upon so many factors (genealogy, residence, age and sex, religion, rank, mode of relationship, and temperament) that decisions must always be made through open discussion about real events rather than derived ready-made from an abstract creed. Let us consider briefly two areas of ethical ambiguity which figure in several narratives: friendship and motherhood.

Friendship ties are ethically uncertain because of their ad hoc, mutable character. Friendship falls, as it were, part way between kinship and strangerhood, between putative altruism and suspended morality. The dilemmas of friendship form the central subject of several narratives in chapter 6. Motherhood also involves considerable ambiguity. A mother is expected to care for her own child and for any other child placed in her care. Her duty to the children is clear, yet there is a very real distinction between one's real child (*dan gbere*) or "blood child" (*dan yeli*) and a nominal child. Affections may conflict with duty, and the ambivalence felt toward a co-wife's child is the theme of many narratives in chapter 8.

Ambiguity arises wherever there is a situation or relationship which involves contradictory frames of reference. Since Kuranko morality is relative to social position, this ambiguity implies ethical dissonance.

Perhaps the best examples of this are joking relationships, where ridicule and laughter are resorted to in order to get around the uncomfortable fact that people find themselves related in mutually contradictory ways (Jackson, 1977b:109–112, 172–175). In a social world dominated by overlapping kinship and affinal connections it is inevitable that people will be related in ways which imply conflicting moral imperatives. Choices arise as to which mode of relationship will be preferred, and this means negotiating a continually changing ethical perspective. In the absence of absolute moral decrees which obtain equally for everyone in all circumstances, every relationship has to be thought through anew. It is out of this kind of dialectic, which Kuranko call *sosole*, that the narratives emerge.

Moral Sensibility

I have said that Kuranko ethics is focused upon problems of maintaining harmony in relationships, and that the field of relationships is allegorized to include mankind, totemic animals, ancestors, bush spirits, and a divine creator. I want to now consider in a little more detail two other areas of Kuranko ethical concern which have been only touched upon so far: relations between positions and dispositions, and relations between intentions and actions.

Social being is the ground of human being. Within this gestalt, the Kuranko recognize two poles of existence: the man-made and the God-given. Thus, the field of custom (*namui*) and law (*ton; seria*)— including social rules and roles—is regarded as given according to ancestral decree. It is a legacy of the first people (*fol' morgonu ko dane*), the ancestors. This domain stands in contrast to personal attributes such as intelligence, strength, beauty, *miran*, and temperament, which are randomly distributed according to some inscrutable design of God (Ala). It is implied that Man has determined what the rules are and who will occupy the roles, but Man can never determine to what extent the rules will be followed or the capabilities of those who fill the roles. For instance, the social rule of primogeniture fixes things so that *A* will be his father's heir, not *B*. But there is no guarantee that *A* will prove best-suited to the role. It is quite possible that *B* will be naturally more gifted. In a society with fixed rules and roles, a crucial moral problem is the indeterminate relationship between birth and worth, position and disposition, the man-made and the God-given. I hope to show that fictional narratives are ways in which these poles of existence are brought into harmony.

The second area of ethical concern is the relationship between thought (*miria koe*), speech (*fo koe*), and action (*ke koe*). Like other Mande-speaking peoples, the Kuranko sometimes define themselves linguistically as speakers of the "true/pure language" (*kan gbe*). The word *gbe* (white, clear, pure, true) is also used in expressions which refer to openness and integrity in human relations. "The hearts of those who live together should be open," say the Kuranko. A person whose heart is pure (i.e. whose actions and words are without ulterior motive) is happy. People say of an honest person, "this is a true person" (*morgo gbe le kela*). And one may declare one's trust in a friend with the words *n'de ya n gbe i le ye*, "I open myself for you." Enemies and aliens are called *morgo fiennu* (lit. "black persons"), and if a neighbor behaves in an underhand way one might comment, *i maiye? a l ko l dan bole, i ko morgo fiennu* ("Do you see? His way of doing things is the way of aliens"). Alternatively, an honest person may be described as "straight up and down" (*morgo telne*), by contrast with a devious person (*morgo dugune*) whose "words are crooked" (*kuma kan wo ro dura*). The epithet *latelan* means straightforwardness. It implies a fidelity between intention and action. It is perhaps the one quality for which the Kuranko are best known nationally.

In ritual practice whiteness and straightness imply harmony between man and man, and between man and ancestors. Conformity to ancestral values makes for harmony among contemporaries. But harmonious *social* relations are also thought to be conditional upon a *personal* harmony between thought and deed. Thus a sacrifice can be "spoiled" if there are people present who nurse undeclared grievances against each other. In particular, adulteries "spoil" sacrifices. It is for this reason that the correction of imbalance (*yiriyara*) in social relations usually requires some form of personal confession in which inward grievances or wrongs are publicly announced. Confession is said to "clear" or "straighten" the path between people. Opening one's heart purifies the relationship. Occasionally one hears of a person who has harbored ill will against someone and then decides to declare his feelings to that person. Such declarations are often prefaced by the words *koe dime n to*, "there is pain in me." The Kuranko take the view that interpersonal tensions may lead to physical pain (*dime*), illness (*kiraiye*), or misfortune (*fuguriye*). This is shown dramatically in witchcraft confession during extreme illness when a woman retrospectively connects her affliction with undeclared wrongs and ill feelings in her past (Jackson, 1975). Even in ordinary sickness a diviner often suggests that the sickness is caused by some misdeed. Confession is advised to effect a cure, and sacrifice is ordered to harmonize relations with God and the ancestors. Sometimes too a woman will declare her adultery and name her lover in the presence of her husband. This is a way of forestalling possible sickness or disgrace. In such cases she will plead with her husband, "let not your *hake* befall me."

The concept of *hake*[3] covers the whole field of moral anxiety. It is a difficult word to translate because, as we have seen already, moral sensibility among the Kuranko is a reflection of social relations; it does not reflect processes like guilt and conscience which are usually considered to center on the inner life of the individual. Neither does *hake* imply religious sanctions following from a rupture in relations between a person and God. Although Krio-speaking Kuranko translate *hake* as "sin," *hake* pertains to the world of social relations, not that of personal emotions. *Hake* is a form of retributive justice according to which ill befalls a person who does ill to those who do him good. It is believed, for instance, that if you do wrong to some innocent person then the offense will hit back at you. The other person's *hake* will come out in you: *a hake si bo i ro*. That is to say, the *hake* of the offended person will cause you to fall ill or have bad luck. *Hake* thus mediates a restoration of the moral balance. It does so in ways which cannot be fully explained, but it is clear that the offended person does not need to know he has been wronged or slighted. *Hake* operates independently of man's knowledge and will. Although *hake* is an impersonal and neutral force, its effects can be nullified by confession. It is, however, the confession itself which prevents the *hake* afflicting the wrong-doer. The wronged person himself does not "forgive" the offender, and he may not even be aware that he has been wronged. Yet *hake* arises out of personal relationships. Infringements of social rules are more readily detected than moral deceits. Thus, while social delicts are taken to court, clandestine wrongs between individuals tend to precipitate the more mysterious sanctions of *hake*. Moreover, unlike punishments ordered by courts, the retributive effects of *hake* are quite unpredictable. For this reason *hake* is usually invoked as a retrospective explanation after a person has suffered some reverse in his fortunes.

When Kuranko people asked me what prevented me from wronging others, I would endeavor to explain that my conscience and scruples did so. I would say that a kind of voice inside me spoke out against my "bad thoughts" (*miriye yugume*). Such a view was regarded as downright ridiculous, and I would be assured that it was the fear of the other person's *hake* which made me do right, not the inner voice. I espoused the European view that there is some abstract moral principle, such as the Kantian categorical imperative, centered within the Self. Guilt is a consequence of violating that principle. Kuranko people took a different view. They stressed a practical morality based on mutuality: respect for rules, honoring contracts, keeping promises, and fulfilling the obligations of one's role. *Hake* is a consequence of a failure of mutuality. For Europeans, confession is usually regarded as a way of restoring harmony between Self and God. It salves one's inner conscience. For the Kuranko, confession and begging are seen as ways of restoring harmony to immediate social relations. The notion of personal redemption is of little significance to them.

Explanation and Evaluation

Perhaps the greatest problem in social anthropology is the problem of knowing how others experience the world rather than merely how they explain it. The Kuranko refuse to speculate about other people's experience. "I am not inside them" (*n'de sa bu ro*), you are told, or "I do not know what is inside" (*n'de ma konto lon*). It is widely acknowledged that what people say often belies what they feel. Thus the adage *morgo si bage to i bu ro le i ni nogoyi l bo*, "a person has blood inside him but it is saliva he spits out." In bringing this chapter to a close I want to consider briefly the relationship between experience and expression.

The foregoing account of *hake* may suggest that Kuranko lack internalized guilt feelings, and that the superego is externalized in social rules and authority figures. It may seem that moral correction depends entirely on external constraints and the diffuse sanctions of shame rather than on inner conscience. But such an interpretation rests on a confusion between empirical and conceptual realities. The fact that Kuranko conceive retributive justice as coming from without is a reflection of their system of values, not of empirical psychological reality. As I have noted elsewhere, many confessions of "guilt" are prompted by inner qualms, not by outside pressure or discovery (Jackson, 1975). There seems no doubt that moral anxiety and conscience are just as much part of Kuranko psychology as of European psychology. It is therefore at the level of belief and explanation that cultural differences should be explored. Here it is important to stress that all explanations reflect moral values and human interests. It is because the Kuranko place value on relatedness rather than individual selves that their conceptions of moral processes, of intelligence, and of personhood differ from European conceptions.

This difference in values was borne home to me time and time again during fieldwork. Quite simply, the more energy and time I devoted to my research project the less energy I had for socializing with villagers. For the Kuranko, existence does not consist in the realization of singular personal projects but in the harmonization of relationships through a wide field of Being. This may entail dancing in a close circle of villagers for hours on end rather than sitting alone in an isolated room writing up field notes. The Kuranko emphasize the person in relation to others, not in relation to his idiosyncratic unconscious, his past, his personal plans, or his inner conscience. However, it is not that Kuranko lack an inner personal dimension to their existence; it is rather that this dimension has little conventional significance. It is for this reason that spontaneous biographies are almost impossible to elicit from Kuranko individuals.

Perhaps the problem of understanding how others experience the world is better rephrased as one of understanding the *relation* between conventional ideas and personal experience. From this point of view the status of Kuranko and European beliefs is very much the same. Beliefs do not define how people think or feel, but how people prefer to think and want to feel on certain occasions about things which they value most. In other words, beliefs are largely ideals, and they are occasional. They tend to be invoked and manipulated during crises, to provide explanations. Or people pay lip service to them when obliged to formulate ideals. From this point of view beliefs are a rough synthesis of personal experience and social values, a synthesis which is realized differently for each person but which nonetheless presents to the world an image on which everyone can find some agreement. I hope to show that Kuranko narratives work out such syntheses, and create these agreements.

2 Form and Play in Kuranko Fiction

Once possessed of consciousness, mankind is continually faced with alternative possibilities of understanding and action.[1] The faculty of language likewise enlarges the scope of human choice. Since words are only arbitrarily related to the things they designate, they are always open to metaphorical reassignment.[2] However, this awareness of alternity is usually deliberately limited, and human cultures come to conserve and enshrine choices made by others at other times, fixing them as habits and customs. Thus, man entertains more possibilities than he is prepared to allow or realize, and culture is often seen as something given and immutable. Occasionally, however, conventional habits of thought and action are broken; in certain ritual settings and in fiction man makes imaginative forays beyond the customary, deliberately promoting moral contrasts and ambiguities.

Kuranko dilemma tales belong to a genre which is widespread in Africa.[3] The ethical character of such tales is immediately apparent. L. V. Thomas refers to them as "riddle cases of conscience," and William Bascom notes that they invariably raise difficult problems of morality, proposing choices that involve keen discrimination on ethical and legal grounds (Bascom, 1975:1). Dilemma tales do not call upon fixed answers. Listeners present their different views and an ad hoc solution is accepted at each telling, depending upon the consensus of those present and the weight of the arguments advanced (c.f. Berry, 1961:10). The following Kuranko dilemma tale will serve to introduce some of the main features of Kuranko narratives.

N.1: *The Three Sons*

Narrated by Keti Ferenke Koroma. Recorded at Kondembaia, January 1970.

There was once a paramount chief who had three sons. One day he called his sons and said, "How are you all renowned?" He said, "Each of you must make a name for himself."

The three sons set off. They came to the country of another chief. They went to the chief and said, "Chief, we have come as your strangers." The chief said, "Why have you come?" The first man said, "I have come to ask you to let me sleep with your senior wife. In the morning you can kill me." The chief said, "All right, I agree to that." He asked the second man to tell him why he had come. The second son said, "I have come to ask you to let me sleep with your eldest daughter. In the morning you can kill me." The chief said, "All right, I agree to that." Then the chief asked the third man to tell him why he had come. The third son said, "I know that you have only one cow. I want you to kill the cow and cook it so that I can spend the whole night eating it. In the morning you can kill me." The chief said, "All right, I agree to that." The chief then gave his senior wife to the man who had asked to sleep with her. They went to one house. He gave his eldest daughter to the man who had asked to sleep with her. They went to another house. He killed his only cow, cooked it, and gave it to the man who had asked for it. He went to another house. They all slept.

Very early in the morning, the chief's eldest daughter said to the man she had slept with, "Let us run away. My father is merciless. If he says that he will do something, then he will do it." So they ran away. Soon after they had gone the chief woke up. He said, "Go and bring the man who slept with my first wife." They went and fetched that man and the chief cut his throat. The chief said, "Go and bring the man that ate my only cow." They went and fetched that man and the chief cut his throat. The chief said, "Go and bring the man who slept with my eldest daughter." They went and came back and told the chief that the man was not there. They said, "Your daughter is not there, and the man is not there." The chief sent all his people out in search of them.

The chief did not know that his daughter and the man had gone along a big road, just like this Alkalia road here.* They reached a river, just like the Seli, and found that the bridge was broken.

*A motor road runs south from Kondembaia to Alkalia; the road crosses the Seli River about two miles south of Kondembaia.

There was no bridge, and there was no hammock-bridge* either. Then a *nyenne* came and sat down at the crossing point. Whoever came there, before the *nyenne* would allow him to cross over, that person would have to give some other person to the *nyenne*. If you didn't give a person to the *nyenne,* then you would not be able to cross the river.

Now, the man and the woman reached the riverside and there was no way to cross the river. At the same time, two other people had come from Alkalia and they were on the other side of the river. It was a woman with her only daughter. Since the day she was born, that was the only child she had borne. The woman had decided the date of her daughter's initiation, and so the daughter was going to inform her kin of that date. Because the woman loved her daughter so dearly, she had decided to accompany her. They had reached the riverside only to find the bridge broken and no way to cross the river. As they were standing on the other side of the river, the woman looked across the river and saw the young man and the chief's daughter. The woman said, "Eh! You young man. Is that your wife?" The man said, "Yes." The woman said, "Will you marry me?" The man said, "Woman, we want to cross to the side where you are because people are pursuing us. But there is no way across and the *nyenne* here says that we should give him a person. We are only two here, and I have no one to give him." The woman said, "Well, I will give you this, my only daughter, to give to the *nyenne* so that you can be crossed over. Then you must marry me." The man said, "Now, mother, if you do that for me I will be very happy." So the woman took her only child and gave her to the *nyenne*. The *nyenne* swallowed her. After he had swallowed her, he divided the waters and the man, with his wife, crossed to the other side. Then the man had two wives.

Just after getting his second wife, the man set off and reached Alkalia. As they approached the place where people draw water, they met the eldest daughter of the Alkalia chief. The daughter said, "Where are you going?" They told her that they were going to Alkalia. The daughter said, "Oh, you handsome young man, my father is paramount chief there. Whenever a stranger comes, he takes out his medicines. As many as twenty he takes out. Then he

---

*A native bridge made of raffia ropes and resembling a large hammock.

asks you to tell him which medicine helped him to become paramount chief. If you point out the medicine, then you will become chief. If you fail to point out the right one, you will be killed and my father will seize all your property. Now you have come and I have fallen in love with you. Therefore, I wish to kill my father so that you can marry me." The man said, "Eh! That will make me happy." The girl said, "Go. My father will give you lodgings. Tomorrow morning he will take out the medicines. I will change myself into a tsetse fly. I know the medicine that helped my father to become paramount chief. You must watch that tsetse fly; the medicine that it settles on is the medicine that helped my father to become paramount chief." The man said, "All right." He went on to the town.

He went to the chief. The chief gave him kola and told him the laws of the place. The chief gave him lodgings, and in the morning he took out as many as twenty medicines. He called the young man and said, "Now, we have a law here that if a stranger comes, he must point out which of these medicines helped me to become paramount chief. If you point out the medicine, then you will become chief. If you fail to point out the right one, you will be killed and all your property seized. Now that you have come with your two wives, here are fifty different kinds of medicine. You must point out the one which helped me to become paramount chief." As the man was looking at them, the chief's eldest daughter went and changed herself into a tsetse fly. The young man watched the fly. It flew over the medicines and settled on the one which had helped the girl's father to become paramount chief. As soon as that happened, the man got up and pointed to that medicine. He said, "Chief, this is the medicine that helped you to become paramount chief." Then there was a great commotion. They caught hold of the chief and killed him. They took the staff of office and gave it to the young man. He became paramount chief. He married the late chief's eldest daughter. Now he had three wives.

The man decided that he would not marry again. His first wife became pregnant. She gave birth to a baby boy. The second wife became pregnant. She gave birth to a baby boy. The third wife became pregnant. She gave birth to a baby boy. All this happened simultaneously. The three sons grew up together. And they were initiated on the same day. After their initiation, the chief, their father, lived for five more years. Then he died. When the chief died, one of the sons got up and said, "I will take my father's place." Another son said, "I will take my father's place." The third son said, "I will take my father's place."

Now, of these three sons which one should be chief? Which do you think?*

Is it the one that survived, when they killed the other two men and the woman told her own man that they should run away? Is it her son that should be chief? Or the son of the woman that gave her only daughter so that the man and his wife could get across the river? Or the son of the girl who killed her father† to save the young man and make him chief? Of the three women, whose son do you think should be chief? My problem is, I want to know the woman whose son should be made chief.

Now, the woman whose son should be chief. You know, before a man explains something he should first of all give examples. Here is my example.

Big Thing and Small Thing had a quarrel. Small Thing said that he was the elder. Big Thing said that that was nonsense. "I am the elder. You hear people saying that I am big." They went to the chiefs. The chiefs told Small Thing not to be cheeky. They said, "Everyone calls Big Thing big and Small Thing small." Small Thing said, "I am the elder." The people said, "No, Big Thing is the elder. Have you forgotten the word 'big'?"

Then Small Thing asked Big Thing to accompany him. They went out of town. Wherever they went and found people quarreling, Small Thing would say, "Let us sit down and listen." The chiefs would summon the people who had quarreled and ask them to explain themselves. When the explanations had been given, the people would tell the troublemakers what a small thing it was that they had quarreled over. Small Thing would say to Big Thing, "Have you heard that?" And they would go on to another place.

At one place they came upon a palaver over a man who had beaten his wife badly. Small Thing said, "Let us sit down and lis-

---

*At this point, Keti Ferenke pauses for an answer. No one can suggest a satisfactory way of solving the problem, so he continues by first rephrasing his question and then giving an answer to it.
†Even though the girl did not actually kill her father, she is held to be culpable for his death for she betrayed the secret of her father's medicines to the young man.

ten." They listened, and when the explanation had all been given, people again said how the quarrel had arisen over a small thing. Small Thing said to Big Thing, "Surely I am the elder, because people are always referring to me." Finally, Big Thing agreed that Small Thing was the elder.

Therefore, everything begins with small things.

Now, they summoned the son of the woman who had killed her father. They asked him why he wanted to take his father's place. He said, "I should be chief in my father's place because my mother killed my grandfather so that my father could become chief. Now that my father is dead, I should be chief. Who is there here that should be chief before me?" The people said, "All right, we have heard you."

Then they asked the next son why he wanted to be chief. He said, "My mother had an only daughter. They met my father at the riverside. My father and my 'mother'* were on the other side. There was no way across the river, and the *nyenne* was at the crossing point demanding a person from my father. My mother came with her only daughter and gave her daughter to my father to give to the *nyenne,* so that he and my 'mother' could cross the river. After that he married my mother. Now that my father is dead, there is no one who should be chief before me." The elders said, "We have heard you, now go and sit down."

Then they called the son of the first wife and said, "Come and tell us why you want to be chief in your father's place." The man said, "I have very little to say. To everything there is a beginning. People should never be surprised at the way things end, they should think of the way things began. My father went with his two brothers to a chief. My father's elder brother slept with the chief's wife. In the morning he was killed. The other brother ate the chief's only cow. In the morning he was killed. My father slept with the chief's eldest daughter, who is my mother. Very early in the morning my mother advised him to run away. They fled. If my mother had not told him to flee, would they not have been killed? Therefore, since my mother was the first to save my father's life, every other fortune originates with my mother. Therefore I should be chief. If a man is fortunate he should never forget how his for-

---

*Here 'mother' signifies "mother's co-wife."

tune began. My mother saved my father first, then the second wife saved him, then the third wife saved him. But they saved him only after my mother had saved him. If a person trips over a stone and falls down somewhere, he should not think of the place where he falls, he should think first of the place where he tripped. Therefore, all the fortune that my father enjoyed originated with my mother. Therefore I should be chief."

Because of that argument—that of the son of the first wife, who was the first one to save the chief's life—he became chief.

The problem treated in this narrative turns on the status ambiguity of the three sons. Because they were all conceived at the same time, born on the same day, and initiated together, the principle of birth-order position is nullified. And, since succession is ordinarily based upon primogeniture, there is no means of deciding unequivocally which son is the rightful heir. The ambiguity and confusion are reinforced here by the apparent similarity of three crucial episodes in which women save the life of the protagonist in return for promises of marriage. In each case the promise is kept.

Each intervention by a woman occurs when an impasse is reached, and each intervention occurs in a liminal setting. In the first episode the protagonist must die for having slept with the chief's eldest daughter; the woman and the man flee the town at dawn. In the second episode the man and the woman are unable to cross a river which divides two chiefdoms; the river and the *nyenne* symbolize liminality in this instance. In the third episode the man's life depends upon a 20 to 1 chance of choosing a certain medicine; the chief's eldest daughter and the man meet at the edge of town and strike a bargain there. The women's interventions, therefore, not only save the man's life, they move on the action of the narrative from one stage to another.

The ambiguity created in the narrative is finally resolved by the narrator himself. On this occasion, no one in the audience could judge the claims of the three sons. Keti Ferenke approached the "trilemma" by shifting attention from the dominant principle (birth-order position determines status distinctions) to a "submerged" principle, namely that differences in the fortunes of men originate in differences in the behavior of their mothers. This implies the notion that a person's destiny is decided by his origins. This shift of focus opens up a way of resolving the problem. We are told that the actions of the second and third women are conditional on the actions of the first. Moreover, in discussing the narrative further with Keti Ferenke, it became clear that the actions of the three women can be evaluated from another point of view.

At the very beginning of the narrative, three sons set off in search of renown. The fate of the men reflects their moral choices or preferences: the first son commits adultery with the chief's wife; the third son is gluttonous; the second son (whose life is saved) marries the chief's eldest daughter. The merciless nature of the chief is contrasted with the compassion of his daughter. In the case of the second woman, she sacrifices her daughter's life in order to save the life of the protagonist. As for the third woman, she sacrifices her father's life in order to save the life of the protagonist. The actions of the second and third women are ambiguous: the life of a kinsman is given so that the life of a stranger can be saved. The action of the first woman is wholly compassionate; it does not have negative repercussions. From this point of view, therefore, the son of the first woman should be favored because of the exemplary actions of his mother.

In the story of Big Thing and Small Thing, the narrator reveals a further dimension of the main narrative. The argument is that cleverness is more important than mere seniority of position. Although this view is more typical of Keti Ferenke than of most Kuranko, it does illuminate a recurrent dilemma in Kuranko life. Cleverness is ideally an attribute of elderhood, but in practice elders are not necessarily more clever than youngsters. This kind of indeterminate relationship between social position and individual disposition is, as we shall see, one of the basic moral concerns in Kuranko narratives.

The story of the three sons shows how explanations and principles of conduct emerge from a context which, at first sight, seems ambiguous. By invalidating one principle of social classification—birth-order position—the narrator is able to bring more informal and diffuse frames of reference into focus. In this particular narrative it becomes clear that a person's destiny reflects the behavior of his mother (not merely his birth-order position), that one's origins are as important as one's attainments, and that compassion toward a stranger is as meritorious as regard for a kinsman. These contemplations are occasioned by the narrative; they do not spring from it as explicit and unambiguous propositions. In this sense the meaning of the tale is indeterminate. It reflects the interests of the listeners, the personality of the narrator, and certain recurring problems in everyday social life.[4] Moreover, the initial ambiguity of the narrative means that a great variety of idiosyncratic views will find expression or outlet in a shared activity. While the story begins in ambiguity, open to interpretation, it concludes in clarity and consensus.

By overthrowing the normal order of things and suspending disbelief, Kuranko narratives create an ecstatic situation in which each person must redefine the world for himself.[5] As such, storytelling sharpens skills of moral discernment and may be compared with certain masked rituals (see Turner, 1970:105–106; Duvignaud, 1972:54–55), notably the Manykomori plays among the neighboring Malinke which function as a form of institutionalized self-criticism of society, revealing and resolving its inner contradictions (Huet, 1978:100).

Modes of Ambiguity

I have already alluded to the indeterminate relationship between social position and individual disposition. While social positions such as roles, statuses, and estates are associated with particular rights and obligations given by ancestral fiat, individual dispositions—moral, intellectual, physical, and emotional—are at once more randomly distributed and more quixotic. Each person must therefore work to bring his temperament under control. This mastery of self creates the appearance of a fit between the individual and the role he plays. But growing up in Kuranko society does not entail a passive accommodation of the individual to his role. The individual does not learn to repress his nature, but rather to express it in ways conducive to the creation of community. This active integration of self and community may be effected in dance, in collective work, in greeting, and in giving. It may also be effected through the subtle devices of narrative art.

Most Kuranko narratives are built around key concepts such as cleverness (*hankilimaiye*), strength (*gheleye*), and goodness (*kin*) which are semantically ambiguous. They refer simultaneously to attributes of social positions and to randomly occurring psychophysical traits. Such concepts mediate between social and personal poles of existence. They are critical indications of the Kuranko endeavor to fashion a determinative relationship between social forms and individual particularities.

The major semantic expression of the contrast between the free energies of the individual person and the bound energies of social roles is the opposition between town and bush.[6] In Kuranko narratives the passage to and fro between town and bush signifies the alignment of the free energies of physical, emotional, and intellectual life with the as-cribed attributes of social being. Learning self-mastery is thus a kind of regularization of ambiguous energies. In certain narratives discussed in chapter 7, sexuality is seen as a kind of free energy (libido) which has to be channeled into the maternal role and not expressed promiscuously. In other narratives the heroic ideal is symbolized by a man with ex-traordinary powers who, rather than satisfying merely personal whims, uses his powers to rejuvenate a disheartened community. In Kuranko thought, correct speech, proper comportment, and self-control are the keys to creating a balance or harmony between given mores and "wild" energies. The goal is not to subdue or repress natural energies but to integrate those energies with collective purposes. But this goal can only be attained when each person *choses* to bind himself or herself over to the collective ideal.

A second mode of ambiguity may be termed (after Quintilian) "schematic." Schematic ambiguity includes allegory and figura, the clas-sical forms of which have been the subject of a notable study by Auer-bach (1959:11–76). Dramatic irony is a kind of schematic ambiguity. It occurs when one character in a tale knows something of which another character is ignorant, or when the audience is privy to some information which the characters in the story lack. In numerous Kuranko narratives the storyteller alerts his audience to the dramatic irony of a situation by interjecting such remarks as "The hyena did not know what the hare knew" or "So-and-so did not know such-and-such." Schematic am-biguity also involves rhetorical obtuseness, where the listeners must fathom for themselves the meaning of a narrative. But unlike the modes of ambiguity referred to so far, schematic ambiguity depends on struc-tural transformations and order of events as much as upon sustained irony. Schematic ambiguity can only be discerned when we consider a narrative in its entirety. Thus, the figure of chiasmus, which I have used to elucidate structural transformations in the narratives, reveals how ambiguity is first dramatized, then annulled. An initially ambiguous situation is created when a person of high status is shown to have in-ferior moral qualities, while a status inferior has all the talents which men of rank should ideally possess. The displacement of the status superior by the gifted underling signifies, schematically, a merging of valued attributes with an elevated social position. But this schema, whose impact springs from a contrast between initial ambiguity and a surprising final clarification, has to be comprehended as a gestalt even though it unfolds serially.

Vladimir Propp observed that "identical acts can have different meanings, and vice versa" (1968:21). As Todorov has shown (1970:914), two forms of schematic ambiguity arise from this. The first is when different semantic units have the same syntactical functions. For example, we may note that greed, overweaning emotional attachments, promiscuity, deceit, betrayal of secrets, and breaking of promises can have the same syntactical functions in various Kuranko narratives. Each semantic unit is thus, in a sense, interchangeable with others, and can be used to convey the same message. The second form of schematic ambiguity which Todorov refers to occurs when the same semantic units have different syntactical functions. For example, if we consider the first seven hare-hyena narratives (N.11–N.17) we find that cleverness is approved. In N.18, however, the hare's cleverness is disapproved and duly punished. Again, while extramarital sexual love is disapproved in most of the narratives in chapter 7, it becomes in N.32 a symbol of constancy and devotion. In both these examples, the first turning upon the ethical ambiguity of cleverness and the second upon ambivalent attitudes to sexual love, the whole narrative as well as its relationship to others must be considered in order to appreciate the meaning given to the core image.

Yet another mode of ambiguity reflects the storyteller's personality and degree of skill. In his famous study of ambiguity in literature (1953), William Empson noted evidence of ideas which had been realized in the process of writing, of unintended irrelevancies, ambiguities, and tautologies, and of confusions and complications in the author's mind. Similar ambiguities occur in Kuranko narratives. In another version of N.1, Denka Marah of Kabala relates how the hero marries four women, but at the close of the narrative he refers to only three. In many narratives I recorded, memory lapses or a loss of interest, particularly by a young narrator, would create confusion, and the storyteller might even be criticized for his lack of skill.[7] It is, of course, sometimes hard to distinguish between tediously discursive passages and delayed denouement. Sometimes, what seems to be deliberate hyperbole is actually the narrator's bombast, and understatement may betray an indecisive mind. It is also difficult to draw a clear distinction between calculated allusiveness and indeliberate obscurity.[8] What is quite clear, however, is that the Kuranko applaud the fluency, command, coherence, and histrionic skills of a storyteller like Keti Ferenke Koroma. Fragmented tales, rambling narration, and indifferent performance are regarded as faults. The Kuranko value eloquence and clarity of speaking. Figurative language and rhetorical ambiguity are acceptable only when a speaker is in full control of what he is doing. It may be recalled that Aristotle considered ambiguity to be a form of deception, a perversion of language (Stanford, 1939:2–20). The Kuranko also admit the negative side of ambiguity which can emerge when a speaker is muddleheaded or when there is no consonance between a speaker's intentions and his actions. Before he can transform a story with his dramatic skills, a narrator must know the story by heart. As Walter Benjamin puts it, storytelling is first of all an "art of repeating stories, and this art is lost when the stories are no longer retained" (1970:91).

One of the most important modes of ambiguity in Kuranko narratives is semiotic ambiguity. Lévi-Strauss has shown that ambiguity is a definitive characteristic of a "mediator." A mediator "occupies a position halfway between two polar terms," and it "must retain something of that duality—namely an ambiguous and equivocal character" (Lévi-Strauss, 1963:226). A mediator is thus endowed with "contradictory attributes" (ibid:227). For convenience of exposition I will consider the mediators in Kuranko narratives under several headings: mediatory figures, mediatory objects, and mediatory settings.

It is striking that the protagonist in a great number of narratives is a young man, *initiated but not yet married*. The category term—*kemine* (lit. "young man")—is often used in the narratives in lieu of a personal name. The mediatory or ambiguous character of the *kemine* is determined by the fact that he is in one respect like a child (not married) and in another respect like a fully responsible adult man (initiated). A *kemine* is, in other words, marginal with regard to the politico-jural community. Separated from the domestic world, yet not fully integrated into the community, the *kemine* is freed, as it were, to symbolize the "unhoused" and the extraterritorial. He is the voyager who risks his life to and froing between village and wilderness.

The second narrative character with obvious mediatory functions is the youngest son, usually portrayed as the hare. The youngest son is marginal with regard to the structure of the generations; he has as much affinity with the junior generation as with his own senior generation, and is a sort of very senior "elder brother" in relation to the generation below his own (Jackson, 1977b:163). With regard to the corporate functions of the family, the youngest brother occupies an extremely peripheral position. He is not likely to ever succeed to a position of authority within the family or to inherit property, partly because by the time his elder brothers are deceased, his elder brothers' elder sons will be of an age to compete with him for control. The youngest brother is what Turner (1970) would call a liminal person; he is neither of one generation nor of another. He is marginal, he is the lastborn (*den na ban*). In the narratives he is assigned attributes of mobility, agility, adroitness, and irresponsibility. He embodies indeterminate powers, particularly cleverness, which are contrasted with the determinate attributes of positions of authority. As Hare, he is the trickster hero. He mediates between center and periphery. He personifies ambivalent attitudes to authority and rigid routine. He is the means by which the inflexible and unjust actions of the elder, the hyena, are corrected.

The third mediatory figure is the old woman (*musu korone*). In the narratives she is often associated, both physically and logically, with the young man. The old woman is past childbearing age, is usually married (in many cases to a bush spirit), possesses extraordinary powers, and lives in the bush. In ordinary life, old women are regarded as trustworthy; their wisdom is respected and they may be admitted into the male *duw* cult association. Many old women establish a reputation as herbalists. In these ways, the figure of the old woman in the narratives mediates between male and female domains. This distinction is expressed in terms of the contrast between town (domain of male control and authority) and bush (extrasocial, peripheral domain). But, like the young man, the old woman is marginal both to the domestic domain (the young man is not yet married, the old woman is past childbearing age) and to the politico-jural domain. The logical relationships between the three mediators considered so far may be expressed as follows:

> *kemine* : elders :: youngest brother : elder brother
> :: old women : men :: bush : town

A fourth set of mediatory figures comprises *jeliba*s (praise-singers), *finaba*s (bards, genealogists) and Muslims, all of whom are marginal to the ruling estate. Their marginality with respect to secular authority is, however, compensated for by their possession of crucial powers. The

Muslims are ritual officiants, diviners, and sorcerers; they mediate between man and the divine. Their power derives from their control over supernatural agencies and forces. The power and influence of the *jeli*s and *fina*s derive from their knowledge of chiefly traditions and genealogies. The legitimation of secular authority thus depends upon the skills and knowledge of individuals who belong to marginal estates.

Other mediators take the form of supernatural intercessories. Shape-shifters are human beings who are able to transform themselves into animals.[9] In such cases a trait of human behavior is associated with an animal form. For example, in N.34 the seductiveness and cunning of a beautiful woman is associated with the grace and wiliness of a female buffalo. Another mediatory figure is created when God assumes human form in order to intervene in solving an earthly dilemma (N.28). The figure of the mentor (*yigi*) is central to several narratives; the mentor's ambiguity derives from the fact that he is a nonkinsman who assumes paternal responsibilities. In other words, he mediates between strangerhood and kinship. Often the mentor-figures in the narratives are insects or animals. It is clear that the contrast between town (humanity) and bush (animality) is the prevailing metaphor for social and behavioral ambiguities.[10] Ambiguity is perhaps most clearly expressed in the figure of the *nyenne*, capricious spirits of the bush whose domain is halfway between the world of man and the world of wild animals.[11] The *nyenne* embody ambiguity and ambivalence, and it is not surprising that they should appear in so many narratives.

The Kuranko *nyenne* is a kind of daimon, a "distributor of destinies," and the *nyenne* is a point of dramatic focus for the interplay between givenness and possibility. It is the *nyenne* who alters one's fortunes, and thereby redistributes possessions or redresses injustices. Like other mediators, the *nyenne* are "part way between the human and divine spheres, touching on both" (Fletcher, 1964:68). The *nyenne* are central to narratives which concern problems of reciprocity and justice; they have the power to intervene in human affairs, and to redistribute scarce material and spiritual resources in the interests of social harmony and equity. Their mediatory roles will be examined further in chapter 6.

The *nyenne* and other mediators are often associated with fetishes and medicines which embody extrasocial powers.[12] The fetishes are frequently personalized, and are addressed as if they possessed intelligence and will (see for examples N.27, N.28, and N.35). A fetish is thus ambiguous; it is a thing, yet it has human attributes. The ambiguous character of a fetish is also indicated by the way in which it combines, in its manufacture, a variety of liminal elements. Many fetishes are made of debris from the marginal domestic area (the *sundu kunye ma*). To protect garden areas, a calabash may be drilled full of holes and the holes stuffed with cotton wool; or a piece of matting and a charred stick from a fire may be used. Other fetishes are made from tree bark, especially red bark. Door lintels are often hung with protective fetishes, such as miniature cane "gates" and *fele. Fele* is a fetish made of black and white cotton thread twisted together. The white symbolizes self, the black symbolizes the other (external evil, a witch, an enemy, etc.). The *fele* is placed on the threshold of a room or at the entrance to a house. Some informants claim that it undermines the self-possession of a potential enemy; others say that it forces an evil-wisher to declare his hidden intentions. Still other fetishes are made from animal skins or body exuviae: urine, excreta, perspiration, hair, etc. But in every case, the fetish is made up of liminal elements and serves to enclose, and thus protect, a unit of social space.

It is significant also that fetishes are made and distributed by old women. This kind of association between mediatory figure and mediatory object is demonstrated in several narratives. In N.27 for example, a young adventurer encounters a *nyenne* in the bush; the *nyenne* gives the young man a fetish, as well as some charcoal, an egg, a piece of bamboo cane, and a stone. These objects are used by the young man in his flights from the hyenas (whose drum he has stolen); when he throws down each object a barrier springs up between him and his pursuers. In N.28 a young adventurer meets an old woman in the bush; the old woman gives the young man a fetish which enables him to accomplish his purposes.

Let us now turn to a consideration of mediatory settings. Once again the contrast between town and bush is the prevailing image. Crucial transformations in the narratives are usually associated with liminal situations. We have already noted this in N.1: the first crucial transformation occurs at dawn (on the threshold between night and day), the second takes place at a riverside (midway between two chiefdoms), and the third occurs at the edge of a town (on the boundary of village and bush). In several narratives (for example N.31) it is a flat expanse of rock which divides village from wilderness. Narrative action on this *faragbaran* (lit. "dividing rock") is usually associated with a crucial transformation in the narrative. Many narratives are set on farms or in farmsteads. This may be in part because the tales are the main form of entertainment during the months when families are living on their farms. But farms are clearings in the bush; they mark the points where cultivation and wilderness meet. Farms are, therefore, appropriate settings for narratives concerned with the interplay between human virtues, such as courage and fortitude, and the brutal, destructive forces of nature, often personified by an intractable *nyenne*.

A second important mediatory setting is the riverside or lakeside. Rivers are often the boundaries between chiefdoms; they are the margins of the main political units in Kuranko society. An even finer distinction is often made between a deep riverhole and the riverbank. Transformations are, in such cases, centered upon actions taking place on the surface of the water or river. A major group of narratives in chapter 8 concerns victimized or disadvantaged individuals: orphans, junior wives, abandoned children, deserted wives, and others. The structure of episodes in these narratives is always the same. The luckless individual is fostered or favored by *nyenne* who live in a riverhole or in a deep lake. Continued communication between the fosterling and the social world is mediated by an old woman who is also a herbalist, by a *jeliba*, and by songs.

The associations between mediatory figures, objects, and settings tend to reinforce one's impressions of the ambiguous episodes and images. The songs which tend to be associated with such episodes and images heighten one's awareness of the significance attaching to these moments of hiatus and suspense. N.32 is a perfect example of these associations. A *young man* has a love affair with a chief's *young wife*. The *young man* is killed and burned; his *ashes* are thrown into the *river*. The ashes are eaten by fish which live in deep riverholes. The woman journeys along the banks of the river, *singing* to her lost lover.

Songs provide an opportunity for audience participation; this is also the case elsewhere in Africa (Finnegan, 1970:246, 386). A narrator often extends the time devoted to a song if his audience includes many children. The songs have their greatest appeal among children. Adults are less interested in the songs; they sing them in order to encourage the participation and enjoyment of children rather than for their own pleasure. It is not surprising, therefore, that the most complex and intellectually demanding narratives seldom include songs.

Songs occur at points of impasse, crisis, and transformation: they mark breaks between crucial episodes.[13] In this way, the songs engage the active participation of the audience at those points in the narrative where uncertainty and tension are greatest. The song sustains a moment of suspense; it presages but at the same time it delays the denouement. One narrative is made up almost entirely of an extended sung exchange between a *nyenne* and a small boy: the *nyenne* tries to tempt and trick the boy into the bush; the boy uses his wits to thwart the *nyenne*. While the song continues, the outcome of the exchange is uncertain. Again, in N.22 the protracted song of the girl who has decided to go into the bush and be killed by a bush spirit rather than marry her father is a way of bringing into relief the nature of the quandary. In the structural interval which songs mark, everyone who shares in the singing of the song tends to identify with the plight or fortune of a central character. One is also inspired to puzzle out a solution to the problem which has been presented. Participation and identification are results of the strongly affective nature of song (Lundin, 1953:132–154), of the hiatus in the narrative plot, and of the ambiguous character of the song itself, which partly springs from the fact that "the shapes of the sound terms are so weak and uniform that there is only a minimal basis for expectation. The feeling is one of suspense and ambiguity" (Meyer, 1956:51).[14]

Songs also provide moments of relief from the often complicated plots of the tales. For many very young listeners, songs are breathing spaces or welcome distractions.[15] The Kuranko sometimes say that the sung parts of the tales are the "sweetest" parts, the occasions of greatest pleasure and personal interest in a storytelling session. It is therefore worth noting that "sweet" music or "sweet" words (which in many songs mimic a musical instrument) are used by characters in several tales as means of distracting a person's attention (N.14, N.15), seducing or beguiling a man, conveying a hidden message (N.13, N.15), or interrupting a routine. In everyday life, music is regarded as a way of distracting attention from pain or toil. But music, like "sweet" words can also corrupt. Like the people of Benin (Ben-Amos, 1975) and the Ashanti (Rattray, 1928; 1930), the Kuranko often refer to stories as being "sweet." Sweetness connotes pleasure-giving, amusing, distracting. Yet too much of a good thing spoils one's appetite for it (*koi l timbine yi' ma di*: "water is not sweet when one drinks beyond the limit"). For this reason sweet things are regarded ambivalently, and in describing the tales as sweet, the Kuranko may mean not just that the narratives are amusing but that they lie ambiguously between truth and falsehood.

Marginal figures, objects, and settings are the objective correlatives of ambivalent feelings, moral dilemmas, and intellectual uncertainties. Quite often, marginal situations are established as fictional means of exploring extreme emotions, attitudes, and actions. This is very clearly shown by the set of hunger narratives in chapter 3. I will later discuss how the various *symbolic levels* in these narratives—economic, techno-logical, geographical, sociological, psychological—can be analyzed in terms of an underlying *logical structure* which is itself the means for generating discourse on certain problems of social conduct. This method is directly comparable to the method employed by Lévi-Strauss in his study of a Tsimshian myth and its versions (1977:146).[16]

In the foregoing account of ambiguous imagery I have emphasized that ambiguous terms are objective correlatives of certain subjective states. The ambiguous images are, moreover, part of common parlance. They are metaphors shared by all Kuranko, metaphors which articulate inchoate meanings in a variety of narrative, ritual, and mundane con-texts. These root metaphors give structure to sentiment; they transcend the essential privacy of experience, and they mediate transformations in awareness (c.f. Fernandez, 1971:41–44). The images and metaphors in the narratives are thus abstract and impersonal. These characteristics have been often misinterpreted. For example, Northrop Frye takes the view that:

> Folk tales tell us nothing credible about the life or manners of any society; so far from giving us dialogue, imagery or complex be-haviour, they do not even care whether their characters are men or ghosts or animals. Folk tales are simply abstract story-patterns, un-complicated and easy to remember, no more hampered by barriers of language and culture than migrating birds are by customs officers, and made up of interchangeable motifs that can be counted and indexed. (1963:27)

Frye's error is to consider the folktale out of context. The complex-ity, depth, and meaning of any narrative are established at the level of interaction between audience and text. The subjective engagement of the audience is, moreover, facilitated by the objective and abstract character of the narrative itself. Frye confuses method with purpose. What he sees as a paucity of subjective detail is really a vast scattering of clues. The impersonality of the narrative makes it more accessible to individual use. Devereux has explained how this occurs. He points out that myths and folktales constitute a kind of "cold storage" for individual fantasies that cannot be successfully or easily handled by means of subjective defenses (Devereux, 1961:378–379; 1969:123). Such fantasies (or the dilemmas and conflicts which generate them) are taken out of private circulation, so to speak, and given conventionalized, impersonalized expression in myths and folktales. Different individuals can then "borrow" the narratives for personal use, while pretending that their motives and interests are purely artistic or merely social.[17] This "intrapsychic alibiing," as Devereux calls it (1961:378), explains why people pass off the narratives as make-believe or "merely for amusement," why narrators disavow responsibility for creating the narratives, and why narratives are bracketed apart from everyday normal social life. Many students of folktales disparage the narratives in similar ways. Some regard them as childish entertainments, others, accepting that they are composed by adults, claim that adults compose them on the basis of retrograde infantile fantasies (Rank, 1959:84); some take the view that folktales are little more than trite and abstract story patterns (Frye, 1963:27), while others simply catalog folktale motifs (Thompson, 1955–58), thus belying the richness of the subjective and social contexts in terms of which all narratives must be interpreted.

The Narratives as Play

The Kuranko distinguish several kinds of oral traditions. The most important distinction is between *kuma kore* (lit. "talk/words/speech old/senior/venerable") and *tileinu* ("folktales"). Any narrative classified as *kuma kore* is regarded as true, a legacy of the ancestors. *Tileinu* are readily admitted to be make-believe. While "old speech" is always taken seriously, *tileinu* are for entertainment" and are "told for amusement." Other forms of Kuranko oral literature are songs (*sigeinu*), proverbs, parables, adages, and sayings (*saranenu*), and riddles or riddle stories (*sosogoma tileinu*).[18] Most *tileinu* include sung portions, which are known as *sigenu* (songs). A storyteller is called *til'sale*, "one who sets down stories."

I have endeavored to avoid definitive terms such as myth, oral history, folktale, and legend, preferring the more neutral word "narrative" in describing both *tilei* and *kuma kore*. To some extent, however, *tileinu* may be compared to *kuma kore* which have been reduced in scale. In Lévi-Strauss's words, "the great logical or cosmological contrasts have been toned down and reduced to the scale of social relations"

(1970:333). In the Kuranko corpus there are several examples of narratives which are classed as *tileinu* but which are actually episodes from epics or myths or Mande. The pursuit sequence in N.27 is a good example.

Lévi-Strauss has also pointed out that the tale contrasts with myth in another respect. "The tale offers more possibilities of play, its permutations are comparatively freer, and they progressively acquire a certain arbitrary character" (1977:128). This comment comes close to conveying the differences subjectively felt by the Kuranko, who are often ambiguous about the exact classification of narratives. In my view, this ambiguity reflects the fact that they make a distinction between the truth of *kuma kore* (founded upon the assumption that the ancestors did not lie) and the fictional character of a *tilei*, while affirming that *tileinu* nonetheless are concerned with moral truths. It is, therefore, the *essence* of the *tilei* which is true; its images, characters, and settings are make-believe. The *events* around which a *tilei* revolves may also be true. Keti Ferenke emphasized that a good *tilei* must make reference to actual social events; it should never be wholly abstracted from the quotidian. He also explained that some *tileinu* may be true because each has been handed down over many generations and "the first person that told it may have been speaking of an actual event." Sinkari Yegbe gave a similar view: "The stories have been handed down to us from our ancestors' time; even if the events in the stories occurred, it was not in our day. But we think those events really did occur because otherwise our ancestors would not have spoken of them."

As Lévi-Strauss suggests, the play element in tales indicates the extent to which individual narrators are free to remodel or vary the content and code. Variability is a fundamental attribute of the Kuranko narrative, and I will have occasion to refer frequently to different versions and to alternative interpretations suggested by them. The play element in the narratives also reflects the fact that they are only tenuously anchored in the mundane and familiar world. They break free of the constraints and organizations of everyday life and entertain new possibilities of thought and action. In Steiner's terms, they exemplify the capacity of language for "counter-factuality," for misconstruction, illusion, and play (1975:224–226).

The function of *tileinu* as entertainment is the most obvious one. Most narratives inspire laughter. Keti Ferenke, a risible man anyway, was often incoherent with laughter occasioned by his own narrations. I have known people to have to leave storytelling sessions because they were unable to control their laughter, and it is not uncommon for people to collapse with hilarity and giggling. The deadpan expression of a skilled narrator while he describes ludicrous actions (the man-baby in N.6 is a fine example) is a certain recipe for success. The second function of the *tilei*, as moral instruction, is more implicit, and the Kuranko do not usually verbalize the meanings contained within the narratives. This is, however, the task of the anthropologist.

The comic and ludic elements of the *tileinu* reflect their incongruous character. The narratives concern real events, yet they use surreal characters and break the unities of time and place; they inspire ambivalence, yet they move toward the resolution of problems and the clarification of ethical issues; they invert or pervert the norm, yet they reinforce ideal principles. The dialectic between form and formlessness is, as I have already stressed, dependent upon a relationship between "figure" and "ground." Mary Douglas has made the same point. She notes that any funny story "offers alternative patterns, one apparent, one hidden: the latter, by being brought to the surface impugns the validity of the first" (1968:364). Kuranko narratives, like jokes, are plays upon form; they tend to subvert the dominant structure of ideas by showing that "an accepted pattern has no necessity" (Douglas, 1968:365). The play element in the narratives thus implies a kind of experimentation. In N.1, for example, the dominant principle of birth-order position is nullified or subverted because all three sons are conceived at the same time, born on the same day, and initiated together. Moreover, they all seem equally well-endowed. The nullification of the dominant principle produces ambiguity. The attention of the audience is then focused upon hidden factors—the different ethical values associated with the behavior of the mothers—and a new awareness of the factors underlying personal destiny is created. It may be suggested that this shift of focus entails a search for a transcendent morality, a morality which is not wholly determined by such dominant principles as birth-order position, estate and clan identifications, and sex. This transcendent morality, which Turner designates "communitas," plays up subjectivity and seeks to accommodate the uniqueness of individual existence within the matrix of inflexible rules and general ethical prescriptions.

The Kuranko emphasize that *tileinu* are mainly for amusement, for entertainment, for passing the time, and for enlivening periods of dullness, particularly during the rainy season when many families are isolated in remote farmsteads. No less important, though less frequently referred to, is the pedagogic value of *tileinu. Tileinu,* in this sense, are means of moral instruction, of changing one's experience of the world. For example, in his discussion of the dilemma tale *The Three Sons* (N.1), Keti Ferenke improvised a proverb as a way of reiterating the moral of the narrative:

> If you strike your foot against a stone, and go elsewhere to sit down, you should not forget the place where you received the injury. Never ignore your beginnings. You children should always be grateful to those who help you. If someone sends you to school and you become well educated and an important person besides, you should not forget the person who sent you to school in the first place. Nor should that person forget the person who helped him achieve his important position.

This indicates how a narrative is frequently a catalyst for generating discussion. It also cautions us to consider narratives in their contexts of telling.

The pedagogic function of the narratives is closely related to the entertainment or play function. The narratives indicate to a child that the social world is largely contingent. It is not something external and preestablished; it is a product of human activity. In Piaget's words, "In order for a child to understand something, he must construct it himself, he must re-invent it" (quoted in Erickson, 1972:132). The narratives occasion this reconstruction and reinvention of the world. They inspire reflection upon subjects which are usually taken for granted, and they encourage people to express preferences and to make judgments upon matters which are normally decided for them. These interests are shared by both children and adults. The narratives help children "grasp" the world and seize upon the ethical principles that underlie social order.[19]

For adults, the narratives provide exercises in the casuistry of everyday life; they are, to use Manfred Stanley's phrase, concerned with legitimacy and human agency. The narratives are not merely means of legitimating given norms, dogma, rules, or structures based on sex, age, genealogy, and class. They are not "charters" for social action. They are explorations into the problem of right conduct. Legitimacy, in this context, connotes "a sense of the fitness (rightness and propriety) of the human world—the institutions, rules, and procedures in terms of which one discovers oneself to be related to society," while legitimation is regarded as "a dynamic hermeneutic process—a struggle for meaning whereby an acceptable moral interpretation of the human world is actively sought for" (Stanley, 1973:401).[20] The problems of legitimacy and doubt arise because general rules and ideal prescriptions cannot be applied unambiguously to all concrete situations. The indeterminate relationship between knowledge and event (which, in the Kuranko case, implies a contrast between the abstract past of the ancestors and the concrete now of contemporaries) means that the interpretation of moral meanings is a task that falls to everyone. It is a never-ending task because ethical structures can never really be complete. And it is this task which is central to the narratives which dramatize the discrepancies between general rules and the "mosaic of immediate situations" (Stanley, 1973:419).

Experimentation and creativity in the narratives occur within certain limits. As Stanley puts it, "Constituting the world does not mean inventing it, but interpreting what is already there" (1973:419). The narratives awaken new responses and attitudes, they encourage a new awareness of familiar problems, but the solutions for quotidian problems which emerge from the narratives are fictional, products of a kind of legerdemain.[21]

The ludic aspects of the narratives reflect the ways in which they annul normal orders, blur categories which are ordinarily distinguished, scorn rigid codifications, and juxtapose elements that are usually kept separate. The ambiguities and incongruities arise from two main situations. Either some peculiar circumstance makes a social rule untenable (as in N.1), or there is a discrepancy between individual temperament or ability and the requirements of a social role. In such situations the social rule or role *cannot be taken seriously.* Since the Kuranko *tileinu* create such situations, it is logical that the *tileinu* should be regarded as make-believe, as entertainments. It is also possible to understand why *tileinu* must never be told in the daytime.

Night in the Bush

The Kuranko think of the daytime (*teli ro,* lit. "sun in") as a time of normal social activity; "day" connotes routine, order, openness among people, community.[22] Night (*suiye*) is associated with antisocial activities, such as witchcraft (witch = *suwage,* lit. "night owner/agent"), intrigue, conspiracy, and disorder. It would be perhaps more accurate to say that "night" connotes a suspension of normal order, an interregnum between days. While genealogies, proverbs, and clan myths are regarded as "true," the *tileinu* entail explorations of the extraordinary; they require a suspension of disbelief, a toleration of momentary disorder. But *tileinu* are told not in the deep of night (when witches are active) but during the evening, on the edge of night. Tales are told on moonlit nights on verandas, in the *luiye* (public courtyard) around a fire, in farmhouses when the day's work is done, or indoors in the light of a candle or hurricane lamp. If we adopt the Kuranko metaphor we might say, therefore, that the narratives are told in the penumbra of the social order. While darkness connotes a suspension or perversion of the social order, the half-light in which the tales are told connotes an ambiguous zone between normal and extraordinary awarenesses. Horner describes a similar situation among the Bulu of southeast and central Cameroon:

> Night is always the setting for storytelling among the Bulu. Night plays games with one's senses. The tropical night falls swiftly as if by a magician's wand. The storyteller, a magician with words, tells his tale facing a group of ten-year-old boys (*bongô*) over a low-burning flickering fire. The boys are ready to learn the daily customs (*yembam*), ethical norms, and goals of Bulu society. In a year or so they will be sent to live and socially "die" as children in the forests, to return as men. This story is for them. It will teach them what to avoid and how to act. (1966:155)

Horner's remarks suggest a fascinating analogy between storytelling and enculturation.[23] In Africa, initiation entails a physical movement from the community into the bush; there, after enduring a period of sequestration and instruction, the neophytes return to the community with a new moral awareness of their roles and responsibilities. Among the Kuranko, initiation involves a suspension and even an inversion of many normal patterns of social behavior. It is during a period of status ambiguity in the bush that the neophytes undergo their transition to adult status. It is a dangerous time, which is why the bush house where initiation takes place is called the *fafei* (from *fafa*: hot, troubled, perturbed). Momentarily displaced from the social and moral world, the initiates comprehend their part in affirming and upholding the principles upon which that world depends. The spatial contrast between town and bush is thus analogous to the temporal contrast between day and night. The narratives, like the liminal phase of initiation ritual, belong to the borderlands between social and extrasocial worlds. Indeed, story-telling is often a prelude to sleep, and the drowsy ambiance of many narrative sessions makes credible, paradoxically, the bizarre characters and events which figure in the tales.[24]

The Kuranko prohibition upon telling stories during the daytime is reinforced by the widespread notion that a parent will die if one does so.[25] The idea of telling *tilei* in the daytime is, however, a cause of amusement, an incongruity. Storytelling is a form of play and it is in-compatible with work. When I once asked Keti Ferenke to explain why he did not hesitate to narrate *tileinu* to me in the daytime, he laughed and said, "My parents are both dead; it is all right for me!" The sanction was, he remarked, intended as a means of keeping children's minds on their work, particularly during the farm season when they had to be vigilant and scare birds from the crops.

I have drawn an analogy between narratives and initiations: both oc-casion a temporary annulment of the social and moral world in order to remodel it and foster a new awareness of its underlying principles and problems. This analogy is also based upon the fact that narratives and initiations center upon certain core images of the contrast between social and extrasocial worlds: day/night, cool/hot, white/black, town/bush. But a more exact analogy may be drawn between the narratives and hunting. It is an analogy recognized by the Kuranko themselves. Keti Ferenke even ascribes the origins of storytelling to a praise-singer of the hunters, Fa Braima Yanka, who accompanied the ancestral hunter Mande Fabori and sang of his remarkable deeds.[26] The connec-tion between the narratives and hunting arises from the fact that both are marginal activities. Hunting is always done at night, and hunters journey from villages into the deep bush. They enter extrasocial time and venture into extrasocial space.[27] Moreover, the values stressed in narratives are directly comparable to those which hunters emphasize: control over emotions and appetites, wariness, skill, bravery, fortitude, cleverness, cooperation, and a willingness to share the gains of the hunt with one's fellow villagers.

In Parenthesis

Like initiation and hunting, narratives are disengaged from ordinary space and time. One is immediately struck by the manner in which stories are set in the remote past, usually in a far-off place. Narrators often use the phrase *wo lai yan la* and *wo le yan be la* ("far-off and long ago") to signify this disengagement from the here and now. Nevertheless, most narrators endeavor to achieve a balance between the strange and the familiar, achieving an ambiguity with respect to the reality of the narrative settings and the credibility of the narrative events. Thus, a narrator might say of a chief in a tale, "He was like Chief Sewa here in Firawa," or of a fictional village, "It was like Sukurela here." In several narratives the relative distance between fictional locations is established by using local references and landmarks. Teina Kuyate sets one narrative in a remote forest long ago, but she then compares the great tree under which the hero sits with the cotton tree that stands outside the chief's house at Kondembaia (the town in which the tale is being told). Narrative movements from the vicinity of the tree into the wilderness and back thus suggest oscillations between the immediate and the imaginary, between a real town and a miraculously created one. The story is "neither here nor there." And it may be this ambiguity which underlies the uncertainty expressed by informants when they are asked whether or not the *tileinu* are true.

Another kind of equilibrium must be kept between the abstract, impersonal character of the narrative and the specific, personal interests or interpretations of the narrator.[28] One of the characteristics of a myth or folktale is that it occasions thoughts, feelings, associations, and recollections which go far beyond the narrative itself. Yet these subjective, concrete, and idiosyncratic elements are pruned out or played down in the narratives. Devereux has suggested that this is because a myth or folktale becomes widely accepted only when concrete incidents are generalized, superfluous details omitted, the narrative fitted into the conventional mold of narrative technique, and the basic plot "ground down to its universally valid nucleus" (1948:238). In order that it be generally available, a narrative must seem to transcend the private worlds of the myth-maker and the myth-teller. And in order that it convey with authority the official meaning assigned to it, a narrative must always retain a veneer of impersonality. I have made the point elsewhere that the problem of myth analysis is comparable to the problem of myth-making, for, in both cases, the "made thing" must facilitate or mediate a dialectic between subjective particularities and conventional or universal meanings (Jackson, 1979). The myth or narrator must organize and represent subjective, idiosyncratic elements of his own life in ways which enable others to discover their own meanings of his work. The myth analyst must establish a similar rapport: between his own response to a narrative and the meanings it has for people in another society.

This "degré zéro," to borrow Barthes's phrase (1967), which is generated in the narratives, raises important problems for the analyst. The difficulty of myth analysis is one of avoiding a reduction of the meaning of the myth to particular subjective realities, whether of a narrator, an informant, or of oneself. At the same time, one must avoid a reduction of subjective realizations to conventional authorized meanings. We cannot expect to develop an inductive science of mythology. Professional and personal predilections will always influence the mode of analysis: the same tale cannot be told twice. The art of myth analysis is to make a virtue of these contradictions. The concerns and interests of the analyst, and the ways in which a narrative varies from context to context and from person to person and from performance to performance, should be regarded as means for attaining new syntheses rather than as obstacles to attaining a set goal. In this way, the myth analysis becomes like the myth, continually transcending the conditions that fostered it.[29]

The disengagement from subjectivity, which is characteristic of the Kuranko narratives, is accomplished first of all by the formal, impersonal, stereotyped organization of each narrative. Personal interpolations by the narrator are minimal. When, as rarely happens, a narrator is telling a tale which he himself has composed, he will not declare his part in the authorship of the tale. All *tileinu* are told as if they were parts of a traditional corpus handed down unchanged over many generations. Individual variations are similarly masked. For these reasons a collector of narratives can be easily led into assuming that idiosyncratic alterations, interjections, elaborations, and interpretations either are insignificant or do not exist. Most narrators, moreover, disavow that tales are created through human inspiration. The following comments by Keti Ferenke, who actually does compose *tileinu,* are interesting in this regard.

> To start with, my great-great-grandfather was a chief. Down to my grandfather, they were all chiefs. Until my father, they were all chiefs. Now, when you are born into a ruling house you will be told many things. If you are a fool you'll be none the wiser, but if you are clever you will scrutinize everything.[30] And when you lie down, you will think over certain things. If you do this, it is good. This is how I think of things. But it is only God that gives thought to a person.

> When you are told something, it is good if it stays in your mind.
> What I have to say about the stories is this: I only think of them.
> They just come into my mind, just like that. I am not asleep. I am not
> in a dream. But when I think of them, I put them all together into a
> story.

Keti Ferenke Koroma insisted that a storyteller's gifts are "God-given" and that it is God who puts the ideas of the *tilei* into the narrator's head.[31] Thus, a narrator simply "sets down" or "lays out" something which has been given to him; he is called *til'sale* ("one who sets down *tileinu*"). In this sense the storyteller is like the diviner. The diviner is "one who lays out pebbles," but it is God who puts the idea of how to interpret the patterns into the diviner's head (see Jackson, 1978a). Just as diviners disavow subjective interference in the business of interpreting pebble patterns, so the narrators disown the narratives. The Kuranko never regard *tileinu* as being in any way the property of individuals. The only prestige associated with storytelling is the prestige that comes from a person's skill in "setting down" the tale.

We have already seen how *tileinu* are set apart from everyday life and ordinary social activity. Work characterizes the quotidian; the narratives, by contrast, are play. The various conventional techniques for signifying that the *tileinu* are disengaged from normal order and from subjectivity are ways of "framing" or bracketing the narratives.[32] The statement "this is play" denotes that "the actions in which we now engage do not denote what those actions *for which they stand* would denote" (Bateson, 1973:152). The functions of this paradox and ambiguity may now be considered in greater detail.

I have already suggested that the *tileinu* involve several ambiguities: true/false, real/not real, subjective/nonsubjective, here/not here, past/present, dominant principles of social structure/submerged principles of social organization, social positions/individual dispositions. By playing down habitual or dogmatic patterns of thinking, the narratives dramatize the problematic of everyday life. The ambiguity which they create inspires audience participation in searching for moral meanings and in clarifying ethical issues. But the narratives not only inspire participation, they allow the expression of normally repressed or forbidden impulses.

In Africa, the cathartic function of folktales is closely related to their satirical function. As satires on chiefs, elders, and priests, or as ways of ridiculing the infirm, the greedy, and the stupid, narratives achieve vicariously what is normally unacceptable. In his analysis of Akan-Ashanti narratives (1930), Rattray makes it quite clear that these functions, which are so much in evidence in the Ashanti spider tales (*anansesem*), must be understood in terms of the fact that a "period of licence" exists on storytelling occasions.[33]

In his introduction to the study of the Mandinka *tali* (c.f. Kuranko *tilei*), Sory Camara refers to the narratives as "enigmatic tales of uncertainly imminent acts" (1972). He also comments upon the parenthetical situation:

> Declared to be a telling of deeds which are not of any time, which have not taken place anywhere, the *tali* concern nonetheless the fundamental experience of every Mandenka individual, an experience which breaks free from the trappings of age and primogeniture:
> "At that moment
> "I carried my mother on my back
> "My father trotted at my feet."
> [my translation]

All these functions obtain in the Kuranko *tilei*. Satires on authority and the stupid and inept are particularly well illustrated by the hare-hyena narratives in chapter 4. But satire, ridicule, and laughter are not always turned against others. These devices mediate private reflections as well as external criticisms. Thomas Lambo points out that "Tales make use of the principle that laughter is the supreme corrective, and poke fun at people who make fools of themselves in various ways" (1961:62). But this is, Lambo stresses, a mode of teaching and of socialization as much as it is a way of inculcating a sense of critical judgment of others.

These references to psychological functions do not, unfortunately, help us to understand the structure of satire or the efficacy of its forms. In the following pages I will endeavor to show how certain cognitive and emotional changes are occasioned by various narrative techniques. Such changes depend first of all upon the conventions of bracketing which I have referred to above. The narratives are set apart from the contexts of everyday life. They are disengaged from subjectivity. The narratives work like magic: they enable personal emotions to be rephrased according to the conventional formulations of the culture; only then does subjectivity become comprehensible and manageable. At the same time, the conventional cultural formulations suggest certain ideas and promote emotional response. T. S. Eliot speaks of this interplay between the subjective and the objective as follows:

> The only way of expressing emotion in the form of art is by finding an "objective correlative"; in other words, a set of objects, a situation, a chain of events which shall be the formula for that particular emotion; such that when the external facts, which must terminate in sensory experience, are given, the emotion is immediately evoked. (1951:145).

The appearance of objectivity, which the narratives contrive, has another purpose, which Eliot only hints at. All morality springs from the consideration of what it is to be another. Moral reasoning begins in empathic understanding, rather than in projective understanding. To empathically understand the experience, reasons, avowals, and actions of another person, one must to some degree achieve detachment from self. An abstract attitude must be fostered. Thus, the purpose of the narratives as means of encouraging moral reasoning is assisted by the abstract, objective, and stereotypical form they take.

The understanding of Kuranko narratives thus depends upon an elucidation of the interplay between certain emotions (the "problems" at the heart of Kuranko social life) and their "objective correlatives." I have already suggested that the narratives may be compared with divination. In divination, emotions which seem at first to be unamenable to organization and control are rephrased in terms of standard cultural formulas. The client is then advised upon a certain course of action as a consequence of the diviner's interpretation of patterns of river pebbles (see Jackson, 1978a). The emotions are thus objectified in two ways: they are expressed in terms of verbal stereotypes, and they are represented by physical objects. The manipulation of things then provides the means of transforming emotions and ideas. The dialectic of subjectivity and objectivity which underlies divinatory practice is equally important in the narratives.

Subject and Object:
Patterns of Composition and Description

Many Kuranko *tileinu* are allegorical. In the first place, allegory "says one thing and means another." Fletcher notes that "It destroys the normal expectation we have about language, that our words 'mean what they say'" (1964:2). It is noteworthy that the word "allegory" is from *allos* + *agoreuin* ("other" + "speak openly, speak in the assembly or market"). Fletcher points out that *agoreuin* connotes public, open, declarative speech. This sense is inverted by the prefix *allos;* thus "allegory is often called 'inversion'" (Fletcher, 1964:2). The Kuranko *tileinu* are, as we have seen, set apart from everyday life in exactly the same sense. They are never told in the *luiye* (public courtyard), but on verandas at the edge of this domain.

In the second place, allegory does not have to be read exegetically; "it often has a literal level that makes good enough sense all by itself" (Fletcher, 1964:7). But, allegory typically lends itself to deeper interpretations and associations. As Fletcher puts it, "Even the most deliberate fables, if read naively or carelessly, may seem mere stories, but what counts . . . is a structure that lends itself to a secondary reading, or rather, one that becomes stronger when given a secondary meaning as well as a primary meaning" (1964:7). The presence and possibility of secondary meanings are what make the *tileinu* ambiguous. The narratives occasion explorations of the particular subjective background or problematic that lies beyond the level of dogma and manifest behavior. But it is the very formality and impersonality of the *tilei* which make these explorations possible. The *tilei* belongs to everyone. Unlike the apologue, which tends to convey a definite moral lesson, the *tilei* invites participation in the process of constructing moral meanings and evaluating actions. It is because these narratives are stripped of all idiosyncratic and subjective trappings that they are available for use in these ways.

Personal names are usually stereotyped. Sira is the usual fictional name for a woman, Tamba for a man. In some instances names are not names used in everyday life. In N.20 the name of the hero, Gbentoworo, is derived from *gbelan* ("shin"), *to* ("in"), and *woro* (perhaps meaning "calf of the leg"); Gbentoworo is born from the shin of his mother's leg. In many cases personal names are dispensed with altogether and the characters of the story are referred to by personal pronouns. Characters address each other by formal terms, rather than by personal names. Thus, *m'fa* ("my father") is used widely as a formal term of respect, similar to the English term "sir" or "mister." The trickster, Hare, is often referred to, as well as addressed, as *Fasan*. And the narrators of *tileinu* tend to depersonalize characters by using category words such as *gberinya musu* ("junior co-wife"), *baramuse* ("beloved wife"), *biranke* ("male affine"), *sunkuron* ("young, newly initiated woman"), and *kemine* ("young initiated man").

Narrators often disguise their normal speech in order to assist characterization. For example, in one tale nasalization of speech signifies a change from human to animal form. Some narrators assume deadpan expressions when telling a story, since it is felt that the narrative must stand apart from the individual who is relating it. But gestures and verbal expressiveness are essential aspects of storytelling, and the projection of the narrative requires histrionic and performative skills. Considerable amusement is generated by a narrator who can mime movement and imitate voices. Laughter is greatest when the incongruity is greatest: for example, Keti Ferenke's imitation of the whimpering, wheedling man-child in N.6, and his ability to dramatize the differences between the clever hare and the stupid hyena.

Stock descriptions, figures, phrases, and sequences also help define the *tilei* as something outside of ordinary reality. Many actions and movements are described by ideophones, most of which are conventionalized; they are used in everyday speech as much as in the narratives. The range is very great, but some examples may be given:

faso faso faso . . . cutting rice (N.6)
gburutu . . . a hoe striking the ground
wado wado wado . . . cutting through a cane with teeth (N.27)
morto morto morto . . . chewing something hard (N.27)
gbodon . . . a stone plopping into water
gbogbon . . . a person plunging into water (N.32)
woooorum . . . a gun being fired
biribiribiri . . . guns being fired
kupukupukupukupu . . . beating of bird's wings
figifigifigi . . . bird flying from a branch
gbusukuru . . . bursting out laughing (N.21)
nye nye nye . . . a man crying like a baby (N.6)
feeeeee, boro . . . falling from a tree and landing
wunya wunya wunya . . . woman running to feed her baby (N.6)
pila pila pila . . . running a race (N.18)
dege dege dege . . . running with a load
barabarabara, barabarabara . . . hyenas running (N.27)
tagbara tagbara tagbara . . . awkward gait of a man who is dressed in woman's clothes
fafa fa fafafa . . . hastening and bustling (N.29)
logbo . . . a hand falling limply to the ground
nolinoli . . . an indolent movement

funsan . . . the sound of a dress being swept back
wurma wurma wurma . . . picking objects up off the ground while walking quickly along
wurtu . . . sound of a calabash plant being uprooted (N.38)
kunduborso kunduborsoborso . . . heavy, reluctant work
kakubatabata kaliamba . . . easy, joyful work
dondon . . . silence

The Narratives in Context: A Storytelling Session

The classification of narratives reflects the interests of the classifier.
But the variety of meanings conveyed by any one narrative makes it
impossible to arrive at a determinate scheme of classification for the
texts (c.f. Propp, 1968:5–19). Apart from a few references to "animal
narratives," the Kuranko themselves do not take any interest in arrang-
ing the *tileinu* into classes or sets; we cannot, therefore, rely on any
indigenous scheme of classification. My own organization of the *tileinu*
reflects the kinds of problems they deal with as much as the plan and
development of the argument in this book. Different theoretical interests would require other groupings.

Although the researcher arranges texts according to an imposed
scheme, it is important to consider the actual sequences in which the
narratives were related and recorded. An analysis of an actual storytelling session gives us insights into the connections between narratives as
well as into the styles and techniques of narrative performance. On 15
February 1972 I recorded a complete storytelling session at Kondembaia. The session lasted 43 minutes, and included ten *tileinu* and a song.
The storytellers were Keti Ferenke Koroma, Kenya Fina Marah, and
Sulimani Koroma. About a third of the session (13 minutes) was taken
up with the narration of *The Origin of the Yimbe Drum* (N.27) by Sulimani Koroma. Keti Ferenke and Kenya Fina told stories for the same
amount of time (8 minutes), and they shared the telling of two stories
(6.5 minutes).

Many of the features of this storytelling session are typical. Sessions
may last only half an hour or go on for as long as two hours, but most
are about an hour long. Usually between eight and fifteen narratives are
told. Most *tileinu* take 2 to 4 minutes to tell, and lengthier stories, such
as *The Origin of the Yimbe Drum,* are not usually told when there are
children in the audience: long and complicated narratives lacking songs

and comic elements do not appeal to children. In most sessions, the storytelling is shared by two or three narrators. In this particular case, each of the three narrators told three stories; two shared the telling of a further two. Variety characterizes the stories told.

In this session, Keti Ferenke began with a just-so story (3 minutes) which explained why cats chase rats. The story included three songs, and each song was chorused several times. The children in the audience were immediately engaged by this story, and they joined in the songs with enthusiasm and delight. For his second story (2 minutes), Keti Ferenke chose a *tilei* with greater adult interest. Yet this story also contained a song with a catchy chorus line, and the children sang it with gusto. The third story (13 minutes) was told by Sulimani Koroma. Although this story was long and involved, the children sat through, entranced. When he had finished, Sulimani allowed Kenya Fina to take over. Her first was *The Melodious Sound of the Yimbe Drum* (3 minutes), which I had previously recorded in March 1970. The second (4 minutes) related how a woman once made an enormous fishing net and fished from the Seli River one of every kind of fish. The woman sings the names of the fish as she takes them from the net. Kenya Fina kept the song going for 3 minutes, the children joining in the chorus. She then sang a song for the children (1.5 minutes), the song of the Siaman bird which was able to mimic the sounds of flutes, drums, and xylophones. Kenya Fina has a beautiful voice; it is relaxed, mellisonant, and expressive. Her love of singing comes through in her treatment of *tileinu*. I knew no other narrator who actually instructed children in how to sing the song before beginning the narration. Even when the audience said they knew the narrative song, Kenya Fina would sing it several times before telling the story. Her narratives (N.32, N.35) are characterized by beautiful singing and superb narrative skill, and she is renowned in Diang chiefdom as a storyteller.

The remaining stories in this session all dealt with relationships between men and women. Although the subject matter of these stories probably held little interest for children, the stories contained songs which the children could share in singing. Narrators keep the attention of all members of the audience by varying the subject matter of the stories, by including songs with stories, and by mixing levity with seriousness of tone. In this storytelling session there was a gradual increase in the spirit of fun and play as the session progressed. The audience was fairly quiet and circumspect during the narration of the first few stories,

but by the time Keti Ferenke and Kenya Fina had decided to share in
the telling of a story, laughter came freely and frequently, and the narrators' antics dominated the narration. It seemed to me that the children identified with fictional characters and situations through the
songs, and that the narrators gradually began to perform rather than
merely tell the stories. Full performance was presaged by the way in
which Keti Ferenke and Kenya Fina lent vocal support to Sulimani
when he was telling the story of the *yimbe* drum. Sulimani often repeated phrases thrice in order to emphasize a point. Keti Ferenke
would often echo or repeat a phrase to the same effect. Keti Ferenke
and Kenya Fina frequently interjected such exclamations as *ha, heh, eh,
oho,* or *fiu,* and murmured their approval of the story with such asides as
mmm, mmmhn, and *hnn.* Such exclamatory remarks abound in the narratives themselves, and must be regarded as dramatic devices for
enlivening interest, and creating surprise or emphasis.

Gifted storytellers never flag in their efforts to astound their audience and maintain a high pitch of excitement. Rapid narration alternates
with slow buildups to a surprising event, and direct speech gives dramatic immediacy to exchanges between characters. In their telling of
one story, Keti Ferenke and Kenya Fina used many of the techniques of
theatrical performance. Indeed, they acted and played the story rather
than told it (Keti Ferenke acted the part of the devoted Muslim; Kenya
Fina played the seductress). The quickness and ease of the dialogue,
and the subtle use of innuendo, indicate how well these two narrators
know each other and how familiar they are with the story. It may be
argued that true theater develops out of oral narration once the stories
have become sufficiently fixed and familiar to allow narrators to perform dialogue, improvise appropriate dramatic expressions, and call
upon song and chorus at given intervals.[34]

While some narrators achieve great fluency and familiarity with their
own versions of certain narratives, the actual sequence of stories in any
session is always different. It is likely that associations of words and
ideas prompt storytellers to offer a particular narrative. For example,
after Sulimani had told *The Origin of the Yimbe Drum,* Kenya Fina told a
story about a town where it was forbidden to sound the *yimbe* drum.
This story is structurally and thematically similar to one of Keti
Ferenke's tales, and it probably inspired Keti Ferenke to tell (with
Kenya Fina's help) his three stories about beguiling women. These
stories in turn suggested another which Sulimani told. The thematic

continuity which can be traced out here must, however, be related to the thematic variations developed by individual narrators. In this case, the three narrators gave different interpretations of women's charms. During the last 14 minutes of the storytelling session, when the four narratives about beguiling women were told, a subtle counterpoising of different points of view was achieved. This is discussed in detail in chapter 7.

Another good example of how a variety of perspectives on a single theme is established during a storytelling session is a sequence of stories recorded at Benekoro on 10 March 1970. The first story told established the themes: the ethical ambiguity of cleverness, and the relationship between the status of elderhood and the personality of elders. The next five stories (four of which are given here: N.15, N.12, N.17, N.11) all illustrated the cleverness of the hare (the proverbial youngster) and the hare's use of cleverness to redress injustices. An old man, Nonkowa Kargbo, who had told four of these stories, then developed a different view in another tale where the youngster is shown to be irresponsible, using his cleverness to deceive an old woman. This view was repeated in the next story, and further stories by six more narrators all concerned aspects of bad conduct. These examples show exactly how the interpretative process takes place within a sequence or set of narratives, united by a single theme but all giving variations upon it. While the dilemma tales provoke discussion of difficult problems of morality, the same kind of casuistry can be promoted by simply telling another story presenting a new angle on the problem raised by the first.

3 During a Time of Great Hunger

GLO: These late eclipses in the sun and moon portend no good to us. Though the wisdom of nature can reason it thus and thus, yet nature finds itself scourg'd by the sequent events: love cools, friendship falls off, brothers divide; in cities, mutinies; in countries, discord; in palaces, treason; and the bond crack'd 'twixt son and father . . .

EDM. This is the excellent foppery of the world, that, when we are sick in fortune, often the surfeits of our own behaviour, we make guilty of our disasters the sun, the moon, and stars; as if we were villains on necessity; fools by heavenly compulsion; knaves, thieves, and treachers, by spherical predominance; drunkards, liars, and adulterers, by an enforc'd obedience of planetary influence . . .

King Lear (Act I Sc.II)

Most Kuranko can tell, in narrative form, how their particular clan came to be associated with a particular animal species which they are prohibited to kill, eat, or injure in any way. These clan narratives also usually explain the origins of the privileged joking relationship, the *sanakuiye tolon*, existing between certain clans.

Although the totemic species and the joking partnerships recognized by a clan differ from place to place, it is everywhere apparent that these clan narratives are forceful expressions of the basic moral precepts surrounding the concept of personhood (*morgoye*). The narratives relate how an animal became a totem (*tane:* "prohibited thing") and was elevated to kinship status when it rescued a clan ancestor from certain death in a far-off wilderness long, long ago (e.g. N.2). In other narratives using the same setting (e.g. N.3) a status inferior saves the life of a chief. In both cases these acts of magnanimity on the part of a normally inferior being are commemorated by the respect accorded the totemic species and by the privileges accorded the descendants of the underling.

Totemic symbols do more than simply affirm the identity of each clan. I have argued elsewhere (Jackson, 1974) that it is by recourse to

totemic metaphor and to historical fictions of clans merging or inter-
mingling that the Kuranko give enduring expression to moral and political choices which effectively enlarge the domain of recognized humanity. Thus, throughout the Mande-speaking area totemic classifications
extend a vast system of clan correspondences over the West Sudan,
preventing the closure of each group and promoting an idea "something
like that of a humanity without frontiers" (Lévi-Strauss, 1966:166). Although people and customs differ from place to place, the various natural species on which the totemic system is based are ubiquitous. Ironi-
cally, therefore, the animal world affords man the means of affirming
his humanity and of extending it.

The clan narratives emphasize values which bind people together:
cooperation, trust, mutual respect, conviviality. Such values may be regarded as "religious" in the strict sense of the word (L. *religio*-"obligation, bond"). All crucial social bonds are seen to begin in supererog-
atory acts of magnanimity, courage, and altruism. Society reflects, according to these narratives, conscious choices by ancestors to extend
humanity to outsiders, passing acquaintances, and neighbors. In their
application to contemporary life, the narratives exemplify an impartial
and rational justice, a justice which transcends self-interest and narrower social identifications and is responsive to the interests of several
groups equally.

Underlying the clan narratives is a search to redress the bias of contingencies in the direction of equality, reciprocity, and complementarity
(c.f. Rawls, 1971:100). Thus, an ancestor's life is saved through the
benevolent intervention of an outsider or animal (N.2), or a status disadvantage (a contingency of birth) is made up for by some complementary advantage (usually some special natural endowment). The theme of
reciprocal altruism which runs through all the clan narratives implies a
transformation of linear dominance hierarchies into systems of balanced
complementarity characterized by mutual aid, interdependency, and a
merging of interests. This transformation is very clearly shown in the
story of Saramba and Musa Kule (N.3). Asymmetrical relations are effectively masked, for the *finaba* is lowborn yet endowed with superior
moral qualities, while the chief has high status but inferior personal
qualities.[1]

This reciprocity between social positions and personal dispositions
implies an ability to identify empathically with another human being. It
is essentially a reciprocity of viewpoints and of identifications. It implies

an awareness that the other is in some fundamental way like oneself.[2] It is this ability to impartially empathize with others which the Kuranko regard as one of the ideal attributes of those in authority.

In order to approach the problems of reciprocity and justice in the narratives, I will make use of John Rawls's concept of "justice as fairness," a concept which implies the transformation of hierarchy into mutuality. Rawls notes that two principles of justice would emerge from an "initial situation" in which the ordinary interests of groups and persons were nullified or suspended: first, equality in the assignment of basic rights and duties, and second, inequality of wealth and authority, which is justifiable only if it results in compensatory benefits for all, in particular for the least advantaged members of society (Rawls, 1971:14–15).

> Once we decide to look for a conception of justice that nullifies the accidents of natural endowment and the contingencies of social circumstances as counters in quest for political and economic advantage, we are led to these principles. They express the result of leaving aside those aspects of the social world that seem arbitrary from a moral point of view. (Rawls, 1971:15)

It is my view that the Kuranko narratives seek such a conception of justice by "leaving aside" certain aspects of the ordinary social world. As we have seen, dominant principles of social structure such as birth-order position are nullified or played down, and the narratives are bracketed away from ordinary social reality, so that this search may be carried out. We have also seen how ambiguity fosters a greater number of perspectives on any single issue than would ordinarily be given. These different perspectives permit the impartial and sympathetic identifications with the positions of others which characterize the quest for justice.

In the totemic narratives there is a recurring situation. A clan ancestor finds himself stranded, hungry and thirsty, in a wilderness; through the altruistic actions of an animal, his life is saved and the continuity of his line ensured. These myths deal with three variables: natural contingencies (finding oneself in a wilderness without food or water), individual endowments (the superior virtue of the totemic creature), and social positions (the superior status of the ancestor, compared with that of the animal). As in other clan myths, we find the following situation: a status superior (ancestor, ruler, religious leader) becomes dependent upon a status inferior (totemic animal, *finaba, jeliba*, commoner) who is endowed with superior qualities. This state of dependency is brought about by some natural contingency: being lost and starving in a wilderness (N.2); eating an animal which brings disease or death; birds which scavenge a rice crop; dying of hunger; a fire accident. These crises and impasses lead to a reversal of the normal social order: status superiors become dependent upon and indebted to status inferiors.

It is not uncommon for natural calamity to lead to inversions and perversions of the normal moral order. Such inversions may serve to symbolize the close kinship between the cosmic, natural, and social orders. And this kinship can then be regarded in two ways, as shown by Gloucester and Edmund in the quotation which prefaces this chapter.

While Gloucester makes social disorder appear to be a consequence of cosmic or natural turmoil, Edmund forbids such false consciousness and perceives that man is the true and only arbiter of his lot. It is precisely this point of view which informs rituals where role reversal is a simulacrum of a natural disaster and a means whereby people achieve a vicarious mastery over external events (see Rigby, 1968). In narratives, this point of view leads to using natural calamities as images of social disorder and as means whereby people can ponder problems of justice and morality in everyday life. In both cases, however, the connections between social, natural, and cosmological planes are metaphorical; they do not imply a doctrine of intercausality.

In the Kuranko case, the contrast between nature and culture is phrased sometimes as a contrast between bush and town, sometimes as a contrast between marginal and central social positions. The narratives create circumstances in which a crossing over, real or figurative, between these contrasted domains takes place. The real crossings involve, of course, journeys to and fro between town and bush. The figurative crossings take the form of a chiasmus. In both instances the crossings are occasioned by some natural crisis. This system of interconnections can be expressed diagramatically as in the accompanying figure.

The second set of narratives in this chapter (N.4–N.10) all relate to events during a time of great hunger, a time which is variously known as "the hungry time," "the hungry season," or "the famine time" among African cultivators. The Kuranko refer to this critical period of the agricultural year as *same konke* (lit. "rainy season hunger"). This is the time when rice is in short supply, the time toward the end of the rainy season when families await the first harvests of early-maturing varieties of

Toward nature   Epitomizing culture
Marginal positions   Central positions

BUSH	fictional journeyings	TOWN
Children Younger brother Women *Jeli*s *Fina*s	fictional connections	Parents Elder brother Men Rulers

rice. Secondary foodstuffs like yams, cassava, and sweet potatoes must often serve instead of rice. It is a time too when families, who have spent several months isolated in sometimes remote farmsteads, begin to look forward to the conviviality of dry-season village life. The "hungry time" is therefore a period of physical and social hardship. Many Kuranko point out that the acute shortage of rice often causes dissensions among kin and neighbors. People are reluctant to share what little food they have, and some may conceal rice or lie about the amount still stored in granary baskets in order to avoid meeting commitments to distant kin or importunate neighbors. In July 1970 I found myself helping some villagers buy rice at the Kabala market (not everyone has such resources); they then took it home by night and the next day smuggled it to their farms so that they could enjoy it without their distant kin knowing about it. Kuranko readily admit that such underhand and stingy practices make them feel ashamed, but they point out that generosity is absurd during times of rice scarcity. They willingly risk attacks of sorcery or witchcraft from those whom they have denied help.

In the narratives, the "hungry time" implies a suspension of normal social order. Reality is transmuted into allegory.[3] The "hungry time" lies outside the usual course of events. By annulling hierarchy and suspending law, the possibilities of communitas can be explored. The "hungry time" is liminal in two ways. First, it is a period out of time; it lies halfway between the two agricultural seasons, *same* (rainy season) and *telme* (dry season), both of which are of equal length (*same keri woro, telme keri woro*: "rainy season six moons, dry season six moons"). Second, it is a period of sociospatial marginality: the farmstead or farm hamlet is a social unit but it is situated in the bush.

The narratives exploit the ambiguous space-time attributes of the "hungry time"; the stories take place on farms (cultivated clearings in the bush) during the "hungry time" (toward the end of the rains, just before harvest). In almost every case, ambiguity is also created by playing down those values which characterize the "morality of association": fairness, cooperation, justice, reciprocity, trust, and impartiality.[4] Following the suspension of these values, there is a moral regression toward egocentricity. This is signified in several of the narratives by a man behaving in a childlike way. But the metaphors of regression are based on more than infantile actions. In some cases they involve a return to the womb—the unsealed grave from which the man returns to life—(N.4), and in one case the regressive behavior is accompanied by a return to the cultural past (N.7), a period when the men's *due* cult was "in the hands of women." In the latter case, the infantile or regressed person's approach to social behavior reflects a cultural-psychological lag. He is an anachronism, since he reverts to childish behavior at the same time as the narrative returns to the past. The psychological regressions and fixations of the male characters (fathers and husbands who are gluttons or who make unjust laws which advance their own selfish interests) are further depicted as role reversals. For example, in N.8 the man goes fishing, ordinarily an occupation restricted to women, and later, when he has his head stuck in the country-pot, he refers to himself as a child. Again, the country-pot may be regarded as a womb, from which the man will be reborn as a responsible adult.[5]

It is also noteworthy that the point of maximum regression marks the moment of greatest suspense, the point where the narrative begins to bring back into relief the very values which it has initially played down. These points are not necessarily midway through the narrative, but they are nevertheless points where the narrator's purposes merge with those of the audience and a tacit agreement is reached about the importance of cooperation, self-restraint, ingenuity, resourcefulness, and the like. In N.4, this moment of merging and of dramatic focus occurs at the very end of the narrative; in N.6 it occurs when the *nyenne* surround the strange-looking child and we wonder whether or not they will see through the woman's ruse; in N.7–N.9 the songs mark the dramatic intervals when a re-reversal of the situation and a return to justice is presaged.

The regressive behavior of the father/husband is also counteracted by a reversal of other roles. Thus, while the husband or father becomes an egocentric and incontinent child, his wife or youngest son comes to exemplify the values ordinarily associated with his role: resourcefulness, self-control, courage, and fairness. The momentary suspension or playing down of these values has the effect of making them emerge with greater force as the narrative unfolds. And those who are listening to the story find themselves participating actively in the discovery and restitution of basic ethical principles. By contriving such fictional annulments of ethical principles, and by inspiring people to share in the process of reconstituting them, the narratives afford the Kuranko means of controlling vicariously events over which they ordinarily have little real control. Hunger, which in reality is a threat to physical survival and to the moral order, is made the occasion in the narratives for rehearsing the very principles it actually threatens.

The inescapability of hunger is often turned into a metaphor for perdurance, as in the common response to the salutation *i kende* ("Are you well?"): *n kende i ko konde* ("I am as well as hunger" i.e. I am very well, since hunger never flags). But it is the calamitous side of hunger that the Kuranko usually emphasize. There is an adage—"A hungry person does not think of tomorrow"—which conveys two meanings: first, that hunger strikes at one of the crucial principles of social maturity (the ability to defer immediate and instinctual demands), and second, that hunger leads to death, in which case there is no tomorrow. One informant told me that "hunger could make a man do anything, even steal from his affines." It is worth noting in this context that the *nyenne* who exploit the woman in N.6 refer to her as "affine" (*biran*). Other informants observe that rice shortages drive people to shamefully antisocial behavior: lying about their real resources, concealing rice reserves, using trickery to avoid having to share rice with needy kin or neighbors. Hunger is regarded as being inimical to the social and moral order as well as to physical well-being. In the narratives, the physical and behavioral consequences of hunger are dramatized as metaphors for the breakdown of the social order. Thus, in N.4 and N.10 death is feigned as a ruse for pilfering the scarce resources of the group (a piece of cassava and a field of corn); death is also a metaphor for the abandonment of the values upon which social life depends. In other narratives (N.4, N.6, N.7), regression to infantile behavior or pretending to be a child have identical significance. The contrast made between two *patterns* of behavior—instinctual demand versus ego-control—is a way of dramatizing a difference between two *principles* of conduct—egocentricity versus cooperation. It is the problem of this balance between self-interest and group-interest which defines the problem of justice.[6]

The hunger narratives focus a morality of cooperation and fairness by first negating such a morality. The "hungry time" is a fictional image of the suspension of the normal social and moral order. In two of the narratives, however, hunger is seen to have real rather than merely fictional value. According to Denka Marah (N.5), hunger promotes hard work and respect among people. In N.6, Keti Ferenke points out that hunger inspires resourcefulness. This leads us to another aspect of these narratives: not only do they focus general concerns, they also afford individual narrators opportunities for advancing viewpoints which reflect personal emphases and interests. Thus, Denka Marah stresses stern and authoritarian values: the value of hardship (N.5), the value of self-discipline (N.7). Keti Ferenke stresses the values of cleverness, ingenuity, and resourcefulness (N.6, N.9, N.10).

The following table shows the key structural relationships among the narratives, and indicates how various ambiguous figures assist the transformations from injustice to justice, egocentricity to cooperation.

The significance of the hunger narratives in the Kuranko corpus derives not from the fact that the Kuranko are obsessed by food shortage but rather from the value of hunger as an image or metaphor; hunger is appropriated and transformed in fiction so that it serves as a means for exploring problems pertaining to the morality of cooperation. Nevertheless, some of these narratives do make reference to actual institutional ways of redressing injustices, such as the women's cult (N.7) and the use of sorcery (N.8). The ideal reciprocity between the troubled wife and the old woman in N.8 contrasts with the lack of reciprocity between the husband and wife. While the husband eats all the rice himself, the wife gives rice to the old woman until her stomach is full, and in return the old woman gives her the means of retribution (the country-pot fetish). The link between the old woman and the country-pot is explicit: the old woman eats until the cord around her stomach breaks, while the country-pot is a symbolic belly, bound round with red threads. This figure reappears in several narratives, also concerned with the theme of justice, in chapter 8, and the symbolic equation country-pot = belly = womb is explicit in the narrative presented in the Appendix.

Most of the associations of ideas and persons in these narratives are entirely fictional. They are based upon the figure of chiasmus, in which

Initial Situation (regressions, reversals, and changes caused by hunger)	Mediator (whereby the initial situation is transformed)	Resolution (means by which justice and reciprocity are restored)
N.4 A gluttonous man feigns death when his child takes the cassava which the man will not share.	Wife	The wife returns the cassava to the husband, thus making public his shame and disgrace.
N.5 Hunger (personified) ruins the crops.	Rice (personified)	Rice saves the life of Hunger; Hunger makes people work hard and respect one another.
N.6 The *nyenne* have rice; people have none, but an impossible condition prevents people receiving the rice which the *nyenne* allow them to harvest.	Wife	The wife makes her husband pretend to be a child; she thus outwits the *nyenne* and takes the rice she worked for.
N.7 A gluttonous man, pretending to taste the sauce, eats it all.	Women's cult	The man is beaten and learns self-restraint.
N.8 A gluttonous man eats the rice set aside by his wife for the next day.	Old woman and country-pot fetish	The wife eats the fish sauce which the husband intended to keep for himself.
N.9 A gluttonous man imposes an unfair condition which enables him to get the cooking water.	Youngest son	The boy outwits his father and then shares his ruse with his brothers.
N.10 A man finds himself a victim of his own absurd decree.	Man disguised as a *nyenne*	The man saves face and the decree is cancelled.

socially marginal persons, particularly women and youngest sons, are attributed the very characteristics which should ideally be exemplified by persons in positions of authority. This surrendering of control to marginal persons occurs occasionally in real life. Cults may intervene when secular means of justice fail. Sorcery may be used to complement and support secular modes of social control. And sometimes, during crises such as drought, epidemic, or witchcraft attack, persons or groups which are marginal to the politico-jural domain and which command extraordinary powers are appealed to by the chief and his council. For example, the women's cult, *segere*, was asked to bring an end to the rain (which was preventing the burning of underbrush on farms around Kamadugu Sukurela in 1971) after the "rain-catcher" and then the men's cults had tried and failed (Jackson 1977b:232). Just as sorcerers and cult leaders are marginal yet complementary to the domain of secular authority, so too are women and younger sons. In the narratives, injustices are redressed through women and youngest sons. But the chiasmus involves a contrast between two sets of terms, the first pertaining to social positions, the second pertaining to individual dispositions. By consistently attributing superior abilities to those in inferior positions, and vice versa, the narratives attempt to mitigate the arbitrariness of natural contingency and social fortune.

N.2: *How Totemism Begins*

Narrated by Bala Kamara, a *finaba*. Recorded at Kabala, February 1972.

When you are in a faraway place where there are no towns and there is no food to be found anywhere . . . you suddenly hear a sound. You go to where the sound is coming from and you find something to eat there. But it is a bush thing and you are afraid of it. But it does not harm you. So you take it as food. You then return to town and explain to your lineage what happened . . . how you lost your way in the bush, had no food, heard a sound, and went there and discovered such-and-such in the bush . . . how that is how you found food and survived to return to town. Then you say that no member of your lineage should ever eat that creature again, or harm it. It becomes your totem. It is your kinsman. You tell your *sanaku* [clan joking partner]: "That creature that saved my life is my kinsman." That is how totemism began.

The Kuyate do not eat the monitor lizard [*kana* or *kurumgbe*]. Their ancestor went to a faraway place. There was no water there. He became thirsty. He was near death. Then he found a huge tree and in the tree bole there was some water left from the rains. The monitor lizard was also there. The ancestor of the Kuyate sat under the tree. The monitor lizard climbed into the tree bole, then got out and shook its tail. The water splashed on the man. The ancestor of the Kuyate realized there was water there. He climbed up and drank. He said, "Ah, the monitor lizard has saved my life." When he returned to town he told his lineage about the incident. He said, "You see me here now because of the monitor lizard." Since that time the monitor lizard became their totem. If any Kuyate eats it, his body will become marked and disfigured like the body of the monitor lizard. His *sanaku* will have to find medicines to cure him.

N.3: *Saramba and Musa Kule*

Narrated by Lansana Gibate. Recorded at Kamadugu Sukurela, February 1972.

Saramba was a *sunike* [ruler] and also a warrior of great renown. His *fadennu* [half brothers] became jealous of his fame and decided to kill him. They plotted to ambush him along the road. The conspiracy was discovered, but by that time Saramba was unable to delay the journey. Musa Kule, a *finaba*,* decided to disguise Saramba in his clothes. He donned Saramba's clothes so that he would die and so save Saramba's life.

When the day of the journey came, they left together. A little way along the road Musa Kule took off his hat, gown, and trousers, and gave them to Saramba, his lord. Musa Kule then dressed in Saramba's clothes. They went on, riding on horses.

As usual Saramba was riding ahead. When they reached the place where the ambush had been laid, Saramba, in disguise, passed by.

---

*The *fina*s (genealogists and orators) are divided into two groups: the *finaninghe* ("little pure *fina*s") and the Musa Kule *fina*s. Both belong to the Kamara clan. Saramba, according to Arafan Sise of Kondembaia, was a descendant of Yilkanani. Sayers also reports the same connection (1972:79–82). However, Mara genealogies which I collected seldom give the name of Saramba though Salia Kamara of Mongo Bendugu observed that Saramba and his eldest son, Mamburu, were the first settlers of the country as far west as Lake Sonfon.

The man in hiding said, "Oh no, not that one, it is only his poor *finaba*." Musa Kule then came, dressed in Saramba's clothes. They shot him.

Therefore, since the time of Saramba and Musa Kule, they have always been together. Therefore, they say, "Musa Kule and Saramba," meaning that they "go together."

N.4: *The Man Who Said He Would Die Rather than Share His Cassava with His Child*

Narrated by Bala Kargbo. Recorded at Benekoro, March 1970.

There was once a time of great hunger. Everyone was troubled by hunger. There was a man who had a family: a wife and a child. The child had only just started walking.

The man was very hungry. He went to an abandoned farm and was lucky enough to find a cassava plant growing there. He uprooted it and found that the root was very small. He cut it into four pieces. He put the pieces in a pot and cooked the cassava. When it was cooked, he took the pot from the fire and drained off the cooking water. Then, his child, who had only just been weaned, came and took a piece of the cassava. The man said, "Ah! I have never before seen such cheek. I'll kill myself. Before Ala, I will die." His wife said, "Ah, you, why are you such a glutton? This child of yours has only just been weaned. Instead of struggling to find food for it, you go on about how you will die because it took a piece of your cassava. Have you no shame?" The man said, "Before God, I am dead, I have killed myself. I am going to wrap myself up. Bring me a covering. I am already dead." Then his wife said, "Shall I go and tell people that you are dead?" He said, "Yes, go and tell them."

Everyone came and began to cry. Some said, "He killed himself over a piece of cassava." They measured his body and went away and dug the grave. Some went to cut *ture* branches.* They washed his body. As they were washing him, his wife said, "Can I say goodbye to my husband?" They said, "Yes." She went and said, "Now husband, do you really think you can die over a piece of

---

*ture branches are laid across the midsection of a grave.

cassava? They have already washed you." The man said, "Yes, I must die. Let them wash me."

They took him to the graveside. His wife said to the people, "Before you bury my husband can I say goodbye to him?" They said, "Yes, you can say goodbye." She said, "Eh, my husband, do you really think you want to kill yourself over the tiny piece of cassava that your child took? You are already in the graveyard and people are just waiting for me to finish saying goodbye, then they are going to bury you." He said, "It doesn't matter. Let them bury me."

They put him in the grave, laid the *ture* branches down, placed the mat and leaves over him. His wife said, "Please don't cover his head. I want to see my husband's face for the last time."† So they left the head uncovered. They put earth on his feet. She leaned down and whispered in his ear, "Eh! My husband, do you really intend to kill yourself over that tiny piece of cassava that your very own child took during the time of great hunger when every parent is struggling for the survival of his or her child? That tiny piece of cassava that your own child took . . . you will kill yourself over that? Then you have no shame, and this is further shame upon you." He said, "I don't care. Let them bury me or you give me back my cassava."

During all this time the child had not eaten the cassava. The wife went and got it. When she came back, she said, "I have brought the cassava. Your child did not eat it." As soon as she said that, the man jumped out of the grave, throwing the leaves and branches aside. Everyone fled, thinking that the dead man had come to life. He snatched the cassava from the woman and swallowed it in one gulp. He sat down without shame.

N.5: *The Force of Hunger*

Narrated by Denka Marah. Recorded at Kabala, July 1970.

A hunger came. It was a great hunger. The hunger became boastful. It said, "I will deal with the world this year." So the cassava built a fence. The potato built a fence. The millet built a

---

†Ordinarily a widow is not allowed near the graveside; her farewell to her late husband must be made before the body is prepared for burial.

fence. The benniseed [sesame seed] built a fence. And the groundnut built a fence. Finally, *suma* [rice] built a fence.

I am now going to tell you how *suma* became known as *kore*.* Whenever that hunger came, it would say, "Hah, by the grace of God I will break down this fence. Two days, three days, I will break it down." It went to the millet. Seven days it took and the millet's fence was broken down. It went to the potato. In eight days the potato was finished. It went to the cassava. In four days the cassava was finished. It went to the benniseed. In three days it was finished. It went to the guinea corn. It took only one day to finish it. Then it reached the groundnut. The groundnut said, "You will not break this fence down." The groundnut got up and ripped off a piece of country-cloth. It held the hunger by its neck and threw it to the ground. Then the groundnut shouted to the *suma*, saying "Elder brother, come here." When the *suma* came, the groundnut said, "Now that we have got it, let us cut its throat." The *suma* said, "Let's not kill it, lest in times to come there will be people who try to avoid work and who, in the absence of hunger, fail to respect others. Let us not kill it."

Therefore we still have hunger in our midst. And since that time, *suma* became known as *kore*. The groundnut started that. Therefore, if a man is married and he and his wife have an argument, then the wife will refuse to cook for him . . . but only during harvest time.†

N.6: *The Woman Who Tricked the Nyenne into Telling Their Names**

Narrated by Keti Ferenke Koroma. Recorded at Kondembaia, March 1970.

There was once a time of great hunger. Only the *nyenne* [bush spirits] had rice. People went about searching for food. Some died of hunger. There was no rice to be found.

---

suma = "rice" (in the context of this narrative). Rice (uncooked) is *kore*, a word which may be cognate with *koro* (elder sibling; elder). This association is exploited by the narrator, who is about to explain how rice becomes the "senior" and most respected of all foodstuffs.

†The implication is that in times of plenty people quarrel and become lazy; hunger keeps the mind on important matters such as work and respect and cooperation.

*I also recorded this narrative from Kanku Pore Kargbo at Kamadugu Sukurela, June 1970.

There was a man and a woman who had nothing at all to eat. The husband had become very emaciated. But they found out that the *nyenne* had rice. The woman said to her husband, *"M'berin*, let us go. Maybe we will get some rice from the *nyenne*." The man said, "Ah, that is a very bad place. No one who has gone there has returned with any rice. The *nyenne* let you harvest the rice, but just after you have finished harvesting and threshing it, the *nyenne* gather round and ask you to call their names, one after the other. If you cannot call their names, you are not allowed to take any rice." (The *nyenne*, his wife, and his children lived in a farmhouse. When a person had finished harvesting and threshing the rice, they would ask him to call their names. If that person could not call their names, then he was not allowed to take any rice. Not even a single grain. And in those days, only the *nyenne* had rice. The story I am about to tell you is to show how we came to have rice.)

The woman and her husband set off to where the *nyenne* lived. As they approached the farm, the woman told her husband that he should get on her back so that the *nyenne* would think that he was a child. (The man was so thin that he looked like a baby.) She said, "I will put you in the farmhouse and cover you up. While I am cutting the rice you can listen and see whether or not they say their names. If they say their names, then pretend to cry. I'll come and place my breast against your mouth and you can whisper the names to me." The husband said, "All right, that is all right." She put her husband on her back. And she left most of the hampers she had brought at the edge of the farm. She wanted it to seem as if she had brought only a few.

She came with her husband on her back and met the *nyenne*. She said, "Greetings to you all." They greeted her. She said, "I have come to you to get some rice. It has been a month since I last ate rice." The *nyenne* said, "All right, that is all right. We are always ready to give rice to people who come for it. Here is the farm, you can harvest what you need. When you have finished harvesting and threshing the rice, let us know. We will want to say something to you." The woman put her "baby" in the farmhouse and started cutting the rice—*fasu fasu fasu fasu fasu*.

The *nyenne* came and looked at the baby. One said, "Heh, this is amazing." The *nyenne*'s wife called her husband, "Tamba Turugbofo, this is amazing! Look at this child." Her husband said, "This is indeed amazing, Kumba Yigi Tege. What do you make of this child? It has confused me. It has teeth, and the teeth are all red.* This really does confuse me. Other children are not like this one. Our children, Tenna Ko and Tabiyane, are not like this one. This really confuses me." Then the "baby" started to cry—*nye nye nye nye nye*. The *nyenne* husband said "Heh, Kumba Yigi Tege, call its mother to come to give it the breast. Call the mother of this astonishing child." The *nyenne* wife left the farmhouse and called to the woman, *"M'biran, m'biran*, come now, your child is crying." The woman said, "Ah, this wicked child has begun to annoy me. Here I am harvesting the rice and it begins to cry. The little dog!" She came—*wunya wunya wunya wunya wunya*—and sat by the child and placed her flat breast against its mouth. The "baby" said, "Heh . . . Kumba Yigi Tege, Tenna Ko, Tabiyane . . . these are their names." He said again, "Kumba Yigi Tege, Tenna Ko, Tabiyane, have you heard them all?" He was whispering, whispering to his wife. The *nyenne* were away on the farm, saying, "Ah, this is amazing. We have never seen such a child."

The woman went back to the farm and continued harvesting the rice—*faso faso faso faso faso*. She cut and cut and cut. Then she threshed the rice and measured out four Fula women's pans [fulamusu panne]. The *nyenne* said, "This woman is hard-working. She can harvest well." Then the woman called to the *nyenne*, "Come on, I have cut the rice." The *nyenne* came. She said, "Here is the rice." The *nyenne* said, "Well *m'biran*, we have a law here that says that whoever comes and harvests our rice, after threshing it and before taking it away, he or she must call our names, one after the other. If you fail to call our names, then you cannot take the rice away." The woman said, "Eh! I have heard you." She got up and stood there and said, "Kumba Yigi Tege, Tanna Ko, Tabiyane."† "Eh," said the *nyenne*, "how did she come to know our names?" They said, "Well, take our rice." She took load after load. She took each load to the edge of the farm and returned and took another load. At last she came and took the "baby." As she left the farm she set down this enormous "baby" and the husband dressed in his ragged trousers and clothes again. The husband bound two

---

*That is to say that his teeth are stained by kola.
†The names are sung several times, with the children in the audience chorusing the names of the *nyenne*.

bags together. The woman bound two bags together. And they went away.

If you hear that a person is clever, well, hunger could make him do many things. They might say that this person is stupid. But he is well-fed. If he were hungry he would become clever. Even a stupid person knows what hunger is. That is the end until another day.

N.7: *The Man Who Ate the Sauce before It Was Served*

Narrated by Denka Marah. Recorded at Kabala, July 1970.

There was a gluttonous man and his wife. Whenever his wife prepared a sauce for the rice, the man would go to her and say, "Let me taste the sauce." The woman would give him a ladle full of sauce, and the gluttonous man would eat it. He would lick the ladle and lick his fingers until he had eaten the last drop.

One day the woman told her friends that she was getting upset over this. She said, "Before I get to serve the sauce, my husband has eaten the best part of it." The other women said that they would help her.

One day, the women told the men to take off their shirts. The women said, "We want to take out our secret thing today,* and so the men must assemble dressed in their trousers only, and wearing blindfolds." The men undressed. The women all had canes. Then the women began to sing:

Sort them out, sort them out, *kole*,†
Sort out the gluttonous men, *kole*.

The man's wife came and whipped him on his back. The women went on singing and the wife went on whipping her husband until his back was raw. Then the other women told her to go back to her house. When she had gone, the women released the man. He went back crying to his wife. His wife said, "Here, I have prepared some sauce and rice for you." The man said, "Leave me. Don't you see

---

*Denka interjects at this point, "The *due* cult was in the hands of women before it came into the hands of men." The *due* cult celebrates ingenuity, cleverness, and skills related to problem solving and mind reading.
†*kole* = the bush spirit whom the women of the cult employ as an ally in seeking out the gluttonous men. By invoking a spirit, the women can disclaim direct responsibility for the punitive measures they take. And, being blindfolded, the men cannot identify their persecutors.

my back?" His wife looked at his back and saw the bloody welts. She began to cry. She pretended to be crying.

Since that time, men do not taste the sauce when the women prepare it.

N.8: *The Gluttonous Husband*

Narrated by Fiti Marah. Recorded at Firawa, December 1969.

There was once a man and his wife. They lived on their farm, but although the husband slept in the farmhouse, his wife returned each evening to the town to sleep. Each evening, when she left to return to town, she would leave some washed rice in the farmhouse. As soon as she left, the husband would cook and eat the rice, and each morning when she returned she would not be able to find the rice. She would ask her husband, but he would say that he knew nothing about it.

Things went on like this until one day the woman decided to go and seek the help of an old woman. She said, "I am confused. Every time I go back to town, I leave some washed rice in the farmhouse, but when I return to the farm in the morning, the rice has gone." The old woman said, "Well, you must first feed me until this rope around my waist breaks." The woman gave the old woman plenty of food. Then the old woman bound seven threads around a country-pot.

The woman took this country-pot with her when she returned to the farm the next day. Then, that evening, she said goodbye to her husband and went to town. As soon as she left, her husband went to fish. He brought some fish back to the farmhouse, and he began to cook them. He cooked them in that country-pot which his wife had left. When the fish sauce was cooked, the man went to sleep. He did not eat anything. But very early the next morning he got up and began to eat the food before his wife returned. He put some of the fish sauce on the rice, then he took the country-pot to drink the rest of the sauce from it. But his head became stuck in the pot and he could not get the pot off his head. He ran around the farmhouse, and began to sing:

> *Gbon gbon fio gbon gbon fio gbon, na m'bi yo, ke dan ma kin kin*
> *ta, na m'bi yo . . .*

*(Gbon gbon fio gbon gbon fio gbon,** come and take me, all right,
this child is not happy . . .)*

He sang this over and over, and ran round and round the farm
until his wife found him. The woman then went and ate the food
which he had prepared. When she had finished eating the food, she
caller her husband. He came. Then she read the verses [*haye*]
which made the pot remove itself from her husband's head. When
the pot was off his head, he said, "Where is the food?" The woman
told him that she had eaten it.

N.9:   *The Man, the Boy, and the Cooking Water*

Narrated by Keti Ferenke Koroma. Recorded at Kondembaia, March
1970.

A man, his brothers, his wife, and his children were all in a
farmhouse. It was a time of great hunger. The first rice had
ripened,† and so the first rice was cooked.

As the rice was cooking, the man said that the cooking water
should be drained off. He said, "No one should drink that except
me. If anyone else wishes to drink it, then they must drink it while
it is hot." Whoever tried to drink it would say, "Eh, no one could
drink this while it is hot. It should be allowed to cool." Then that
person would put it down and go away. Everone who tried to drink
it would end up saying the same thing, until at last the man would
come and say, "All right then, no one else wants it." He would take
it and drink it all up. He went on doing this, and the others suffered as a result.

During this time, the lastborn son was growing up. The man did
not know that this son would be the cleverest of all the brothers.
One day the cooking water was drained from the rice. Everyone
tried to drink it, but everyone was obliged to put it down. Then,
the lastborn son took it and and said, "Father, I am going to drink
this cooking water today." His father said, "Do you know of the
law which I laid down concerning the cooking water? Have your

---

*The nonsense words suggest the hapless movements of the man staggering around with
the pot on his head. The song is sung six times.

†Farmers grow some early-maturing rice so that they will have rice to eat during the
period of rice scarcity before the main harvest. This narrative stresses that people are so
hungry at this time that even the cooking water is regarded as delectable.

elder brothers* told you about it?" The boy said, "What is the law?" His father said, "In my house, when the cooking water is drained off, if you want to drink it, then you must drink it while it is hot." The boy said, "Oh, father, if that is all the law is, then I can drink it without cooling it." His father said, "All right, take it." He gave the cooking water to the boy. The boy said, "I must not cool it, eh? But I can pass it around to show my elder brothers, can't I?" His father said, "Yes, you can show it to your elder brothers. The only thing is that you must not cool it." The boy said, "Well, that is all right."

The boy took another pan and dipped it into the cooking water. (He poured the water back and forth from pan to pan. He did this to cool the cooking water without his elder brothers' knowledge.) As he did this he sang:

Le le le le dini ti fen do a ma yira kinanuna

(Up up up up, a child should not eat something without letting his elders see what it is)

He went on doing this until the cooking water became cool. He then drank it.

One day his elder brothers called him and said, "Younger brother, we are all afraid of drinking this cooking water because it is so hot. But you manage to drink it without burning your mouth. How do you do it?" The boy said, "Well, it is all your fault. Our father is old and he has a clever way of deceiving us. Therefore, we, the young ones, should find a way of meeting his cleverness. If we don't, it will be no good for us." He said, "Now, if you see me putting the pan up like this before pouring the water into the other pan, well, it is because it loses heat in the process. This is how I cool the cooking water."

---

kinenu = elders. In this context it refers to the boy's elder brothers; in the context of the song the term includes the boy's father and elder brothers, since none understand how he manages to cool the cooking water.

N.10: *The Man Who Would Not Eat Millet*

Narrated by Keti Ferenke Koroma. Recorded at Kondembaia, March 1970.

There was once a man who told his wives that he would never eat millet. One year passed, two years passed, three years passed, and there came a time of great hunger when the only food that could be found was millet. Because this man had told everyone that he would never eat millet, no matter what the circumstances, he did not want to lose face by eating it now. He became very thin. He wanted very much to eat the millet but he had told everyone that he would never eat it, no matter what the circumstances. His family knew this.

One day he said to his wives, "I will not be sleeping in the farmhouse tonight, I am going to sleep in town." They said, "All right, that is as will be. You'll find us here tomorrow." He left the farmhouse. But he did not go directly to town. He waited around the farm until it was almost the middle of the night. At midnight he approached the farmhouse and put his hands over his mouth and said, "Good evening, good evening, good evening . . ."* The people in the farmhouse were afraid. They said, "What is that?" A voice said, "It is I, it is I. Is your husband Tamba not there?" They said, "He isn't here. He didn't sleep here tonight." The voice said, "Yeh, is he coming back in the morning?" They said, "Yes, he'll be here in the morning." The voice said, "Well, when he comes back in the morning, tell him that our bargain has been fulfilled and so he can now eat millet. All right? There won't be any trouble if he eats millet."

Soon afterward the man went on to town. In the morning he came back and said, "Good morning." Then his son came up to him and said, "Father, something came here last night." The man said, "Ah, wait a bit, there are older people here. They can explain this to me properly." He said, "Sira, what happened here yesterday? What is this lie that these children have been telling me?" Sira said, "Eh, *m'berin*, it is not a lie. Something really did come here last night. It really terrified us. It said 'good evening' and we answered it. We had nowhere to go. It said 'isn't your husband sleeping

---

*He muffles his voice to disguise his identity, pretending to be a bush spirit.

here?' and we said 'no.' Then it said 'well, if your husband comes back tomorrow tell him that our bargain has been fulfilled, so he can now eat millet.'" The man laughed and said, "Well, a man does not say that he will not eat something without there being a good reason for it. It was a bargain between me and a *nyenne*." Then he said, "Now put some in the mortar and pound it, then cook it quickly. You see, had I eaten this because I was starving I would have been killed and you would have been without a husband and the children without a father. But now that the *nyenne* has decreed that I should eat it, I will eat it without hesitation from now on. A person can say that he should not eat something. For one year, two years, three years . . . it was a bargain." Then the man ate the millet.

No matter how clever a woman is, a man is cleverer.

4 *Hare and Hyena*

Most Kuranko animal stories center upon the relationship between Hare and Hyena.[1] The hare-hyena narratives explore the same themes as the hunger narratives. Sharing food and ensuring the welfare of dependents are dominant themes in both sets. Problems of reciprocity and justice are approached by playing up such antisocial actions as greed, covetousness, and imposing unfair laws. The redress of bias and injustice is accomplished through the cleverness and guile of the hare. The hyena, who exemplifies inflexible virtue and the blind voice of custom, is inevitably the dupe. But while the scarce resources in the hunger narratives are foodstuffs, the key resources in the hare-hyena tales are talents and gifts such as cleverness, guile, insight, and intellectual subtlety. In both sets of narratives, however, the problem is the same: the unequal and random distribution of resources, both natural and personal, and the problem of creating a just and complementary apportionment of resources and roles.

Hare and Hyena are persons in animal form; they are masks or personae. Ambiguity is established by having the animals act, think, and speak like persons. It is also denoted by the use of the human personal pronoun *fa* ("father," but more generally "sir"). Thus, in the narratives, the hare is usually spoken of as *Fasan*, the hyena as *Fasuluku*. This device also distances the characters and dramatizes their artificiality. Hare and Hyena are personalized in yet another way. The hare is often spoken of as *doge* or *dogone* ("younger sibling," but more generally "junior" or "smaller"). The hyena is *koro* ("elder sibling," but more generally "senior" or "bigger").[2] In Kuranko, the terms for smallness and bigness refer to both physical size and relative social position. Because it is understood that Hare and Hyena are male, they are related as younger brother–elder brother. But this relationship has broader significance and connotes a general contrast between small and big, subordinate and superordinate positions, peripheral powers and central authority.

The choice of Hare and Hyena as allegorical characters reflects, according to the Kuranko, various aspects of their behavior. At the same time, the place of these characters in folktales in countless African societies of the savanna lands attests to a traditional characterization which goes back hundreds of years.[3] It endures even in areas, like the Kuranko area, where hyenas are not found. Kuranko descriptions of hyenas and their habits indicate that these fictional characterizations need not be founded upon actual observations: the fictional creatures convey impressions and insights derived from the observation of people, not animals.

The hare which figures in Kuranko *tileinu* is the Togo hare (*Lepus capensis zechi*). Most informants associate the hare with cleverness, ingenuity, adroitness (*hankili*), and with cunning (*kio*). The hyena is stupid (*hankili ma*), clumsy, inflexible, and lacking in insight. Hare and Hyena are thus related in much the same way as Prometheus ("foresight") and Epimetheus ("afterthought"). In some narratives the hyena's *numorgo* (joking partner: elder sister's husband or wife's younger brother) is mentioned; he is equally stupid. It may be that *suluku* is the spotted hyena (*Crocuta crocuta*), while his *numorgo*, who is called *lei*, is the much rarer striped hyena (*Hyaena hyaena*). The juxtaposition of similar and dissimilar details of appearance thus provides an image of the *numorgo* relationship, which involves mutually contradictory frames of reference (Jackson, 1977b:109–112).

Kuranko hunters say that the hare is very cunning, quick, elusive, and alert. They observe that the hare is particularly skilled at camouflage and will sit or stand stock-still in the grass while hunters pass close by it.[4] If wounded, it may feign death only to run for cover as soon as a hunter touches it. It is said that it is difficult to trap; it sees concealed traps and avoids them. Many informants point out that the physical swiftness and alertness of the hare are indications of quickness of mind and cleverness. Other habits of the Togo hare may explain why it is such an appropriate symbol of attributes which are marginal to the normal social order. It is nocturnal and solitary, and ranges far in search of food (Booth, 1960:36); in this case, night and solitariness are symbols of antisocial activity, while the far-ranging habits of the hare recall the greater geographical mobility and freedom of movement of younger sons (Jackson, 1977b:170). Again the ambiguous sexuality of the hare has often suggested to the European mind that the hare is fickle, untrustworthy, and an omen of misfortune (Rowland, 1973:90–91). The "ethical ambiguity" of the hare derives, in my view, from the ethical ambiguity of the faculty most commonly associated with it—cleverness. But it is the semantic ambiguity of the Kuranko term *hankili* (c.f. Arabic *al'aql*, reason and intellect) which makes possible the exploration of the ethical ambiguity of cleverness.

Homer made clear that intelligence is ethically neutral. It may take the form of selfish cunning or of altruistic wisdom, and, as Stanford has noted, Odysseus's character vacillates between these two poles throughout the literary tradition which has used and reused him as hero (Stanford, 1968:7).[5] The Kuranko trickster, Hare, uses his superior intelligence to double-cross and dupe his status superior, Hyena. But, although cleverness here entails disrespect toward an elder, it is justified because the elder has first reneged upon his obligations. Cleverness is regarded ambivalently; it implies personal power, a faculty whose appearance and use are never entirely determined by social factors; but at the same time it is the means of righting wrongs and of reconstituting a moral order based upon justice and reciprocity. Although Hare embodies ambiguous talents, he is not depraved, vain, lecherous, and greedy like the Zande trickster, Ture (Evans-Pritchard, 1967:28), nor is he as unrestrained as Legba, the Dahomean trickster and youngest child of Mawu the Creator. Yet, in his capacity as a corrector of injustice, Legba is directly comparable to the Kuranko trickster (see Herskovits and Herskovits, 1958:35–46). The antinomian character of the Kuranko trickster, Fasan, places him outside the moral and jural order. He epitomizes play, surplus energy, and high spirits. Like Pan, son of Hermes and god of the woodlands in Arcadia, Fasan belongs to the margins of the social order. And, unrestrained by it, he symbolizes, paradoxically, the energies, skills, and forces which maintain it.

While the cleverness of the hare is an ambiguous factor, the hyena's stupidity is always regarded as a vice. The hyena symbolizes the weakness inherent in positions of authority, a weakness which results from a discrepancy between the ideal attributes of an office and the actual character of the individual who holds it. The hyena occupies a superordinate position, but he forfeits his right to be respected and obeyed because he reneges upon his obligation to look after the welfare of his dependents. This is precisely the same in Kaguru hare-hyena narratives.

> Hyena's right to this authority rests upon his own nature as a just person quite as much as upon his seniority. His kinsmen's obedience

is conditional upon Hyena's having their interests at heart. But Hyena proves himself a bad person and thereby forfeits his right to be obeyed. (Beidelman, 1963:62)

The general principle underlying both Kuranko and Kaguru hare-hyena narratives may be phrased as follows: If a senior position is occupied by a person with a weak or bad disposition, then an individual occupying a junior position but possessing the qualities ideally associated with the senior position has the right to take over (c.f. Beidelman, 1961, 1963).[6] When the capable subordinate takes over the position held by a corrupt or inept status superior, the discrepancy between social position and personal disposition is made good. As we have already seen, this transposition takes the form of chiasmus. It also implies a transformation of cleverness into wisdom, since an indeterminate quality—*hankili*—is brought into association with the role of elder. Wisdom is simply cleverness which is socially bound to a status position.

The Kuranko make two observations about the hyena, even though no Kuranko has actually seen one. It is said to be spotted, and its hind legs are said to be longer than its forelegs. As a result, it walks with its head down, and it cannot see where it is going because it is always looking back under its belly to where it has been.[7]

The distorted image of the spotted hyena which Kuranko informants give does, however, contain a kind of truth. Young men sometimes allege that elders tend to be overconservative, inflexible, backward-looking, and lacking in foresight. The shambling, awkward, and purblind gait of Fasuluku, the fictional hyena, is an image for them of the dogmatic, self-interested, biased attitudes of the old. Cleverness, flexibility, cunning, adroitness—the attributes of the hare—are seen as compensatory advantages, not just in the psychological sense but in the moral sense as well. Cleverness is a means of redressing injustices, of challenging corruption, and even of escaping the constraints of one's lot.

That the hyena symbolizes moral depravity and perversion may reflect other aspects of its behavior. The spotted hyena is a voracious and ill-disciplined eater (it often wounds other hyenas while tearing at a kill), and it is filthy in feeding habits and in toilet (van Lawick and van Lawick-Goodall, 1970:164–165, 187). This may explain why the hyena is often associated with greed, lack of self-control, filth, and stupidity.[8]

Considered in relation to the nocturnal and free-ranging or rootless habits of both the hare and the hyena, these various beliefs and observations may help explain why Hare and Hyena are so frequently paired as ambiguous characters in African folklore.

It must be emphasized, however, that the relationship between the animals and the concepts associated with them is arbitrary. Hare and Hyena are fictional creatures. They are personae. Their reality lies in the context of the narratives, where normally repressed desires and ambivalent attitudes are brought into focus. The use of animal characters as masks to enable comment upon ordinarily forbidden subjects has been noted in studies of folktales in numerous African societies.[9] But key concepts and relationships may find their expression in a variety of animals. Thus, the Zande trickster, Ture (lit. "spider"), or the Ashanti trickster, Anansi (lit. "spider"), exemplifies similar characteristics to the Ba-Ila Fulwe ("tortoise") and Sulwe ("hare"), and the Kuranko Fasan ("hare"). Tortoise and Spider in fact do appear occasionally in the hare's role in Kuranko narratives (N.26), and it is worth noting that in Sierra Leone the trickster among the Temne is the royal antelope, the same animal which is known as "Cunnie Rabbit" among the Krios of the peninsula (Cronise and Ward, 1903). Similar terminological overlap is shown by the Kono conventions of calling the spider trickster Fasaluku (c.f. the Kuranko, Fasuluku, "hyena"), and the "coney rabbit" Fason (c.f. the Kuranko, Fasan) (Parsons, 1964:119).

It must be stressed, however, that whether the trickster is symbolized in different societies by the same animal or by different animals, we should never assume that he will have identical attributes in every society. For example, the Kuranko trickster, Fasan, may be compared with the small, shy but clever antelope in Limba narratives, but he does not share the stupid, gluttonous, selfish, and irresponsible traits which the Limba trickster, the spider (Wosi), possesses (Finnegan, 1967:37). Nor does Fasan have the vain, treacherous, greedy, and antisocial tendencies of the Zande trickster, Ture, or the licentiousness of the Winnebago trickster, Wakdjunkaga. Even when Hare and Hyena are found paired in the folklore of different African societies, quite different relationships may be signified. Among the patrilineal Kuranko, Hare and Hyena signify the relationship between younger brother and elder brother, though elsewhere in the West Sudan Hare is the nephew of Hyena (Monteil, 1905:7). Among the matrilineal Kaguru of Tanzania, the key relationship is also between mother's brother (Hyena) and sister's son (Hare).

It is also the case that contrasted ideas which are symbolized by animal characters in one society may be depicted differently in another. The Kuranko animal characters signify a contrast between cleverness and stupidity. Stupidity connotes both absence of intelligence and the use of cleverness for selfish advantage. A similar emphasis is placed upon these attributes by the BaMbuti Pygmies of northern Zaire:

> . . . the one quality to which these BaMbuti attach the greatest importance is cleverness, a term which in certain circumstances also means "trickery." Conversely, while selfishness, greed, laziness, and gossiping women are mildly condemned in a number of legends, the sin of sins is stupidity. (Turnbull, 1959:51)

The BaMbuti attribute the same value to cleverness as the Kuranko do, but the BaMbuti associate cleverness with smallness, with themselves, while bigness, clumsiness, stupidity, and the selfish use of cleverness are traits associated with the village Negroes (Turnbull, 1959:51, 54, 58). Both BaMbuti and Kuranko narratives betray a concern with the ethical ambiguity of intelligence. This ambiguity arises from the fact that intelligence can be used for perverse and selfish purposes; it is at the same time the principal means by which justice is maintained and the social order is continually reinvigorated. The problem of intelligence is closely related to a recurring social problem which we have already touched upon. Although cleverness and wisdom are associated with the old, many elders abuse their positions of authority or are unable to discharge the duties of their offices. Younger Kuranko men often remark the senility and ineptitude of old men, the self-centeredness and inflexibility of their attitudes. They would undoubtedly share the BaMbuti view that old age, when accompanied by disability, is loathsome (Turnbull, 1959:52). In the Kuranko case, the disability may be physical or moral, but the consequences are the same: corruption or ineptitude in the exercise of power, and a failure by elders to meet their commitments to dependents. The key problem in the hare-hyena narratives is one of contriving the simulacrum of a fit between personal disposition (intelligence and self-restraint) and the social position of elder or chief.[10]

The Kuranko hare-hyena narratives work to deny or reduce the ambiguity inherent in authority, an ambiguity which results from the indeterminate relationship between person and role.

Stanley Diamond has argued that Plato's *Republic* and the Book of Job are also concerned with the problem of justice and "bent upon denying human ambivalence and social ambiguity" (1972:xiii). This denial of ambiguity is accomplished, Diamond points out, by showing that good and evil have *different* sources (divine and human respectively). A similar polarization occurs in the Kuranko narratives. While the hare is associated with *extrasocial faculties* (symbolized by the figure of the clever youngster), the hyena is associated with *antisocial traits* (symbolized by the figure of the corrupt or stupid elder). Hare signifies intelligence, mobility, flexibility, unorthodox improvisation, and play. These attributes are all implied by the term *hankili* (cleverness). Certain physical characteristics of the hare serve as metaphors for the intellectual skills implied by this term. *Hankilimaiye* is, as we have seen in chapter 1, regarded by the Kuranko as an innate factor, something which is not determined by heredity or by birth, rank, sex, or estate. It is always randomly and unpredictably distributed in any population. Hyena, by contrast, signifies dogmatic inflexibility. Hyena also signifies corrupt, inept, and selfish behavior, the use of rules and of power for personal gain. In the narratives at least, these proclivities are regarded as inevitable aspects of elderhood (*koroya*). Cleverness is, on the other hand, always associated in the narratives with youngsters.[11]

As we shall see, the usual plot in these narratives involves the hare outsmarting the unjust hyena and usurping his position. In this way, fortuitously distributed but highly valued abilities like *hankili* come to be associated unequivocally with the position of elder. The displacement or death of the inept and corrupt elder implies a return to justice, a revitalization of the social order.

It is not that the narratives abandon the hierarchical distinction between elder and younger; rather, the distinction is suspended, only to be reinforced as soon as there is a merging of superior ability and superior status position. Because the status inferior (Hare) has superior ability, ambiguity is created. In other words, there is an *effective* symmetry between Hare and Hyena. The superior status position of the latter is cancelled out by the superior ability of the former. This ambiguity is reduced as soon as the superior ability is associated with the superior position. And with this reduction of ambiguity goes a restoration of justice. These narratives may be compared with a "zero-sum" game in which effective equality between the players at the outset of the game leads toward a new inequality.[12] The play situation is comparable to the situation which is developed in the hare-hyena narratives: in both instances, equality and role alternations are simulated as ways of resolving problems. The narratives simulate an ideal situation, one that cannot possibly be realized, a situation in which there is a determinate relationship between personal ability and social position. In the present context, such a situation would imply that chiefs and elders are always just, impartial, and wise.

But the narratives do not merely simulate impossible situations; the unlikelihood of these situations is fundamental to the fictional mode itself. Narrative resolutions, like all simulative modes of action, are not simply artificial and vicarious; they *must* be so, and be bracketed away from everyday reality. The license given to youngsters in play activity and in narratives would, if it became incorporated into the workings of the politico-jural order, have destructive rather than constructive results.[13]

It is now possible to show in what way the hare-hyena narratives are allegorical, saying one thing but meaning another. Younger sons and younger brothers are not enjoined to outsmart their elders. The fictional schemes are ways of generating a new awareness, of encouraging people to engage in thinking about problems which arise in everyday life, and of showing that intellectual control and determination can be achieved over events which, paradoxically, remain always unpredictable and refractory. The narratives are means of changing one's consciousness, but not of changing the world.

N.11: *The Hare and the Thornbush*

Narrated by Nonkowa Kargbo. Recorded at Benekoro, March 1970.

One day the hare summoned all the other animals. He said, "Let us meet together and try to catch whoever it is that divulges all our secrets." The animals all looked at one another. Then they fell upon the hare and said they were going to kill him because he was the one who was guilty of divulging all their secrets.

As they held him, the hare said, "I have one plea to make. If you want to kill me, then kill me. But you see that thornbush? Don't throw me into it or I will escape. You see that open grassland? When the other animals caught my grandfather they sent him there and he died. So please don't send me there. If you do, I will die a dreadful death."

The animals said, "Well, we are going to throw you into that open grassland." The hare started crying out, saying that they should not throw him into that open grassland, that they should throw him into the thornbush instead. They said, "No matter whether you cry or not, we are going to throw you into that open grassland. Where your grandfather died, there shall you die too."

Then they threw him into that open grassland. He jumped up and laughed at the other animals. They ran after him, but they couldn't catch him. So he got away. Since that time, if you chase a hare in the open grassland you will never catch it. I have also told you how tricky the hare is.

N.12: *The Hare, the Hyena, and the Fishing Weir*

Narrated by Nonkowa Kargbo. Recorded at Benekoro, March 1970.

Once the hare told the hyena that they should make a fishing weir.* He said, "Hyena, you should be content to listen to the sound of the water falling over the weir. People passing along the path will hear the weir water falling and they will say how strong you must be to have dammed the river." The hyena said, "Younger brother [*n'dogo*], you have spoken the truth. Let us go." They went and made the weir.

Very early every morning, the hare went and collected the fish that had been caught in the weir. After this, he would go to the hyena and say, "Elder brother [*n'koro*], let us go to the weir." They would go and look in the fishing trap and not find any fish. The hare would say, "Eh, *n'koro*, we have not caught any fish. How is that?" And the hyena would say, "I don't care about the fish. The weir is making this great noise and I am content with that. I know that people are praising me, saying how strong I am. The weir is going *woooooo*, and everyone that passes this way is saying how strong I must be. That is all I want from the weir."

So the hyena got a name† and the hare got the fish. He deceived his elder brother.

---

*One Kuranko fishing method is to construct a fishing weir: a gridwork of branches is built across the river, the openings blocked with palm leaves. A free passage is left in midstream and a tapered cane basket-trap is lowered into the gap.
†This is to say that he earned a reputation for his strength.

N.13: *The Lioness, the Hyena, and the Hare*

Narrated by Karifa Sise. Recorded at Kamadugu Sukurela, February 1972.

There was a lioness. She had two cubs. The lioness gave one of her cubs to the hyena, and she gave her other cub to the hare. She asked them to look after her cubs.

The hare went to the hyena and said, "Let us eat the cub that was left in your care." The hyena said, "Eh, what would our elder say?" The hare said, "Don't trouble yourself about that." So the hyena killed the lion cub, skinned it, made a shirt and a pair of trousers from the skin, and ate the meat.

Before long the lioness came back from the place where she had been looking for food. She said to the hare, "Where is my cub?" The hare brought the cub to the lioness. The cub was well fed and looked well. The lioness said, "Where is the hyena?" The hare said, "Well, I don't know where he has gone, but he has killed and eaten your cub and sewn a complete outfit from its skin. He's wearing that outfit now and boasting among the other animals about his ability to sew clothes from lion skins." The lioness said, "How can I catch him?" The hare said, "I will bring him to you, but first you must give me something for my trouble." The lioness went off and killed many animals. She brought them to the hare. When the hare had eaten his fill, he went off in search of the hyena.

He met the hyena. The hare said, "Oh, *n'koro*, you are marvelous, there is no one like you, you are the only person who can sew clothes from lion skins. Let us go and show you off to all the animals. I have a song for you." The hyena went along with the hare. Wherever they went, the hare sang:

> Our elder's child, the one that went missing,
> Is on the hyena's head as a cap;
> Our elder's child, the one that went missing,
> Is on the hyena's body as a shirt;
> Our elder's child, the one that went missing,
> Is on the hyena as a pair of trousers . . .
> He is a man of strength and power.

The hyena was very pleased. They went from place to place and wherever they went the hare would sing (as before).

At last they reached the place where the lioness lived. The hare said to the lioness, *"N'koro*, didn't I tell you I would bring him to you? Here he is in his fine outfit, made from the skin of your cub. Look at him."

The lioness fell upon the hyena and ate him up.

N.14: *The Great Laugher*

Narrated by Keti Ferenke Koroma. Recorded at Kondembaia, March 1970.

There was a man who said that no one could laugh as much as he could. So they invited him to a *korfe** sacrifice to see if he could laugh more than anyone else. They wanted to see how he laughed, because there were many others who could laugh too. He decided to attend the *korfe*.

As he approached the town, he sent the customary kola to the chief, announcing his arrival and conveying the message that all the town laughers should come and meet him. Now, the *korfe* was in the name of the hyena's mother.† The hyena had decreed that everyone be serious and that no laughter should be heard during the *korfe*, because the *korfe* was in the name of his mother. There were many animals who wanted to laugh, but they were not able to, because of that decree. If a person tried to make others laugh, they would not laugh, because the hyena had passed this decree in order to get food for himself. He would fall upon whoever he saw laughing and eat that person. He was looking at everyone's face. As soon as he saw a smile he would fall upon that person.

The hare said, "Wait, I am going to get everyone laughing." He had made a little drum called *tamban*. As he approached the town, he sent a message that he was coming to attend the *korfe* for the hyena's mother. He said, "I am coming with all kinds of tricks." They said, "Well, you are welcome." He entered the town and said, "I have got some songs. When I sing one of my songs, everyone

---

korfe or *kofe* = a kind of sacrifice, offered by a chief to the memory of a recently deceased parent. Visitors are invited from other chiefdoms and a *korfe* is frequently an occasion for festivities and entertainments.
†This is to say that the *korfe* is dedicated to the memory of the hyena's mother.

present should join in. Everyone should join in the singing. There must not be a person who does not join in." He began to sing:

N'de lar magade, yenawe lar maga yo, yenawe

(I have been amused, this great laugher has
been much amused, this great laugher . . .)*

Everyone started laughing. Everyone was laughing, even the hyena. And the hyena was not telling people to stop laughing, because everyone was laughing. They all laughed until they were exhausted. The hyena said that his decree should be forgotten and that the *korfe* was over. He went away.

Therefore, it is always wise to have a clever person amongst you, be it on the occasion of a gathering or on any other occasion. The hare used his cleverness to get around that bad decree that the hyena had passed. Through the cleverness of the hare, all the animals laughed as much as they liked.

N.15: *The Animals Who Ate Their Mothers*

Narrator's name not known. Recorded at Benekoro, March 1970.

The lion, the hyena, and the hare formed a farming cooperative [*kere*]. No sooner had they formed this *kere* than they decided that they would make their mothers into sauce to be eaten with the rice.

They went to the hyena's farm. They killed the hyena's mother, cooked her, and ate her. They went to the lion's farm. They cut off the lion's mother's head. They made her into sauce to be eaten with the rice.

Now the hare was a clever animal. Before the time came when they were to come to the hare's farm, the hare made a small drum and he told his mother the secret of the *kere*: that they had decided to eat their mothers. He then told his mother that they all had

---

*The refrain is chorused many times. As soon as the audience was chorusing the refrain, Keti Ferenke started to imitate the hare's cheeky and irreverent manner. He then began to laugh uproariously, as a kind of counterpoint to the refrain, "Ha ha ha ha ha, ho ho ho ho ho . . ." In other words, the hare's behavior and laughter infected everyone around him, including the hyena. And, in just the same way, the narrator's laughter and antics infected everyone in the audience.

different names. The mothers had to name them properly; if they failed to do so they would be eaten. The hare said, "They have already eaten the mothers of the lion and the hyena." He told his mother that one of his companions was called Tensara, another Konkofekenkie, and another Almantuporo. Then the day came when they were to come to the hare's farm to work.

Since they had eaten the mothers of the other animals, the hare did not want his mother to be eaten. So he decided to play some music on his little drum as the others worked. While they were enjoying the music, he could remind his mother of their names. When he saw his mother approaching the farm, he sang:

> Konkofekenkie, *tintimatima, a tima tintima*
> Almantuporo, *tintimatima, a tima tintima*
> N'*de l togo* Tensara, *tintimatima, a tima tintima*
> (I am called Tensara . . .)
> *Ni nyina ra wo l ko i le toge konkon mangfa, tintimatima, a tima tintima*
> (If you don't remember that, your name will be sauce to be eaten with the rice . . .)*

Then they asked the hare's mother to tell them what their secret names were. She named them all correctly and she went free.

This shows the cleverness of the hare.

N.16: *The Hyena and the Pangolin*

Narrated by Keti Ferenke Koroma. Recorded at Kabala, July 1970.

The animals formed a *kere* [labor cooperative]. The hyena came and said, "I would like to join your *kere*." They said, "All right, join us." So the hyena and his small son joined.

Now the hyena had only joined the *kere* because the pangolin was in it. When he saw the pangolin's scales, he thought that it was fat all over the pangolin's body. That is why the hyena joined the *kere*, so that he could eat the pangolin.

One day the hyena felt hungry, very hungry. He said, "Heh,

---

*Each line is sung twice; the refrain suggests the sound of the drum music. The cleverness of the hare lies in his ability to use the drum music to distract the attention of his companions while he reminds his mother of their secret names.

tomorrow I am going to eat that pangolin and enjoy all that fat which is all over its body." At daybreak they went to the farm. The hyena chose a patch of ground to hoe that was near the patch which the pangolin had chosen to hoe. They worked for a while. Then, at noon, the hyena jumped up and pounced upon the pangolin. The pangolin held him to its hard shelly back and ran with him among thorn bushes, across streams, through swamps, over mountains, into valleys . . . through every bad place. The hyena's son followed them, saying, "My father is dead." He followed them, shouting, "My father has left me, my father has left me, my father has left me, my father has left me. Pangolin has carried my father away, the pangolin has carried my father away." For the whole day the pangolin was running around with the hyena on its back, but at dusk he let him fall off. When the hyena was free, he went home. At home he found that his other children had killed an animal and cooked it. (The hyena had only joined the *kere* because of the pangolin. He was such a glutton that when he saw the pangolin's scaly back he thought it was all fat; so he joined the *kere*.) One of his children said, "Eh, father, why are you so bruised?" The hyena said, "You know that hoeing is hard work. It is only the work. It is not that anything happened to me." They said, "Eh well, that is that." (Before then he had warned his son not to say anything about what had happened.)

They prepared the meat. They said, "Father, share out the meat." The hyena picked out all the bones and said, "All you children, here is your share." He picked up all the meat and said, "I work in the *kere*. This is my share." That is how he shared the meat. Then his little son, who had been with him during the day, said, "Look what our father is doing to us. He has gathered all the meaty parts for himself and given us the bones." Then he went outside and stood there for some time. After a while he said, "Father, the pangolin has come!" At once the father hyena opened the back door and jumped out of the house, leaving all the meat behind. He went into the bush and hid. The little boy came back and said, "*N'koro*, let us eat the meat. I know that we will finish it before father gets back. I know what happened today in the *kere*. Father won't be coming back. Let's eat." So they ate everything.

Therefore, it is very bad to be covetous. That which you covet, you will seldom get. This was what happened between the pangolin and the hyena.

N.17: *The Hare, the Hyena, and the Yam*

Narrated by Nonkowa Kargbo. Recorded at Benekoro, March 1970.

Once the hare got a yam to plant. He showed it to the hyena and asked the hyena how to plant the yam. The hyena said, "First of all, boil it, then peel it, then plant it." The hare cooked it and planted it. That night the hyena came and took the yam and ate it. So the yam never grew.

Before long the hare discovered that he had been tricked by the hyena. So he decided to have his revenge. He told the hyena that he was sick and that the hyena should come the next day and examine him. Then the hare pounded some *dege* [rice flour], mixed it with honey, and smeared it all over his body. He lit a fire and lay down by it. Then he sent for the hyena, his elder brother. He said, "May my elder brother come to tell me whether I will live or die."

The hyena came. He said, "What is this all over your body?" The hare said, "It is my sickness. Will you taste my sickness and tell me whether I will live or die?" The hyena licked a part of the hare's body. "Eh, *n'dogo*, this sickness of yours is very sweet." He kept taking the rice flour from the hare's body and eating it. He said, *N'dogo*, this is a sweet sickness you have." And finally he said, "*N'dogo*, can you show me how you got your sickness?"

The hare said, "There is nothing wrong in that. You must return home now. Tomorrow you can come and I will show you how I got my sickness." Then he said, "*N'koro*, will I die?" The hyena said, "No," and said, "All right then, I will come and visit you tomorrow."

Before the hyena came back the hare washed all the rice flour from his body. The hare kept the dried flour and honey. When the hyena came back the hare said, "Well, this is the rest of my sickness." The hyena sat down and ate it all. Then the hare said, "Well, come back tomorrow and I will show you how I got my sickness."

The next day the hare went to the hyena and said, "*N'koro*, I have come to make you sick." The hyena said, "All right, explain it to me." The hare said, "Call your sons." The hyena called all his sons. The hare said, "Well now, tell them to go and find some firewood." They went and fetched firewood and stacked it outside the house. The hare said, "*N'koro*, do you think you will be able to

stand it?" The hyena said, "Yes, I will bear it." The hare said, "Well,
tell your sons to each bring a long pole." The sons each brought a
long pole. The hare then told the hyena to light a very big fire.
"You should jump into that fire and when you say 'get me out, get
me out' your sons should use their long poles to push you further
into the fire until you say 'push me into the fire, push me into the
fire,' when it will be time for them to pull you out." The hyena
said, "All right." Then he jumped into the fire. He said, "Get me
out, get me out, get me out!" His sons pushed him further in with
their long poles. Soon after, he shouted again, "Get me out, get me
out!" They pushed him further in again. When his body had
roasted for some time he shouted, "Push me in, push me in!" They
pulled him out. They took him to his house and laid him down
there. Then the hare said, *"N'koro*, in two days time I will come and
visit you." The hyena said, "Mm mm, that is all right."*

After some time the hare came. He found flies everywhere. The
hyena had begun to putrefy. The hare said, "Hmmm, something
smells around here." The people said, "It is your elder brother,
who is sick." The hare said, "Eh, well, this sickness is just like the
boiled yam. My elder brother told me to boil my yam before plant-
ing it. I boiled it and planted it. Then my elder brother went and
took the yam and ate it. Now then, if a boiled yam can grow, then
my elder brother will live." And he jumped through the window
and ran off. No sooner had he gone than his elder brother died.

N.18: *The Hare, the Old Woman, and the Lion*

Narrated by Keti Ferenke Koroma. Recorded at Kondembaia, March
1970.

There was an old woman who lived in a far-off place. She lived
alone in that distant place. She had many sheep and goats. There
was a hare. The hare would go and look at the sheep, go away, and
come back again. The hare coveted the sheep and wanted to steal
them from the old woman. But there was no way in which it was
possible to do this.

---

*Spoken in a very rueful tone.

The hare went and got a ram. He brought it to the old woman and said, "Grandmother, I have come to leave you my ram for safekeeping." The old woman said, "All right, leave it here." He left it. The hare went away.

One month, two months, three months passed. In the fourth month the hare came back. He said, "Grandmother, how are you and all my sheep?" The old woman said, "You only have one sheep here. It was only one that you brought." The hare said, "Eh, grandmother, you had all the ewes, and I brought the ram. The ewes had lambs because of my ram." The old woman said, "Eh! You only brought one sheep." The hare said, "Give me my sheep and I'll go." The old woman gave him one sheep, and he went away with it. He ate it.

One month, two months, three months passed. In the fourth month he came back. He said, "Grandmother, how are you and all my sheep?" The old woman said, "Eh! You have no more sheep here." They argued for some time. Then the hare said, "All these ones here are from my ram." He took one of the sheep and went away with it.

One month, two months, three months passed. In the fourth month he came back again. He greeted the old woman as usual: "Grandmother, how are you and all my sheep?" And so, in this way he got all the old woman's sheep, leaving only the ram with her.

One month, two months, three months passed. The old woman went to the lion and said, "My child, I am in trouble. The hare has stolen all my sheep. He has left only a ram to me. He has taken all my sheep and left me only this ram. And I know that he will come tomorrow and take the ram as well. I have no way of stopping him. That is why I am asking you to help me stop the hare from taking that one last ram away from me." The lion said, "Now go, I will meet you in the evening." The old woman went away.

When she returned in the evening, the lion came. He said, "Grandmother, what shall I do?" The old woman said, "I will tie a rope around your neck and take you to the pen. When the hare comes, because he usually comes at night, I will hand you over to him. Then, when you have left my place, somewhere along the way you can eat him." The lion said, "Well, that is all right." The old woman tied a rope around the lion's neck, took him to the sheep pen, and tethered him there. No sooner had she come back than the hare appeared. He said, "Grandmother, how are you and my sheep?" The old woman said, "You are after my sheep. But the only one left is in the pen. Come, let us go and I will get it for you." But as the hare was going, he called an old hyena to accompany him. He told the old hyena that they were going to collect his sheep and then to eat it. As soon as they reached the pen, the old woman took the lion and said, "Here is the only sheep that is left." The place was quite dark. The hare took the sheep tether, not realizing that it was a lion tied to it.

The hyena was driving the sheep for the hare. As they went along, the lightning flashed. The hare turned and saw that it was a lion. He said to the hyena, "*N'koro*, take our sheep. I want to go have a shit." The hyena did not know that it was a lion, so he took the rope. When the hare handed the so-called sheep to the hyena, he ran away and escaped. The hyena waited for some time. The hare didn't turn up, and the lion didn't say anything. So the hyena took the "sheep" to the hare's farm.

At the hare's farm he found the hare's wife. He said, "Here is your husband's sheep. I waited for him but he didn't turn up. So I want to leave the sheep with you. When he comes back in the morning you can give it to him." The lion said nothing. The hare's wife took it and tied it to one of the veranda posts. The lion lay down and the hyena went away.

The hare had gone and slept in a grove of raffia palms. In the morning he made a harp from the pithy stems of the palm. As he approached his farmhouse he started playing the harp and singing:

Kindi kindi, * *ko fora n'kuma kunu kindi*

(*Kindi kindi*, I say something just missed me yesterday *kindi*)

He sang this song because he had seen the lion when the lightning flashed. And he had given the lion to the hyena and now thought that he was out of danger. That is why he was singing about something just missing him. He didn't know that he was about to find the lion there.

As he neared the farmhouse, his wife said, "Eh, hare, this behavior of yours is no good. The hyena brought your sheep last

---

*This describes the sound of the harp (*seraima*). The line is sung thrice.

night. I have been waiting for you for a long time but haven't seen you." The hare said, "What! Is that a sheep? You wait and see!"

The hare ran away, his wife ran after him, their child ran after them. The lion severed the rope and ran after them. It was a great race. *Pila pila pila pila pila*—they ran and ran and ran. When the lion got near them, the hare leaped up and hung from a tree branch. His wife leaped up and hung on, and their child also leaped up and hung on. The lion came and sat down beneath them, and watched them. They hung for some time. Then the hare's child said, "Hmm, father, my hands are tired." The hare said, "Then hang on by your feet." Then the child said, "Hmm, father, my feet are tired." The hare said, "Then hang on with your teeth." As the child was about to grasp the branch in his teeth, he slipped and fell. The lion pounced on him, cut him in two, and swallowed him, first one half then the other. Then he sat down again, watching the hare and his wife. The hare's wife said, "*M'berin*, it is getting harder and harder." The hare said, "Well, what am I to do now? We are both fighting for our heads." And he said, "Well, there is nothing to be done." Before long the hare's wife fell from the tree. The lion pounced on her and cut her in two. He swallowed the first half, then he swallowed the second half. He sat down, looking up at the hare.

The hare hung on for some time. He hung by his hands, and when his hands got tired he hung by his feet, and when his feet got tired he hung by his hands again. He did this for some time. But finally he slipped from the branch. He tried to grab hold of the branch with his ear. But it did not hold. He came down shouting. He fell in front of the lion. The lion cut him in two and swallowed this half, then swallowed that half. The lion went away.

Therefore, it is not good that people get things by deceit. Whatever does not belong to you, don't lay claim to it. It may take a long time, but one day you will suffer for it.

One of the main characteristics of the hare is that he is unable to keep secrets, and unable to hold his tongue. The continual mobility and twitching of the hare's mouth may make this animal an appropriate symbol of these traits (c.f. Werner, 1925:291). But not all aspects of the personality of the fictional hare are as easily traced to physical features. The childlike and irrepressible personality of Fasan sets him apart from the group; Fasan is a loner, a law unto himself. His solitary habits and small size imply, in the narratives, social marginality (youngest son) as well as a detached and irresponsible attitude. His detachment from the other animals is both physical and psychological. His cunning and resourcefulness are contrasted with the rather inflexible, stolid, law-abiding character of the other animals, who always remain undifferentiated, their individual personalities eclipsed by their group identity. This contrast is expressed in terms of a difference between laws, contracts, and sworn oaths on the one hand—things which are *binding*—and music and song on the other hand—activities which *lighten and loosen*. The hare's irrepressible and lawless nature is usually signified by his inability to stop himself singing and making music. His failure to keep secrets or to respect bargains sets him outside the domain of law, oath, and contract. His tendency to sing and make music is, by contrast, the thing which isolates him from the politico-jural order *and* the means by which he corrects faults within that order.

The marginality of the youngest son can be established in several ways. From a structural point of view his position is halfway between the senior and junior generations (Jackson, 1977b:163). In terms of birth-order position, the youngest brother is the last in the line of inheritance; he must run errands for and do the bidding of his older brothers, he is the recipient of hand-me-downs, often a victim of bullying elders, and isolated from the centers of authority and property control within the family. As Nonkowa Kargbo pointed out to me, the youngest son often feels neglected and misused, but, free from the responsibilities of a determinate status, he may travel around, living with different brothers until he finds a secure niche. Nonkowa also noted that younger brothers may cause dissensions among their elder brothers by playing them off against each other and by spreading rumors (see Jackson, 1977b:170). In cunning, deceit, quickness of mind, and cleverness, a youngest brother or son finds compensation for the social disadvantages of his marginal position. It is because of this that many Kuranko informants say that the youngster in the narratives is always the cleverest person. An inevitable loser in the game of life, he can nonetheless win by manipulating the fortunes of the other players by chicanery, cheating, and deception.

However, I think that it is important to emphasize once more the allegorical character of the hare: the fictionalized younger brother or youngest son. The narratives do not simply provide socially approved fantasized successes for disadvantaged younger siblings; they are not merely compensatory or consoling in their function. This point is confirmed by the fact that many of these narratives are related by elderly men (like Nonkowa Karbgo) or by men (like Keti Ferenke) who emphasize that the hare-hyena narratives have much wider implications and concern the problem of the discrepancy between talents such as cleverness and social positions such as elderhood. In other words, the narratives deal with a recurrent ambiguity which springs from the indeterminate relationship between individual capability and social expectation. It was in fact Keti Ferenke who first afforded me insight into the importance of this ambiguity, an ambiguity which, as we have seen in chapter 3 (N.3), reflects the contradictory connotations of the principle of *fisa mantiye*: it can refer to relative superiority/inferiority with respect to age-status position or it can refer to relative superiority/inferiority with respect to personal qualities and talents. In the following remarks, Keti Ferenke uses lexical ambiguity (*kina wo* and *kina wo* are homophones) to clarify the situation.

> We say *kina wo* and *kina wo* [respectively "beehive" and "elder"]. They are not one [the pronunciation of each word differs slightly]. If you hear *kina* [elder], he knows almost everything. But if you hear *kina* [beehive], it does not know anything. The elder could be found in the younger and the younger could be found in the elder.
>
> Even if a person is a child, but behaves like an elder, then he is an elder. If he thinks like an elder, then he is an elder. Even if a person is old and senior, if he behaves like a child then he is a child. Therefore, this matter of seniority comes not only from the fact that one is born first, or from the fact that one is big and strong; it also concerns the manner in which a person behaves and does things. For example, you will see some old men who have nothing; they are not called "big men" [*morgo ba*, "elders"]. But some young men have wealth; because of that they are called *morgo ba*. Therefore, whatever God has put in your head, that will make you what you are. I am speaking now, but some of these words of wisdom [*kuma kore*] which I am explaining to you are not known by everyone. You may ask a man and he may know of them. But I have explained them. Therefore, am I not the elder? There are some elders who know of these things, but I have explained them. Therefore, if you hear the word *kina* you should know that it is *hankili* [cleverness] that really defines it. [my translation]

Keti Ferenke chooses to play up the value of cleverness over the importance of elderhood per se. He does this in his narratives as well.

Other Kuranko informants tend to play down such attributes as cleverness, preferring a fairly doctrinaire definition of *fisa mantiye* which emphasizes birth-order position alone. Others, like Keti Ferenke himself,
may refer to the manner in which status is conferred by wealth or
achieved through the manipulation of fetishes and supernatural properties. Indeed, *fisa mantiye* can be said to connote social position, material
wealth, and personal "properties." Different connotations emerge in different situations.

The narratives exploit the ambiguity intrinsic to the concept itself.
Attention is shifted from personal attributes like cleverness and play-
fulness (associated with the hare) to status attributes such as jural control and command (associated with elderhood and chieftaincy), until
there is finally a merging of the status position and the superior ability.
In this way ambiguity is reduced; this is accomplished at the level of
event by the clever youngster usurping the position of the corrupt or
inept elder.

Apart from N.11, which focuses attention upon the hare, most of the
narratives in this set dramatize the *relationship* between hare and other
animals, usually the hyena. In one narrative, not published here, the
animals meet together to discuss what they fear most. All agree that the
elephant is the most fearsome of all the animals. The hare then boasts
that he can ride the elephant like a horse. He goes to the elephant and
tells it that the other animals believe that if the hare sat upon its back
the weight would prove too much for it. Tricked by this ruse, the
elephant allows the hare to caparison it like a horse, and to ride it into
the town. Impressed, the animals declare the hare the cleverest of all
and appoint him chief.[14] In another version of this tale, God rewards
the elephant for carrying the chief on its back by making it the largest
of all the animals. This is seen as compensation for its slow-wittedness.
In N.12 a similar complementarity is established between the stupid
and gullible hyena, who asks only that his superior strength be recognized, and the clever and artful hare. The interplay between cleverness
and brute strength is often depicted in African folktales as a physical
contest, a tug-of-war, between the hare and an elephant or hip-
popotamus. Such tales, and stories like *The Hare and the Thornbush*
(N.11), have frequently found their way, often via Afro-American culture, into European children's lore. These themes have a universal appeal and distribution.

N.13 dramatizes the stupidity and gullibility of the hyena. The hyena,
without any moral hesitation, acts upon the hare's suggestion that he

kill and eat the lioness's cubs (which have been left in their care). In another version of this narrative, given by Denka Marah, the stupidity of the hyena is also played up. The hyena thinks that the hare's song is in praise of him, whereas it is the hare's means of telling the lioness that the hyena has eaten her cubs and clothed himself with their pelts. The same narrative was also told to me by Keti Ferenke, with the spider as trickster and the chimpanzee as dupe.

From these narratives we gain insight into the Kuranko notion of individual responsibility. The hyena's stupidity lies in his inability to empathize with others; therefore he cannot form moral judgments by putting himself in another person's place. In N.13, he acts blindly, selfishly, and instinctively: he readily kills the cub which had been left in his care by the lioness. The hyena can never integrate his intentions with the consequences of his actions; he lives in a world of emotion and impulse, a world pervaded by his own subjectivity. Hare, by contrast, takes a detached view of things, assesses each situation, considers the possibilities inherent in the situation, and acts with control and judgment. Since the hare is the hero in most of these narratives, it is clear that the Kuranko view is that there is no excuse for ill-judged actions, no external agency to lift from each person the burden of choice.[15]

In chapter 1 we saw that the Kuranko refer to a variety of innate or contingent factors, as well as postnatal influences and external forces, which together shape a person's destiny and temperament. Yet, as I have argued elsewhere (Jackson, 1977b), the Kuranko do not take the view that a person should abnegate control and forfeit his will in favor of external and adventitious factors. Ideally, each person must strive to seek control over the destiny which happens to be his. It is this conception of moral responsibility which pervades the narratives. Many of the narratives in chapter 3 deal with straitened circumstances—food shortage and hunger—which threaten and weaken man's control over his emotions and sympathies. None of these narratives allows any moral excuse for submitting to hunger or for regressing to infantile behavior. Food-sharing and cooperation in food production are factors which characterize human evolution and constitute the foundation of any social order. But ethical systems are never wholly determined by these material circumstances, and in the narratives which we are concerned with here the contrast between greed and sharing serves as a metaphor for exploring moral problems related to such contrasted tendencies as judgment/impetuosity, self-interest/group-interest, self-control/

immoderation. Food-sharing is, of course, one of the most universal images of correct behavior (Richards, 1969:30), and it is already clear that greed is the dominant metaphor for injustice and irresponsibility in Kuranko narratives.

It is also interesting that the notion of retributive justice (*hake*) is often expressed in terms of food. In N.18, for example, where retributive justice is a central theme, Hare and his family are eaten by the lion as a result of Hare's having deceived an old woman. The notion of *hake* is also applied to sorcery, one of the most common means of redressing injustices in everyday life. If one has been wronged, then the sorcerer often uses the weapon of wrongdoing in working to injure or harm the malefactor. But if one is making an unjust accusation, then the sorcery will rebound and afflict the accuser. This boomerang effect of sorcery safeguards it from being misused. In Kuranko narratives, retributive justice is often achieved by turning the tool of injustice back against the wrongdoer.

N.14–N.17 are perhaps the most important narratives in this set. All except N.15 specifically involve relationships between elder and younger, and in most cases the "elder" is the hyena and the "youngster" is the hare (in N.16 the key relationship is hyena and hyena's youngest son). These narratives echo the hunger narratives, particularly N.9, where unscrupulous and greedy fathers use unfair strategies to keep all the food for themselves and are outwitted and corrected by their youngest sons.

In the hare-hyena narratives, a person in authority imposes an unjust or absurd law on the community in order to satisfy his greed, or he violates his obligations to others, again for selfish reasons. In N.14 the hyena chief decrees that no one may laugh; if anyone laughs, the hyena will eat him. In a narrative not included here a chief hoards all the rice during a time of great hunger; he refuses to distribute it among his subjects, whom he is duty-bound to protect and feed. N.17 is comparable. The hyena misinforms his younger brother because he wants to eat the yam which the latter wishes to plant. N.15 and N.16 involve violations of contracts. In N.15 the animals agree to kill and eat their mothers, a complete perversion and misuse of the contractual and reciprocal bonds of the *kere*. In N.16 the hyena joins a *kere*—a cooperative work group founded upon mutual interest—merely to kill and eat a member of the group, the pangolin. The fact that the *kere* is referred to in these narratives confirms the view of Dundes that the theme of the making and breaking of friendship in African folktales is "closely related to contractual relationships and to mutually reciprocal behavior" (1971:180). But in most of these narratives the unethical behavior refers not to friendship but to kinship. The crucial relationships—elder brother/younger brother, chief/subjects—imply a particular kind of reciprocity in which respect accorded by the subordinate is reciprocated by protection and welfare given by the superordinate. In every case, the person in the senior position fails in his responsibility to those under him, usually because he is inept, corrupt, greedy, covetous, or simply stupid.[16] It is the person in the subordinate position, the hare, who redresses the injustice. In some cases the stupid law is abandoned (N.14), sometimes the law is circumvented to the advantage of the youngster (N.15), and sometimes the corrupt elder is hoist with his own petard (N.17).

I wish now to reconsider the significance of the narrative setting, and then turn to a discussion of the means used in redressing injustices or escaping from the impasses created by them. N.15 is an example of a narrative well known throughout Africa, in which two friends or kinsmen agree to kill their mothers for food. One violates the agreement and saves his mother's life. Examples are: *Cunny Rabbit Tricks the Animals (Feasting on Their Mothers)*—Krio, Sierra Leone (Mudge-Paris, 1930:319); *How Turtle Deceived Leopard into Eating His Own Mother*—Bulu, Cameroon (Schwab, 1914:267); *The Tale of Hyena and Rabbit*—Kaguru, Tanzania (Beidelman, 1961:61–62). Only in the Kaguru and Kuranko examples is the crucial relationship one of kinship; in the Krio, Bulu, and other instances (Brain, 1977:37) friendship is the key relationship. But in every case, the bargain is struck during a time of hunger and food shortage. The moral dilemma which the narratives deal with arises out of a choice which has to be made between individual survival and the survival of the moral community. Eating their mothers or sisters means that the continuity of the social group is no longer possible, even though each animal guarantees his own personal survival. For the matrilineal Kaguru, women are biologically and genealogically indispensable, and the crime which the hyena commits in killing his mother strikes at the heart of the social and moral order (Beidelman, 1961, 1963). For the patrilineal Kuranko, the prevailing image of kinship, *nakelinyorgoye,* means "mother one partnership." Thus, even when the bargain is made among friends (N.15), it implies a threat to kinship and to the continuity of the social order.

The moral choice in these narratives is one between momentary personal gain and deferred social advantage. Because the hungry-time is marginal to the dry season, which is the period of intense social activity and community life, and because hunger itself tends to drive people to selfish and regressive behavior, it is understandable that it should provide the temporal setting for narratives concerned with the conflict between self-interest and group-interest. Moreover, since the narratives "play up" and "play out" normally repressed and antisocial tendencies, the hungry-time is an appropriate image in another sense. During times of hunger and famine, the male world—associated with rice (the staple crop), farming, and politico-jural control—goes into abeyance, while the peripheral roles of women and children—associated with gathering wild fruits and tubers in the bush, with gardening and secondary foodstuffs—come to the fore. The various ways in which hunger and deprivation lead to switchings and changes in social and individual consciousness may explain why "famine" is one of the commonest settings in African folktales. Furthermore, the metaphorical use of food, food shortage, greed, and sharing for discoursing upon problems of reciprocity and justice is found throughout the continent (Paulme, 1975b:621; Innes, 1964:9–10).

The Sweetness of Retribution

I have emphasized that the hare's deceits and ruses are justified only when they serve to right a wrong; cleverness should not be used for merely personal gain. This point is made nicely by Beidelman in his first essay on the hare-hyena stories of the Kaguru: "Rabbit's disobedience to Hyena rests upon the assumption that Hyena does not deserve such authority and respect if he is found to be motivated merely by selfish reasons" (1961:63).

In her typology of trickster tales, Denise Paulme stresses the complementarity of trickster and dupe, and of the characteristics they embody: deceiver and deceived, clever and stupid, immoderate and moderate, provident and impulsive (1975a:596–597). She also makes the same point as Beidelman, only with reference to trickster tales throughout Africa:

> To speak for Africa of one trickster and one only, whosoever the actor—Hare, Spider, Tortoise—whichever the society assigns the role, is not enough. In the first place, the trickster does not always

succeed, and it is important to specify the occasions of his failures.
Let us say, to summarize, that he succeeds when his goal, while assur-
ing him of a personal advantage, does not gravely disturb the social
equilibrium. [Paulme, 1975a:596, my translation]

The same principle applies to both Hare and Hyena. Hare should not
use cleverness if it upsets the social equilibrium; nor should Hyena, the
embodiment of authority, use his authority if it is to the disadvantage of
others. The misuse of cleverness is illustrated by N.18, in which the
hare uses trickery to steal the sheep of a solitary and defenseless old
woman who has done the hare no harm. The old woman seeks the aid
of the lion, the embodiment of stern justice. The hare, unsuccessful in
his attempts to make the hyena the scapegoat for his misdemeanors, is
finally killed and eaten by the lion. The ethical ambiguity inherent in
cleverness and other talents also attaches to fetishes and medicines.
These extraordinary objects can also be used for personal gain just as
readily as they can serve to restore social justice. The problem of the
ethical ambiguity of fetishes will be discussed in chapter 6 when I deal
with a group of narratives in which the hero manipulates magical *objects*
rather than using innate *talents* such as cleverness.

Let us now consider in greater detail exactly how the hare uses his
cleverness and what means are employed to redress the injustices he
suffers.

It will be readily apparent from the summary chart that the means
employed to redress unjust situations are drumming and singing. The
Kuranko often point out that cleverness is a great asset because people
think twice before crossing or offending a clever person. But, as one
informant put it, "cleverness without skill with words is worthless." Di-
plomacy, cunning, fine judgment, and skill in argument—all aspects of
cleverness—depend upon an ability to use words. *Miran,* or presence,
is derived from a person's oratorical prowess as much as from any other
factor. But while the association of intelligence and verbal ability is emphasized in ordinary discourse, the narratives tend to play up a connection between cleverness and musical ability. In both cases, however, the
faculty of intelligence is expressed by an ability to make words or
sounds communicate more than they appear to. In ordinary speech, this
skill is shown in the apt use of proverb, allusion, pun, innuendo, allegory, and other forms of verbal indirectness. This kind of rhetorical
ambiguity is often used to give gentle expression to unpleasing facts or
to disengage the speaker from the latent meaning of his own words.[17]

Impasse or injustice	Means of escape from impasse or means of redressing injustice	Result
N.13 Hyena kills and eats lion cub left in his care.	Hare invents and sings a song and the lioness learns thereby that the hyena has eaten her cub.	Lioness kills and eats the hyena.
N.14 Gluttonous hyena uses a stupid law (banning laughter) in order to kill and eat his guests.	Hare drums and sings and makes everyone laugh, including the hyena chief.	Hyena forgets and abolishes the stupid law.
N.15 Animals decide to kill and eat their mothers.	Hare plays his drum to distract his companions; he sings a song to communicate to his mother their secret names.	Hare's mother is not killed.
N.16 Gluttonous hyena joins a *kere* in order to kill and eat the pangolin; he gives his children only the bones.	Hyena's youngest son pretends to be the pangolin.	Hyena is frightened away and his children get all the food.
N.17 Hyena double-crosses the hare.	Hare pretends to be sick and the gluttonous hyena wishes to contract the same sweet sickness.	Hyena is roasted alive and dies.

In the narratives, the hidden things "left for the hearer to discover" are of course the messages contained in the lyrics of the songs. The musical ambiguity in these narratives springs from the simultaneous expression of *sung lyrics* and *drummed melody*. While the dupe is distracted by the melody and rhythm of the trickster's drumming and singing, we attend to the meanings conveyed by the words of the song. In other cases, the drums simulate or approximate speech, so that they suggest or signal verbal messages *and* mere rhythmical sound *at the same time*. The closeness of drumming to speaking may reflect the highly tonal character of African languages (Finnegan, 1970:482), and it is typical of Kuranko narratives that drumming is expressed by narrators as nonsense or quasi-nonsensical words. Whether the drumming is accompanied by singing or not, the musical sections in these narratives involve the simultaneous use of two codes: one which is merely melodic or rhythmic, another which is verbal or *suggests* speaking. We might refer to the former as an elaborated code and to the latter as a restricted code (Bernstein, 1973), because the verbal messages are missed or misread by the dupe.

Hare's cleverness would seem, therefore, to consist of an ability to manipulate two codes of communication at the same time. His duplicity depends upon the different consequences of the verbal and melodic signals. Thus, his songs or drum-playing are never what they seem. In some cases the music leads people to do things which are the very reverse of that they want or intend: the hyena chief forgets to follow his own decree in N.14. In other narratives, the music conveys a concealed message: in N.13 the hyena fails to realize that the hare's song, which the lioness readily understands, seals his doom. The opposite situation occurs in N.12, where the hyena is duped into thinking that the sound of the river falling over the fishing weir is a praise-song celebrating his strength.

Pretense, disguise, dissembling, and feigning are common to both the hunger narratives (chapter 3) and the hare-hyena narratives. Cleverness implies an ability to deceive and dissimulate. This ability is censured when it serves as a means of denigrating another for personal advantage. But in its positive aspect, pretense is the very faculty which enables a person to identify and sympathize with the plight of another. This vicarious and empathic *exchange of viewpoints* is, in my opinion, more important and fundamental than all other institutionalized modalities of exchange—whether mediated by women, goods and services, words, or nonverbal signals. From an evolutionary standpoint, empathic understanding precedes acts of alliance, since the latter are simply the means of realizing or making permanent the merging of interests and the recognition of common identity established by empathy.

Yet it is not easy to isolate the faculty of pretense from the faculty of language. It is language which enables man to falsify reality, to misinform, to "say otherwise," and to disguise certain persuasions in the interests of entertaining others. George Steiner emphasizes that "To pretend to be another, to oneself or at large, is to employ the 'alternative' powers of language in the most thorough, ontologically liberating way" (1975:225). Fiction itself has its source in this peculiarly human ability to pretend, to shift one's ethical ground (Popper and Eccles, 1974:106). But the use of language for "alternity" has more than banal survival value in misinforming others about the location and accessibility of scarce resources. The creative power of language enables man to deny injustices, to bypass the realities of an imperfect world, and to manufacture mythologies of justice. In the Kuranko narratives with which we are concerned here, the hare is the heroic contriver. Playing tricks with words and with sounds, he counters and outdoes the hyena.

We have already established that the hare's ruses almost always involve an artful use of drumming and singing. The Kuranko usually refer to such music as "sweet." Sweetness is also associated with persuasive words,[18] seductive women, and appetizing food. Something which is "sweet" is inevitably something which both attracts (binds) and distracts (loosens). Sweet things thus imply ambivalent attitudes, in particular a conflict between personal desire and social duty. For example, sexual pleasure is "sweet"[19] but promiscuity and infidelity have disastrous social consequences: a woman's children will suffer and ill-feeling will be bred among the men of the community. Scarce foodstuffs, especially meat, are said to be "sweet," yet an uncontrolled appetite for meat signifies gluttony and self-interest. A euphemistic way of referring to corruption in high places is to cite the adage "old people have an insatiable appetite for sweet things." "Sweet" words imply rhetorical skills, but "sweet talk" can persuade people to follow courses of action which may prove ill-judged or calamitous. Wherever "sweet" music appears in the narratives, several or all of these kinds of incontinent behavior are implied. We will later have occasion to note the explicit connection made between "sweet" music and women's allures, and a key narrative (N.27), discussed in detail in chapter 6, explores the social consequences of immoderate love of "sweet" music—the music of the *yimbe* drum.

In the dialectic of self-interest versus group-interest, images of sweetness figure prominently as the ambiguous terms. If self-interest be considered as a kind of regression to nature, as it is indeed in the hunger narratives, then it is possible to show a relationship between images of sweetness in the Kuranko narratives and the "alimentary seducer"—honey—in South American myths. As Lévi-Strauss has shown, honey "radiates ambiguity in all its aspects" (1973:296), and whenever the social order is momentarily broken or about to be reaffirmed, honey appears as the symbol of transition. On a purely formal place, "sweet" music marks points of disjunction, doubt, ambiguity, and suspense in the Kuranko narratives. The music is often spellbinding or distracting; it brings the narrative to a hiatus and signals the imminent resolution of a difficulty, the righting of a wrong, or a reversal of fortunes.

One narrative in particular, N.17, exploits the ambiguous connotations of sweet things in ways reminiscent of several South American myths. The theme of the *bicho enfolhado,* in which the fox deceives the jaguar by smearing itself with honey (Lévi-Strauss, 1973:112), appears in this Kuranko narrative along with another theme widespread in Africa—that of feigned sickness (Paulme, 1975b:620). The plot of the narrative is simple: the hyena (elder brother) tricks the hare, but the hare employs the same mode of deceit in turning the tables on the hyena. The imagery of the narrative is more complex. First, the hare boils, peels, and plants a yam, which the hyena comes and steals and eats during the night. Second, the hare takes his revenge by pretending to be sick: he smears his body with honey and raw rice flour, both of which are sweet to taste, and the hyena craves the "sweet" sickness. Third, the hyena follows the hare's instructions, not realizing that the hare is motivated by thoughts of revenge, and is roasted alive in a fire built by his own sons; the hyena becomes putrescent and dies.

There is a "culinary triangle" here which marks out a semantic field. The contrast between the boiled, peeled, buried yam and the roasted, charred, putrescent hyena is mediated by "sweet" foodstuffs which are eaten raw.[20] Yet, both honey and *dege* are, in one sense, cultural products, since honey is collected from man-made beehives (lodged in trees in open forest areas) and *dege* is prepared by pounding rice in a mortar. Gathered or prepared by cultural techniques, yet consumed in their natural state, honey and *dege* may be regarded as occupying an inter-mediate position between roasting (which is "close to nature") and boil-ing (which is "close to culture," since boiled food is mediated twice, by the cooking water and by the cooking pot) (Lévi-Strauss, 1969).

If we review the events of the narrative in their given sequence, we find that the initial situation is characterized by the abuse of a cultural precept: that the elder brother should look after the welfare of a younger brother. As a result of his unjust treatment of his younger brother, the hyena falls victim to the hare's ruse and is "roasted"—is symbolically cast out of society to putrefy and die. The culinary metaphors rely upon a further contrast—between external aspect and internal reality—in effecting this transformation.

The ambiguities within this narrative depend upon the way in which external appearances belie internal realities. As Lévi-Strauss has pointed out, roasting implies an "intrinsic ambiguity" (charred on the outside but undercooked on the inside), while boiling implies an "extrinsic ambiguity" (this mode of cooking makes use of an external object, the cooking pot). The deceptive appearances of the buried yam, of the hare covered with honey and *dege,* and of the burned hyena are thus appro-priate metaphors for the deceit and dissimulation around which the nar-rative revolves. In the case of the hare's ruse, the contrast between covert motive and apparent intent is fully developed. This contrast may be compared with the contrast intrinsic to the musical episodes in which a melodic or rhythmic pattern overlays a concealed message.

It must be emphasized that the Kuranko give considerable impor-tance to the consonance between real motive and declared intent. This concern is usually expressed in terms of the ideal of "clearness" or "plainness" between people. Prevarication, lying, deceit, and concealing one's true intentions from others are all regarded as inimical to com-munity life. Communications between persons should be like com-munications between man and the ancestors; they should be "pure" or "clear," and this is possible only when there is a fidelity between out-ward expression and inward feeling. The fault which the narratives find with elders is the fault which is inherent in all positions of authority: the discrepancy between the ideal requirements of the position and the ac-tual abilities or inclinations of the person holding the position. In the narratives, the deceitfulness of the elder consists of his use of his posi-tion as a kind of disguise for self-interested acts. The corruptibility of elders is expressed, as we have seen, in terms of their unassuageable

	Initial situation	Intermediate situation	Denouement
Culinary mode	boiled	raw	roasted, rotted
Internal reality	cooked yam	Hare pretending to be sick	duped and dying Hyena
External aspect	yam is peeled and buried and planted, *as if* to be grown and not to be eaten	Hare's body is smeared with honey and *dege, as if* he had a skin disease	Hyena's skin is burned and begins to putrefy; the hyena acts *as if* he were merely sick

appetite for sweet things, their lack of restraint, their easy seduction by women, sweet music, or sweet foods. The trickster uses these very things as the means of accomplishing his revenge and of redressing injustices. Not only do the actions of the trickster make good the discrepancy between persons and positions; they bring about a harmony between outward appearance and subjective attitude. In this sense, the narratives reduce the ambiguity which springs from the continual interplay between the apparent and the real.

5 *Prevented Transitions*

In Kuranko thought trueness of heart, moral straightness, self-possession, and clarity of speech are all intimately connected. In each case mastery of self implies a merging of personal purposes and community mores. To control one's tongue, to limit one's sexual impulses and appetites, to withstand adversity, and to make individual talents such as cleverness serve the commonweal are all expressions of one overriding value.

Throughout Africa a prevailing metaphor for loss of control is the garbling, forgetting, or corrupting of messages and speech. As Hans Abrahamsson has shown (1951), this metaphor often appears in myth, linking the origins of human mortality to the perversion of messages.[1] But the mythical events pertaining to the origins of death must be read allegorically; they are metaphors of the disruption of *social* order, not just personal existence. Irregular communication implies discontinuity where there should ideally be continuity.

In the narratives discussed in chapters 3 and 4, acts of negligence, sins of omission, abuses of authority, and failures of mutuality bring about a disruption of the moral order. Because the moral order consists of a system of explicit and shared codifications, amoral or antisocial behavior may be defined as behavior which is based upon wholly private, egocentric, nonconventionalized meanings and purposes. Gossip or songs with concealed meanings are significant markers of such idosyncratic language use. In Kuranko terms, such behavior causes "darkness" in human relationships, or it "blocks the pathways" that connect people in a community. What is often implied by these expressions is a discrepancy between what is expected and what occurs, a contradiction between private intentions and public avowals.

Although there is no Kuranko narrative which deals explicitly with the origin of human mortality, several narratives are concerned with the problem of irregular communication, the same problem which underlies those African myths in which the origin of death is explained. In this chapter I have brought together two groups of narratives, the first of which deals with discontinuities in communication *between the generations,* the second of which deals with discontinuities in communication *between lineages.* The problems underlying the first group refer to problems of intergenerational succession, while the problems dealt with in the second group pertain to marriage and affinity. The social repercussions of disjunctions between the generations and between exogamous lineages are comparable. A reluctance to surrender or assume a position of authority in the lineage has the same social consequences as a reluctance to surrender sisters or daughters to another lineage in marriage *or* the reluctance of women to get married. Prevented successions lead to a breakdown in the continuity of the lineage; prevented marriages lead to a breakdown in the alliance networks which link lineages together. This structural comparability may help explain why Oedipal and incestuous themes are frequently found together in myth.

N.19: *Why the First Child Comes First*

Narrated by Keti Ferenke Koroma. Recorded at Kabala, July 1970.

Why the first child* comes first. There was once a chief in this world. After the birth of his first child he married a second wife. He made the second wife senior and he made the first wife, who bore him his first child, junior.† The first wife became despised.

Before long the second wife bore a child. Both children were boys, but the junior wife's child was really the elder. The second wife's child was loved. The first wife's child became despised.

One day the second wife (whom the chief had made the senior), said to the chief, "Chief, your first son doesn't like me. Indeed, he has it in mind to sleep with me. Therefore, if you don't make him go from this *luiye* I will leave." The chief said, "All right. I will kill that firstborn son. I must kill him." He got up and went as far as from Kabala here to One-Mile.** He took a gun and a white cloth,

---

den fole = "child first," The firstborn son is called *den ke sare* ("child male firstborn"), and the firstborn daughter is called *dimusu sire* ("child female firstborn").

†*bare* or *baremusu* = senior wife (in the context of narrative this often implies "beloved wife" or "preferred wife"); *gberinya* = junior wife.

**My wife and I lived about one mile from Kabala and the location was known locally as "One-Mile." Keti Ferenke told the narrative at our house and thus gave it a local setting.

which he gave to the people who lived at One-Mile. He said, "Keep these things here. Tomorrow morning you should kill the son of mine who passes here first. He will be on a horse. As soon as he comes by, cut off his head. Put his head in this white cloth and wrap it up. The son of mine who passes here next . . . give him the head wrapped in the white cloth." The chief returned to his place. In the evening he called his two sons. He said to the firstborn son (whose mother he had made the junior), "I am going to send you to Makakura, very early tomorrow morning." The son said, "Yes." He said to the second-born son (whose mother he had made the senior), "I am going to send you to Makakura tomorrow morning." The son also said, "Yes." Then, that night the chief called them to tell them why they were going. But he first called the junior wife's son and said, "Here is a white cloth. Very early tomorrow morning you will leave for Makakura. When you get there, ask the town chief to give you what I left in his charge." (He wanted him to be killed.) The chief said, "Now you can go to bed." He went. Then the chief called the "senior" wife's son and said, "Tomorrow morning you will go to Makakura. I left something with the town chief there. It will be given to you to bring to me." (He had planned that the senior wife's son should be given the head of the junior wife's son, to bring it back to him.)

Very early in the morning the junior wife's son mounted his horse and rode off. As he passed the place where the veterinary station is, he noticed an old woman standing by the roadside. She said, *"M'fa togoma,** good morning. Where are you going?" He said, "I am going to Makakura. My father sent me." She said, "Would you share my morning meal with me?" The old woman was a leper, but the boy decided to join her. He dismounted and went to the old woman. All her fingers and toes were missing. She said, "Come and share my food, won't you?" He said, "All right."

Not long afterward the senior wife's son came by. The old woman called loudly to him, *"M'fa togoma,* good morning. *M'fa togoma,* good morning." The boy said, "Ah, grandmother, leave me be, don't come near me. Your fingers and toes are missing. I don't

---

**m'fa togoma* = "my father's namesake." The firstborn son is conventionally named after its father; the name is thus inherited by the firstborn son generation after generation. A woman often addresses her grandson as *m'buin togoma* ("my husband's namesake"), sometimes as *m'fa togoma* (in which case she identifies with her late husband).

know why you should be calling me. Why do you shout out '*m'fa togoma*'? I am on an errand for my father. Don't waste my time." He went off.

Now, the chief had not told the people how to tell one son from the other. He had not made a distinction between the firstborn and the secondborn. All he had said was "the son of mine who passes first." So, as soon as the senior wife's son reached that place, they cut off his head and wrapped it in the white cloth. Then they waited. By then the old woman had finished preparing food. She said, "*M'fa togoma,* rice." The boy said, "Thank you, grandmother, I have already eaten. I stopped because I did not wish to offend you by turning down your kind offer."* He mounted his horse and left. When he reached One-Mile the people stopped him and said, "Your father sent you here. He said that we should give you this." The boy took the head and returned home, but he did not know that it was his brother's head or that a plot had been made to kill him.

While he was on his way home, the senior wife was rejoicing, saying, "My son's *fadan* [half brother] has been killed today." But soon they saw the junior wife's son approaching on his horse. When they saw him they looked at each other and said, "Eh, what is wrong?" Then the boy gave the chief what had been given to him at One-Mile. The senior wife began to cry. The chief beat the drum. All the big men came. Then they asked the boy to explain what had happened. The boy said, "After you had given us the message, I left very early in the morning and soon reached the old woman's place. She invited me to share some food with her. I know that it is wrong to turn down an invitation so I stopped there awhile. While I was with the old woman my companion [*m'bo*] came by. The old woman invited him to eat but he did not want to stop. He went on. After some time I left, and when I reached One-Mile they gave me something wrapped in a white cloth—my companion's head."

The chief said, "Eh! Till the end of the world, if you are going on a journey and you are told to stop, then stop, do not go on. Second, whoever you despise in this world, him you will end up with.

---

*According to Kuranko etiquette an invitation to partake of food should not be declined. Even if one has eaten, one should sit down and eat a morsel of food offered before declaring that one is not hungry.

I plotted that you should be killed because my senior wife told me that you intended to sleep with her. I arranged for you to be killed when you reached that place. My senior wife's son was to return with your head. Now that everything has happened the wrong way around, I have nothing to say and can do nothing. This has shown that no matter how much you dislike your firstborn son, he is second to you in authority."

The chief then killed that senior wife and said, "You caused all this." And the junior wife was made the senior. Therefore, you should never forget the first person you move with.* Don't ever forget the person you first started life with. Even if you become wealthy, don't despise that person. If the person is your wife, you should not forget her. If the person is your first child, you should not despise it. If the person is your brother, do not despise or ignore him because he is second to you. If the person is a friend, do not forget the person you first befriended. If you forget your beginnings your end will be bad. People should never forget the first things in their lives.

N.20: *The Story of Gbentoworo*

Narrated by Keti Ferenke Koroma. Recorded at Kondembaia, July 1970.

There was once a chief and his wife. The chief had no children, so he went to a diviner. The diviner told him that he would get a child but the child would kill him. The chief said, "Heh, well, let me see this child."

Now, all the time the chief was punishing the woman for her failure to bear him a child. Every morning he would call her and say, "Come and braid my hair." She would come and say, "Eh, your hair is not long enough to braid." Then he would beat her. He would then tell her to go and get milk from his bull. She would say, "Heh, I have never known people to get milk from a bull." He would beat her again.

Before very long the shin of the woman's leg became swollen. Her shin remained swollen for seven years. One day the woman

---

*This is to say one's firstborn child and one's first wife.

took an axe and went to find wood. She stood by the woodpile and said, "Ah, God, all this time my husband beats me because I have failed to bear a child for him. But whenever we go to the diviners, they say that I will bear a child that will not die by fire or by water, a child that will take my husband's place. May God give me that child now." Then, as she chopped the wood a splinter flew up and hit against her shin. It opened. A little boy jumped out. He stood there and said, "My mother, greetings."

The woman said, "Eh, *n'dogo,* where are you from?" He said, "This is my seventh year in your shin." He had a small bag hanging round his neck. In the bag was a palm nut and a calabash seed. The mother said, "Eh, where are you from?" He said, "You are my mother. This is my seventh year in your shin." She said, "What is your name?" He said, "Gbentoworo."* He took the wood that his mother had found and he said, "Let us go to town."

When they reached the town he went and greeted his father and said, "Father, I am the child that you have been beating your wife for. I have spent seven years in my mother's leg. Now you have a child. I am your child." His father said, "Eh! Is this my child, who was born today and yet speaks like this?" The child said, "Yes, I was born today and so I should speak today." The father did not mind this too much. They went to sleep.

The next morning the chief said, "Sira, Sira, hurry up and come and braid my bald head." Then the boy came. He took out the palm nut and said, "Father, plant this palm nut today. Let it germinate and grow today. Let it bear fruit today. Then we will gather the fruit today and mill the oil from it today. If you do all this today, then that will be the oil that my mother will rub on your head. And if hair doesn't grow on your head today after all this has been done, it means that I did not spend seven years in the shin of your wife's leg." The people said, "Heh! This is amazing, chief." The chief said, "Sira, Sira, go and milk my bull." Then the boy put his hand into his bag and took out the calabash seed. He said, "Now, look here, father. Plant this calabash seed today. Let it germinate and grow today. Let it bear a calabash today and the calabash be strong today. Let us pick it today and put it down and

---

*Gbentoworo's name is a contraction of *gbelan* (shin of the leg), *to* (in), and *woro*. Some informants say that *woro* is his personal name, but Yeli Fode Gibate is of the opinion that *woro* means "calf of the leg."

let the seeds rot away today. And let it split open today. If you do all this today, then, if my mother is unable to get milk from the bull, it means that I did not spend seven years in the shin of my mother's leg." The people said, "Heh friends, this is a problem." The chief also became troubled.

One day the chief called all his big men and said to them, "I am troubled and confused. What shall I do with this child?" The big men said, "Well, chief, the only answer is to kill the child and get rid of him from this lineage altogether." The chief said, "How am I going to do this?" They said, "You must give him a house. Tell him that he should sleep there by himself. At night we will set fire to the house." The chief said, "Good. Go and call him." They went and called Gbentoworo. He came. The chief said, "I have longed for a child. Now that I have got you, I love you very much. So, you see that house over there? It is your house. You should sleep there by yourself so that no one will disturb your sleep." (All houses were thatched then.) Gbentoworo said, "There is nothing wrong with that. I am happy about that. A thing should trouble only a man when he does not understand it."

Gbentoworo entered the house. No sooner was he inside than he started digging a tunnel from the house to his mother's house. At night he entered the tunnel and went to his mother's house and lay down on the bed there. In the middle of the night the chief called his big men and they set fire to the house. It burned all night. In the morning the big men came to the chief and said, "Haha, Gbentoworo is finished! He is burned to ashes. Now, chief, you are free. This kind of child would have been very dangerous, a threat to the whole lineage. It was a human being for seven years in its mother's shin, and when it came out it brought all these problems. Well, now everything is all right. But chief, you must offer a sacrifice for him."

Now, in the morning Gbentoworo had told his mother not to tell anyone that he was there. He told his mother to pound some rice flour [*dege*] for him. She prepared the *dege* and kept it in the house. Then the father also gave instructions that they should pound the *dege* for his sacrifice for Gbentoworo. The *dege* was prepared and brought to the chief. The chief called the elders to sacrifice the *dege*. But, as they were about to place their hands upon the *dege*, Gbentoworo came out with his own basin of *dege* and said,

"Father, here is my contribution, but only if you are offering the sacrifice for another child and not for me." His father said, "Heh, Gbentoworo has come back to life." Everyone became afraid. The people said, "This is a very difficult problem, chief." The chief said, "Well, I think I should leave him be."

One day Gbentoworo went for a walk. He met one of the chief's children coming from a farm. He shot and killed him. Now, in the town there was a notorious thief who would steal at night and put the things he stole into a large hamper. Gbentoworo knew of this, so when he had killed the chief's son, he put him in a hamper and that night brought it to the house of that notorious thief. When he reached the house, he stood outside the fence and called to the thief's wife, "Sira, help me, Sira, help me." The thief was away, so Sira came and helped. She thought it was her husband. She came and took the hamper with the corpse in it, and put it in the house. Gbentoworo went home.

When the thief returned to his house, his wife said, "That thing you brought yesterday, it is here." He said, "Eh, did I bring something last night?" She said, "Yes." Gbentoworo now pretended that he was coming only to greet them. He stood by the porch of their house. And he overheard what they were saying. He went up to them and said, "Aha, I know what you have done. You have killed the chief's child." The thief became afraid. He gave everything he had to Gbentoworo. Gbentoworo said, "Now bring me everything you have ever stolen from other people, everything." The thief went and brought all that he had ever taken. He gave everything to Gbentoworo. Then Gbentoworo went and took the corpse in the hamper. He went off to look for some honey.

When he found the honey he put it in the hamper and brought the hamper back to the town. (In those days, when a chief was in bed no one was allowed to disturb him. If you opened the door when a chief was in bed, you would be killed.) Gbentoworo came with the corpse and the honey, put them on the veranda, and knocked at the door. The chief opened the door immediately and, without stopping to see who was there, he fired his gun at the child who was already dead. He went back inside and lay down. In the morning he came out. Who did he see? He saw his child lying there. And the child had told his father that he was going to look for some honey. The chief said, "Eh, Gbentoworo, you are becoming a menace. You have made me kill my own child. He went to find honey. Now you have made me kill him." He summoned his big men and told them what had happened.

The big men said, "Eh, chief, this is all the doing of Gbentoworo. We have done everything possible to kill him, but without success. Now let us tie him up and throw him into the river." They caught Gbentoworo and tied him up securely and took him away. As they neared the river, Gbentoworo said, "Oh, you people, wait. Look at those vultures flying over yonder. They are flying over some dead animals. Go and get the animals so that, after dropping me in the river, you will have something to take back to town with you." They put him down and all rushed into the bush in search of that dead animal.

No sooner had they gone than a certain trader came by. He had cows, goats, sheep, money, everything. The trader found Gbentoworo tied up and said, "Eh, *n'dogo,* why are you tied up like this?" Gbentoworo said, "Never mind. They told me that I should be chief, but I am young and small and I told them that I did not want to be their chief. They became annoyed and tied me up and said they were going to throw me into the river." The trader said, "Eh, *n'dogo,* you turned down the chieftaincy!" He said, "Mm, I am young and small, I don't want to be chief." Then the trader said, "Well, let me untie you so that you can tie me up instead. When they come back I will tell them that I've accepted their offer. They will make me chief." Gbentoworo said, "No, I am not going to put the chieftaincy into your hands. You do not belong to a chiefly house." The trader said, "*N'dogo,* please do. You can take everything I have here if you will go away so that I may become chief." Gbentoworo said, "Well, untie me." The trader untied him. Gbentoworo tied him up, took all his possessions, and went into the bush.

The people who had gone to find the dead animals found nothing. And Gbentoworo had tied the trader up. The people came back, saying angrily, "You dog, Gbentoworo, you *kafiri* [infidel], you have really upset us today. We are going to deal with you now." Then the trader began to say, "Now I am willing, I am willing. Let us go and I will be your chief." The people said, "What are you saying? Are you going mad? Even if you pretend to be mad, we will not abandon you. You have done other things apart from this. No matter what tricks you play now, we will not free you. We are going to throw you into the river." The trader was thinking of what Gbentoworo had told him, so he kept on saying, "I consent to be your chief, I consent to be your chief. Let us go back now, let us go back." The people said, "Hurry up, he is mad." They went and threw him into the river.

For one day, two days, three days, Gbentoworo wandered about in the bush. On the fourth day he came to town. He went to the chief and said, "Father, sound the drum, let everyone come." The chief sounded the drum and all the big men came. Then Gbentoworo took out £10, and five ounces of gold. He said, "I am from *lakira*.* Your father greets you. He said that you are enjoying life here so much that you do not intend going there to greet him. So he sent you this. He is a very wealthy man there and if you go there he will give you all you want." Then he gave £10 to some of the big men, saying, "Your fathers said that I should give you this." He gave £5 to some £2 to others, giving false messages to them. The big men gathered. They said, "Oh, Gbentoworo, how can we get to *lakira*?" He said, "Eh, what did you do to me? Didn't you tie me up and throw me into the river? Whoever is tied up and thrown into the river will go to *lakira*." Then the chief said, "Now, I am your chief. You should tie me up first and throw me into the river. I should go first. I know that there is more wealth where this came from."

They tied up the chief securely. As they were carrying the chief away, some of his wives whose parents were dead began to say, "If you go, greet my mother, if you go greet my father. Tell them to send us some of the things they gave to Gbentoworo." Then they threw the chief into the river. The crocodile caught him. Then the big men began to say, "Oh, they have welcomed him." And whoever came forward would say, "Tie me up quickly and throw me in. Don't let the chief leave me behind." So they tied up all the big men and threw them into the river. Then they went back to town.

When they reached the town, Gbentoworo called the few that were left. He asked them, "Who is in my father's place?" Nobody answered. He asked again, "Who should be chief?" They said, "You should be chief." Then Gbentoworo became chief. He was chief there forever.

---

lakira = abode of the ancestral spirits.

Prevented Successions

N.19 is typical of several Kuranko narratives which I have analyzed in depth elsewhere (Jackson, 1979). These narratives begin with an unjust inversion of the proper birth-order positions of the first- and second-born sons of a ruler. The identity of the true heir is thus masked, and the rightful succession is placed in jeopardy. In other narratives, of which N.20 is a good example, the succession is prevented by other means. In some instances the birth of the true heir is delayed (N.20), in others there is difficulty in conceiving an heir, in others the birth of the true heir is concealed, and in others the heir's infancy is artificially prolonged or his physical growth is retarded. Most of these motifs appear in various versions of the Mande epic of Sunjata (Niane, 1965; Pageard, 1961; Bird, 1971; Innes, 1974; Ames, 1975), and several occur in a Kuranko version of the epic (Jackson, 1979:101). But these motifs all have the same significance. By preventing the succession of the rightful heir, the continuity of the lineage is threatened. Whether it is the heir who is reluctant to displace his father, or the father who tries to kill, banish, or deny his son, the social consequences are the same. The passage of social time is interrupted.

This impasse is usually the result of a conflict between social imperatives and self-interest. For example, in many of the narratives the "beloved wife" (*baramusu*) of a ruler is barren, and, taking advice from a diviner, the ruler marries a second wife who is dumb. When the second wife becomes pregnant, the first wife feigns pregnancy by placing a stone against her belly. When the dumb wife delivers her child, the first wife, with the connivance of the midwives, steals it, and subsequently the dumb wife is ostracized for having deceived her husband. The lie is finally discovered through the benevolent intervention of bush spirits, and the injustice is redressed. In N.19 the self-interest centers on the chief's preference for his second wife. He wrongly grants her superior status and heeds her malicious advice. In N.20 the chief is so mindful of the prophecy that his wife will bear him a son who will become his murderer that he maltreats his wife. In each case fatal flaws of character lead to a loss of *self*-control which creates a *socially* ambiguous situation in which a status superior is wrongly made subordinate.[2] Moreover, these uncontrolled personal emotions or ambitions have the effect of interrupting the passage of social time.

Redressing this injustice takes the form of a re-reversal of birth-order positions or the displacement of a ruler. As Keti Ferenke Koroma suggests in N.19, the narratives thus emphasize the priority of the firstborn and of the senior wife, and stress the undeniable importance of the primary bond between a mother and her uterine child. But there is more to the narratives than this. In each case the denouement brings about an alignment of positive personal qualities and high social positions.

In many African societies the rule of primogeniture could not guarantee that the most capable person would accede to a position of authority. In practice, the rule was sometimes waived,[3] and in myth and folklore we see how fictional modes provide an even greater latitude for manipulating the world and synthetically resolving recurrent problems. Clearly it is improbable that a nominal heir will always be the cleverest, strongest, or most incorruptible person around. The discrepancy which often follows, between a determinate principle — primogeniture — and indeterminacy, in practice is made good through fictional devices which contrive the semblance of a fit between high ability and high status. In those narratives where an ineffectual ruler is deposed or killed by a strong and precocious son, or where a weak and corrupt firstborn is displaced by a youngster, the fictional plot conforms to a social ideal: that a ruler should also be strong and clever. We may therefore interpret the reversals and exchanges of ascribed positions as examples of fictional legerdemain, accomplishing through chiasmus the appearance of a determinate relationship between social positions and individual dispositions. The narratives do not merely confirm dogma; they afford Kuranko an occasion for manipulating their social order and achieving a vicarious mastery over it. Random and biogenetic distributions of such traits as cleverness and strength are seen to give way to determinate patterns of systematic attribution which are the result of human design.

From a psychological point of view, succession implies growing up. The moral and physical strength of the mature individual is made to invigorate the office to which he accedes. In several Kuranko narratives (N.20 for example) the successor is symbolically associated with the leg.[4] The leg signifies the strength and potency of a complete person.[5] It also signifies the active aspect of human being.[6] Thus, in the narratives, the *social* succession of the generations often depends upon the heir's *physical* strength and ability to move.[7] As a result, the formal movement in the narratives which brings strength of character into alignment with high office is expressed in terms of images of physical movement: walking, journeying, overpowering rivals, and the like.

References to strength are significant in yet another sense. The

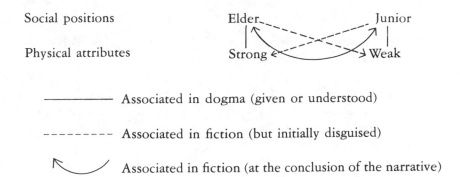

Social positions

Physical attributes

Elder .... Junior

Strong .... Weak

———————— Associated in dogma (given or understood)

-------- Associated in fiction (but initially disguised)

⌣ Associated in fiction (at the conclusion of the narrative)

Kuranko concept *gbeleye* (strength), like the concepts of *fanke* (power) and *tianye* (weakness, lassitude), refers to both social and physical attributes. *Gbele* can mean enduring, hard, or strong in both physical and psychological senses.[8] *Fanke* also means strong, but is usually used to mean powerful in the sense of "having authority." *Tianye* can mean weak or lazy, but it can also denote irresponsibility and indifference. It is because such concepts have connotations which link them to both social and psychological domains that they can mediate and facilitate movements between different poles of being.

Like cleverness, strength is also ethically ambiguous. It implies abilities which are innate as well as acquired, and it can only be used legitimately by a junior when it is wrongly used by a status superior. In one sense, *The Story of Gbentoworo* (N.20) is a discourse upon problems of knowledge and power, since here the chief's misuse of his powers justifies Gbentoworo's use of cunning and subterfuge to wrest the chieftaincy from his father. The problem of intergenerational succession is not simply one of replacing the incumbent (who is often unwilling to be replaced) by an heir (who is often unwilling to succeed); it is one of bringing moral and physical strength, as well as wisdom, to the high offices of society. I have also suggested that this endeavor implies another, namely to make the world of natural distributions appear to conform to the world of cultural attributions. To facilitate adjustments between these two domains, the narratives make use of ambiguous terms whose fields of meaning refer as much to social positions as to natural talents. Narrative strategies can thus be compared with certain ritual practices such as initiation in which natural processes (birth and death) are brought under the imaginative control of men; rather than being suffered, they provide metaphors for the intentional construction of a social and moral order.[9]

N.21: *The Girl Who Never Laughed*

Narrated by Sulimani Koroma. Recorded at Kondembaia, February 1972.

There was once a chief who had a daughter called Sanson. Sanson never laughed. The chief said, "Whoever makes my daughter Sanson laugh can marry her." Many people came and jested and joked, but none could make her laugh.

A certain man set off for that place. When he reached the middle of the bush, he went to the *nyenne* and asked them to give him the leprosy-gown.* They gave it to him and he became a leper. He also got some millet. Then he went on to the town.

When he reached the town he told the chief that he had come to court his daughter. The people said, "Oh, better men than you have come, but they have all failed. How can a leper succeed?" The man told them that he was going to try. He said, "I will cook my millet rice, but that girl should be here while it is cooking." He asked for a pot. They gave him a country-pot. He put it on the fire. The girl was sitting there, watching him.

The millet was soon cooked. (Now, we know that lepers have no fingers.) He made to take the pot from the fire. But as he tried to grasp it, the pot fell from his hands. Then—*gbusukuru*—the girl laughed. The man leaped up and sang:

You Sanson, Sanson has laughed at me today, Sanson.†

He moved about the town singing this song, saying how he had got himself a wife by making the girl laugh. The chief sounded the drum and said, "Everyone who came to court my daughter failed to make her laugh. Now this leper has succeeded. Take her away, she is your wife." The girl wept, but to no avail. They went away.

When they reached the place where he had borrowed the leprosy-gown from the *nyenne*, he took out a kola nut and split it. He gave one half to the girl. Then he told her to wait there. He said, "I am going to have a shit." He went into the bush. There, he gave the leprosy-gown back to the *nyenne*, and he became once more a very handsome man.

---

*This is a cloak or second skin which, when donned, changes the man into a leper.
†The refrain is chorused nine times.

He returned to where he had told the woman to wait. He said, "Let us go." She said, "No, I am waiting for my husband." He said, "I am your husband." She said, "No, my husband is a leper." The man said, "All right, give me what I gave you before I went away." She said, "What did you give me?" He said, "The kola nut." She took out her half, the man took out the other half, and they put them together. It was the same kola nut. Then she became very happy and they went back to her father, the chief.

The chief gave them horses and many other things. They went away happily.

N.22: *The Girl Whose Father Wanted to Marry Her*

Narrated by Minata Konde. Recorded at Kamadugu Sukurela, February 1972.

There was once a man who had one wife. This wife bore him many children. The lastborn child was a girl. She was the most beautiful of all the children.

Then, her father said, "This girl is going to marry me." The girl said, "Eh! Marry my father!" They said, "Yes, you are going to marry him." Her mother said, "My husband is going to marry you. You are now my co-wife." All the children said, "You are going to marry our father. You are now our *na kura* ["mother new" = mother's co-wife].

The girl went to fetch water. When she came back with the water, she said, "Mother, come and help me get the water down from my head." Her mother said, "Say 'co-wife, come and help me'." She went to her father and said, "Father, come and help me." He said, "Say 'husband, come and help me'." She went to her *tene* [father's sister], and said, "Aunt, come and help me." She said, "Say *'dinyon* [brother's wife], come and help me'." Then the girl threw down the bucket, took her bag, and put it on her back, and went away.

They began to sing:

Where are you going oh, Bala,* going oh, Bala, going oh?

---

*Bala is the girl's name.

The girl sang:

> My father who bore me said that I am his wife, go away oh,
> Bala, go away oh.
> My mother who bore said that I am her co-wife, go away oh,
> Bala, go away oh.
> This aunt of mine said that I am her *dinyon*, go away oh, Bala,
> go away oh.
> Even my brother said that I am his mother, go away oh, Bala,
> go away oh.
> I am going to the *kome*, oh *kome soro,** so that he kills me.

Wherever she went she sang this song. At last she reached the
place where the *kome* lived. As soon as she got there, the *kome*
began so sing:

> Where are you going oh, Bala, going oh, Bala, going oh?

The girl sang [as above].
Then the *kome* sang:

> Am I to make you my wife?

The girl sang back:†

> Aha, I did not come for marriage.
> Am I to make you my child?
> Aha, I did not come to be your child.
> Am I to kill you with my sword?
> Aha, I came to be killed, aha.

The *kome* took his sword and pierced her through the breast and
killed her.

N.23: *The Sun, the Moon, and the Star*

Narrated by Keti Ferenke Koroma. Recorded at Kondembaia, February
1972.

The sister [*tersan*] of the sun and moon is the star. The sun and
the moon used to be as one. They did not burn people. They were

---

Kome = a powerful bush spirit; *kome soro* is a particularly nefarious species.
†These final sung lines alternate between the *kome* and the girl.

both like the moon. There was no difference between the sun and the moon.

One day the sister of the sun and moon was going along the path. She came upon a stream and she said, "Let me bathe here." As she was bathing, the sun came by and found the star having her bath. The sun went away immediately. As the sun was going from there, he met the moon. The moon said, "My companion, what has happened?" The sun said, "Our sister [*tersan muse*] is taking her bath." The moon said, "I am going there." Then he went to the stream and sat on the bank while the star took her bath.

Not long afterwards, the star called them both. She said, "You, moon, if *tersan koe** is a fact, then you have seen me clearly.† May the whole world see you clearly." She turned to the sun and said, "If *tersan koe* is a fact, then you have not seen me clearly. May the whole world not see you clearly.**

Since then the moon remained as it had been. But the sun became brighter. No matter how bright the moon is, you can gaze at it. No matter how dull the sun is, you still cannot gaze long at it.

Therefore, if you see the night and the day, this is how they began. Their sister cursed the moon.

N.24: *The Girl and Her Crocodile-Brother*

Narrated by Denka Marah. Recorded at Kabala, July 1970.

Once there was a woman who had two children, a boy and a girl. The boy was the elder. He was so handsome that the girl declared that she would marry no one but her elder brother, Kansamori. Her father tried to dissuade her, but to no avail. Wherever her brother went, she would follow.

The brother made a tobacco garden. Each time that he went to water the tobacco plants the girl followed him. By now she was a grown woman. Her mother said to Kansamori, "Eh, this garden you have begun to make, I hope you will not do anything bad there. If you do then your *fadennu* will laugh at you."

---

*_tersan koe_ = "sister thing/act," i.e. incest (prohibition) between brother and sister.
†This is say, "you have seen my naked body, my private parts." The phrasing signifies that the sister is cursing her brother (*tersan danka* = sister's curse).
**This is to say, "you averted your gaze from my naked body; therefore, no one will be able to gaze easily upon you."

(Kansamori was able to transform himself into a crocodile, and his garden was near a river.) One day he went to water the tobacco plants. His sister followed him. And their mother followed them secretly because she was concerned that Kansamori might interfere with his sister. When they reached the garden, Kansamori told his sister to go for water. As soon as she had gone he transformed himself quickly into a crocodile. He then caught his sister and carried her down into his riverhole. When the mother saw this she began to sing:

> You Kansamori, Kansamori: may the crocodile not carry my little one away, oh you Kansamori.

The crocodile replied:

> If she calls me brother then the crocodile will not carry her away, Kansamori.
> But if she calls me husband the crocodile will carry her away, Kansamori.

The girl, held by the crocodile, then sang:

> My mother and my father, my husband is Kansamori, Kansamori, my husband is Kansamori.
> I am not telling a lie, Kansamori and I are one.
> Kansamori, my husband is Kansamori.

The crocodile pulled her down into the river again, and swam away. The mother walked along the bank of the river, crying. Then the crocodile brought the girl to the surface once more. And the mother sang [as above].

The crocodile pulled her down into the river again. This time it held her under the water until she was almost drowned. The mother was crying bitterly. Once more she sang [as above]. The girl replied:

> My mother and my father, my brother is Kansamori, Kansamori, my brother is Kansamori.
> I am not telling a lie, my brother is Kansamori.
> Kansamori, my brother is Kansamori.

Then the crocodile threw her up onto the sand. They went and picked her up. As they carried her away she said, *"N'koro*, when you give me in marriage I shall be there." Since that time brothers do not marry their sisters. That is how *tersanye** began.

N.25: *The Girl Who Was in Love with Her Dead Brother*

Narrated by Kumba Doron Sise. Recorded at Kamadugu Sukurela, June 1970.

Once there was a chief who had many wives but only two children. The two children, a boy and a girl, lived together. They had the same mother.

Then the boy died. The girl grew up to be a very beautiful woman. Everyone admired her beauty.

(Now, in those days, the dead would sometimes return to the town. What made the dead return to town is what I am about to tell you.) The girl's dead brother used to come to the town every night. He came every night. One night the girl saw her brother, but not knowing that he was her brother, she felt free to love him. So one evening she went to greet him. She said, "*M'biran*, I have come to greet you." (She did not know that he was her brother.) He took a kola nut and gave it to her. In the evening they played and danced. Then the young man said, "Well, *m'biran*, should I come and greet you?" She said, "No, but, *m'biran*, we are going to sleep together tonight."† (She did not know that he was her brother.) Then he said, "Mmhmm."

Now, when the young man made to return to his grave he told the girl to wait for him awhile. But because the girl was so much in love with the young man she said, "No, I will accompany you to where you are going." He said, "All right." (She did not know that the young man was going to his grave.)

As they started off, the young man began singing:

Eh, segi ka n'dogone
*Eh, segi ka yan. A ma na ka***
Bale yi kenkenne
Kuma be fola kunu, i ma wola memba ba? A ma na ka

---

*Tersanye ("brother-sister relationship"), from *tersan*: a term of address and reference for a sibling of the opposite sex.
†The word *sabi* connotes both "sleeping together" and sexual intercourse.
**These first two lines are the chorus. They are sung thrice and repeated at the end of the song.

Fule yi te re te re
Kuma be fola kunu, i ma wola memba? A ma na ka
Yimbe yi kudu kudu kudu kudu
Kuma be fola kunu, i ma wola memba? A ma na ka*

(Eh, go no further my young one
Eh, go no further than there now. Let it be so
Xylophone was sorrowful
All the words said yesterday, didn't you hear them? Let it be
    so
Flute was making the sound te re te re
All the words said yesterday, didn't you hear them? Let it be
    so
The Yimbe drum was making the sound kudu kudu
All the words said yesterday, didn't you hear them? Let it be
    so)

Then the girl said, "I think I understand." The young man said,
"What?" She said, "No, the words I spoke yesterday were 'let us
go'." So they went on until they reached another place. But the
young man was crying. The girl was so much in love with him,
however, that she did not see the tears in his eyes or realize that
she had fallen in love with her dead brother. The young man said,
"Eh, go back." She said, "No, let us go on. I must follow you."
They went on until they reached the path that led off to the
graveyard. The young man started to sing again:

[As above, except that after the line beginning *Yimbe yi kudu
kudu*, another refrain is introduced.]

Ma fa yi di la lu'bama kunu sini, i ma wola memba? A ma na ka
*Ma na yi di la bum'bala kunu sini, i ma wola memba? A ma na
ka*

(Our father was crying at the big *luiye* the day before yester-
    day, didn't you hear him? Let it be so
Our mother was crying at the big house the day before yester-
    day, didn't you hear her? Let it be so)

Then the young man said, "Eh, *m'biran*, stop now and go back."
The girl said, "No, I so love you that I will follow you wherever

---

*The refrain *a ma na ka* is chorused.

you go. I will stop where you stop. Only death will separate us. Where you end your journey today, there will I end mine." The young man said, "Go back!" The girl said, "No, I will not go back. We are going to sleep together tonight. We must sleep together before this day is over." He said, "All right." By this time they were near the grave. He turned around and looked at the girl. Tears ran from his eyes. He began to sing [as above].

The young man said, "Eh, *n'dogo*." He reached the grave and stood by it. As he stood there the graveclothes covered him. The clothes hung upon his body. She recognized him now as her brother.* The young man began to sing [as above].

Then the girl said, "I will never return." Soon the grave swallowed up the young man. Since that time the dead have ceased coming to town to mingle with the living. It was because of those two people.

N.26: *The Man Who Tried to Seduce His Sister*

Narrated by Keti Ferenke Koroma. Recorded at Kabala, July 1970.

Once there was a man who had many wives. One wife bore a boy and a girl. The girl, who was second-born, was called Kore [uncooked rice]. The man had many daughters by other wives. He named them Fona [millet], Benke [cassava], Wusan [sweet potato], Fofoke [cocoyam]. He named all his children after foodstuffs.

Then his firstborn son said, "Why don't people marry their sisters? I will try to marry one of my sisters." They said to him "Heh, people do not do that." He said, "I will try to do it. If something happens to me, well, people will not do it any more. But if nothing happens, then people will know that it can be done."

The young man went off to work on the farm. They prepared food and gave it to Fona and said, "Go and take it to your brother." Fona brought the food but the man said, "I don't want it. Go and let Kore bring it. I want my real sister to bring it."

(Now, he had planned that if she brought the food he would fall on her and have sex with her.) Fona had also noticed that her brother wanted to have sex with his sister. She went back and said, "Heh, our brother says he will take the food only if Kore brings it

---

*The phrase is *na keli nyorgo* ("mother one partner"), i.e. blood kinsman.

to him." They said, "All right." They prepared another dish and gave it to Kende [sesame] to take to him. The young man said, "I don't want it. You should give the food to Kore to bring. If Kore doesn't bring it, then I do not want to eat it." Kende also went back and said, "I took the food to my brother but he says he doesn't want it unless Kore brings it to him." They did everything they could and all the other sisters of the same father went with the food. The man said no to each one "unless Kore brings it." (This was a ruse so that he could make love to his sister.)

Then they prepared rice and gave it to Kore, saying, "Now, Kore, you take this food to your elder brother. Everyone has taken food to him and he has said that he will not eat unless you bring it to him. Since things are getting desperate, you take the food. Whatever happens, we will explain it to the generations to come." They gave the rice to Kore. She took it and carried it to him. She found her brother sitting in the middle of a hammock-bridge which crossed a very wide river. As she approached she was weeping. She called out to her brother, "My elder brother, I have come with the rice." He said, "Come with the food and find me here." (He felt that if his sister came to him in the middle of that hammock-bridge over the river she would be afraid and more readily surrender to him).

Then the girl said, "My elder brother, you are in this world, yet you have eyes for no other woman but me, who was born after you. Now God is watching us. If it were right for a brother and his sister to have sex together, well, I should still regard you as a human being and people would know that a brother could have sexual intercourse with his sister. But if it were not right, then, before I reach you, may God make you fall from the hammock-bridge into the river and turn you into a crocodile, and may I also fall into the river and be made into a river turtle so that I will be with you always, though we remain brother and sister. And when we fall may this rice be turned into sand and the sauce become river stones." Then she stepped onto the bridge. As she reached the middle of the bridge, it broke. The sauce became river stones, the rice became sand, the man became a crocodile, and the girl became a river turtle.

They are the ones which live in the river today. Wherever the crocodile goes, the river turtle is always nearby. But there is no sexual intercourse between them. Since that time people came to the conclusion that no sex should occur between brother and sister. Therefore, people should not have any sexual contact with the ones who are their *tersannu* [sisters]. With some other kin it is possible, but not one's *tersan*.

You see the crocodile living in the river. So too the turtle. They were brother and sister but they have different names and bodily forms. This is because of the different ideas they had. If anyone intends to have sex with his sister, he will be made into something which you cannot think of. Therefore it is prohibited.

Prevented Marriages

Infant betrothal was traditionally the most usual kind of marriage among the Kuranko. In the years immediately before her initiation, a betrothed girl spends brief periods in her prospective husband's household to become accustomed to the people among whom she will pass the early years of her married life. But adjustment to married life is not easy. A young bride may occupy a subordinate position in her husband's household, under the supervision of her mother-in-law or senior co-wife, and her husband may be old and quite indifferent to her. I was often told that some girls cry and hang back when the time comes for the formalities of the marriage to be concluded. The transfer of rights *in genetricem* and *in uxorem* is regarded as absolute and in perpetuity, and a young bride must face the prospect of severing many sentimental as well as formal ties with her natal family.

There are several narratives (not published here) which may be taken as evidence of the problems outlined above. In one such narrative (which is reminiscent of the naming problem in the story of Rumpelstiltskin) a beautiful girl called Dorondia vows that she will marry no one unless he guesses her name. Many men hazard their guesses and fail, until one day a *jeliba* is passing the place where the girl is washing her clothes. His dog walks over the clothes which she has laid out to dry and in a fit of temper the girl blurts out, "Nothing annoys Dorondia more than the behavior of undisciplined dogs." The *jeliba*, overhearing this, arrives later in the town and sings Dorondia's name as he plays his xylophone. He marries the girl. In another narrative, a young woman called Yeneba refuses to go to live with her husband. The young husband steals the girl's clothes and her breasts (which she is able to remove) while the girl is bathing. He promises to return them to her on condition that she sleep with him. The girl accepts defeat, spends a night with her husband, and discovers that married life is less trying than she had imagined.

These narratives should not be interpreted merely in terms of affect. In the first place, the narratives in which a girl appears reluctant to marry are complementary to others (N.21 for example) in which a father is reluctant for his daughter to marry. Unless we postulate that the father is unconsciously motivated by incestuous desires, it is difficult to explain the second group of narratives in terms of affect. It would be confusing anyway to use a sociologistic explanation for the first group of narratives and resort to a psychologistic explanation for the second group. Moreover, I have no wish to attribute to the narratives meanings which the Kuranko would regard as generally inapplicable. Incest between father and daughter has no special term to describe it; it is "unthinkable" and "it never happens." I see no virtue in assuming that these denials are necessarily evidence of unconscious preoccupations. Second, the ambivalent attitudes in these narratives are expressed in ways which do not suggest intended verisimilitude (pretended lameness in the tale of the reluctant wife; bizarre or impossible conditions imposed upon suitors; breasts which can be removed and stolen). Third, the formal resemblances between these narratives and others already discussed in this chapter indicate that all are variations on a single theme, aspects of a single problematic. Thus:

The heir reluctant to grow up and displace his father *is to* the father reluctant to be superceded *as* the girl reluctant to marry and leave home *is to* the father reluctant to have his daughter marry.

Although I collected twelve narratives of the prevented marriage type, I have included only one here (another narrative in which this theme is secondary is N.30). But the main details of all these narratives are given in the accompanying summary chart.

Women prefer these tales more than men do and tell them more frequently than men. Most women I interviewed said that the competitive element in the stories appealed to them: the situation in which men compete for the hand of a beautiful and highborn woman. This response may reflect the fact that women do not choose, in real life, whom they will marry, and there tends to be a discrepancy between the judgment of a father and the preference of his daughter. In the narratives, marriages follow from choices made and strategies used by the *junior* generation. These choices and strategies express personal desires, individual talents, idiosyncratic and fortuitous factors. They may be contrasted, therefore, with the bases upon which marriages are arranged in real life—lineage interests, political considerations, and even economic necessities.

Implicit in the narratives is a dialectic between social necessity and individual choice. The dialectic is developed in terms of a contrast between social and psychophysiological elements. It is, for example, characteristic that the narrative begin with a chief who has a very beautiful daughter. The juxtaposition of references to *rank* and *appearance*[10] is paralleled by subsequent references to lowborn suitors with extraordinary talents. The domain of the social connotes inflexible positions and absolute rules, while the domain of the psychophysiological is associated with organic images pertaining to appearances, talents, disease, and bodily functions. The narratives make possible an interplay between social and psychophysiological orders. Thus, absurd and inflexible rules are broken by socially marginal figures characterized in terms of organic and physiological functions. For example, one suitor splits a stick (signifying the inflexible rule) with a fart. In two other narratives, the suitors "borrow" diseases in order to break the chiefs' rules, and in several others the breaking of an impasse is marked by laughter (N.21), trickery, or sweet music. As we have already observed (chapter 4), laughter, music, and deceit are closely related and recur as markers of liminal episodes. It could also be argued that the transition to marriage is characterized, both socially and biologically, by an "opening up," in the first case of relations between groups and in the second of relations between bride and groom. As Lévi-Strauss has shown in his study of South American myths, laughter is frequently associated with opening, particularly bodily opening, and it serves as a symbolic marker of the boundary between nature (incontinent behavior) and culture (continence) (1970:120–134).

The Kuranko narratives open up a dialectic between social necessity (signified by mechanical rules and impersonal demands) and individual choice (signified by organic and psychophysiological metaphors). The "organic" reinvigorates the "mechanical" order, so throwing into relief a moral perspective in which personal predilections and social demands are never in conflict. Moreover, this moral perspective abolishes the

Marriage prevented by	Means of prevention	Solution
Girl	Impossible condition (that her husband have an unblemished skin)	Girl marries a *nyenne* and goes into the bush; her younger sister (who tried to prevent this misalliance) prospers.
Bride	Pretends to be lame	Husband feigns death and so shocks the woman into walking.
Girl	Impossible condition (that her suitor guess her name)	A *jeliba* and his dog trick the girl into revealing her name.
Betrothed girl	Refuses to sleep with any man	Husband steals the girl's breasts and so inveigles her into sleeping with him.
Girl	Pretends to be dead	Girl awakes only when her chosen man sings to her.
Girl	Impossible condition (that her suitor prove capable of digging up bush yams with his penis)	The narrative is not really resolved. The girl sets this condition so that she and her orphan brother will be able to remain together always.
Man	Impossible condition (that he would marry the girl who guessed the name of the insect whose skin covered his drum)	A girl is successful in naming correctly the insect.
Parents	Impossible condition (that their daughter will marry a man who can split a *tile* branch with a fart)	A man is successful in splitting the branch with a fart.

Marriage prevented by	Means of prevention	Solution
Father	Impossible condition (successful suitor must have elephantiasis of the testicles)	A man borrows the disease from an old man, and marries the girl. But the old man runs away when the young man tries to return the affliction to him.
Father	Impossible condition (successful suitor must have trousers which can sing)	A man puts a songbird in his trousers, and marries the girl.
Father	Impossible condition (that suitor get milk from a lioness, a live hyena, a live bushfowl, and a live python)	Hare uses various ruses to meet the conditions and marry the girl.
Father	Impossible condition (make the chief's daughter laugh)	A man gets a leprosy-gown from the *nyenne*, and by mimicking a leper without fingers makes the girl laugh.

distinction between group-interest and self-interest and so avoids reducing itself to either. In every case, the marriage with which the narrative concludes satisfies social imperatives as well as personal desires. The narratives also imply that recourse to indeterminate and ethically ambiguous factors such as cleverness, cunning, and "sorcery" is justified only when an impasse has been caused by the imposition of an absurd rule. The rules which prevent marriages taking place are absurd because they are unjust and inflexible. Not only do they impede the passage of social time by preventing exchange between groups, they deny the importance of individual choice and sentiment. We may now understand why these narratives are among the most amusing and popular in the Kuranko corpus. In practically every case, an infexible rule is juxtaposed with organic images or allusions to personal feelings. This "artificial mechanization" of an area of social life dominated by emotionality and biological processes is ludicrous. The incongruous relationship of personality and role is sometimes expressed by comic disguises in which a person is embarrassed by his body (N.21). And the ways in which various suitors meet the conditions laid down for marriage are similarly incongruous and surprising. Bergson has observed that laughter and comedy serve the purpose of converting rigidity into plasticity, and, through ridicule, counteracting the tendency of social rules and personal desires to become increasingly discrepant (Bergson, 1911:177). Or, to use Bateson's terms, the comic element in these narratives offsets the "complementary schismogenesis" which tends to create an ever-widening hiatus between the rules laid down by the old and the preferences felt by the young (Bateson, 1958:175–177). Bergson seems to summarize the spirit of these narratives when he notes that a "flexible vice may not be so easy to ridicule as a rigid virtue" (1911:138).

An unpublished text provides a bridge from the narratives concerned with prevented marriages to the "incest narratives" (N.22–N.26). In that text, a brother and sister, whose parents are both dead, agree to impose a condition which will prevent any man from marrying the sister: each suitor is told that he must dig bush yams from a thorny field with his penis. The storyteller, Denka Marah, was overcome with laughter as he sang the suitor's song ("The bush yam is hard to dig, digging-stick oh!"), interrupting it with cries of pain as the unlucky suitor hurt his penis on the thorns, and so the narrative was left unresolved. But Denka implied that the brother and sister remained together, caring for each other in a quasi-incestuous union. Most of the incest narratives deal explicitly with brother-sister incest (N.23–N.26), which, in Kuranko, is known as *tersan koe.*

The social consequences of incest are the same as those that follow from prevented successions and prevented marriages. A father who refuses to let his son succeed him, and who seeks to kill his son (N.20), may be compared with a brother who refuses to let his sister marry, and who seeks to marry her himself. Killing one's son, like marrying one's sister, or daughter, puts the "eligible" out of circulation, preventing the exchanges which ensure the succession of the generations and which create alliances between groups. The fact that the person who prevents the marriage (or the succession) is often a chief or his child reflects perhaps the greater importance attaching to alliances between ruling lineages (or to chiefly succession). At the same time, the choice of the ruling estate for the narrative events helps dramatize the problems underlying them. A direct parallel may be found in Indo-European folktales where contrasts between rulers and peasants (mediated by wealth, beauty, and cleverness) indicate at once an underlying concern with social mobility. While Kuranko narratives emphasize exchange between the generations or between lineages, Indo-European stories give greater emphasis to problems of exchange between estates and classes.

Lévi-Strauss has noted that "Even if the incest prohibition has its roots in nature it is only in the way it affects us as a social rule that it can be fully grasped" (1969:29). The incest prohibition is first and foremost a rule of reciprocity enjoining exchange between groups, and incest is socially absurd before it is morally wrong. In Kuranko narratives which deal explicitly with incest, as well as in Kuranko hermeneutics, it is the symbolic significance of incest which is stressed. That incest is mentioned often as a metaphor in discourse upon ethical problems in social relationships does not mean that incest actually occurs or is even of real concern. Informants speak of incest as a form of greed or theft, an expression of excessive selfishness. To give women in marriage to other groups signifies, according to the Kuranko, a desire for the continued life and well-being of others. The gift of a woman is the highest gift; it guarantees that another lineage will not "die" and it keeps the "paths" between different lineages "open" and "alive." Not to give one's sisters or daughters in marriage is tantamount to refusing to communicate or share food with others. It is sometimes said that incest with a clan sister is like eating one's totem. Respect—*ghiliye*—implies distance and disjunction. Thus, one should not injure or even touch one's totem, and a man should not offend or touch his sister. To offend one's sister implies incest, since disrespect connotes inappropriate conjunction or contact. In such cases, a sister had the right to curse her brother by invoking their common kinship and then standing naked before him (see Jackson, 1977b:129). Incest signifies a denial of life to others (and the sister's curse brings impoverishment and even death to her brother), while harming one's totem signifies a denial of life to members of one's own group, since the totemic animal is a metaphorical kinsman. In both cases, the illegitimate conjunction is expressed in terms of eating and self-assimilation.

Minata Konde's narrative (N.22) develops an interesting aspect of the prevented marriage theme. Here the father's decision to marry his youngest daughter is approved by everyone in the family except Bala, the daughter. The narrator plays off the *emotional attachments* of different family members to the girl against the *social necessity* of severing these attachments so that she will be free to marry legitimately. Incest is shown to create role conflicts and terminological confusions within the family, and the girl chooses death rather than become her father's wife.

Underlying all the incest narratives is a recurring contrast between inappropriate emotional ties and appropriate social disjunctions. Immoral desires are symbolized by sexual and alimentary images, while formal disjunctions are symbolized by contrasted images, such as living/dead (N.25), sun/moon, night/day (N.23), garden or farm/river (N.24, N.26). The sexual and alimentary images coalesce in N.26, where the brother demands that his sister, Kore, bring rice (*kore*) to him. His plan is that he will have sexual intercourse with his sister when she comes with the rice. The pun on *kore* (rice; elder sibling) allows the narrator to juxtapose images pertaining to illicit desires and to excessive greed. But no matter what images are used, the narratives work from an inappropriate conjunction toward an extreme separation of the initially conjoined terms. In N.23, another version of which has already been published (Jackson, 1977b:128), the moon cannot control his lust for his sister, the star. The moon is cursed, which is why one can gaze at it and see it in its nakedness today. The correct distance between brother and sister is symbolized first by the relation of disjunction between the sun and the stars (the sun belongs to the day, while the stars belong to the night), and second by the fact that one cannot gaze at the sun without being blinded any more than a brother can gaze with lust upon his sister without being cursed. The daytime is, moreover, auspicious (*teli* means both "day" and "sun"), while the night is a time of clandestine and sinister activities. It is interesting that in N.25 the sister falls in love with her dead brother at night because she does not recognize him. Confusion and immoral conjunction are associated with the night, distinctness and moral separations with the day.

In N.24, which is also addressed explicitly to the problem of explaining the origin and function of the incest prohibition, a contrast is made between the sentiments which the girl expresses the first time she sings ("Kansamori and I are one") and the sentiments expressed once she realizes that her incestuous desires will lead her to her death. When she finally sings "Kansamori, my brother is Kansamori," she acknowledges the disjunction between brother and sister and accepts that in due course her brother will give her in marriage to another group. In the sad and tragic narrative told by Kumba Doron (N.25), an analogy is drawn between mortuary and marriage ritual. Indeed, Kumba Doron goes as far as saying that the incest prohibition and the prohibition against the spirits of the dead returning to the world are closely connected. In the Kuranko view, grieving, pining, and uncontrolled weeping signify unduly prolonged and over-sympathetic identification with the dead person. It is thought that weeping must cease before the reluctant and abandoned spirit of the dead person will detach itself from the world of the living and undergo transformation into ancestorhood (Jackson, 1978b). The commingling of dead and living is thus compared with the incestuous ties between brother and sister, while the girl's infatuation is compared with the overprolonged emotional ties between the bereaved and the deceased. This is clearly established when the girl presages the resolution of the problem by saying, "Only death will separate us." Just as mortuary customs enforce a disjunction between the living and the dead by various isolating and protective rites, so marriage customs demand a severance of a girl's emotional attachments to her natal group before she is given in marriage to another group.

The last narrative in this group (N.26) makes use of the curse in effecting a disjunction between brother and sister. But the curse is not worded like the usual *tersan danka* ("sister's curse"), which appeals to uterine kinship bonds and to the brother's repudiation of them (Jackson, 1977b:129). The curse in this narrative plays up a contrast between the domain of humanity and the domain of animals and things. Incest is shown to be a reversion to animality; the brother and sister are changed into river creatures and are thus separated for all time from the world of humanity. Moreover, while brother and sister normally call each other *tersan*, a reciprocal term, the relationship between the turtle and crocodile is nonreciprocal. The narrator exploits a further aspect of the metamorphosis by pointing out that the river turtle (*batonton*) and the crocodile (*bambe*) share the same habitat, just as brother and sister share the same home and parentage. Similar in this respect, they are, however, different in another: the river creatures have different names and different bodily forms, and they therefore cannot interbreed; brother and sister have different destinies in different groups, and they therefore should not marry each other. Brother and sister are certainly bound to each other by sentimental ties, but there must be no sexual relations between them.

In the narratives, it is *excessive* sentimentality, expressed in terms of sexual desire or attraction, which is censured. Transformations are contrived in order to eclipse excessive emotionality by rules which demand separation and impassivity. The incest narratives thus reverse the pattern of transformations which we traced out in the prevented marriages group. In the latter case, impersonal and inflexible rules gave way to intimate emotional unions (marriages). In the incest narratives, improper unions and misplaced emotions give way to extreme separations and depersonalizations (the incest prohibition). These separations and depersonalizations are depicted in terms of metamorphoses: from humanity to animality, and from person to thing. In one narrative (not published here) the guilty woman is changed into an anthill, in N.22 the girl seeks death at the hands of a bush spirit, in N.23 the brother guilty of incestuous wishes is depicted as the moon, upon whose impassive visage all can stare with impunity. The contrast in N.25, between the living and the dead, is an image of the ideal disjunction of sister and brother. Finally, the threatened "assimilation" of the girl by the crocodile in N.24 may be compared with the actual transformation of the brother into a crocodile in N.26. Kansamori's threat to eat his sister brings home to her the implications of incest. Her fear of death is perhaps an image of the social death which, in the absence of exchange between groups, would follow from incest. But while the sister relents in N.24 and is returned to the riverside, the brother in N.26 remains obdurate in his desire to marry his sister. Considering his adamantine attitude, the following transformations seem appropriate:

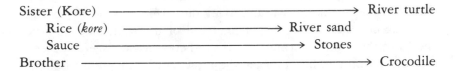

Sister (Kore) ⟶ River turtle
Rice (*kore*) ⟶ River sand
Sauce ⟶ Stones
Brother ⟶ Crocodile

Clearly, this narrative exploits the analogy which we have already re-marked between *inedible food* and *unmarriageable women*, and there is a direct parallel between the food which is turned into inedible things and the siblings who are turned into animals which cannot interbreed. The analogy is assisted by the pun on the word *kore*, but there is another connection between the relation between rice and sauce and the relation between brother and sister which is worth noting. If a sister gives her daughter in marriage to her brother, she customarily observes: "This is my *dogoma* price. I am paying for the *dogoma* that you have given me." The sister's claim upon her brother is often expressed by her privilege to take food from his plate. *Dogoma sonke*, which may be translated as "handful of rice and sauce price," is the term used to describe the privileged form of marriage known as the avunculate. Thus, if a sister gives her brother a wife, it is regarded as an expression of gratitude for the help and respect, symbolized by the *dogoma*—the rice and sauce—which her brother has given her (Jackson, 1977b:115). But this situation can only occur if the sister has married into another group in the first place, bringing bridewealth to the family so that her brother can marry with it. If no *dogoma* is given by a brother to his sister, then this would imply no indebtedness on his part, and that his sister had not married. Thus, figuratively speaking, the sauce would be as stone.

The structure of these narratives depends upon contrasts between life/death, humanity/animality, person/thing, and domestic/wild. The key transformations occur in liminal settings: in the domain of *kome*, a bush spirit (N.22), at the edge of a stream (N.23, N.24, N.26), and at the burial ground on the outskirts of the village (N.24). Rivers are natural as well as political boundaries in the Kuranko area and, in the past, were zones of periodic trespass and ambiguous control. In two of the narratives (N.24 and N.26) the riverine area is divided into three zones: the river proper, where the crocodiles live; the river shore; the tobacco gardens and farm areas along the riverside. Movement through these zones signifies a transformation from the world of people to the world of things (sand, stones) and the world of wild animals. In N.26, liminality is even more precisely established. Here, the crucial transformation occurs in the middle of a bridge over the river. It is on the bridge, wavering between the worlds of man and of the wild, that the sister speaks of the choice that must be made between marriage and incest. Because her brother fails to make the right choice, she prefers isolation from human society, just as Bala (in N.22) chose death. In the narratives we have examined in this chapter, problems of choice are central, and we discern here more poignantly a point of view implied elsewhere: the decision to exchange with others must not be prevented lest unwilled changes lead to downfall and death.

6 *Reciprocities*

It is useful to regard the protagonists in Kuranko fiction as figures rather than characters. They are not identified by idiosyncratic features, motives, mannerisms, or personalities. Rather, they exemplify modes of action and kinds of choice, thereby affording insights into an interplay of forces, influences, and possibilities which always retain an abstract definition.[1] Unlike the characters in European literature, where "being" and motivation are of great significance, the figures in Kuranko *tileinu* are neither individuals nor types. The struggle between the heroic individual, epitomizing a universal idea, and a contingent historical or social reality, which is at the center of so many European novels, would be foreign to Kuranko thought, which does not polarize such autonomies as the "social" and the "individual." In Kuranko narratives the *experience* of individual being is either disregarded or considered arbitrary. It is for the listener (and the anthropologist) to realize this aspect in his own way. But the consequences of individual *action* are of the utmost importance. The "person" in Kuranko narratives is a synthetic unity, defined by implication as the active agency of change in a vast system of interactions and fortuitous contacts. The "self," so it is implied, is a varying or steadying monitor, an agent of choice and judgment in a universe whose pathways cross, conflict, and converge. Indeed, the Kuranko make use of the metaphor of pathways in describing their world. And, as we have already seen, the motif of the journey recurs as a metaphor for conduct and of life, and suggests images of crossing-points and boundaries which enable allegories of choice to be constructed.

The congruence of past and present is set as one of the ideal goals of human endeavor. This goal is attained by unanimity and consensus in legal deliberations, or by conformity, in ritual and moral contexts, to the "words" of the ancestors, the "first people." It is thus appropriate that moots and court hearings are held in the *luiye*—the open spaces within the village—where paths converge. Rituals, such as sacrifice, which promote "agreement" and openness between men and ancestors as well as among men, are also held in the *luiye* areas. Relationships are thought of as like paths, and gift-giving, greetings, and hospitality among villagers are said to be ways of keeping the paths "alive" or "clear." The imagery of paths (*kilenu*) is closely associated with the Kuranko ideal of pureheartedness and openness (*gbeyekan:* lit. "pureness of language"). Having an open heart and speaking openly implies a consonance between one's feelings and one's words. In this way, the paths that link lineages and subclans in the local community (actually and figuratively) are kept open. But the pattern of recipirocal respect, which ideally characterizes relationships within the community, must be continually reinforced by *deliberate* acts of sympathy, concern, and magnanimity. Reciprocity is not a self-sustaining system; only through human mindfulness and choice can it be maintained. Thus, greatheartedness and openheartedness are aspects of the same ideal. In the network of interdependency which is created in the course of everyday life, harmony, trust, unanimity, and mutual adjustment must be consciously striven for and rigorously approved. Whatever generates discord or prevents flow and exchange is censured. Excess and rigidity, like selfishness and dissimulation, are the cardinal offenses in the enclosed world of the village. Such offenses "block" or "darken" the paths between people.

The narratives in this chapter have a common theme: reciprocity. This theme is explored in the contexts of kinship (*nakelinyorgoye*), affinity (*biranye*), and friendship (*dienaye*). These are for the Kuranko the three major modes of relationship; strangerhood (*sundanye*) and neighborhood (*siginyorgoye*) are aspects of friendship. The theme of reciprocity is also explored in a more abstract way. In several of the narratives, formal, not interpersonal, relationships are central, and there is considerable emphasis on the ethical ambiguity of extraordinary powers, magical objects, and heroic talents. These narratives often make use of the motif of the heroic journey into the wilderness, so that the hazards and bravery of the hero, or encounters and pacts made by him with powerful spirits of the bush, provide the raw materials for disquisitions on problems of power and responsibility.

N.27: *The Origin of the Yimbe Drum*

Narrated by Sulimani Koroma. Recorded at Kondembaia, February 1972.

The story which I am going to tell is about the *yimbe*.* That is the *yimbe* which the children dance to. It used to be in the bush. Many people know the *yimbe,* but they do not know how it came into the hands of man.

The *yimbe* was in the hands of the hyenas. Every evening they used to play it, play it, play it. And every evening the chief's people would go along the path listening to the sound of the *yimbe.*

One day the elders assembled and went to the chief and said, "Chief, that thing which makes such a sweet sound, if you don't try to bring it to us in town here then all your people will go into the bush." The chief sent a message around the chiefdom: whoever brought that thing to town would be given a hundred of everything.

On the way to where the hyenas lived there was a *tutufingbe.*† It lived on nothing but human flesh. Whenever it saw a person, it would cut off that person's head and eat him.

One day a certain man decided to go. He said goodbye to his mother. "Mother, I am going to get that thing. If I come back, all right. If I fail to come back, all right. The chief said that he would give a hundred of everything to the person who brought that thing to him." (They called it "thing" because they did not know its name.) His mother said, "All right, try your luck." So off he went.

When he reached the place where the *tutufingbe* lived he could not find it. It had gone off in search of food. The man stopped and waited for the *tutufingbe.* He sat down on the skulls of people that the *tutufingbe* had killed. When the *tutufingbe* came, it found the man sitting on the skulls. It called out, "Heh, you, what have you come to do?" The man said, "I have come to ask that you accept my apologies. I am going to get that thing which the hyenas play every night. So, for the sake of God and Muhammed, forgive my intrusion and allow me to pass. The chief said that he would give a hundred of everything to the person who brings that thing to town.

---

yimbe = a small hand-drum played by neophytes during the entertainments at an initiation rite.
†*tutufingbe* = a cannibalistic ogre or bogeyman.

So, if you please, don't eat me. Let me pass by so that I can go and get it." The *tutufingbe* said, "Well, I do eat people, but I will accept your apologies for intruding because you are so brave. You have confronted me face to face."

The *tutufingbe* then made him a *fele* [a fetish]. The man's name was Sarafin Mara. The *tutufingbe* said, "Now take this. Whatever you want to do, first consult it. You should say '*Sarafin Mara inse*,'* then it will reply '*Sedu Mara haba*' and tell you what you want to know." Apart from the *fele*, the *tutufingbe* gave the man some charcoal, an egg, a bamboo cane, and a stone. It said, "Put these in your pocket."

The man went on until he reached the place where the hyenas lived. There was a courthouse where the *yimbe* drums were kept. Upon entering the hyenas' village, the man said to hyena Sira, "Blessings to you and to hyena Tamba. I have come to spend a night with you." Hyena Sira called all the hyenas to a meeting. She said, "Heh, this young man has come to steal our *yimbe*." Another heyna said, "Heh, you, enough of such words. Do you think that a human being could come and steal our *yimbe*? Even if he takes it and travels as far away as Saralon,† it will take me only a few steps to catch up with him. So let's not worry about him." Then they went and showed the man his lodgings for the night.

Before long the man started to cry out, "Hah, I have got diarrhea. I took some medicine before coming here and now I am wanting to shit all the time. Please let me sleep in the courthouse." They said, "All right, that will be no bother." So they lodged him where the *yimbe* drums were kept.

In the evening the hyenas came and began to dance. They beat all the *yimbe* drums. The man took note of the loudest drum. After the dance the hyenas put the *yimbe* drums back in the courthouse, then retired to their houses. But hyena Sira said, "Heh, I have told you that this man has come to steal our *yimbe* drums." But the others said, "We have told you to forget about that. Do you really think that a human being could come and steal our *yimbe* drums?"

That night the young man took out the *fele* and said the words

---

*Sarafin Mara inse . . . Sedu Mara haba. The exact meaning of the words is unclear, but *inse* is probably a contracted form of *in sene*, "greetings," and *Sedu Mara haba* probably means "Greetings to you, Mara."

†Saralon = Freetown. The Kuranko think of Sierra Leone and Freetown as one and the same place, as somewhere beyond Kuranko country.

"*Sarafin Mara inse.*" The fele answered, "*Sedu Mara haba,* lie down for a while. All the hyenas are asleep except for the hyena Sira." Some time later he took out the *fele* again. "*Sarafin Mara inse.*" The *fele* answered, "*Sedu Mara haba,* now take the *yimbe* and go." He took the *yimbe* and ran—*gharamgbaram, gbaram.* Hyena Sira woke up immediately and roused the other hyenas, saying, "He has made off with your *yimbe.*" They all rushed to the courthouse and checked, only to discover that the man had stolen the loudest of all the *yimbe* drums. They started off after him—*barabarabara, barabarabara.*

Quickly they closed the distance between themselves and the man. The man took out the *fele* and said, "*Sarafin Mara inse.*" The fele answered, "*Sedu Mara haba,* run, and drop the bamboo cane." He dropped the cane. A wall of bamboo sprang up from east to west. The hyenas ran east along the bamboo, west along the bamboo. Hyena Sira said, "I told you that this man came to steal our *yimbe.*"

Then hyena Sira seized the bamboo and cut it with her teeth— *wado wado wado.* She broke it down. The hyenas burst through. They ran after him. As the man saw the dust rising he took out the *fele* again and said, "*Sarafin Mara inse.*" The *fele* answered, "*Sedu Mara haba,* drop the stone." He dropped the stone. A huge stone wall rose up from east to west. When the hyenas came to the wall they ran east along it, west along it. Hyena Sira said, "I told you that this man would go off with our *yimbe,* but you all said no, it would not happen."

The hyenas said, "Hah, we could cut through the bamboo, but how will we get through this stone wall?" Hyena Sira put her mouth against the rock and chewed at it—*morto morto morto.* She broke it down. The hyenas burst through.

When the man again saw the dust of the hyenas he took out the *fele,* and said, "*Sarafin Mara inse.*" The *fele* answered, "*Sedu Mara haba,* drop the charcoal." It became a huge fire which stretched across the world from east to west. The hyenas said, "Ah, we could get through the bamboo, we could break through the stone wall, but fire is too difficult to pass through." They ran east, they ran west. Then hyena Sira said, "Hah, I told you people." She turned her backside to the fire and went—*sa sa sa sa* [urinated]. She put out the fire. They crossed that place.

Now it was only about one mile from the town. But the hyenas drew near again. The man took out the *fele* and said, "*Sarafin Mara inse.*" The fele answered, "*Sedu Mara haba,* drop the egg." It became an enormous lake which crossed the world from east to west. The hyenas could not cross it. The man went on into the town with the *yimbe* and presented it to the chief.

Long before this, the *tutufingbe* had told the young man, "As soon as your task is done you must kill a red bull as a sacrifice to the *fele*. Dip the *fele* in the blood so that whatever in the world you ask of it, so will it do." The young man had agreed to this. But when he returned to town he forgot.

Hyena Sira now transformed herself into a human being and crossed over the lake. The young man's mother had told him already, "If a young woman comes today, do not love her. She is one of the creatures from whom you stole the *yimbe.*" In town everyone was dancing and celebrating. The chief had given the man a hundred of everything. But the man had forgotten to sacrifice the red bull to the *fele*.

Late in the afternoon a strange girl arrived in the town. The man went and told his mother. She repeated what she had said to him before. "If you go, she will love you, and I have told you to beware of her." The young man said, "All right, mother." But as soon as he left his mother he went to the place where that young woman was. By then many young men had gathered. The girl looked through the crowd, watching for him. Suddenly she saw him standing by the door. She said, "It is that man over there that I love, it is that man over there that I love." The man went back and told his mother what had happened. He said, "Mother, that girl says that she loves no one but me." His mother said, "Well, I did tell you." She went to the house where her son was going to sleep. She said to the door, "My son is in your care." There was a dog there. She said to the dog, "My son is in your care." She said to the hearth, "My child is in your care." She said to the bed, "My child is in your care." She said to the smoking-basket over the fire, "My child is in your care." She placed her son in the care of all these things.

That night, hyena Sira, who had transformed herself into a human being, came to sleep with the young man. He was so happy that he went to sleep immediately. Late in the night hyena Sira got up and was just about to kill him when the bed said, "No." Then the smoking-basket said, "Don't trouble him." The door said, "I will not let her through." The hearth said, "We will roast her." So the woman went to sleep.

In the morning she told her lover that she was leaving and that she would not be sleeping in his house that night. She asked him to accompany her. The man took a machete. But the girl said, "What? Are you going to kill me?" He took a stick. She said, "Why are you taking that stick? Are you going to beat me?" So the man left the machete and the stick behind. He went off empty-handed.

Some way along the path out of town he said, "I will stop here." (He had forgotten about the *fele* in his pocket.) The girl said, "I think that you do not love me. Why should you stop here so soon? If you love me you will accompany me as far as the lake."

When they reached the water's edge the man said, "Well, I must go back now." The girl said, "Eh, so you do not want to cross over the lake with me?" So he crossed to the other side of the lake with her. No sooner had they reached the other side than the girl called out, "I have come with that *kafiri* [unbeliever]." The other hyenas emerged from where they had been hiding and hyena Sira transformed herself into a hyena again. The young man climbed up a locust tree. Hyena Sira said, "Now let us fell the tree." They began to gnaw at it with their teeth.

The man was utterly without hope. He put his hand in his pocket. He found the *fele.* He took it out and said, *"Sarafin Mara inse."* Dondon* . . . the *fele* was silent. He repeated the words, *"Sarafin Mara inse."* Dondondon . . . the *fele* remained silent. The young man cried out, "Oh, God, how am I going to be saved from my plight? If my misfortune is because I did not sacrifice a red bull to you *fele*, then, if I am saved I will sacrifice two bulls." At once the *fele* spoke. "You do not listen to your father, you do not listen to your mother. But take hold of one of the branches of the tree." He took a branch in his hand, and the branch changed into a gun. The *fele* spoke again, "Take some leaves now." They became cartridges. Then the *fele* said, "Shoot." He began firing. After some time he took the *fele* and said, *"Sarafin Mara inse."* It said, *"Sedu Mara haba,* hyena Sira is not dead yet. Shoot her again." He shot her dead.

The young man came down from the tree and went home. As

---

don = quiet. Variations on the word are common in Kuranko narratives, signifying stillness, hushed silence, quietness.

soon as he arrived there he sacrificed two red bulls to that *fele*. That is the way the idea of going to people to make magical medicines [*besenu*] began. That is all.

N.28: *The Abuse of the Killing Word*

Narrated by Keti Ferenke Koroma. Recorded at Kondembaia, January 1970.

There was a woman who was greatly admired by many young men. They all decided to go and find bridewealth with which to marry her. One man said, "I am not going to find anything but meat with which to marry this woman. I am going to kill animals and come and pay the meat as bridewealth." Another man said, "I am going to find clothes. That is what I will bring as bridewealth." Another man said, "I am going to bring money. That is what I will bring as bridewealth." Everyone announced what he was going to find and bring. Then they all went off.

The man who said that he was going to kill animals spent three years in search of game. All his clothes were worn out, but he failed to find any animals. Meanwhile, his companions returned to town. Some brought money, some brought clothes, some brought cows. But they were not able to give these things to the woman because one man had not returned. They said, "Well, let us wait for the one who went off in search of animals. When he comes and gives what he has, then we can decide who will have the woman." They sat down and waited for him. They waited for two years. All this time he was in the bush.

One day he came upon an old woman, deep in the bush. She was surrounded by dried meat. He went up and greeted her. "How are you?" The old woman answered, "How are you?" She said, "Why are you wandering about here?" The young man said, "My companions and I are competing to marry a certain woman. Everyone announced what he would bring. I said that I would bring meat to pay the bridewealth. This is now my fourth year of wandering in the bush and I have found no meat. Grandmother, since I have found you here with all this meat, I want you to give me some." The old woman said, "All right. Now sleep here." He slept there.

In the morning the old woman gave him some dried meat. He said, "Eh, old woman, you are living here in this faraway place in the bush, no man with you, yet you have plenty of meat. Now, instead of giving me some, tell me by what means you get it." The old woman agreed. The old woman had a tied-up thing. Each morning, if she wanted bushcows, she would say, "You, bushcows, come here." When they came she would say, "You, bushcows, I have *nyemakara* this at you." She would point the tied-up thing at the animals. All those animals would die. The tied-up thing was wrapped inside a kerchief which she held in her hand. Whatever she pointed it at, saying "I have *nyemakara* this at you," that creature would die. The old woman took out the kerchief and gave it to the young man. "When you go, whatever animal you want, just stand on the veranda of your house and call it. When it comes running toward you, say 'I have *nyemakara* this at you.' Then it will die." The young man said, "All right." He took the kerchief and returned to the town.

When he arrived in the town, nobody recognized him because he was so emaciated. He said to the other men, "Your companion has come back today." They told him to go and rest until morning. At daybreak they called him to come and give whatever he had. They said, "We have spent four years waiting for you. The woman could not be given to anyone until you came back. Now, how did you come?" He said, "This is how I came. I did not get meat." Then he gave the few lumps of dried meat that the old woman had given him. They said, "Well, if this is all you have brought, you are not going to get the woman." He said, "Heh, wait a moment." That morning, in front of all the elders, he went behind the houses to the outskirts of the town. He called as he went, "Bushcows, come!" All the bushcows in that area came running. As they neared the town he took out the kerchief and said, "I have *nyemakara* this at you." All the bushcows died. He told the people to go and get the animals. Everyone went, butchered the animals and shared the meat. The man went to the other side of the town and said, "All you wild pigs in this area, come!" They also came. He said, "All you that have come, I have *nyemakara* this at you." They all died. He went to the other side of the town and called the antelopes. They came. He said, "All you that have come, I have *nyemakara* this at you." They all died. The other men grew afraid. They took the woman and gave her to him. She remained with him for one year.

The old woman said, "Heh, this young man has not returned to me the thing I gave him. I must go and get it back." When she reached the town she went to the young man and explained why she had come. She said, "Is this our agreement? Since you left my place last year you have not been back." The man got up. "You obstinate old woman, why should you come and ask me this? Now, I have *nyemakara* this at you." The old woman fell down dead.

The young man struck fear into the hearts of all. The men who had competed with him to marry the woman held a meeting. He went there and found them. "Oh, so you are plotting against me. Now, I have *nyemakara* this at you." They all died. The young man became a terror in the town. Wherever he went and found people gathered together he would say, "Oh, you are all plotting against me. Now I have *nyemakara* this at you." They would die too. He became a burden on the whole world, a burden on the world. His father-in-law and his mother-in-law decided to discuss the matter. He went and found them sitting together. He said, "Oh, my in-laws, so you have come together to plot against me. Now I have *nyemakara* this at you." They died too.

He went on in this way. But Ala was watching everything. Then Ala said, "Heh, this is a terrible thing. If I do not go and free the people from this thing it will cause great trouble." Ala changed himself into a very beautiful woman. She came down. The woman went to the young man and said, "I have come for you to marry me. Your name has traveled far and wide." (Women cannot fail in their plots against men.) She told the young man that they should sleep together. "I have really come for you to marry me." The young man said, "Well, you are welcome." (Now, we all know that Ala never fails in what he sets out to do.) She spoke sweet words to him. Finally she said, "Please show me your secret for killing animals." The young man got up and opened his box and took out the kerchief. "This is what I use for killing whatever in the world I want to kill." He gave it to her. The woman said, "So this is what you use for killing." He said, "Yes." Then she said, "Well, you, young man, who is lying down here, I have *nyemakara* this at you." He fell down dead. Then she took the kerchief and went up with it. That is the kerchief that Ala now has. Therefore, whenever Ala says to someone, "I have *nyemakara* this at you," that person will die that very day. That thing is owned by Ala and by no one else.

Whenever he says, "I have *nyemakara* this at you," that person will die that very day. Whoever is sick and unable to recover, Ala will say, "I have *nyemakara* this at you."

N.29: *The Three Brothers and the Fetish Called "Repayment of Kindness"*

Narrated by Keti Ferenke Koroma. Recorded at Kondembaia, March 1970.

There was once a very wealthy chief who had three sons. The chief died. His three sons shared the inheritance. The inheritance amounted to nine *lankono*.* They said, "Now that we have this wealth amongst ourselves, if any one of us prospers, then so be it, and if any one of us fails to improve upon his fortune, then so be it." The first son got three *lankono*, the second son got three *lankono*, and the third and last son got three *lankono*. They said, "Whoever wants to waste his wealth, let him waste it. Whoever wants to keep his wealth, let him keep it."

The second brother used his wealth to trade with. From the profits he married two wives. He came. The last brother used his wealth too, and he married a wife. He came. The first brother had kept his wealth. He saw that his brothers had got wives and children.

They all lived in the same house. Behind the house there was a huge cotton tree. The vultures lived in that cotton tree. They laid and hatched their eggs there.

One day someone's dog came into the house and overturned the plate of food that the youngest brother's children were eating from. They said that they were going to kill the dog. The eldest brother said, "Eh, you, don't kill that dog. It has no way of speaking." They said, "Ah, *n'koro*, we are going to kill it." The eldest brother said, "Don't kill it." They said, "Well, if you like the dog and don't want it to be killed, give us one *lankono* of your wealth and we will let it go." He went and took one *lankono* from the three

---

lankono or *lankone* was the traditional Kuranko unit of value in barter exchange. One *lankone* was equivalent to 10 mats, 10 rattan containers of rice, 10 *gbalgbalan* of cloth (a *gbalgbalan* was 4 lengths of cloth measured from elbow to fingertip), or 10 bunches of tobacco leaf. It is important to note that the three sons are half brothers (same father, different mothers); the rivalry between the younger brothers and the eldest brother is thus a case of *fadenye*.

that had been given to him. He gave it to his younger brothers.
They let the dog go.

They were there for one month, two months, three months.
Then someone's cat came into the house and ate the groundnuts of
the second brother's wife. They seized the cat and said they were
going to kill it. The eldest brother came and said, "Eh, don't kill
that cat. It has no way of speaking and it would be wicked of you to
kill it." They said, "Eh, *n'koro*, we are going to kill it. But if you like
the cat, give us one *lankono* of your wealth and we will let it go."
They were doing this in order to make their elder brother less
prosperous than they were. The eldest brother went and took one
lankono from the two that remained. He gave it to his younger
brothers. They let the cat go. The eldest brother now had only one
lankono out of the three that had been given to him.

One day a strong wind blew up. By that time the vultures had
hatched their eggs. The wind blew one of the fledglings from the
tree. The children of the two younger brothers went and picked up
the fledgling. The eldest brother came and said to the children,
"Leave the bird alone. This is a vulture. One may not eat it, let it
go." He took the bird from them and set it free. The children cried
and went to their fathers and told their fathers that their elder
father had taken the bird away from them and set it free. The
younger brothers came, *fafa fa fafafa*, and said, "*N'koro*, why did
you take the bird away from the children?" He said, "It was no
other bird but a vulture. You know that one may not eat the vulture." Now, because they wanted to see their elder brother with
nothing at all, they said, "Well, if you like the fledgling vulture then
bring us one *lankono* to pay for it." The eldest brother said, "Eh, it
was a fledgling vulture. One may not eat the vulture." They said,
"Oh, no, no, no! If you like the vulture, then give us one *lankono*."
He went into the house and took out the one remaining *lankono*
and gave it to them. His mother cried and cried and cried and
cried.

He took the fledgling vulture and raised it. He fed it until it was
full-grown. By that time the mother vulture had flown off to a
distant country. He had fed the fledgling until it was full-grown.
The vulture decided that it was time to go away. It said, "Thank
you very much. Now I am going to find my mother." It flew off to
find its mother. (Heh, the day that vulture was reunited with its

mother, that was a great day.) When it found its mother, they were happy. The vulture's parents said, "Who raised you?" The vulture said, "A certain man raised me. He gave three *lankono* to save my life and, besides, he took care of me. When I grew up I asked him if I could go and find you. Now that I have found you, I would like you to do something for that man, to repay the kindness that he has shown me." They said, "All right, but do you think that you could pick that man up and fly with him?" The vulture said, "Yes, I can do that." They said, "All right, go and fetch him."

The vulture flew back to the man and said, "I have seen my father and my mother. They told me to come and bring you to them." The man said, "How can I go?" The vulture said, "I will take you." The vulture picked him up and flew with him right up to Mande. On the day they reached Mande, everyone was very happy. It was a great day and they prayed for him. They called all the old vultures, and they prayed for him. Then God sent a piece of red taffeta tied in a knot. The vultures took the taffeta and gave it to the man. They said, "*M'fa*, we have nothing that can repay the kindness you showed us, but take this as your gift. From now until the day you die this taffeta will do whatever you ask it to do." The man took the red raffeta and said, "You, Repayment of Kindness, if a person does good, then goodness shall be his reward. I am here, but I want to be in my own house." As soon as he said that, he found himself sitting in his own house. It was because of the power of that red taffeta.

His younger brothers were laughing at him now. They thought that they had succeeded in making him poor. They did not know that he was the wealthiest of all of them. One day he took the red taffeta and said, "You, Repayment of Kindness, if a person does good, then goodness shall be his reward. I want to find myself in a wide level place in the bush." As soon as he had said that, he found himself in a wide level place near the Seli River. Then he said, "You, Repayment of Kindness, if a person does good, then goodness shall be his reward. I want there to be a large town here." Immediately, a large town appeared. He said once more, "You, Repayment of Kindness, if a person does good, then goodness shall be his reward. I want this town to be filled with people, and I want to be chief in this town." As soon as he had said that, the town became crowded with people and he became chief. He was the wealthiest person there. He had everything he wanted. But he was on the other side of the Seli River and he had not bridged the river yet.

His renown spread far and wide. One day the second brother said, "Heh, I must go and visit this famous town." He went. When he arrived, he found that the chief had gone to his farm. The chief's senior wife was there, looking after the house. The man went to the chief's *luiye*. He met the woman. He greeted her, "*M'biran, in wali*." She answered him, "*M'fa, in wali*." He said, "Where is your husband?" She said, "He has gone to the bush." He said, "Eh, well, this town surprises me. Do you know that your husband is our eldest brother? I am second to him. But we did not know that he had built this great town. Still, we are happy that he has become chief in such a great town." Then they began joking with each other.* The woman said, "I am older than you." The man said, "What! Don't be so cheeky, I am older than you." The woman said, "I can prove to you right now that you are not older than me." The man said, "Oh, come now, don't be so cheeky. I am older than you. But if you can prove otherwise, then go ahead." (He wanted to learn the secret of how his elder brother had become chief in that town.) Now, because the woman was the senior wife, she had a key to each of her husband's boxes. She got up and went into her husband's room. She opened one of the boxes and took out Repayment of Kindness. Then she brought a basin and set it down. She said, "You, Repayment of Kindness, if a person does good, then goodness shall be his reward. Let his basin be filled with rice." As soon as she had said that, the basin was filled with rice. The man said, "Oh, if this is all there is to it, then I can do it myself. I can say what you said." The woman took Repayment of Kindness and gave it to the man. The man went away with it.

Upon arriving home, the man said, "You, Repayment of Kindness, if a person does good, then goodness shall be his reward. May everything on the yonder side of the Seli River be ruined, and may I be chief here." As soon as he said that, everything vanished except the senior wife. She remained, but everything else came to that man. He became chief, a great chief, and his town was filled with people.

---

*A joking relationship (*numorgoya tolon*) exists between a man and his elder brother's wife; this banter is a typical joking exchange. The woman endeavors to prove that she is "older" than the man by demonstrating her extraordinary powers (using the red taffeta fetish). The man sees this as an opportunity for stealing the fetish from his elder brother.

When the eldest brother returned from his farm that evening, he found an empty place. He went to his house and found his wife sitting there. He said, "Why is this place deserted?" The woman said nothing. He said, "Give me the key." She gave it to him. He opened his box but he could not find Repayment of Kindness. He said to his wife, "Where is the thing that was here?" His wife said, "A certain man came and took it away." He said, "Eh!" He cried and cried and cried. (Now I will tell you why dogs and cats do not get on well together.)

The dog and the cat came and asked, "*M'fa*, why are you crying?" He explained everything to them. He said, "My younger brother came and stole my Repayment of Kindness from my wife. That is why I am crying." The dog said, "*M'fa*, do you remember the day that you took one *lankono* of your wealth and used it to save my life?" The man said, "No." The cat said, "*M'fa*, do you remember the day that you took one *lankono* of your wealth and used it to save my life?" The man said, "No." They said, "Well, be patient, all right? That Repayment of Kindness will be returned to you here." The man said, "All right." They set off.

They reached the river. The dog could swim but the cat could not. But people like cats more than they like dogs. The dog said, "Now, cat, sit on my back and I'll cross you over. Then I'll wait for you while you go on to the town." The cat said, "All right." They crossed over the river. The dog waited at the riverside, and the cat went to the town to get Repayment of Kindness. Whether the cat would get it or not, the dog did not know. He waited for some time. The cat did not come. He became angry. (This is why we see today that dogs do not laugh.) Before long the cat came with Repayment of Kindness. The dog said, "Now tell me, who got this Repayment of Kindness for the man?" The cat said, "I did." The dog said, "So, you claim that you got it. But would you have got it if I had not crossed you over the river?" They began to quarrel. Finally, the cat said, "Let's not go on quarreling here. Let's take the man's property back to him. We can settle our argument later." (But they still haven't settled their differences. Whenever they meet, they resume their quarreling.)

They went and gave the man his Repayment of Kindness. They said, "*M'fa*, we have brought it to you. You once showed us a kindness by saving our lives, therefore we have helped you today." The man held Repayment of Kindness and said, "You, Repayment of Kindness, if a person does good, then goodness shall be his reward. Let everything that was taken away be returned." As soon as he had said that, everything reappeared. He became chief, just as before. His younger brothers' place became as desolate as ever. Then he called his senior wife. He said, "You are not going to betray any man ever again." He cut her throat. He was chief in that town. Therefore, no matter how much you love a woman, never let her know your secrets. If she gets to know your secrets, you are done for.

N.30: *The Two Friends and the Sequestered Woman*

Narrated by Keti Ferenke Koroma. Recorded at Kondembaia, January 1970.

There was once a woman in this world. Although she had been initiated four years before, she said she would marry no one unless he could understand the secret meaning of human actions, a man as clever as she was.* For a further three years she did not marry. Whenever a suitor came to her she would do something and then ask him to tell her the meaning of the action. The suitor would not understand. To those that came and were unable to explain the meaning of her actions, she would say, "I do not want you."

Now one man was cleverer than most people in that country. He called one of his friends and told him that he wanted the daughter of that chief to be his wife. His friend said, "Many men have tried to marry that woman but they have all failed. Now you say that you are going. You will not succeed in marrying her." The man said, "Never mind, let us go anyway." He and his friend set off. They reached the town. When they reached the town the man said to his friend, "This evening go and greet the chief's daughter. Tell her that I greet her." The man's friend went to the woman and said, "I have come with a friend and he has sent me to greet you. He said that he has come as your suitor."† The woman said, "I am happy about that."

---

* It is customary for a girl to take up residence with her husband in the same year as her initiation.
† *sundan* = stranger, guest; in narratives it often means "prospective lover."

They stayed there all day. In the evening the woman prepared some rice. She gave a basin of rice to her younger sister and told her to take it to the strangers. The girl went and took the rice to them and said, "My sister said that I should bring this rice to you." They said, "This is good." They ate the rice. They slept. In the morning the man's friend asked him why he had not gone to sleep with his lover during the night. The man said, "Be patient. Sit down." Then he asked his friend again to go and greet the woman. His friend went and greeted her. He returned and told the man that he had gone and greeted her. They stayed there all day. In the evening the woman prepared rice and placed a red kola nut on it. She gave the basin of rice to her younger sister and told her to take it to the strangers. The girl took the rice to them. When the man's friend saw the red kola nut on top of the rice he said, "Eh, friend, I am not going to eat this rice with the red kola nut on it." The man said, "Friend, don't be afraid. I brought you here. I bear the responsibility for whatever befalls you. Let us eat the rice." They sat down and ate. They slept.

In the morning the woman prepared rice and put a white kola nut on it. She gave a basin of rice to her younger sister and told her to take it to the strangers. The girl took the rice to them. The man's friend said, "Eh, friend, I am afraid. Yesterday red kola, today white kola. This makes me afraid." The man said, "Now look, don't be afraid. Look at me. I brought you here. The woman and I are passing something between ourselves that you cannot understand. Let us eat the rice." They sat down and ate. They stayed there all day. In the evening the woman prepared rice. She put it in a calabash. She broke the side of the calabash. Then she took three bones and placed them on top of the rice. She also took a piece of charcoal and put it on the rice. And she took a scrap of country-cloth and put it on the rice. She called her younger sister and told her to take the rice to the strangers and tell them that it is their gift. The girl took the food and said to the strangers, "My sister told me that I should bring this for you." The man's friend said, "Eh, friend, I am afraid. Since we came here everything that the woman has done has made me afraid. Once again she has done this curious thing, putting all these things on top of the rice. I will not eat it." The man said, "Friend, oh friend, don't be afraid. Let's eat the food. There is nothing wrong with us. Let's eat." He took the three bones and put them in his pocket. They sat down to eat. He threw the charcoal and the cloth away.

Evening came. At the time when people go to bed the man said, "Friend, I am going to sleep somewhere else." His friend said, "Where will you sleep?" The man said, "I am going to sleep with my woman." His friend said, "But you have not sent word that you are coming to sleep with her." The man said, "Just watch me, that's all." The friend said, "All right, go. Whatever happens, you will find me here." The young man left the house and went off.

There was a high fence around the chief's *luiye* and only one way through it. Inside the fence the chief kept his three dogs. If anyone entered the *luiye* at night the dogs would drive him away. But the young man had the three bones in his pocket. As soon as he entered the *luiye* the dogs came running and barking. He put his hand in his pocket and took out the bones. He gave each dog a bone. The dogs took away the bones to chew them at the back of the house. The young man had the *luiye* to himself. But all the chief's houses looked alike. He did not know which house he should go to. He looked around. Then he saw that one house had a veranda which was broken away at the edge. He went to that house and said to himself, "My lover is in this house." He entered the house. It was dark. He went to the hearth and mended the fire. He saw many people asleep in the room. He didn't know which person to wake. Then he noticed that one woman was covered with a country-cloth bedspread. He went and sat on the mat by her side. He woke her and said, "Friend, good evening." He had awakened her but she pretended to be asleep. He shook her. She still pretended to be asleep. He got up and took off his shirt and hung it on the wall. Then he lay down and drew the bedspread up over himself.

The woman said, "Who is this?" He said, "I." She said, "Who are you?" He said, "I am your suitor." The woman got up and asked him, "How did you get here?" He said, "You told me." She said, "How did I tell you?" He said, "On the day we arrived here my friend came to you and told you that I had come as your suitor. Didn't you hear him?" The woman said, "Yes, I heard him." The man said, "Didn't you cook rice and put it on the head of your younger sister that she should bring it to us?" The woman said, "Yes." The man said, "On the second day, in the morning, didn't you again prepare rice and put a red kola nut on it and send it to us?" The woman said, "Yes." The man said, "Didn't you mean to inform me that you were indisposed?"* The woman said, "Yes, that was exactly what I meant." The man said, "This morning didn't you prepare another dish of rice and place white kola on it, and didn't the white kola mean that you were well again?" The woman said, "Oh yes, that is exactly what I intended." The man said, "This evening you prepared food and put it in a broken calabash to tell me that if I should come I should look for the house with the broken veranda." The woman said, "Yes, that is what I was thinking about." The man said, "And you put three bones on the rice to show that there were three dogs in the *luiye* which drive away intruders at night. You meant that I should use the bones to keep the dogs quiet while I came to your house. Was that not what you sent the bones for?" The woman said, "Exactly." The man said, "Again, you put the scrap of country-cloth on the rice to tell me that I should look for the person covered by a country-cloth bedspread. That person was you. Was that not why you sent the country-cloth?" Then the woman said, "Heh, I have found a husband."

The woman told the man to wait. "Let us go and inform my father that I have found a husband." She went and knocked on her father's door. She said, "Father, I have found a husband." Her father said, "Have you found a husband?" (Because the father, like all the people of the town, was worried about the way in which the woman had refused to get married.) The father got up and ordered that all the *jeliba*s should assemble. They brought out the horses. They danced. They spent the entire night dancing. In the morning the chief gave many gifts to the young man. The chief gave gifts to his daughter as well. Then finally the chief gave his daughter to that young man. The young man was happy. So too was his friend. His friend said, "If a person accompanies or follows a trusty friend he will never regret it." The young man said that since everyone was happy about his marriage to the chief's daughter, he should go and find bridewealth. He said, "In that way, chief, the marriage will prosper. Therefore, I will leave your daughter here with you while I go off to find something to give as bridewealth. Whatever I find I

---

* In polite usage, a woman's menstrual period is referred to as "her sickness." This has no pejorative connotations, and I have translated "sick" as indisposed.

will bring as bridewealth." Then he told his friend, "Friend, let us go off once more." His friend agreed. They set off.

II

Now, they had heard of another chief who had a very beautiful daughter. This chief had put his daughter in a special house. She had been there from the time that she had been weaned. The chief had said, "This child of mine shall not desire anyone and no one shall desire her." So he had put her in a special house (enclosed within two other houses). This was to prevent anyone except the chief entering the house.

The clever young man heard about this chief. He said to his friend, "Friend, let us go to this chief's place and find out whether or not what we have heard is true." They set off. On the way they met some traders, driving a herd of cows. The clever young man said, "I wish I could get two of these cows so that I could give them to my affines as bridewealth." The leader of the traders said, "You, you just said something, and if I had had all my wits about me I would have given you four lashes of my whip here and cut off your head with my sword." Then the traders went on their way. When they had gone some distance the clever young man ran after them and said to the leader of the traders, "When you arrive in the town that you are heading for, go to the chief's *luiye* and ask for the chief's firstborn daughter. Tell her that you met a young man who asked you to inform her that he had forgotten his sword and his whip, and that she should keep them for him." The leader of the traders said, "All right, I will go and deliver the message." They parted.

When the traders reached the town the leader asked the way to the chief's *luiye*. He also asked for the chief's firstborn daughter. She came and said, "Here I am." The trader said, "I met a man today who told me to greet you." He delivered the message [as above]. After this the woman fell to the ground. Everyone crowded round her, asking why she was crying. The woman said, "It is this trader. He told my husband that he should have beaten him and cut off his head. This is the message that my husband has sent through him." Then they all fell upon that trader and tied him up. The traders took their cows and begged for their leader's life. They released the leader of the traders, and the traders went off.

When the two young men approached the town of this other chief, the clever young man made a large hamper. He picked some leaves and put them inside, then he asked his friend to get in and lie down. His friend lay down inside it. The young man covered him with leaves and tied the hamper up. Then he took the hamper and went into the town. He went to the chief and told the chief that they were from a country where kola was very scarce. He said, "Since God has helped me get this hamper of kola, would you please keep it for me in a place which no one except yourself will enter. I am going to find more kola to add to my supply. I want you to keep my hamper somewhere safe." The chief said, "Well, the only place is the house where my daughter is." The man said, "Well, chief, if you keep it there I will be very happy." The chief took the hamper and opened the first door, the second door, the third door, and entered the house where his daughter was. He told her not to touch the hamper because it belonged to someone else.

As soon as the chief had left the room, the young man called out to the girl, asking her to untie the hamper. (His friend had told him that if their ruse was successful then he should ask the girl to untie him as soon as the chief left the room.) So, as soon as the chief had gone he asked the girl to untie him. The girl had been there for seven years and had never left the house in all that time. She was wanting to be married but there was no hope of marriage because her father had passed the law: this child of mine shall not desire anyone and no one shall desire her. The young man asked the girl to untie him. She quickly and gladly did so. And they lived together in that house. Whenever the chief came to leave food for the girl the young man went hurriedly and lay down in the hamper. The girl tied it up and put it where the chief had first left it. The chief would come, leave the food, and go away. Then the girl untied the young man and they would eat together.

During this time the other man was roaming around waiting to see what would happen. The man and the girl were in the house for three months. The very same month that the hamper had been put in the room the girl became pregnant. In the fifth month, that other cunning fellow decided to go for his hamper of kola. He came. He went to the chief and said, "Chief, I have come for the hamper that I left in your charge." The chief went and opened the doors and entered the house where his daughter was. He took the hamper. But he did not look closely at his daughter and notice that her belly was swollen. The girl said, "Please, father, let me go out and get some fresh air." Her father said, "Well, let us go out together." The father took the hamper, but as they went out into the light he saw that his daughter's belly was swollen. He said, "Heh, this is a curious thing. My daughter was living alone, now she is pregnant." He dropped the hamper and went off. He sat on the veranda crying. All the townspeople gathered round, saying, "The chief is crying, the chief is crying." They asked the chief why he was crying, but he could not explain because if he told them that his daughter was pregnant they would say that he was the only person who entered the girl's room. The chief was very worried.

Then, the cunning young man told the chief to tell his big men to be quiet. The chief did so. The man told the chief to go for his hamper. The chief fetched the hamper and placed it in the middle of the *luiye*. Then that cunning young fellow said, "Chief, you have done something that no one else in this world could do. Your grandfather married your grandmother. They begat your father. And your father married your mother. They begat you. Then you got married and had a child. Now, if you say that she is not allowed to bear a child, well, that is something I have never heard of before. You said that she should not desire any man, and that no man should desire her. It is you and you alone who decreed this. Therefore I put my friend in this hamper and gave the hamper to you for safekeeping. There was no kola in the hamper. And it was my friend who made your daughter pregnant." The chief said, "Eh! Thanks be to God. You have saved me from disgrace."

The chief assembled all the musicians and led the dancing. He took one hundred of everything, and also his daughter. He gave them to that clever man, and said, "Thank you very much. You have saved me from disgrace. Take these things, and take my daughter." So they all danced. And the friend also got married.

Therefore, if you are clever and you have a friend who is not as clever as you, and you have a way of getting through life in this world, then you should not laugh at your friend, because friendship means that if you are clever and can get certain things through your cleverness you should help your friend get things through you. So this man got a wife through his cleverness, and his friend got a wife through him. Therefore, if someone is clever, be he small or big, we should all live by him. We should all gain. This piece of advice I give you all.

N.31: *Gbeyekan Momori and His Deceitful Friend*

Narrated by Keti Ferenke Koroma. Recorded at Kondembaia, March 1970.

There were two friends. They were both called Momori. One day they sat down together and, since they were friends, they decided to go into business together. So they started selling things. They made about £30. They decided to use the money to get married. They married the same woman. Their wife helped them by selling things in the market.

One day they said, "Well, now, we are two and yet we are married to the same wife. How is this possible?" One of the Momoris—his name was Gbeyekan Momori*—said, "I feel nothing but goodwill toward you.† If you feel the same goodwill toward me, then that is fine. Now because I feel goodwill toward you, and because we have only one wife between us, I am going to give her to you. From now on we can work hard so that it becomes possible for me to get a wife for myself." The woman became the wife of the other Momori. They continued in business. They continued trading until they had earned £20. But they needed another £10 to make up the £30 needed to get a wife.

One day they happened to pass a flat expanse of rock [*faragbaran*]. They stopped there and that other Momori told Gbeyekan Momori to go and fetch water for them. Gbeyekan Momori said, "Eh, friend, we have worked hard and got a wife. Because of my goodwill I decided that she should be your wife. Now instead of asking your wife to fetch water for you to drink you are asking me to go. But it doesn't matter, I will go and fetch the water." So Gbeyekan Momori took the water bowl and went to fetch water. No sooner had he gone than the other Momori said to his wife, "When my friend returns, we must fall upon him, knock him to the ground, beat him up, and gouge out his eyes. Then the £20 will be ours." His wife said, "All right. There is nothing wrong with that."

Gbeyekan Momori returned. As he was putting down the water bowl, the other Momori fell on him. He called for his wife to take Gbeyekan Momori's feet so that they could force him to the ground. His wife came and helped. They forced him to the ground,

---

*Gbeyekan is best translated as "purehearted," connoting honesty, straightforwardness, and openness in one's dealings with another person.
†The literal translation is, "My heart is pure/white (*gbe*) for you."

beat him up, and then the other Momori took out his dagger and gouged out Gbeyekan Momori's eyes. The other Momori and his wife left Gbeyekan Momori lying helpless on the *faragbaran*.

Near the *faragbaran* was a very big cotton tree. After being abandoned, Gbeyekan Momori crawled to the cotton tree. He lay there till evening. He did not know that it was the meeting place of an old hyena and an old vulture. When they met there, the vulture would tell the hyena what he had seen from the air during the day, and the hyena would tell the vulture what he had seen from the ground. So that evening the hyena and the vulture met. The vulture said, "Good evening, hyena." The hyena said, "Good evening, vulture." The hyena asked the vulture what he had seen from the air during the day. The vulture said, "Hyena, I did not go anywhere today. I was laying my eggs in this cotton tree. I had laid five eggs before today, but today I laid the sixth egg. Now, whoever breaks these eggs will have his wishes fulfilled. But, hyena, you were not here today. Something happened here today. A woman and two men came onto this *faragbaran* today. When they came here, one man took the water bowl and went to fetch water. When he came back with the water, they fell on him, forced him to the ground, then sat on him and gouged out first one eye then the other. Then they went away. After they had gone I said, 'This is a remarkable thing, I must tell the hyena about it.' So, have you heard me?" The hyena said, "Well, I have heard you. What a pity that the man is not here. Because if one takes the bark of this cotton tree, squeezes it, and then washes one's face in the liquid, one will be able to see again." All this time Gbeyekan Momori was sitting under the tree, but the hyena and the vulture did not know that. The vulture said, "Friend, I am sorry that I have no mouth with which to speak to that man. I would like to tell him to take a stone and dash it against the cotton tree. The liquid that flows out could be washed over his eyes, then he could see again. But I don't know where he is."

They all spent the night there. In the morning the vulture went away and the hyena went away. When they had gone the man crawled across the *faragbaran*, took a stone and dashed it against the cotton tree. When the liquid began to ooze from the tree, he took some in his hands and washed it over his eyes. He immediately could see. Then he started off. Soon he came to a very flat and fertile land. He decided to retrace his steps a little way. He went back until he found a tree. He cut off a long pole. He went back to the cotton tree. When he reached the cotton tree he leant the pole against it, climbed up and collected the vulture's eggs. There were six eggs. He took three of them. Then he went off in the direction that he had taken before. He reached the flat and fertile country again. He said, "You, egg of the vulture, if I break you here it is because I want a great town here." He dropped the egg on the ground and a large town sprang up. Then he took the second egg. He said, "You, egg of the vulture, if I break you here it is because I want to be chief of this great town." He dropped that egg on the ground and became chief. Then he took the third egg. He said, "You, egg of the vulture, if I break you here it is because I want to be the wealthiest man in the world. I want to own everything that you can think of." He dropped the egg on the ground and he became very wealthy. He was chief there and owned everything he wanted. He had many children, many wives. He had everything in great abundance.

Now that other Momori and his wife had become very, very poor. They didn't have a cent left of the £20 they had seized. It was as if there was something working against them. Whatever they tried to do, they failed in. Now they heard people saying, "Eh, there is an amazing chief. He is the wealthiest chief in the world. He has everything in great abundance." The woman said, "My husband, why don't we go to that chief and ask him to give us something?" The man said, "Ha, that is a good idea." So they started off. They reached the town and went to the chief.

It took them two days to reach the town. They couldn't get to see the chief because they were in rags. But they tried their best, pushed in ahead of others, and at last managed to greet the chief. The chief looked at them. He looked at the man. His face was familiar. He looked at the woman. Her face was familiar. Then the chief said, "I usually give strangers lodgings outside my *luiye*, but I will give these people lodgings in the house next to mine." The chief sent them to their lodgings. They stayed there till night. The chief gave them food and other gifts.

In the middle of the night the chief said that he was going to greet the strangers. He went and knocked at their door. The strangers were afraid. The chief said, "I have come to greet you, don't be afraid." They opened the door and he went in. When he was inside, the chief said to them, "What town are you from?" They told him. The chief said, "How did you come to get into the trading business?" The man said, "Two of us started in business, but my friend died long ago." The chief said, "Your friend died?" The man said, "Yes." The chief said, "How did he die?" The man said, "He had some kind of sickness. It came upon him when we reached a certain *faragbaran*, and he died there. We couldn't take him with us so we left him there." The chief said, "Let us tell some stories." They said, "Chief, but we don't know any stories." They were afraid of the chief.

The chief began, "There were once two men in this world . . ." The man said, "Yes." The chief went on, " . . . and they were great friends. One was called Gbeyekan Momori and the other was called Momori. They were such good friends that they went into business together. They made some money . . ." The man said, "Eh!" He sat down for a while. He said (to himself), "These are things that this chief actually knows about." The chief continued, "That Gbeyekan Momori and his friend Momori made £30. He told his friend to get a wife with the money. They married the same woman. Then they said, 'We are two and yet we are married to the same woman, what are we going to do about it?' Then Gbeyekan Momori said, 'Friend, I feel nothing but goodwill toward you. If you feel the same goodwill toward me, then that is fine. Now, because I feel goodwill toward you and because we have only one wife between us, I am going to give her to you. In the future we can work hard to get a wife for me.' So they did that."

No sooner had the chief said this than the man fell at his feet. He said, "You are my friend!" He shat his pants.* He said, "Eh! Are you not the one?" The chief said, "Keep quiet, don't cry." But the man and his wife were prostrate at the chief's feet, begging him for mercy. They said, "We are sorry, we are sorry, we have suffered disgrace† because of what we did to you." The chief said, "When we first met I felt nothing but goodwill toward you. I will show you that I still feel the same way toward you. In this world, if you

---

*Acute fear and anxiety are expressed figuratively in this way, not only in the narratives but in everyday discourse.
†*yarabiye* = disgrace, impoverishment.

become friends and your friend has goodwill toward you, then you must have goodwill toward him. If you have no goodwill toward him, then no matter how you conspire against him your conspiracy will fail and you will suffer disgrace because of what you tried to do to him.* It is best that people work with pure hearts. Now I will show you that just as I once felt goodwill toward you, I can again show goodwill toward you. First thing tomorrow, I will divide my country into two. You will be chief over one part, I will be chief over the other." The man was very happy to hear this. The chief went to sleep.

When the chief had gone the woman said to the man, "*M'berin*, rather than this chief giving you half of his country, why not ask him how he came to acquire all this land and wealth? Then you can become as wealthy as he is." The man said, "Ha, that is so. I will go and ask him." He went to the chief's house. He was not afraid now because the chief had cleared away the uncertainty between them.† When he reached the chief he said, "Friend, I have come to you." The chief said, "What for?" The man said, "By what means did you acquire this chieftaincy and all this wealth? You that we beat up and blinded and abandoned on the *faragbaran*. . . . how did you acquire this chieftaincy?" The man's friend said, "Friend, you know that just as I once had goodwill toward you, so I still feel the same way. At the place where you gouged out my eyes, there stands a very big cotton tree. I got the means to acquire this wealth from lying under that cotton tree. The vulture had laid six eggs. I took three of them. If you get the other three, then whatever you wish for will be given to you. When you break the egg, God will fulfill your wish. I took three of the eggs, there are three left. If you want to be a chief like me and if you want to become as wealthy as I am, then you must go and get the three eggs. Whatever you wish for when you break the egg, God will give it to you. You know that it is good to have a pure heart. If you have a pure heart, then no matter if a person conspires against you, he will suffer disgrace." Then the chief said, "Don't tell any of this to a woman."

---

*c.f. the exposition of the Kuranko theory of *hake* in chapter 1.
†The Kuranko phrase is, literally, "cleared away the darkness between them." The narrative exploits contrasts between white, pure, open, honest and dark, impure, deceitful, dishonest; these contrasts are expressed in terms of the color words, *gbe* (white) and *afinye* (black).

But when the young man, the accursed man, left, he went and
told his wife everything. He explained it all, just as his friend had
explained it. The woman said, "Well, *m'berin*, you should leave very
early in the morning." Very early the next morning the man went
to the cotton tree. When he reached the cotton tree he climbed up
and took the three eggs of the vulture. He returned to the town.
He didn't go to see anyone except his wife. He said to her, "My
companion, I have come with the eggs of the vulture." The woman
said, "Now let us go and find a remote place in the bush. We are
now chiefs." They went to a very distant and wild country. The
man took the three eggs. When they reached the place he said,
"Now what will we do with these three eggs? What will we do with
them?" His wife said, "Well, if you want these eggs to be a boon
for us, take one of them and break it on the ground, at the same
time wishing for a great town to appear there." They broke the egg
and a great town sprang up. The man said, "What will we do with
the second egg?" The woman said, "Well, you must break this second egg on the ground and wish for a great river to appear there.
People cannot live without water." The man broke the egg and the
river appeared. Then he said, "Now, what about the third egg,
what shall I do with the third egg?" The woman said, "Well, you
know that if a man marries a woman from a family that is wealthy,
then he will never want for anything. You must break the third egg
on the ground and wish that your wife's family were very wealthy."

The man's affines became wealthy and his kinsmen became impoverished. Therefore, if you show goodwill toward someone and
that person tries to deceive you, God will make him suffer disgrace
and impoverishment. When the man's affines became wealthy and
he had become poor, they took the woman away from him and he
was without a wife. Therefore, it is always best to be honest and
straightforward with your friends. If you try to deceive them, then
one day God will make you suffer impoverishment and disgrace.
All the wealthy people in the world are descended from the family
of that woman. All the poor people in the world are descended
from the family of that man.

Journeys and Bargains

Kuranko *praxis* is characterized by a search for equilibrium and adjustment between opposing forces: hunger and plenty, conflict and

unity, self-willedness and communitas. The semantic opposition between "bush" and "town," which serves as the armature in so many narratives, affords the Kuranko a metaphorical means of expressing these contrasts and working toward that equilibrium. But Kuranko thought does not emphasize categorical separations and partitions; rather, it seeks adjustment and balance and regulated flow between contrasted forces. As we saw in the last chapter, ontogenetic development and social continuity are closely linked. And, in both cases, a kind of adjustment is sought between psychophysical abilities or inclinations and social roles and imperatives.

Initiation, which the Kuranko often regard as a ritual "crossing-over," is the most important ritual means of reducing the discrepancy between biological and social dimensions of reality. In adulthood, the expression of a person's will and personality is ideally mediated by his social awareness. Initiation inculcates an abstract attitude, a social conscience. For these reasons, perhaps the most important of the preceding set of narratives is N.27, *The Origin of the Yimbe Drum*. Here, the acquisition of the *yimbe* drum and command of its "sweet" music is vital if the community is not to disband and, as the narrator puts it, "go into the bush." The link between the survival of the community and the enculturation of children through initiation is suggested by the drum itself, symbol of the initiatory passage. Moreover, both in initiatory rites and in the narrative, there is a dramatic polarization of natural and cultural domains, preceded by a blurring of the boundary between them. The hero in the narrative goes on a dangerous journey into the bush, strikes a bargain with a bush spirit, and uses extrasocial magical powers to realize a quest undertaken on behalf of his community. During the liminal phase of initiation, the neophytes undergo ordeals and receive moral and practical instruction in a makeshift house located in the bush. In both cases, the return of the voyagers to the community signifies a triumph of human will and determination over the vicissitudes and contingencies of nature. Like the neophytes, the narrative hero is a marginal person. He is referred to in the narratives as *kemine*, which is to say a young man who has been initiated but is not yet married or regarded as a fully responsible member of the community.

It must be pointed out that journeys and forays into the bush are not only metaphorically significant. Each year, Kuranko farmers must penetrate the dense forests to make new farms, and almost every day hunters and palm wine tapsters brave the real and imagined hazards of the bush. Fortitude, bravery, self-control, and decisiveness are the principal virtues inculcated during initiation, but their importance is most fully realized when men venture alone beyond the world of the village.

An unmediated relation with the bush (which on the psychological plane signified libido) may epitomize freedom, but it also signifies isolation from the moral community. This is why each person's relation with the metaphorical "wilderness" must be mediated by abilities and objects acquired in the context of social existence.[2] In one narrative, related by Kumba Doron, palm wine tapping is said to have originated when a young man dared to enter the bush which the *nyenne* owned. Up to that time the *nyenne* had simply stolen the palm wine which people tapped. The young man's audacity and bravery are rewarded when he meets a clever old woman who, in return for food, gives him the means to outsmart the *nyenne* and tap the wine. The narrative points out that it is a combination of personal fearlessness and social propriety which makes possible the subjugation of the wilderness. The hero is not only brave; he enters into a reciprocal agreement with a wise old woman. In another narrative by the same storyteller, a brave farmer ventures into the bush to make his farm despite the fact that the *nyenne* there assault and menace human beings. The *nyenne* fall upon the man and sever his head, but he uses a special medicine to put his head back on his body. The alternation of decapitation and reparation continues until the farmer has cleared a vast area of the bush and, as in the previous tale, the *nyenne* yield and abandon their ground. Like the ruse of the old woman, the magical medicine is a cultural means of conquering nature. Natural audacity alone is insufficient.

The conditionality of human freedom and power is explored in considerable depth in N.27. The initial situation is one in which creatures of the wild (hyenas) are in possession of something (a drum which makes "sweet" music) which it is imperative to bring to town. Once again a brave young man risks his life in this quest for an object of cultural value—in this instance, the initiation drum. He is aided by a marginal figure who, like the solitary woman in the story about the origins of palm wine tapping, recognizes the principle of reciprocity in a place where it is ordinarily in abeyance. That a bush spirit which habitually kills and eats people should agree to assist the hero creates an ambiguous situation. Indeed the very name of the bush spirit— *tutufingbe* ("*tutu* black white")—suggests its ambiguity. The *tutufingbe*, impressed by the hero's bravery and directness, gives him an ambiguous object: the *fele*. This fetish, which is widely used in real life, is made of twisted black and white threads. In the narrative, its ambiguity is further established by the fact that it is an object yet is able to speak. The *tutu* also provides the hero with four things which, during the final episodes of the narrative, facilitate four successive and increasingly successful disjunctions between the fleeing hero and the hyenas: the bamboo cane, which turns into an impenetrable brake; the stone, which becomes a wall; the charcoal, which creates a barrier of fire; and the egg, which becomes a lake.[3] The function of fetishes and medicines in creating appropriate discontinuities between opposing domains is clearly emphasized in the narrative. Sulimani Koroma ends his narration by saying that it explains how the use of magical medicines (*besenu*) began.

In order to clarify the ambiguities which lie at the heart of this narrative, it is necessary to refer briefly to the distinctions which the Kuranko make between sacrifice, gift-exchange, and protection. A sacrificial offering or gift is always made in the name of a spirit category or dedicated to a spirit. Sacrifice thus mediates relationships between men and ancestors, bush spirits, and God. Sacrifice implies reciprocity: in return for the respect given, welfare may be received or appeasement secured. To protect—*ka kandan*—is, by contrast, to enclose, separate, or safeguard from invasion. Protective things, *kandan li fannu,* such as the *fele* mentioned above, isolate a sociospatial category by preventing uncontrolled traffic across its boundaries. A *fele,* for instance, is placed on the threshold of a room and it will compel anyone of ill will to declare his hidden intentions if he should step across the line marked by the fetish. It is always implied that protection is appropriate against forces and beings with whom there can be no reciprocity: predatory animals, enemies, witches, sorcerers, and the more intractable of the bush spirits. Gift-giving is quite different, and characterizes relationships between neighbors, kinsmen, and friends. Gift-exchange is unlike protection because it promotes contact, dialogue, and reciprocity; it may also be contrasted with sacrifice where communications are always indirect.

Gifts, fetishes, and things offered in sacrifice are all means of regulating or mediating the relationship of self/other. There are, however, some relationships where it is not clear which response is appropriate—exchange, protection, or propitiation. Relationships between man and *nyenne* are ambiguous in this sense. One hears of men and women who have seen and communicated with *nyenne,* who have made pacts with them, or been possessed by them. The authority of cult masters and some diviners is allegedly derived from an alliance with a bush spirit. It is also true that the Kuranko make sacrifices to appease *nyenne* in the forests around farm sites. But in every case, transactions between people and *nyenne* are problematical. First, *nyenne* are capricious and best avoided by most prudent people. Second, in return for favors given, a *nyenne* usually demands the life of a son or daughter. *Nyenne* are thus ambiguous, because while they are generally inimical to the social order, they possess powers which may be tapped by special individuals and used for the social good. The powers of cult masters are derived from their skills in communicating with bush spirits, as well as from their command of dangerous medicines. The cult system provides opportunities for exceptional individuals to participate in the moral and legal administration of the community. Cult masters achieve their positions of power by dint of intelligence, moral strength, boldness, and force of personality. By contrast, chiefs and their councils of elders draw their authority from secular and determinate sources: age, birth, and genealogy. Nevertheless, chiefs depend on fetishes and medicines to increase *miran* and to bolster their capabilities, and they also rely upon the cults when secular powers prove inefficacious. Justice results from a complementarity and adjustment between secular and sacerdotal powers. The complementarity of chiefs and cult masters reflects, moreover, the complementarity and equilibrium which is sought between socially determined roles and indeterminate personal abilities. The relationship between people and *nyenne* is thus to some extent a projection of the relationship between social roles and "natural" abilities, and narratives in which relationships between people and *nyenne* are central may be regarded as allegorical accounts of the interplay between social and personal imperatives.

That marginal beings and objects (*nyenne* and fetishes), like personal talents (intelligence and boldness), are regarded ambivalently is made clear in N.27. The *tutufingbe* and the *fele* combine black and white elements. In the case of the *fele,* the Kuranko observe that the white thread symbolizes "self" or "person"; the black thread symbolizes "other," by implication "nonperson." More generally, white stands for openheartedness, honesty, and reciprocity, while black stands for deceit, dissimulation, and the absence of reciprocity. The problem arises, therefore, of how the young man should regard the *tutufingbe* and the fetish: as persons, like himself, with whom promises must be kept, or as alien creatures or things with whom there is no contractual obligation at all.

But N.27 is not simply about the ambiguous relationships between people and *nyenne.* It is also an allegory of initiation. The hero's relationship with his mother is contrasted with his relationships with the *tutufingbe,* the *fele,* and the hyena who assumes human form. The narrative suggests that growing up involves ceasing to be dependent upon one's mother's care and protection and accepting one's obligations in the outside world. From another point of view, the narrative discusses the relation of personal freedom and social necessity. The young adventurer, whose age and status frees him to some extent from social responsibilities, gambles his life on fortuitous encounters in order to attain a normally impossible goal. He is fatalistic in his attitude, and chooses to rely upon luck and his own boldness in obtaining the *yimbe* drum from the village of the hyenas. His journey is along a path which does not converge with others in any familiar social world. He goes against what is customarily expectable, possible, and even desirable. The narrative thus mixes the calculable and the accidental. It creates a synthesis of the quest for individual choice in a world of ordained routines and the necessity of commitment to a world of interdependent roles. In his essay on the adventure, Georg Simmel notes that the adventure enables a synthesis to be reached between chance and necessity, the "accidentally external and the internally necessary," between activity and passivity, and "between what we conquer and what is given to us" (1959:247, 248).

The problem of the use of extraordinary powers brings us to a third aspect of this narrative. As we have already remarked, the initial situation is ambiguous. The young hero makes a bargain (a *social* contract) with a being which is ordinarily excluded from the human world and belongs to the domain of the wild. By playing up the ambiguity and dramatizing the liminal setting in which the pact with the *tutu* is made, the narrator creates interest and suspense. The listener is confronted with a problem to be solved. His attention is directed to the principle of reciprocity, its field of application, and the implications of repudiating it. As in N.28, the narrative enjoins us to keep promises, honor bargains, and show gratitude by returning favors given. And in every case, it is emphasized that extraordinary powers, although derived from the realm of the extrahuman, must be used for the social good and not for personal advantage. In other words, there should be a reciprocity established between personal powers and the social weal. This point is best made by comparing N.27 with N.28, *The Abuse of the Killing Word.*

N.28 begins with a young hero who decides to risk more than his companies are prepared to risk in seeking bride-wealth with which to marry. He embarks upon an arduous and dangerous journey into the bush in search of game. As in N.27, the hero's quest (which, incidentally, implies a transition from bachelorhood to marriage) can only be fulfilled if he promises to honor a bargain made with a marginal figure and use with discretion the fetish given to him. The "killing word," *nyemakara,* is probably cognate with the Malinke *nyamakala* (Kuranko *nyemakale*), the term which describes the marginal "caste" groups: the *jelis* and *finas*. While the word *kala* means "knot of grass," *nyama* refers to detritus, rubbish, dung, dead leaves, and sweepings from a house, as well as suggesting perhaps "life energy" (*nie*), that is to say "unembodied power" (c.f. Paulme, 1973b:90–91). Many Kuranko fetishes used in cursing are indeed made from tufts of grass or thatch from house roofs, possibly because of the metaphorical connotations of grass and paths; they allude to the principle of reciprocity, which cursing, of course, denies.

Like the *fele* in N.27, the fetish in N.28 is ambiguous. It signifies the problematic interface between socially controlled and indeterminate powers. It provides the occasion, moreover, for focusing attention on the ethical ambiguity of boldness. In the stories about the origins of palm wine tapping and of farming referred to earlier, the audacity and courage of the young men is approved since social benefits accrue from their actions. But in N.27 and N.28 the heroes are overbold. Because of their hubris they forfeit the right to live in human society. However, the hero in N.27 is given a second chance to make good his failure to honor the bargain which he made with the *tutufingbe.* By sacrificing the two bulls to the *fele* in return for the favors received from it, the young man reenters the moral world and his life is spared. Not so the hero in N.28. He receives a powerful fetish from an old woman, and is thereby able to return to his village and marry. At this point in the narrative the disjunction between the domains of bush and town is as it should be. The man kills only *animals,* at the *perimeter* of the town, and he *shares* the meat among the townspeople. But when the old woman requests the return of her fetish, the young man runs wild and abuses the powers which have been placed in his hands for a *social* purpose — to marry and rejoin the community. He behaves without moral scruple, and kills his benefactress, his age-mates, his fellow villagers, and his parents-in-law. At this moment of impasse, the hero having repudiated all reciprocities, God intervenes. Disguised as an attractive young woman, God steals the power of the killing word from the hero, whose hubris is now divinely punished by death.

Discontinuities are thus reestablished, first between the moral world of the community and the world of the wild, and second between human and divine realms. These disjunctions, the first on the "horizontal" plane and the second on the "vertical," serve to moderate or temper powers whose ambiguity stems from the fact that they are as contributory as they are inimical to the social order. Because the paranoid amok of the young man implies a dissolution of the boundary between self and other, his death restores a further balance to the social world. But in every case, the narrator shows that the control of extraordinary powers, whether innate (as cleverness is assumed to be), innate and acquired (like *miran*), or acquired (like fetishes and medicines), depends upon individual choices, and these judgments must reflect a striving for harmony between personal and social imperatives. In the Kuranko view, there is no excuse for wrong choices; "no sacrifice can avert (cut) one's fate" (*latege saraka saa*).

The crucial social imperative is, of course, reciprocity. One must respect the life and contribute to the welfare of others without ulterior motives. One must keep promises, be trustworthy, and honor bargains. The opposite of a bargain is a conspiracy, which in Kuranko terms is a "bargain made against someone." Promises, bargains, contracts, and agreements are associated with the moral world of the village, while conspiracies are associated with the bush. Thus, dreams and omens of conspiracy include such visions as floundering in deep water, kola nuts within the husk, being lost in deep forest, a loaded gun which is not discharged, swimming halfway across a swollen river and being forced to return to where one began, being bogged down in mud or swampland. These references help us understand why narratives concerned with problems or ambiguities of reciprocity are usually set in the no-man's-land midway between bush and town.

The recognition of reciprocity or the fulfillment of a bargain implies that full *social* status has been attained, and this is often depicted in the narratives by the miraculous creation of a town in the midst of a wilderness. For example, in an unpublished narrative by Teina Kuyate on the origins of ingratitude, a fictitious bird whose name is a pun on "word" (*kuma*) cures a leper and provides him with all the attributes of full social existence: a cleared space in the bush, a town filled with people, clothes, a house, and a wife and child. In return for the bird's magnanimity, Mande Braima promises to take care of the bird's eggs while it goes away on a journey. The word *karifa* means trust, care, safekeeping, custody, and connotes a close relationship, as among kinsmen who foster their children with one another. This narrative plays up the same ambiguity which obtains in N.27 and N.28. Is Mande Braima morally bound to keep his word with a creature of the wild? Although a mere bird, the *kuma*'s name as well as its generosity of spirit places it within the world of human society. And the bird sagely predicts the ingratitude of man, repeating the phrase *a aye la firana n de la,* "he will wipe his eyes of me" (i.e. he will prove ungrateful). In another version of the narrative, told by Sumayila Kargbo of Firawa, the contrast between the man's original state (wild) and the bird's deserved status (social) is made by alternating references to a great cotton tree in the bush, under which the man is discovered, and a cotton tree in the town, in whose branches the bird leaves its eggs. In both these versions, however, Mande Braima chooses to regard the satisfaction of a whim of his own child as more important than the physical survival of the bird's young, even though it was the bird which enabled him to have a child in the first place: when his child whimpers for a bird's egg to eat, Mande Braima has little hesitation in giving the child the eggs of the magical bird. Mande Braima makes a wrong choice. He proves incapable of keeping a promise and undeserving of trust; he is returned to his previous condition—a miserable, disease-ridden exile from human society. In these particular stories the passage from the moral to the physical dimension is facilitated by the semantic ambiguity of the concept *kendeye,* which refers to both social propriety *and* physical well-being. Thus, disease is a metaphor for moral baseness and social worthlessness.

Friends and Brothers

Two principles emerge from the set of narratives in this chapter. First, reciprocity must never be taken for granted; it must be continued and extended through deliberate acts of magnanimity and altruism. Reciprocity is not to be regarded as a self-perpetuating *system;* it is something created and maintained by conscious endeavor and by choice.

Second, those in possession of extraordinary powers must choose to balance the use of those powers between personal advantage and social benefit. The adjustment of individual dispositions and the system of social positions depends, again, on individual choices and judgments. These two principles are exemplified by N.29, *The Three Brothers and the Fetish Called "Repayment of Kindness."*

This narrative first establishes an ambiguous situation. Three brothers, who have *different mothers*,[4] receive *equal parts* of their father's legacy. By playing up the equality of endowment among the three brothers, the narrator provides a background for later bringing into relief the moral distinctions among them. The crucial moral distinction is one between the elder brother's altruism and the younger brothers' self-interest. The elder brother gives away his share of the legacy in order to save the lives of a dog, a cat, and a fledgling vulture. The initial episodes of the narrative establish an ethical dilemma: are the dog, the cat, and the vulture to be regarded as mere animals and thus killed without scruple, or are they to be respected as persons? The younger brothers act on the former assumption, while the elder brother takes the view that these creatures are to be treated like people. To dramatize the problem of choice, the narrator makes use of the ambiguous status of these creatures. The dog and the cat are classified as *sotemasowi* ("town-in-animals"), by contrast with "wild animals" (*firarosowi*, lit. "bush-in-animals"). They are thus midway between the world of people and the domain of animals. In the narrative, they invade the human domain entirely, by entering the house. The dog takes food from the younger brothers' children, and the cat takes food from the second brother's wife. The vulture (*duwe*), which is considered to be a mediator between man and the ancestors, also loses its intermediate status. The vulture fledgling falls from the tree into the village. The younger brothers choose to deny human status to the animals; they seek to kill them. The elder brother chooses to incorporate the animals in the social order; he saves the lives of the dog and the cat, and he raises the vulture as if it were his own child. Thus, while the younger brothers attempt to maintain a rigid division between humanity and animality, the elder brother's attitude is more flexible and generous. He acts magnanimously, and treats the animals as persons. Later in the narrative the animals reciprocate his kindness, and the elder brother's superior moral qualities are rewarded.

Unlike the protagonists in N.27 and N.28, the hero in this narrative does not abuse the extraordinary powers of the fetish which comes into his possession. His self-restraint is contrasted with his wife's heedlessness. She is easily persuaded to use the red taffeta fetish to secure a trivial advantage over her *numorgo*. As a result, the fetish is stolen from her and the second brother uses it to ruin his elder brother and to usurp his wealth and position. However, the elder brother remains the rightful owner of the fetish because it was a gift from the vultures in repayment for his kindness to the fledgling bird, and because he does not misuse its powers. Toward the close of the narrative the cat and dog intercede to get back the fetish for the elder brother. The wife is killed for her treachery, and the hero is restored to the high office for which his exemplary behavior has qualified him. Whereas the narrative begins by playing down the distinctions among the three brothers, it concludes by playing up the moral contrast between the self-seeking behavior of the younger brothers and the magnanimity of the elder brother. As in other narratives, particularly those in chapter 4, the formal patterning of events leads to a congruity between superior moral qualities and senior social positions. This congruity is achieved by first nullifying, then polarizing, and finally crossing over elements which refer both to psychophysical attributes and to social positions.

N.29 emphasizes that reciprocity is created and maintained by generous and openhearted actions. Moreover, it is suggested that one should strive to bring outsiders into the ambit of the moral community, rather than reject them as one would reject mere animals. Yet the narrative does not lay down unequivocal or ideal prescriptions; it deals with some of the ethical problems associated with reciprocity *in practice*. These problems center on the question of how one should treat persons with whom there is simultaneously a relationship of identity and difference. Like the *nyenne* in N.27 and N.28, the domestic animals in N.29 are associated with the human world at the same time as they are, in a classificatory sense, divided from it. The *nyenne*, the dog, the cat, and the vulture are all ambiguously situated. They appear in the narratives as figurative "markers" of areas of uncertainty in interpersonal relationships. This uncertainty usually reflects a problem of choosing between different modes of reciprocity. For example, kinship (*nakelinyorgoye*, lit. "mother-one-relationship") connotes mutuality and amity. But residential separation may, in practice, reduce the sense of mutual obligation among kinsmen. The Kuranko acknowledge that genealogically distant kin (and even strangers) who live together may feel a greater sense of "oneness" or kinship than genealogically close kin who live apart. In other words, descent and kinship identifications are not always congruent with residential ties. One of the most common reasons for the dispersal of kin is the latent antagonism and rivalry among nonuterine brothers. The antagonistic relationship among nonuterine brothers, which is known as *fadenye*, is said to reflect the social and emotional differences among their mothers. *Fadennu* (lit. "father's sons") are thus one in terms of common descent yet different in terms of matrifiliation. Since maternal ties have no jural implications, the "problem" of *fadenye* springs from a contradiction between positive jural ties and negative emotional bonds. Thus, *fadennu* are, in theory, obliged to support and help one another as kinsmen, yet in practice they tend to avoid one another and regard any transactions as matters of credit and debt rather than as expressions of goodwill.

It is understood that the three brothers in N.29 are nonuterine brothers, and, as in N.1 (*The Three Sons*), the moral distinctions among the brothers reflect the different moral qualities of their mothers. In my view, *fadenye* is an appropriate image in these narratives concerned with ambiguities in reciprocity because the relationship among nonuterine brothers, unlike the relationship among real brothers, is intrinsically ambiguous. As we have seen, this ambiguity reflects a conflict between jural identifications and emotional ties. The first two narratives in this chapter (N.27 and N.28) deal with problems and ambiguities in reciprocity by focusing upon relationships between men and *nyenne* and between men and birds with human qualities. N.29 is transitional to another group of narratives which deal with problems and ambiguities in reciprocity by focusing upon relationships between friends. Like the relationship among *fadennu*, which provides the image in N.29, the relationship between friends is always characterized by a contrast between jural and emotional ties. But friendship (*dienaye*) is the exact opposite of *fadenye*, despite the fact that both relationships imply the same kind of ambiguity.

	Structure	Sentiment
Friendship	No jural obligations or identifications	Intense emotional bonds and a sense of oneness
Fadenye	Jural obligations and identifications as members of the same descent group	Antagonism and rivalry

The ambiguity of friendship springs from the fact that friendships are always based upon a mutual choice to become one, yet this emotional aspect of the relationship must be adjusted to socially given and inescapable differences of age, sex, clan, and estate. As Robert Brain has observed, there is an element of strain and fragility in all friendships (1977:11), and the mixture of aggression and affection in joking-play among friends in Kuranko society testifies to this. Any relationship which includes adventitious, optional, and temperamental elements, yet at the same time is based upon the principle of reciprocity, is bound to be problematical. It is not surprising, therefore, that the making and breaking of friendship is a recurring structural frame in African folktales. Dundes takes the view that the violations of contracts between friends in the folktales provide "an outlet for protest against the binding nature of interpersonal obligations of the kind imposed by formal or quasi-formal institutional friendship pacts" (1971:180). However, this explanation has limited utility. Many societies, including the Kuranko, do not institutionalize friendship pacts in any formal or quasi-formal way. Nor can we assume that every Kuranko individual finds onerous and binding the various pacts and promises that may be made between friends. In my opinion, the "problem" of friendship ties is a direct consequence of the indeterminate nature of friendship itself. Like kinship, it contains elements of reciprocal obligation, but it also includes the nonobligatory, ad hoc elements which characterize the morally neutral relationships between strangers. It is a domain of choice, a "grey area," and it provides, therefore, a means of bringing into discussion some of the problems of reciprocity in relationships which lie at the edges of the social order. This discussion also touches upon the deeper dialectic of necessity and freedom, and on the indeterminate relationship between structure and sentiment. The surface patterning of events in the friendship narratives adumbrate deeper existential concerns.

N.30 is at once reminiscent of those narratives, discussed in the previous chapter, whose theme is prevented marriages. But this narrative enlarges upon the value of cleverness. Here, as elsewhere, Keti Ferenke emphasizes the importance of cleverness, but he points out that cleverness must be used to attain *social* goals, and that it should benefit others to the same extent that it gains advantages for oneself. Thus, in N.30 cleverness is the means by which the hero gets a wife, first for himself and later for his friend. His choices imply a correct adjustment of personal freedom (afforded by his extraordinary talents) and social necessity (signified by his marriage, and by his decision to help his friend find a wife).

N.31 is related to N.30 in the same way that N.28 is related to N.27. In both N.31 (*The Two Friends and the Sequestered Woman*) and N.28 (*The Abuse of the Killing Word*) there are antiheroes. Incorrect moral judgments are made, and the disastrous consequences bring retrospectively into relief the moral values which have been repudiated. The young protagonist in N.28 reneges on his promise to the old woman, and he uses the fetish to kill people in his own community. In N.31, Momori disregards utterly the magnanimity of his friend. He blinds and abandons him in the wilderness, and when much later he is helped once more by the generous-hearted Gbeyekan Momori,[5] he impulsively and imprudently steals the three remaining magical eggs and uses them for selfish gain. In both these narratives, the protagonists must be regarded as signifying the social order. By denying their own moral nature, they die. This also implies that when reciprocity is denied within the social order, society dies.

We must take the metaphor of self as society quite literally if we are to understand the true import of these narratives. The fictional figures are not autonomous individuals. Rather, they provide insight into and represent aspects of *praxis* in a universe which admits no definite boundaries between self (*personne morale*) and society. This perspective, which I believe is faithful to the implicit Kuranko world view, helps us understand another aspect of N.31. The two Momoris are not just different people; they express different dimensions of the self. At the beginning of the narrative the unity of the two figures is played up. They have the same name, they are involved in business together, and they are married to the same woman. The fact that they are close friends confirms the image of oneness. As the narrative proceeds, there is a gradual polarization of positive qualities such as goodwill and openheartedness on the one hand, and negative qualities such as ingratitude and selfishness on the other. The events and figures in the narrative are simply the concrete means by which these polarizations and transformations are made. Thus Momori's final impoverishment and disgrace signify the extirpation of selfishness from the moral order, while Gbeyekan Momori's success and good fortune signify the coalescence of superior moral qualities and a high social position. At the same time, Keti Ferenke insists upon the need for harmony between public and private aspects of self or society. Gbeyekan Momori has integrity; his inner motives and outward actions are consonant. The other Momori is deceitful; he disguises his true intentions, or pretends one purpose while acting in terms of another. Straightforwardness must be cultivated not only in relationships with others, but also in relation to oneself. As we have seen, the Kuranko emphasize that there must be harmony between intentions and actions, both between people and within oneself. If the narratives make use of concrete events and inter-personal relationships it is often because fiction cannot express directly the moral abstractions and fields of interaction which are its main con-cern. The simplicity of events, settings, and characterizations in these narratives should not be taken as evidence of simplistic purposes, for they are essays in moral philosophy.

Friendship is a recurrent motif in Kuranko narratives, although it is clearly more important to some storytellers (notably Keti Ferenke) than to others. The importance of friendship as a narrative motif may reflect its ambiguity. First, friendship connotes oneness, but it can never oblit-erate entirely the differences of sex, age, estate, and community which it strives to transcend. Second, friendship is closely connected to the fictional motif of the double; it refers simultaneously to relationships between different people and to the relationship between individual conscience and action. Third, friendship implies a morality which is not wholly dictated by the established conventions of the social order; more than any other relationship it is obviously made and unmade by indi-vidual choice. As a domain of choice and indeterminancy, friendship provides a narrative means of bringing into discussion some of the or-dinarily undiscussed modes of human action. In each of the friendship narratives a crisis situation compels the listener to share in discussing and evaluating alternative courses of action. The self-evident, "natural," and orthodox character of the social world is destroyed (Bourdieu, 1977:169). The laughter which these often bizarre crises evoke may reflect, according to this view, the anxiety of being surprised by one's own freedom and confronted by one's own responsibility for the world.

7 *Men and Women*

Occasionally in Koinadugu district one hears rumors of a marvelous town somewhere in the hazy savanna regions to the northeast and known as Musudugu—town or place of women. No men live there, and the women of the town are famed for their skills in divination, curing, and sorcery. Some say that the medicines the women possess are the powerful *korte* and anti-*korte* medicines, ordinarily controlled and used by men. Kola traders and seekers bring reports of miracles accomplished and wealth bestowed, but the town is built of hearsay and fantasy, and no one can confirm that it is actually the mapped Malinke town of Mousadougou which lies in the Konyor country at the edge of the forests on the border between Ivory Coast and Liberia.

References to a town of women occur in several Kuranko narratives, and, like the similarly fabulous Town of Women in Nupe lore (Nadel, 1964:265), it is a place at the edge of the known world or is said to have existed only in the distant past. Like the chimeras and monsters with which the European imagination once populated the margins of the charted world, Musudugu suggests an inverted social order lying beyond certainty. In the narratives, journeys to and from such a place by male heroes are allegories of relationships between the sexes, and they open up inquiry into some of the most crucial moral issues of Kuranko social life.

That the Kuranko fantasize a town inhabited and ruled by women may indicate something of the ambivalence of men's attitudes toward women. I have already referred to a paradox in Kuranko thought which, while stressing male hegemony in both politico-jural and domestic domains, allows that the influence of women pervades every sphere of social action, shaping the personalities and destinies of children, modulating the quality of affinal relationships, and mediating the flow of blessings between individuals and their patrilineal ancestors. This contrast between a dogma of male control and an "unofficial" admission of the actual importance of female influence means that the status of women is ambiguous. First, although the Kuranko ideology of procreation denies that the mother contributes anything to the physical formation of the child, it is acknowledged that the social and personal fate of the child is "in its mother's hands." Second, although the social order is the province of men, it is only through women that it can be perpetuated. This is illustrated by the fact that the ideology of patrilineal descent accommodates a vocabulary in which the ethos of kinship is expressed entirely in terms of motherhood (*na keliye*, "mother oneness"). Third, women's roles are intermediary. The Kuranko say, for instance, that the relationship between brothers-in-law "goes through the sister." Likewise, a person's relationships with his matrikin "go through the mother." The mother is also the most important intermediary between a person and his or her patrilineal ancestors, and in misfortune and fortune alike it is the mother who is held responsible. A person's relationships with his or her half siblings are also mediated by the mother, and the quality of these relationships is thought to be a direct reflection of the quality of the relationships among co-wives. The central role of the mother is nicely shown by the assertion that, in the event of a division of loyalties to a wife and to a mother, a man will always take his mother's side.[1] Indeed, the conventional phrasing of the mother's curse makes clear the priority of natal over conjugal attachments. Thus, if a man neglected his mother in preference for his wife, the mother could curse her son as follows:

> If I did not labor to bring you into the world, and if you did not sleep in my womb, and if it was not I who cleaned up your shit and did everything for you, then ignore my words, but if it was I who labored to bring you into the world, and if you slept in my womb and I cared for you and did everything for you, and you have now forsaken me for a wife, then may God prevent you from prospering, may you suffer, and may your half brothers deride you.

In three of the four versions of the narrative *Mande Fabori and the Animals* (N.34), which I will discuss in detail presently, it is the hunter's mother who saves him from the snares of a female shape-shifter. This theme is reminiscent of one informant's remark that "a man should trust no one, but he should trust his mother more than any other woman."

Clearly, the intermediary roles of women do not imply complete passivity. Nor are women to be considered subservient or entirely inferior in status to men. The active role of the mother in child-rearing, and the active influence of the sister over her brother may be contrasted with the submissive role of the wife and the political marginality of women in the community. Yet even here, at the level of village organization, women have real powers, individually as herbalists and fetish-makers, and collectively in the activities of the women's cults. The narratives dramatize the active aspects of womanhood. The image of the compliant, submissive, dutiful wife does not occur in the *tilei*. The narratives also polarize the negative and positive elements of female power, so that the figure of the wanton or treacherous woman which appears in some of the narratives can be contrasted with the heroine in others who, with magical or intellectual resourcefulness, saves the hero's life, rescues him from disgrace or impoverishment, or brings compassion and love to a rule-bound world. As with the *kemine* (initiated young man) and the youngest son (heroes in other narratives), the powers of the fictional heroines are ambiguous. The narratives can thus propose problems of choosing between alternative courses of action. They occasion discourse on the problem of achieving a balance between the use of extraordinary abilities for personal ends and for the general good.

Another aspect of female ambiguity arises from the fact that women retain emotional and social attachments to their natal groups which may conflict with marital obligations. Young wives often have to reconcile conflicting imperatives: the desire for security, which she finds among her own kin, and her commitment to her children; the desire for love and affection, which she may find among her age-mates or with a lover, and her conjugal duties. The intermediary role of women, considered together with the divided loyalties and ambivalent attitudes which many Kuranko women experience, may account for the fact that women are characterized as indeterminate. They are popularly thought to be untrustworthy, temperamental, weak-willed, refractory, and capricious. It could also be argued that men project their awareness of the ambiguous status of women in beliefs that women are somehow freer to choose than men, that they are less constrained by social conscience or external rules.[2]

Kuranko men advance the view that women instigate adulterous affairs; men are the seduced, not the seducers. Women tend to be blamed, and to take the blame, for misfortunes within the family. In other words, women make choices, but usually make the wrong choices. It is important, however, to note that while some men attribute *actively* malevolent or improper motives to women, others prefer the view that women are simply the passive victims of their own unrestrained emotionality. Women allegedly allow themselves to be easily drawn by passing fancies and emotional persuasions. But in either case, the male view is that women are naturally unreliable. This view finds its most common expression in concerns about women's sexuality. Wanton, illicit, and clandestine sexual behavior is regarded as inimical to the social order. Only procreative sexuality is compatible with maintaining goodwill among men and with ensuring the continuity of each lineage. Men are so concerned that women devote themselves to childbearing and child-rearing that they tend to view shared sexual pleasure in marriage as of little account. It may also be recalled that one of the key purposes of the symbolic enactments during male initiations is to make it possible for men to "give birth to" male children and to "mold" them into men without the intervention of women.

Thus, from the men's point of view, procreative sex is proper, recreative sex is to be censured. This attitude may reflect the fact that procreation is socially determined, while love affairs are based on individual choices and fortuitous encounters. In this sense, love is like friendship, and the same word — *kene* — may be used of both. It is probably also true that it is because marriages are made and controlled by men that men hold the opinion that love affairs are always instigated by women and that the negative consequences of adultery can be blamed on women. Love, like all strong emotions, is difficult to control, and its course is unpredictable. Men, it is said, have greater capacities for self-control, and therefore sexual love is associated more with women than with men. Many women accept these views and even celebrate them. The inflexibility and gravity of men is ridiculed, and the ease with which men can be distracted and seduced is often remarked. Domestic recalcitrance, deception, and clandestine love affairs afford many women the means of outwitting and ridiculing the men who endeavor to control and limit them. These themes are readily apparent in the critical remarks which women informants make about men (Jackson, 1977b:102), and the same themes occur in many of the narratives which women tell. Sinkari Yegbe once remarked to me that although there are no set stories for men or for women, "women like stories which are about the jealousy of men." This is because, "in our ancestors' day, men began to control women, and we have no way of changing this, so we speak our minds in stories." Among the Mende, too, women relate tales which are mostly about relations between husband and wife or between co-wives, an indication of the anxiety which surrounds these "pivotal relationships" (Kilson, 1961).

The Kuranko concern with problems associated with relationships between men and women is evident in the fact that most court and moot hearings are classed as *musu ko kele* ("woman palaver"), and is further demonstrated by the frequency with which these problems occur as motifs in the narratives. Nevertheless, while the narratives are in one sense means of bringing into discussion some of the problems in male-female relationships, they are in a deeper sense explorations of the dialectic of necessity and choice, structure and sentiment, personal inclination and social obligation. An adjustment or complementarity is sought, not just at the literal level, between men and women in the quotidian world, but between alternative modes of action which they exemplify. The narratives tend to establish a "euhemerization of the boundaries" between the sexes, to use Bourdieu's phrase; they do not work toward a hierarchicization of roles. The narratives seek to accommodate rather than expunge those elements such as love, compassion, sympathy, and choice which in real life often constitute a kind of shadow vocabulary. If we succeed in discerning a balance achieved between external rules and personal persuasions, this will be evidence of the allegorical dimension of the narratives, which, for a people without any formal language or tradition of abstract ethical inquiry, make interpersonal relationships serve as means of working out abstract resolutions and harmonies.

N.32: *The Story of Na Nyale*

Narrated by Kenya Fina Marah. Recorded at Kondembaia, March 1970.

Once there was a very jealous chief. No man could reach his wives. So the wives decided upon a ruse. They made several large raffia baskets and tied ropes to them. Then they hung them from the walls of the house. Whenever they made ready to go to the farm, each wife would put her lover in one of those raffia baskets. She would bind up the mouth of the basket and hang it on the wall. The women also prepared food and put food in the baskets. Then they would go off to the farm to do the weeding. In the evening they would return to town with their lovers.

This went on for some time. Then one day one of the wives, who was called Na Nyale, decided to leave her lover behind in the farmhouse because he was too heavy to carry. The wives did not know that the chief was going to visit them that day. Na Nyale had killed a chicken and prepared it well and left it for her lover. All the other wives took their lovers in the raffia baskets to the place where they were going to be weeding that day. But Na Nyale left her lover in the farmhouse.

No sooner had the woman left the farmhouse than the chief arrived. As he entered the house he saw that big basket hanging there. He touched it and said, "Eh, these women are amazing. What have they got in this huge basket? I am going to have a look inside." When the chief said that he was going to look inside it, the basket started shaking, shaking, shaking. He said, "Eh, the basket is shaking! I must look into this." The basket shook twice. Then the chief took his machete and cut the rope. When the rope was cut, the basket fell down—*din*. The basket said, "Mm hmm." The basket hummed. The chief said, "Ah! So the basket can speak. I am going to open it this very day and see what is inside it." He took a knife and cut the rope from around the mouth of the basket. And who did he see? Fara Mara. Then the chief said, "Who is in this basket?" The man said, "I am." The chief said, "Who are you?" "I am Fara Mara," said the man. Then the chief said, "What did you come here to do?" The man said, "God has destined that this happen." The chief said, "Well, God has indeed destined that something happen between us today. Get out so that I may kill you." The man said, "Oh, chief, why don't you just fine me. Whatever the amount, I will pay it." The chief said, "No, I must kill you." Fara Mara got out and the chief grabbed him. He put one foot on Fara Mara's legs, put the other foot on his hands. He took out his little knife and cut Fara Mara's throat. When his throat was slit, Fara Mara's blood splashed onto a cassava plant. The blood splashed over the leaves. The cassava leaf then changed into a little Senegalese fire finch (*tintingburuwe*). The fire finch flew to the part of the farm where the women were weeding to tell them what had happened. It found that the women had partitioned the area. He stood a little way in front of Na Nyale, whose lover had been killed. He stood there and sang:

Na Nyale, oh Na Nyale, Na Nyale, oh Na Nyale
Ni i wara sole to mansa, ni i wara sole to mansa
Wara Kemine ye m'bi yo, oh Na Nyale

(Na Nyale, oh Na Nyale . . .
If you have left the basket, then the chief . . .
. . . has seen a man today, oh Na Nyale)

Then Na Nyale said, "Nnn, my companions, the bird is crying. I
am not going to finish weeding my piece of ground. I am gone, I
am gone, oh. The bird is saying something to us." The others said,
"All right, go. We will see you later." She hurried quickly down the
hill and found herself at the farmhouse. But what did she see? She
saw the basket on the floor, all the ropes cut from its mouth. Then
she saw the chief and asked, "Chief, what happened here?" The
chief said, "Whose basket was that?" The woman said, "Mine." The
chief said, "Are you the owner of it?" She said, "Yes." The chief
said, "Even of what was in it." The woman said, "Yes. But there is
no need to be afraid. What did you do with it?" The chief said,
"Well, I have not left any man in my farmhouse. If I had found a
man in the basket with the bones of a chicken, a pan with traces of
palm oil on it, then it means that the food he eats is sweeter than
the food I eat.* And I killed him." The woman said, "After you
killed him, what did you do with him?" The chief said, "After I
killed him I burnt him and threw the ashes into the river." The
woman said, "Into which river?" The chief said, "The Seli."

Then the woman started following the river downstream. But
first she went to the town and got some money. She said, "Whatever befalls, if I do not see this man today I will not rest. I must
find him." For two years she followed the river. She said that she
had to find her lover. Wherever she stopped she would find palm
birds [*legenu*] in their nests. She would tell the birds to be quiet,
that love is in the air and love is on the ground, and is under the
water. She would say, "I am searching for my lover."

I ya l moina, Fara Mara, i ya l moina? Dondo
I ya l moi, dondo? I ya saya soron n'de le fe
Dondooooo. Don

(Do you hear me, Fara Mara, do you hear me? All is quiet

---

*The circumlocution is intended to convey the idea that women prepare the best food for
their lovers.

Do you hear me, quietness? You died because of me
All is quiet. Quiet)

She heard nothing except her own voice. She would continue on
her way. Wherever she stopped she sang the same song by the
riverside. For two years she followed the river, searching for her
lover.

Then, all the living things of the river met together and said,
"The man who was killed and burnt and whose ashes were thrown
into the river . . . whoever ate some should bring it forth now.
There is someone in search of him, so desperate that she cannot
rest. All those who ate the bones should regurgitate them. All
those who ate the flesh should regurgitate it. All those who ate the
eyes should regurgitate them. And we should put all these parts
together and make the man as he was." Then everyone brought
forth the different parts. All those who could join the bones together came and joined them. All those who could put the flesh on
the bones came and did so. They put all the parts together. Then
they asked who had taken the life [nie]. The one who had taken the
life said, "I took the life." They said, "Well, go and get it." He went
for the life. They told him to put the life back in the body. He did
so.

Then they told the man that someone was looking for him and
that the person was desperate to find him. At that moment Na
Nyale arrived at that spot. That place was so fear-inspiring that no
one would ever venture there. But, so desperate was this woman
that she did not care. She stood there. She found the palm birds
chattering. It was very dense forest. She scattered some coins in
the forest and said, "All you bush spirits [nyenne] who live here,
this is my gift to you. I am looking for someone, the person they
killed on account of me. If I do not find him I prefer to die by this
river. I will never rest content." She put some coins along the
riverbank and said, "All living things, in the water and on the land,
listen to me." Quietness was everywhere. She stood there and sang
[as above]. The man sang in reply:

Ah, n'de Fara Mara; n'ya saya keni i le l le fe dondo

(Ah, I am Fara Mara. I preferred death because of you. All is
quiet)

Then she jumped into the water—*gbogbon*. She said, "He is here.
No person knows my song but Fara Mara. He must be here." She
leaped into the water. And she saw Fara Mara. Those who dwelt
under the water looked after them for two years. They were well-
fed and cared for. In the third year they were given a xylophonist
(*bal'fole*, i.e. a *jeliba*). A horse was given to the lover, and the
woman was given two boxes of dresses. Then they were taken to
the surface. The water creatures said, "Well, we have to tell you
that when you return you should immediately find the man who
killed you and take your revenge. If you fail to do this, we will kill
you. When you return you should ask for him and spend a night
lodged with him. The next morning, tell him you want to dance.
Invite him to dance with you. Sit on your horse and he will sit on
his. As you dance, take your sword and cut off his head, thus paying him back in his own kind.* By cutting off his head you will
satisfy us." The man and the woman said, "All right," and they set
off.

In every town they reached they asked, "Is that chief still there?"
The people would say, "What chief?" "The chief that killed a man
that year, the man who was hidden in a raffia basket on the farm."
Then the people would say, "He is there." That is what they did
until they reached the town where the chief lived. But they could
not recognize the *luiye*. They asked, "Is the chief still here?" The
people said, "What chief?" "The chief that killed a man on the farm
on account of his wife." They said, "Yes, he is here." Then the man
said, "Well, he raised me so I have come to thank him." The people
said, "He is here." The man said, "Well, will you show me the way
to his *luiye*?" They led him right into the chief's house. They all
looked at the two strangers. Then one of the chief's wives said,
"Eh! This man's wife resembles Na Nyale, the one whose lover was
killed by the chief. She looks like her." She went and greeted her.
But she said "I am not Na Nyale." The other woman said, "Well,
people really can look alike!" She went away. But then she said,
"And the man looks like Fara Mara." The talk went on but the
strangers said nothing.

The man took £15 and gave it to the chief and said, "You raised

---

*The Kuranko phrase *ko manni a nyorgo manni* means literally "something happened, its
partner [i.e. the same thing, its counterpart] happened."

me. You have forgotten, but you did raise me." (The chief did not
know that a plot was being laid against him, a way of getting him to
do what the others wanted.) Then the woman gave two lapas and
head ties to each of the chief's wives. Then they went to bed. In
the morning the man told the chief that he was going to offer a
sacrifice because it had been a long time since he had offered one.
He said, "I did not know that I would find my big man here." Then
the chief mounted his horse. The man mounted his. The old
women crowded around them, clapping, and the *jeliba*s were playing the xylophones. The man scattered coins on the ground. And
people scrambled to get them. Even Fara Mara's mother did not
recognize him. But he did not go to her place. The *jeliba*s were
playing. Everyone was happy. But Fara Mara had a sword under his
gown. He put his hand under his gown and grasped the sword. He
said, "Oh God, I did not start this. I was killed by this man. I was
burnt and my ashes thrown into the river. If all this occurred, oh
God, help me take my revenge." As the chief passed him, he drew
his sword and with one blow cut off the chief's head. His head fell
there. His body fell there. There was a great commotion among
the people. Everyone was crying. Fara Mara said, "Heh, heh, heh,
heh, everybody be quiet. Everyone can tell me soon why he or she
is crying." (A killer's word is always feared.)* Then everyone fell
silent.

Next day he sacrificed two cows, one for himself and the other
for the dead chief. He became chief in that town. All the chief's
wives became his wives. Therefore, be you a chief or a nobody,† if
you should find your wife with another man, fine him but do not
kill him. That is not customary. That is not what we have
encountered.** And since these events took place a stop was put
to it. Therefore no one does it now.

---

*Keti Ferenke, who acted as a kind of second to Kenya Fina during the telling of the
story, referred at this point to an event which had taken place in Kondembaia a few days
before. A man had quarreled with another man and inflicted a minor cut on him with a
knife. The offender was feared and people were reluctant to approach him. This interjected anecdote was an elaboration of Kenya Fina's own aside.
†*kemine ghana* = an unmarried young man; an idler, a drifter. Here the term is used as a
synonym for a commoner, someone of inconsequential status.
**The phrase *maiya min ta ra* ("that is what we met") signifies "that which is customary"
or "that which the ancestors decreed should occur."

N.33:   *The Story of Soresawa*

Narrated by Keti Ferenke Koroma. Recorded at Kabala, July 1970.

There was once a man who braided his hair. He was stronger
than any other man. He braided his hair in three parts* and called
himself Soresawa. He went about the world with his hair braided in
this way. Whatever chief he visited, the day after he had enjoyed
the chief's bountiful hospitality he would ask that chief to name
the three braids. If you named the braids correctly you could kill
him, but if you failed to name the braids correctly he could kill you
and take all your possessions.

His elder brother's firstborn son traveled with him. He was a
very small boy. He went about with him. Soresawa had killed one
chief, two chiefs, three chiefs. Wherever he went, if you named his
three braids correctly you could kill him, but if you failed he could
kill you and take all your possessions. He continued in this manner. Then he went to a chief who had heard about him. That
chief's daughter was a grown woman but had not yet been given in
marriage to her husband. When Soresawa reached that town he
went and announced his strangership [*sundanye*] to the chief. The
chief's daughter became afraid for her father's life. She went and
fetched water, heated it, and went to Soresawa. She said, "*M'fa*
Soresawa, I have got water ready for your bath." He went and took
his bath. Then the girl said, "I know that young women in this
town sometimes steal other women's lovers, but whoever steals
this lover of mine, my father will beat the drum for both of us."†
(She wanted to save her father's life by making Soresawa fall in
love with her.) She caught a chicken and said, "*M'fa* Soresawa, this
is your gift." She prepared a very big meal for him and he ate it.

That night the girl went to Soresawa's lodgings and said, "*M'fa*
Soresawa, I will sleep here tonight." (Soresawa had already sent a
message to the chief, telling him that the purpose of his visit would
be made clear the following day.) Soresawa said, "Well, that is all
right." (And you all know about the wiles of women.) She got up
and lay down beside him. During the night she aroused Soresawa,

---

sore = a braiding style with two braids at the temples and one braid at the back of the
head. *sawa* = three. Thus, Soresawa: "three braids."
†That is to say, the matter will be settled by litigation, made public.

so he touched her. She said, "Don't touch me!" He said, "Why?"
She said, "Because I have never been with a man and I am a virgin
[*koin*]. Moreover, I am annoyed because I do not know the names
of your three braids. But if you tell me the names of your three
braids I will let you make love to me. If you don't name them I will
not let you make love to me." Then Soresawa said, "Well, if that is
all then there is no difficulty. The name of the first braid is 'Your
brother's child is your child but not your real child.'" The girl said,
"Yes, I have heard that. What about the second one?" "The second
one is called 'If you are involved in something with a woman you
are not involved in it with a person.'" She said, "Aha, I have heard
that. What of the third one?" He said, "The name of the third one
is 'You should not have only one friend in the world.'" Then she
said, "That is that. Wait for me. Let me go and get a bigger
bedspread from my mother. When I return you may make love to
me."

The girl got up and ran to her father. She said, "*M'fa*, if you do
not bear in mind what I am about to tell you, then you will be
killed tomorrow." She said, "His first braid is called 'Your brother's
child is your child but not your real child.' Have you heard that?"
He said, "Yes." "The second braid is called 'If you are involved in
something with a woman you are not involved in it with a person.'
Have you heard that?" He said, "Yes." "The third braid is called
'You should not have only one friend in the world.' Have you
heard the names of all three? If you forget them, tomorrow he will
kill you." Then the girl went and took the bedspread from her
mother and returned to sleep with Soresawa. Soresawa made love
to her.

In the morning Soresawa went and asked them to sound the
drum. The drum was sounded and all the big men came. When the
big men had assembled he took out his long knife (when he is
ready to kill someone he first dons the clothes that his elder
brother's firstborn son usually wears) . . . and sat on the cane chair
which had been placed in the middle of the *luiye*. Then he called to
the chief and said, "Chief, come." When the chief approached,
Soresawa said, "What is the name of this my first braid?" The chief
said, "Your brother's child is your child but not your real child."
Soresawa said, "That is its name." He asked again, "What is the
name of the second braid?" The chief said, "If you are involved in

something with a woman you are not involved in it with a person."
Soresawa said, "That is its name." He asked again, "What is the
name of the third braid?" The chief said, "You should not have
only one friend in the world." Then the people said, "Catch him,
catch him, catch him!" They caught him and they said, "Kill him,
kill him, kill him. Let us take him to the river and cut his throat!"
They tied him up. But as they were carrying him to the river, his
elder brother's child said, "Heh, *m'fannu* [sirs], wait a little, wait a
little." They stopped. The boy came up to them and said, "Please
take off the shirt he is wearing. It is my shirt. Let it not get stained
with blood." Then Soresawa said, "Well, chief, you see. This boy is
my elder brother's son. If he were my own son would he say 'take
off the shirt and let it not get stained with blood'?" They said,
"Heh, Soresawa, the name of your first braid really does make
sense. This is very true. If he were your own child he would not
have thought of his shirt as we were taking you away to be killed.
But because he is not your own child he thinks more of his shirt
than of your life." That passed.

They went on and said, "Well, we are going to kill you by that
big river." As they went on their way there they met another man.
The man said, "Eh, is that Soresawa?" They said, "Yes." He said,
"Chief, please don't kill him." And he gave £100 in order to free
Soresawa. They said, "We will take your £100 but we will not
spare his life." The man followed them, begging for Soresawa's life.
Then they met another man who also said, "Eh, is this Soresawa?"
They said, "Yes." He also paid £100 and said, "Please, chief, spare
his life. Don't kill him." They said, "We will not spare his life. We
must kill him." That man also followed them, imploring them to
spare Soresawa's life. As they neared the place where they intended to kill him, they met another man. He said, "Eh, is this
Soresawa?" They said, "Yes." He paid them £100 and said, "Chief,
please don't kill him. Spare his life." The money increased to £300
and three people followed them, imploring them to spare Soresawa's life. Then the chief said, "Hnnn, one, two, three people all
begging for this man's life. And they have paid £300 for his life. It
is best that we do not kill him."

Soresawa was acquitted. They did not kill him. Soresawa said,
"Eh, chief, here we are. Had I been loved by only one friend,
would my life have been spared? Were you not going to kill me?

Therefore I named my third braid 'You should not have only one friend in the world.' You should have many friends in this world. Don't ever say that because you have one friend you need not befriend others. When you are in trouble and all your friends plead on your behalf you will be saved. If you are a chief, never say that because you are a chief you need not befriend people."

They left Soresawa. Soresawa said, "Chief, I am not going to journey further. I will remain here and work on your farm. You knew the meaning of two of my braids when you saw what my elder brother's child did and when you saw what my friends did. If my friends had not done what they did, wouldn't you have killed me?" The people said, "Yes." "Therefore I will remain to work for you till you understand the meaning of all my three braids. Then I may decide to move on." So he remained on the chief's farm.

Now, the chief's eldest daughter, who had discovered the names of Soresawa's braids, was no longer polite to people. Whoever addressed her, she would answer with rudeness and insults. Even her father's wives. Whenever her father's brothers spoke to her she would insult them. When her brothers spoke to her she would abuse them. When younger people addressed her she would insult them. One day she abused one of her mother's co-wives. The wife went crying to the chief. She said, "Eh, your child has insulted me. I am not pleased about it." Her father caught hold of her, as one does with one's child, and beat her. When she was released she went and stood outside and said, "It is not your fault. It is my fault because I saved you from Soresawa. That is the reason. Was I not the one who sacrificed myself and let Soresawa deflower me so that I might discover the names of his braids and tell you those names and so save your life?" Soresawa said, "Ah, chief, here we are again. Didn't I say that if you are involved in something with a woman you are not involved in it with a reliable person? Now this girl has brought to light everything that occurred. So this was why you came and lay yourself under me? So that your father would not be killed? Well, chief, you see now. Had you shared this secret with a man, would he have divulged it in this way? Because it is a woman involved, the secret has come out. Therefore, don't ever share your secrets with a woman. A man should never let his wife share his real secret, lest when you quarrel she give it away. Be the woman a lover, a wife, a sister, don't tell her your secrets. Because whenever there is a small misunderstanding between you she will divulge everything. Women don't have a second thought."

N.34: *Mande Fabori and the Animals*

Narrated by Keti Ferenke Koroma. Recorded at Kondembaia, January 1970.

There was once a renowned hunter. His name was Mande Fabori. He had killed so many animals that there were few left. This troubled the animals. The few that were left held a meeting. They met deep in the forest. They said, "Friends, what can we do about Mande Fabori? He has killed all the animals in this country except us, the few who now remain." While they were thinking what to do a female buffalo said, "Wait for me. I will go and bring Mande Fabori to you." They said, "Well, go."

She set off, after telling the other animals to wait for her there. As she approached the town she changed herself into a very very beautiful woman. She entered the town. She asked for Mande Fabori's house. They pointed out the house. She went into the house. There she met Mande Fabori's wife. Now, Mande Fabori's wife could also change herself into a buffalo. When they met each other, Mande Fabori's wife knew at once that the woman was a buffalo in human form. The woman stranger greeted her. Mande Fabori's wife greeted the woman stranger. The woman said to Mande Fabori's wife, "Where is Mande Fabori?" And she said, "I am Mande Fabori's stranger." Mande Fabori's wife said, "Sit down and wait here for him. He has gone to the bush." She cooked rice and gave it to the woman stranger.

That evening, Mande Fabori returned. His wife said, "*M'berin,* while you were away a woman came for you. She says that she is your stranger. She is here." Mande Fabori said, "That is all right. She is welcome." Then he put some kola nuts into a drinking cup and gave them to the stranger. He said, "Tell me why you have come." The woman stranger said, "I came for no other purpose than that you should marry me. Your name has traveled far and wide and you are renowned as a great hunter who has killed many animals. I have come because of your name." Mande Fabori said, "Well, that is all right. You are welcome."

Night fell. When night had come, Mande Fabori's wife called him. When she had called him, she said, "Eh, Mande Fabori, when you see something then you must examine it carefully. Don't confess your secrets to this woman who has come to you. She is not a person of the town." Mande Fabori said, "You are jealous again. There is nothing in you but jealousy. You are saying all this because you are jealous of this beautiful woman who has come to me. You are giving me this bad advice because she has come." His wife said, "All right, that is it. I will sit down and watch you."

When the time came to go to bed, the woman stranger went and lay down on Mande Fabori's sleeping place. Before long, Mande Fabori also came and lay down. In the night the woman got up and woke Mande Fabori. She said, "Mande Fabori, get up." Mande Fabori got up. The woman said, "Mande Fabori, do you see how, in this world, people follow the good names of others. If you see me here, come from a far place so that you will marry me, then it is because of your good name. But there is something that troubles me, something I would like you to tell me about. You have killed many animals, but no one knows the secret of your hunting skill. This is why I have come to you to marry you, so that you will tell me how you do that." Mande Fabori said, "All right. If a person comes from a far place to see you, then it is because that person loves you. If the person does not love you, he or she will not come."

(Now, Mande Fabori had four eyes, the eyes he uses during the day, and the eyes he uses at night. When he comes back from hunting he puts his hunting eyes in a box.) Mande Fabori got up and opened the box and took out his hunting eyes. He put them on a piece of cloth. He then took out one of his own eyes and put it down. He took out the other one and put it down. Then he put on his hunting eyes. The room became as bright as day. The woman sat down, trembling. She said, "Eh, Mande Fabori, take them off. They are fearsome." Mande Fabori took one out and put it down, then took the other out and put it down. At once the woman took the four eyes, opened the door, and ran off. She went far into the bush. She went and said to the other animals, "I have come with Mande Fabori's eyes. He had four eyes. You see these two, these are the ones he uses when he kills animals. You see these two, these are his own eyes. I have brought all of them." All the animals were very happy. They took the four eyes, placed them on some leaves, and began to dance around them.

Now, Mande Fabori was saying, "Friend, bring them to me. Have you taken them? Give them to . . ." (He didn't know that he was alone in the room.) He said, "Please give me the eyes. Are you playing? They should not be handled for too long. Bring them lest they get broken. Please give them to me. This is no good, this is no good. I know that newly married women behave like this, always playing around, but these are not playthings. Give them to me." He kept on talking like this, not knowing that the woman had gone. Then he called out to his first wife, "Sira, Sira." His wife called back, "No, go on, it is only my jealousy. I am not coming." Mande Fabori said, "Oh, that is not it. Something has happened." His wife said, "I'm not going to come. You said that I was jealous. What I see sometimes from a long way off, I tell people about. Therefore, I am not coming to you." Mande Fabori said, "That is not it. Think of the children, and come." The woman said, "No, I am not going to think of any child. You go on with your new bride." Mande Fabori said, "I did something when this girl was here. Now she has gone. I took out my eyes and put them down somewhere. Now I can't find them. Please come." The woman said, "Eh, I am not getting up again." He said, "Eh, I implore you, please come. Ignore me, you were telling me the truth. Come. My hunting eyes and my own eyes are gone. Whether this woman went up or down, I do not know. Come."

Then the woman thought of the children she had borne Mande Fabori. She felt sorry for him, and she got up and went to him and he said, "Look on the ground. Are my eyes there?" The woman said, *"M'berin,* why did you take off your eyes?" Mande Fabori said, "Ah Sira, fate is stronger than any person. This woman said that she had never seen the eyes which I use when hunting. I took them off and put them on a piece of cloth. Then she took them. Now, whether she went up or down, I do not know." The woman said, "Well, didn't I tell you yesterday that you should not confess your secrets to this kind of stranger? Now what are you going to do?" Mande Fabori cried and cried and cried until he was tired. Then the woman said, "Wait for me, all right? I will be back soon."

She went out of the town and changed herself into a buffalo. She traveled far to the place where all the animals had gathered. When they saw her coming they did not know that she was a human being changed into a buffalo. They said, "This is our kinsman. Where do you come from?" She said, "Mande Fabori shot me. This is now the seventh year that I have been curing myself. Then I heard that you had gone and got the eyes of that *kafiri* [infidel] and I came running to look at them, to see the eyes he uses to kill us." They said, "Don't you see the eyes there?" She went and took the eyes and said, "Are these the dog's eyes?" They all started shouting, "These are the dog's eyes, these are the dog's eyes!" They began dancing. She would run away a little, then come back, saying, "These are the dog's eyes, these are the *kafiri*'s eyes. Let us break them." The others said, "Let us not break them just yet. Let us play with them for a while, let us play with them for a while." Then she went up one hill with the eyes and came down the other side. She went up another hill, and came down the other side. Then, away she ran with the eyes.

When she approached the town she changed herself back into human form. She took the eyes and put them in front of her husband. He took one eye and put it on. It fitted well. He took the other eye and put it on. It fitted well. He saw clearly. Then he took his hunting eyes and put them in the box. He said to his wife, "Where did you go?" She said, "You see that mountain there? When you go up it and look down the other side you will see them all on the *faragbaran* [flat rock] there." Then Mande Fabori took his gun and went off. He climbed the mountain and looked down. He pointed his gun at them and shot them all.

An Excess of Love

There are a great number of Kuranko narratives which stress the importance of modesty and continence. "Nothing to excess" is the moral which the narrators invariably draw from them. Although no examples of this kind of narrative are published here, it is useful to summarize some of them in order to indicate the ways in which various cautions are conveyed. One tale tells of a promiscuous woman who had left one town, where all the men have tired of her, for another. Her notoriety precedes her and the young men in the second town scorn her because of her shamelessly unrestrained and importunate behavior. The narrator, Keti Ferenke, brings the narrative to a close with the comments:

It is not good to become notorious for something. If you become notorious for doing something, you will be left alone. Even with eating, you should not be gluttonous. Whatever you do, do it in moderation. This woman was shunned because of her lustfulness.

In another narrative a woman falls in love with a handsome young man who changes into a python before making love to her. The woman is so infatuated that she declares her readiness to follow her lover to the ends of the earth. The python makes demands upon the woman—that she bring him the best food in her husband's house—which the woman willingly meets although this means depriving her own household of food. Finally her affair is discovered by a small child from the woman's house, and the child informs his father (the woman's husband) of what he has seen. The husband dresses himself in the woman's clothes, learns the song she sings in order to entice the python from its hole, and then kills the snake. He butchers it and cooks it. Upon discovering that her lover is dead, the disconsolate woman rushes home, where she finds the python on the smoking-rack over the fire. When she realizes that the child is responsible for the death of her lover, she kills the child and throws his body into the fire. The husband becomes worried about the child's disappearance, and finally learns of his wife's crime when the ashes of the dead child begin to sing as the woman mixes them with water in order to make washing soda: "My mother killed me because of her lover. . . ."

In these two narratives the women are so engrossed in their love affairs that they spare no thought for others. The field of their social consciousness is narrowed and distorted. Prolonged grief and pining can also lead to excessive self-absorption, as in two other narratives which relate the absurd and tragic consequences of bereaved spouses remaining attached to their loved ones. In the first of these tales, a husband cuts the breasts off the body of his dead wife so that he will not be "left empty-handed." After forty days, however, the breasts begin to putrefy and the man disturbs the entire village with his childlike lamentations. He sits by his late wife's graveside, singing and calling to her. But the men of the village hit upon a ruse to bring him to his senses. Some of the men hide in the woman's grave, and when the husband draws near the edge they seize him by the arm and threaten to pull him into the earth. Next morning, having overcome his shock and grief, he returns to the grave and closes it forever. In the second tale, three bereaved women decide to cut the penis off the body of their dead husband. They dry the penis and use it as a dildo.

With both intense love and excessive grief, attachment to the loved one results in a merging of identities which is inimical to a sense of wider social obligations. This may explain why love and grief serve to signify the nature of asocial behavior in the narratives. Unrestrained passions involve self-absorption, distractedness, and a kind of "social blindness," and since they are incompatible with the social order they must be moderated or expunged. In the narratives, ostracism, banishment, divorce, avoidance, and metamorphosis into objects signify that incontinent behavior belongs properly to the world of the wild. In a narrative not published here (narrated by Sara Mantene Mara of Firawa), the key figure is a woman who is "inordinately fond of accompanying men." This is a euphemistic way of saying that the woman is promiscuous. It refers to the custom whereby one accompanies a guest or friend some way along the path when he decides to go on a journey or return to his own village. The custom, known as *bilasalalke,* is often referred to in the narratives because it provides a dramatic means of signifying a movement or transition from the social to the extrasocial world. In Sara Mantene's narrative the love-struck woman is determined to accompany her lover along a path which passes near a huge rock which is able to engorge people. Her mother warns her against going there, and her father repeats the warning, saying that if she must go then she should be careful not to stand close to the rock. But the woman ignores this advice and is swallowed by the rock. As she is gradually engorged, she sings ruefully of her heedlessness and error. In this narrative the woman's obdurate attitude is appropriately punished by immobilization. Her antisocial behavior leads to her becoming a part of the extrasocial landscape. This pattern of events recurs in N.34, in which the heedless hunter loses his eyesight and is temporarily immobilized.

The consequences of sexual incontinence are similar to those already studied in the incest narratives (N.22–N.26). The offenders are punished by being changed into animals or things or by being assimilated into the natural landscape. While incestuous relations are "too close," we might say that promiscuous and adulterous relations are "too distant." It is noteworthy that the incontinent behavior of the promiscuous women in the narratives referred to above is not merely a matter of immoderate appetites; it entails sex with strangers. In short, the customary preference for marriage within the village is disregarded. In the narratives the impropriety of excessive or illicit sex is in fact signified as sex with an outsider. In one of these tales the lover is a gluttonous python who "comes from a far-off place." The lover's status is thus marked as being extrasocial. Moreover, the illicit affairs take place away from the community, in a strange town or in the wilderness. It should be recalled that the Kuranko prohibit sexual relations in the bush lest medicines are spoiled which are placed on the boundaries of the chiefdom to safeguard it against invasion. Finally, illicit sex with a stranger implies a denial of children. Childlessness, immobility, and ostracism are not only punishments for sexual incontinence. They serve as reminders that a women's first duty is to her husband and to her children. Love is regarded as a distraction, and a woman's adultery can harm her children's destinies.

Another relationship can be noted between incest and promiscuity. In my discussion of N.25 I drew an analogy between incestuous relations and excessive grief. In both instances, emotional attachments are inordinately close. In the narratives we are presently concerned with, a similar situation occurs. In two of them excessive grief and prolonged attachment to a dead wife or husband prevent the resumption of normal social life and lead to the neglect of children. In the narratives about promiscuity uncontrolled sexual appetites are shown to be inimical to marital stability and conjugal harmony. Ideally, a wife should suppress all extrafamilial emotional attachments and devote her attention to her husband and children. The wrong choice is to give priority to external attachments, signified in the narratives by liaisons with creatures of the wild, strangers, and ghosts. As we saw in chapter 5, uncontrolled emotionality has the same consequence as ambivalent feelings: social time is brought to a standstill, and social exchange breaks down. According to the Kuranko, adultery "spoils" sacrifices and prevents the communication of messages between men and their ancestors. This is why the presence of a pale-complexioned virgin girl in sacrificial contexts is often advised by diviners. Grief can "spoil" mortuary rites in a similar way since it is said that excessive grief displayed by the bereaved kin will prevent the dead person's spirit from passing from the world of the living to the world of the ancestors.

To summarize: extreme emotionality distracts, narrows, or individualizes the field of a person's social awareness. In Kuranko terms, emotions are "hot" and confusing; correct social relations should be "cool" and "clear." Passionate commitments and sentimental attachments are regarded ambivalently, for they tend to be exclusive, asocial, and they lead to incautious behavior. In the narratives, love and grief are singled out to signify the potentially ruinous consequences of uncontrolled feelings. An obsession with one other person is seen to be a kind of self-absorption or absentmindedness; it implies an antisocial attitude. This may be why the lover in the narratives is often a stranger, a person who does not belong to the moral community. Sexual love in particular gives rise to problems of reconciling personal inclinations and social obligations. And, because sexual love is associated with women, the dangers of excessive emotionality are expressed in terms of such injunctions as these:

> *Musu kai i gbundu lon*
> ("Never let a woman know your secrets")

> *Kele da ma si ban, koni musu ko kele ti ban*
> ("All quarrels resolve themselves in the end, except those caused by women")

> *Yanfe da ma si no, koni musu yanfe wo ti fo*
> ("All conspiracies can be overcome, except those made by women")

Turning now to a second group of narratives, represented by N.32 (*The Story of Na Nyale*) and N.33 (*The Story of Soresawa*), we can explore various other attitudes toward women and toward love. These attitudes are often more tolerant and more positive than those outlined above, and they indicate therefore the profound ambiguity of the subject. This ambiguity is also shown by the different opinions taken by male and female narrators, and by the fact that some narrators draw quite different conclusions from different narratives on the same theme. Thus, love is sometimes equated with an absence of restraint; it is seen as a threat to secular and religious order, inimical to self-control. At other times, love is shown to be a power for good, able to ameliorate, sweeten, or humanize a world of hardship and inflexible rules. If in their narratives men tend to be critical of women, the satirical, poignant, and indignant qualities in the narratives told by women tend to offset and modulate the dogmatic attitudes which men espouse in public and insinuate into their stories.

The men's narratives and the women's narratives must be considered together. If we examine an actual sequence of narratives told at a particular session, we can quickly see how a kind of complementarity or adjustment of viewpoints is reached. In a narrative session at Kondembaia in February 1972, Kenya Fina Marah told a story—*The Melodious Sound of the Yimbe Drum*—which I had previously recorded in March 1970. The story ridicules rigid and self-righteous attitudes in men. It relates how the Muslims have decreed that there should be no drumming during Ramadan. A brilliant drummer comes to the village and soon distracts the Muslims from their prayers with the melodious playing of his *yimbe* drum. Having told this story, Kenya Fina told another which celebrates women's fishing skills. She then sang the song of the bird Siaman Konde, which could mimic other voices flawlessly and beautifully.

At this point, Keti Ferenke, whose chauvinistic attitudes toward women have already been mentioned, shared in telling a story with Kenya Fina. What astonished me at the time was that Keti Ferenke would take an active part in telling a story which satirized and ridiculed men. The narrative is set at a river crossing. Keti Ferenke took the part of a disgruntled ferryman, while Kenya Fina related the story. The narrative dramatizes the ferryman's different attitudes toward men and toward women. Whenever a man asked to be ferried across the river, the ferryman would grumble about the poor condition of his canoe and sing dolefully, "If you drown or break your legs, don't blame me." But when a beautiful woman asked to be taken across the river, the man's tone would change and he would sing of how safe the canoe was, of the smoothness of the water and the steadiness of the current.

When this story had been told, Keti Ferenke volunteered another on the same theme. The narrative concerned a blacksmith who would complain each time a man brought him work to do. He would moan about the poor repair of the bellows, berate the farmers for not taking good care of their implements, and badger his clients for charcoal or payment for the work. But when Sira, a beautiful woman, approached the blacksmith with work, he broke into song, chattering away as follows: "Oh you're welcome, welcome . . . The bellows are working well . . . How many machetes did you bring with you? What, only one! . . . You should have brought several . . . You must spend the night here . . . I will let you have the machetes and hoes which the men brought to me. . . ." As he sang, the bellows made an easy and pleasing sound, *yinnnng*. This contrasts with the labored stuttering of the bellows when male clients came: *kaponkoponk*.

The narrative which followed this one was also told by Keti Ferenke, but Kenya Fina took the part of the woman in the story, seducing the

Muslim with her sweet song. The narrative concerns a Muslim who lives alone beyond the town. There is no one to lead people in prayer, so a woman dresses herself seductively in beads and braids her hair and goes to where the Muslim lives. He is soon captured by her charms and follows her back to town. At the close of this narrative Keti Ferenke returned to his more usual themes: the treachery and mischief of women, the destructive repercussions of illicit sexual love.

The next narrative told, *When Women Took Control*, elaborated on the same themes, although this story by Sulimani Koroma was less explicitly condemnatory of women. It tells of a time when men and women lived in separate towns. The men tried to persuade the women to come and live with them, but each man who went was seduced by the charms and songs of the women and fell a willing captive to them. Before long the women had captured and tied up all the men.

This review of a sequence of seven narratives from an actual storytelling session shows how narrators counterpoise different points of view and vary the tone of their interpretations. While Keti Ferenke accepts Kenya Fina's view of men's inconsistency and gullibility in the story of the ferry crossing, Kenya Fina goes along with Keti Ferenke's cynical view of women in the story of the Muslim and the beautiful woman. This reciprocity of viewpoints between narrators helps create a kind of moral equitability with different interpretations balanced against each other. It must be emphasized once more that narrative viewpoints are largely provisional. Different perspectives emerge through a process of statement and counterstatement, as much within the context of a single storytelling session as within a single narrative. The presentation of alternative points of view in rapid succession heightens the effect of the narratives, engaging the interest and active participation of the audience in thinking through the dilemmas and contrary views advanced. Narrative skill consists as much in an ability to respond appropriately to other narrators as in an ability to descern and play upon the predilections and concerns of the audience. For this reason alone, an expert narrator must have a large repertoire and be able to alter the tenor of tales to suit each situation. The subtle collaborations of Kenya Fina and Keti Ferenke in storytelling sessions are of course reflections of their narrative skills, their love of storytelling, their similar intellectual interests, and their fine sense of the absurd. But a deeper compatibility should be remarked, for it is their friendship itself which exemplifies the ethical ideal toward which many of these narratives strive, an ideal in which love transcends both sexual hankerings and the formal definitions of kinship and marriage, helping to create a social world that does not exclude personal preference and choice.

Love (*kene*) is in one sense like cleverness (*hankili*): it is ethically ambiguous. While sexual love is often regarded negatively, maternal love is synonymous with virtue. Although strong emotions are often condemned, they are nevertheless inevitable concomitants of all great and exceptional endeavor. It is the ambiguity of love which makes it such a compelling theme in the narratives. And it may be because love is as capricious as it can be constant that it is used as a figurative means of bringing into discussion problems of balancing sentiment and rule.

Of Women's Powers and the Fate of Men

The narratives referred to above show that neither medicines, nor renunciation and avoidance, nor the trappings of secular power can safeguard men against the blandishments and allures of women. In the story of how women took control, the sung portion contrasts the power of feminine wiles with the power of men's weaponry. Like medicines, the men's weapons prove to be inadequate defenses against the naked and seductive girls, and the men become their willing captives. In the story about the Muslim and the beautiful woman the *tunkolo fare* beads around the woman's waist and loins are contrasted with the Muslim's prayer beads; the former distract his attention from the latter. Sweet songs and sounds are equated with sexual allures, and the sweet sounds of the *yimbe* drum in the first story referred to have the same subversive effect as the women's sweet songs and beguilements in the others. The way in which sweetness serves as an image of corruption, distraction, or incontinence has already been discussed in chapter 4. A structural parallelism can be noted here between the younger brother who uses disguise and trickery to outwit an elder brother and the woman who beguiles and distracts a man. In both situations, deception is an acceptable way of breaking an absurd law or ridiculing an inflexible attitude. The critique of strict Islamic observances in the tale of the Muslim and his prayer beads is a dramatic way of showing just how ludicrous self-righteousness, overseriousness, and mechanical adherence to routine are.

Several other narratives lampoon overpossessive husbands in a similar manner. In one such narrative a jealous chief is so infatuated by his wife's beauty that he will not let her out of his sight. His wife tells her lover to come to the house dressed as a woman and to announce himself as her "aunt." The gullible chief welcomes the "aunt" and even urges her to sleep in the same room as his wife. The narrator, Keti Ferenke, acted out the clumsy movements of the lover, hampered by women's clothes and jewelry, and he also played up the stupidity of the cuckolded husband. In another tale, told by Barawa Sira Mansare, a jealous husband accompanies his wives everywhere, even to the stream when they go to fetch water or wash clothes. One day one of the wives places a stone under her lapa and when her husband's attention is distracted she lets it fall into the stream. When he asks what made the splash she tells him that "the thing you are always following me to watch over" has fallen into the water. The stupid husband dams the stream, bales out the water, asks the fish if they have seen "the thing I paid money for, the thing I paid cows for," until at last the woman points out how ridiculous he is and so brings him to his senses. In this and other narratives in which jealous husbands invade areas ordinarily prohibited to men we can see how emotional preoccupations lead to an infringement of social rules. For this reason, the men deserve to be tricked or shamed by the women whose rights they have ignored. As in the hare-hyena narratives discussed in chapter 4, the deceptions which are used to redress or correct the errors include songs with concealed messages, disguises, and pretenses. In the tale referred to above, in which the lover disguises himself as the woman's aunt, the lover is eventually found out by the chief. But the woman quickly invents a song and dance, singing that her "real aunt has been changed into a man." The chief is distracted by the song, and the woman and her lover make their escape.

The communication of a hidden message to a lover through a song occurs in another tale in which the woman's lover is hidden in the banks of a stream. As she and her lover make love she sings a song about catching different varieties of fish. I recorded this narrative in Kamadugu Sukurela on two other occasions (narrated by Kumba Doron Sise and by Sinkari Yegbe Sise), and, as Sinkari Yegbe noted, the narrative shows that "no matter how vigilant and clever a man may be, a wife can evade his scrutiny if she wishes to." The narrative is directly comparable to another in which a wife hides her lover in a sesame field, then warns him with a song when her suspicious husband comes to drive him into the open by setting fire to the straw and stubble. I collected two versions of this narrative, both related by women of Kamadugu Sukurela, and in one of these versions the song which distracts the husband's attention goes as follows:

> *I la wuli wo, beni koromgbe an bi kale I*
> *mani ma, yenyen, ben' koromgbe an bi kale I*
> *mani ma, wunan wunan, ben' koromgbe an bi kale I*
> *mani ma . . .*

Translated, the song means, "You get up, oh heap of sesame straw, they are setting fire to you, *yenyen*, heap of sesame straw, they are setting fire to you, *wunan wunan* . . . ," and the phrase *wunan wunan* conveys the movement of the lover as he escapes.

The use of disguise and of song is shown in yet another narrative not published here. The jealous husband refuses to lodge handsome strangers in his *luiye*, so the wife's lover disguises himself as an ugly, filthy beggar. Thinking that none of his wives would want to sleep with such a man, the chief admits him to his house, whereupon, once night has fallen, the man washes himself, dons clean clothes, and spends the night making love to the chief's wives. In the morning, as the man goes on his way, the wives sing to him:

> Are you going, you dusty man,
> Your gifts are not enough,
> Are you going now, you dusty man,
> Here is a cow for you,
> Your gifts are not enough . . .

Of course, the real message of the refrain, "Your gifts are not enough," is that the lover should return and satisfy all the wives. The cuckolded husband, however, thinks that his wives are simply showing charity toward a beggar by giving him a cow, a goat, and so on.

The whole dogma of male control is called into question in these narratives. It may even be argued that the orthodox male view of women is a defensework against anxieties over the real extent of their self-control and social authority, particularly in domestic life.[3]

Yet, among the Kuranko, the negative or the repressed attitudes to love and to women's powers do not preponderate. A spirit of good humor and a sense of the absurdity of rigid demarcations of sexual domains prevail in many of the narratives. It is even admitted that love is stronger than law and more constant than marriage. Many narratives celebrate the happiness and levity which love brings to work. The tales of the ferryman and of the blacksmith have already been recounted in brief. Another story, related by Denka Marah, tells of a woman who laundered her husband's clothes reluctantly, complaining all the while of the perspiration stains on his shirts. However, when her lover gave her his shirts to wash she would sing joyously as she scrubbed them in the river. The song in the narrative includes the ideophone *kunduborso kunduborsoborso*, which signifies the heavy and reluctant work of washing the husband's clothes, and the contrasted expression *kakubatabata kaliamba*, which conveys the joy and easiness of the work of washing her lover's garments. In yet another of Denka's narratives on the same theme, a cuckolded husband decides to punish his unfaithful wife by forcing her to carry her lover on her back around the village. In this way the husband hopes to shame her publicly. But the wife puts her lover in a back-hamper, summons drummers and xylophonists, and goes about the village singing of the lightness of love's labor. The same contrast between the "sweetness" of love and the burdens of conjugal life is made in N.32 where Na Nyale's husband observes the difference between the unappetizing food she sets before him and the feast she prepares for her lover. The bonds of love are stronger than the bonds of both marriage and kinship.

The relative weakness of parental authority is shown in a narrative related by Silan Marah of Firawa. It tells of a girl who is so distracted by lovemaking that she forgets to bring in the rice from the drying-mat when it starts to rain. Her mother berates her and the girl becomes annoyed; she goes into a kind of coma, refusing to talk to anyone. As soon as this occurs, all the rivers dry up and the villagers become parched with thirst. They approach the girl, begging her to accept their apologies; for they realize that the drought is connected with her anger and immobility. Members of the village apologize to her, singing sweetly, but she betrays no emotion. Her mother sings to her "I am your true mother," but she still does not move. Finally her lover approaches her, singing "I am your true lover and I am parched with thirst," whereupon the girl responds with a smile, clouds appear, rain falls, and the rivers run again. The metaphorical connection between seasonal imbalance and social or psychophysical inertia has been discussed in chapter 5 (see also Jackson, 1979:123). Here we find a similar connection between immoderate behavior on the one hand (the mother's overreaction to the girl's negligence, and the girl's catatonic state) and immoderate drought on the other (the villagers nearly die of thirst). Both the passage of social time and the succession of the seasons are interrupted by stormy emotions and ill-governed passions.

The moral value set upon such attributes of love as devotion, constancy, and self-sacrifice is shown in N.32, perhaps one of the most poignant and moving of all Kuranko narratives, and beautifully related by the renowned Kenya Fina Marah. In this narative Kenya Fina plays up the devotion of the heroine, Na Nyale. The narrator thus creates an ambiguous situation, since a kind of equivalence is established between the *legal* bonds of marriage and the *moral* qualities associated with the illicit relationship between Na Nyale and her lover. The equivalence places us in the position of having to make a choice between the legal rights of the husband and the moral virtue inherent in the love affair. Kenya Fina assists the resolution of this dilemma by first exaggerating the husband's zealous and ill-tempered behavior. Since adultery is not a crime punishable by death, the husband's jealous rage, which leads him to kill his wife's lover without mercy, can be condemned legally as well as morally. His behavior is then contrasted with the strength and steadiness of Na Nyale's devotion to her slain lover, Fara Mara. Rather than find fault with her husband, she blames herself for Fara Mara's death. Redeemed by this attitude, she is helped by the river creatures and, with her lover, returns to the chief's town, where Fara Mara kills the chief and takes his place.

In N.32 the structural transformations are identical to those already traced out in our analysis of other narratives concerned with psychophysical attributes such as cleverness, strength, magnanimity, bravery, and compassion. As I have shown, such attributes are fortuitously distributed and semantically ambiguous. Love is another such attribute. *Kene* may refer to sexual as as well as to platonic relationships, maternal as well as conjugal attachments. And love is stronger than, and transcends, both social demands and self-interest. Love can therefore serve both equally; its negative potential is as great as its power to do good. In N.32 there is first a polarization of social relationships and moral qualities. A contradictory situation is then shown to exist: the positive moral qualities are associated with the illicit relationship, while negative qualities are associated with the legal relationship. This situation is resolved by a crossing-over of terms, so that the narrative concludes with a coalescence of a positive moral quality and a legal social relationship. If we consider this resolution in a literal way, then all we need to observe is that the husband dies or goes away, the lovers are married, and, to use a catchphrase from Indo-European tales, "they live happily ever after." But the marriage must also be considered allegorically, as signifying the resolution of a problem which has as much to do with abstract qualities as with actual individuals. Again using the figure of chiasmus, let us depict the relevant transformations:

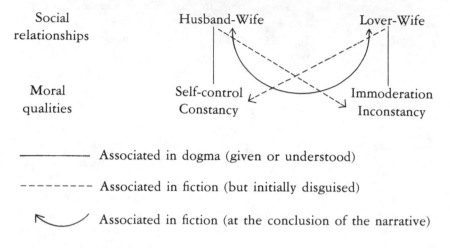

Social
relationships   Husband-Wife   Lover-Wife

Moral
qualities   Self-control   Immoderation
                  Constancy   Inconstancy

——————— Associated in dogma (given or understood)

- - - - - - - - Associated in fiction (but initially disguised)

⌐_/ Associated in fiction (at the conclusion of the narrative)

It should also be noted that the moments of greatest crisis, greatest ambiguity, and imminent transformation occur in liminal settings, and that the liminal and critical episodes are marked by song rather than speech. Thus the burned and dismembered lover in N.32 sings in reply to Na Nyale as she follows the course of the river in search of him.

With N.33 we return to the problems surrounding the ambiguity of love and the ambiguity of women's powers. The chief-slaying and anarchic Soresawa[4] enters a strange town where the chief's virgin daughter, fearing for her father's life, gives herself to Soresawa in order to learn the names of his three braids of hair. With this knowledge she is able to save her father's life. But her self-sacrifice and courage are contrasted with her subsequent rudeness and discontent, and Soresawa points out to the chief that the girl should be rebuked for failing to keep the secret with which she was entrusted. Loyal to her father, she nevertheless betrays her lover, who is almost put to death as a result. At first sight this conflict of loyalties seems irresolvable since loyalty to one necessarily entails a betrayal of the other. However, let us briefly return to a consideration of the conflict of loyalty in real life where a woman is often torn between attachments to her natal kin and obligations to her husband and children. In the narratives this conflict is frequently depicted as one between positively evaluated immediate or specific social bonds and negatively evaluated or diffuse extrasocial attachments.

kin / stranger (N.33)
marriage / promiscuity
husband / lover (N.32)
living kin / dead spouse
community / outsider or lawbreaker
children / outside interests
person / creature of the wild

The particular terms and figures are largely contingent and there is a great deal of substitution and overlap within each set. For example, lovers are usually also strangers or creatures of the wild. The resolution of these conflicts between social and extrasocial bonds is accomplished by breaking and cancelling the latter or, as in N.32, by transferring a positive attribute of the extrasocial attachment to a legitimate social relationship such as marriage. In N.33 another kind of transformation occurs. As we have seen, the girl's conflict of loyalty between kin (chief, father) and stranger (lover, killer) leads to an ambiguous situation, an ethical impasse. But this conflict is gradually eclipsed by a contrast which is drawn between specific and diffuse ties. Thus, while the girl's ties are specific ones, the names of Soresawa's braids suggest contrasts between specific *and* diffuse ties, first in the idiom of kinship ("Your brother's child is your child but not your child"), second in the context of personhood ("If you are involved in something with a woman you are not involved in it with a person"), and third in the field of friendship ("You should not have only one friend in the world"). The problem of the conflict of loyalties thus resolves itself into a question of choosing, not between two individuals but between two kinds of trust, the one specific, the other diffuse. This contrast is then further translated into the language of social categories so that the injunction "Never trust any one person" becomes "Never trust any woman." This is the culminating transformation of a set of terms among which we have discerned the following parallelisms:

one friend : many friends :: brother's
child : one's own child :: women : men

I have also noted the chauvinistic tendency of Kuranko men to displace blame onto women. In this sense, the resolution of the problem
proposed in N.33 may be said to be unsatisfactory. The male stranger,
Soresawa, is finally assimilated into the community; he settles there for
good and works on the chief's farm. The chief's eldest daughter, who
initially belongs to the community, is, however, set apart from it as a
result of her antisocial behavior. She becomes the stranger, the nonperson, and she bears the brunt of the narrator's final attack.

In the Mande Fabori narratives the contrast between the social and
the extrasocial once more finds expression in the contrast between
marital or maternal love on the one hand and illicit sexual love on the
other. The figure of the Delilah-like seductress in N.33 and the figure
of the deceiving old woman (which occurs in other narratives not published here) merge in N.34 in the figure of the seductive female shape-
shifter. But, unlike previous narratives, in N.34 the figure of the
mother plays a crucial role countering the schemes of the seductress.
Problems of "pure-heartedness" dealt with in N.33, such as trust, loyalty, and guarding confidences, also emerge in N.34. Thus we may remark the themes of moral discernment and visual acuity (both qualities
being regarded as aspects of cleverness, *hankili*) which pervade the
Mande Fabori narratives. In N.34 deceptive appearances and misrepresentations bring about a loss or blighting of the hero's vision, and his
clear-sightedness is only restored when his wife (in four other versions
it is his mother) uses similar tricks against the seductress. In some versions, the mother's concern and watchfulness lead her to notice that the
seductive "stranger" has the fetlocks of an animal. In one version the
mother is able to change into a cat, and in another she brings back to
life Mande Fabori's hunting dogs after the seductress has persuaded
Mande Fabori to kill them and serve them to her as food. In every
version, however, the women play active roles; Mande Fabori is passive,
inept, easily duped into giving away his powers. Yet the wife or mother
outwits the seductress and returns Mande Fabori's powers to him. This
suggests the triumph of maternal over sexual love.

The ambiguous identity of the seductive "stranger" may be compared
with the ambiguous status of Mande Fabori[5], and the ambiguous attributes of the hero's wife or mother.[6] In one narrative two female deer
transform themselves into human beings and attempt to kill Mande
Fabori's hunting dogs. But in four other versions the female shape-
shifter is a buffalo which assumes the form of a beautiful woman in
order to steal the hunter's powers of vision. The image of the buffalo-

woman gains its dramatic strength from two facts: first, the buffalo (*Syncerus caffer*) is, according to Kuranko hunters, the most formidable, clever, and dangerous of all animals; and second, the greatest super-natural danger for hunters is believed to be an unfaithful wife or an adulterous liaison. This belief explains why most hunters avoid sexual intercourse before a hunting expedition lest illicit sex "spoil" the hunt-ing medicines and so make the hunters vulnerable to the dangers of the bush.

Although formal discipline and training, special qualities such as courage and fortitude, and medicines are all essential to a hunter's safety, it is the role of medicines which is played up in the Mande Fabori narratives. In one version, Mande Fabori's protectors are his dogs, while in another version his special powers enable him to assume the forms of an egg, a stone, a bamboo brake—indeed the same magi-cal objects we have already encountered in N.27. But the most impor-tant of the special powers attributed to the hero-hunter is the power of "four eyes" which enables him to see in the dark. The hunter's loss of this magical vision is contrasted with the vigilance and perspicacity of his mother or wife who exemplifies the Kuranko adage: "When you look at something, you should look between the toes." But love is blind, and the hunter-hero, who in many ways embodies the ideal attri-butes of Kuranko manhood, is shown to be vulnerable to sexual love. The mother, symbolizing maternal love, helps him regain his powers, and thus the entire narrative takes the form of an allegory in which the male order is maintained and perpetuated only through the constancy and perspicacity of the mother.

The ambiguity of the wife/mother in these narratives is not simply a reflection of the interchangeability of the two figures in different ver-sions; it springs from the fact that a virtuous wife is a woman who be-haves in an emphatically maternal way. Not only does she put her chil-dren's interests before her own; her relationship with her husband is ideally characterized by the constancy and devotion of a perfect mother. Mande Fabori's wife in N.34 and the devoted Na Nyale in N.32 serve to remind us of the high value placed upon maternal love. In the narra-tives it becomes a metaphor for the positive aspects of the conjugal relationship itself. Moreover, the dutiful figures of wife and mother signify closeness and trust over against the figure of the alluring female shape-shifter whose true domain is the bush.

The Mande Fabori narratives all involve dramatic movements be-tween village and bush, and each movement is accompanied by a metamorphosis. These movements and metamorphoses signify "wild" oscillations in which there are losses of social, psychological, and ecological equilibrium. For example, the narratives all begin with a situation in which a hunter with special powers has killed too many animals. In one version, by Yanku Pore Kargbo of Firawa, the excessiveness of the killing is made clear when an argument develops between two hunters, one of whom wishes to kill the young and nursing mothers of several animals, the other of whom is for protecting them. It is this narrative which gives a clue to the meaning of the others. The contrast between sexual and maternal love is analogous to the contrast between excessive killing (killing for pleasure) and moderation (protecting the young and their mothers). The hunter who impetuously wants to kill all the animals is therefore like Mande Fabori in N.34, who cannot prevent himself being seduced by an alluring creature from the bush. The first hunter ignores his friend's counsel and kills the mother animals and their young. Mande Fabori ignores his wife's (mother's) advice and sleeps with the seductress. Both act against nature, and thus against the order and continuity of society itself. One loses his life and the other loses his special powers. In most versions it is the hunter's mother who returns the hunter to the social order, by regaining his powers for him and bringing him back to his senses.

The Mande Fabori narratives unfold simultaneously on social, psychological, and ecological planes, each plane being a transmutation of the others. Thus, a balance between hunting wild animals in the bush and keeping to social rules is metaphorically cognate with incautious sexual adventures with strangers and respecting natal ties. One narrator draws the lesson that "However much people may love you, your mother loves you more," but the allegorical dimensions of the narratives enable us to point to a whole series of balances which are striven for: between personal initiative and respect for the counsel of others, between taking risks and and avoiding dangers, between foolhardiness and courage. In the Kuranko view, a clever person is mindful of the need to achieve these balances, of mediating and moderating contrary forces and contradictory imperatives. Cleverness is thus a kind of attentiveness which consists in discernment and intelligent observation as much as in heeding the advice of others. The problem of choice therefore resolves itself into a problem of moderation, and the problem of controlling the world becomes the same as the problem of self-control.

8 *Co-Wives, Orphans, and Miraculous Interventions*

In the preceding chapters we have been able to chart several transformational patterns and procedures in the narratives which indicate that similar ethical problems keep recurring and that these problems are treated allegorically and allusively with the help of various mediated contrasts such as totemic animal/wild animal, kinsman/stranger, elder/younger, male/female, town/bush. While some of these contrasted terms are sociological, others are geographical, zoological, cosmological, economic, or technical. Each pair of terms has a set of variants, so that, for example, the contrast between elder and younger may take other more specific forms: elder brother/younger brother, father/son, chief/subject. Moreover, each pair of terms has various connotations depending upon the narrative context; thus the contrast between town and bush implies other contrasts: persons/nonpersons, villagers/enemies, close kin/distant kin, maternal love/sexual love, social rules/extrasocial influences. These chains of associations make it possible to correlate different contrasts, as in the formulation

male : female :: elder : younger :: town : bush

Plotting such formal schemes might suggest that the selection of a particular pair of terms in a particular narrative is largely arbitrary. But this is not entirely true, since the personality of the narrator and the concerns of the audience influence the choice of subject, the use of metaphor, and the mode of resolution in each narrative. For the analyst, however, a problem remains, for whether he begins with contrasted social categories or landscape zones he always finds himself at an indefinite point within an interminable world of transmutations which depart from the lineal and causal schemes upon which analysis usually depends, and blur distinctions between the literal and the figurative. He finds himself moving through partial resolutions, endless evasions and transformations until, in exasperation, he seeks an entirely detached position from which to view the world of myth.

In this book I have taken the view that the narratives are attempts to come to terms with problems which are actually insurmountable, such as guaranteeing impartiality in the exercise of authority, achieving perfect reciprocity in exchange, securing just apportionments of talents and abilities, and making correct judgments in everyday life. I have thus sought to show how the transformational patterns in the narratives are anchored in the quest for moral meanings. For instance, the problem of justice as fairness is taken up and dealt with in the hunger narratives in chapter 3 in terms of the problem of achieving an equitable distribution of scarce resources during a time of great hunger. The same problem underlies the hare-hyena narratives (chapter 4), where it is discussed in terms of the problem of the just exercise of secular powers. Problems relating to the proper use of supernatural powers, magical objects, and extraordinary gifts form the main concerns of the narratives in chapter 6, and a close affinity is shown between problems of justice and of reciprocity. In the prevented-transitions narratives (chapter 5), discussion of these problems centers on crises and impasses in exchange relations between groups and between the generations. These narratives also raise the problem of reconciling personal and social interests, a problem which leads to a consideration of pureheartedness, that is, honesty to oneself and honesty to others. Problems of trust, openness, clear judgment, and insight are taken up in the narratives in chapter 7, where the pivotal relationships involve men and women.

The narratives proceed on several levels simultaneously. Although justice is regarded as a form of equality or as a means of compensating for inequalities in the apportionment of resources, these resources may be material (property and wealth), natural (food), supernatural (blessings), social (rights and privileges associated with a certain status), or psychophysical (cleverness, strength, kindness). The narrative schemes involve the reapportionment of resources, and the adjustment of inequalities. Quite often this reapportionment takes the form of chiasmus, so that positive psychophysical attributes come to be associated with persons in high positions, and negative attributes are extirpated by contriving the death or displacement of an unjust ruler, the ostracism of a rogue, or the degradation of a deceiver. But such "events" always have allegorical significance and must be understood as elements in abstract designs which enable the narrators and their audience to shape and interpret their world as they see fit. It must also be stressed that the narratives are not simply means of providing vicarious compensations to the disadvantaged members of Kuranko society, for they occasion the active search for moral meanings and for determinate patterns, thus compensating for the randomness, ambiguity, and inequality that exist in the world.

Ethical ambiguity is first played up, then reduced. The procedures in the narratives are comparable to divinatory procedures where randomness is maximized before it is shown to be a kind of disguised order. In both the divinatory rite and the storytelling session people actively manipulate simulacra of the real world in order to grasp it more clearly and transform their experience of it. The pebbles in the diviner's hands are like the figures and images (*gestalten*) with which the narrator creates new interpretations, and both the diviner and the narrator make possible a transition from confusion to clarity, and an adjustment of individual freedom to its limiting conditions. The reconciliation of personal imperatives and external demands is as much the subject of the tales as it is the purpose of storytelling itself.

The underlying metaphor in the narratives is of balance, adjustment, equilibrium. The association of balance and justice is, of course, found in European lore and literature as well. Justice is the eighth enigma of the Tarot pack, and the bilateral symmetry of the Empress-like figure holding a pair of scales denotes, among other things, the balance between good and evil, and the harmony between inner judgment and social legality. Similar metaphorical contrasts in Kuranko narratives include: the measured step/limping;[1] moderation in eating/gluttony; continence/promiscuity; control over one's speech/gossip, volubility, or betrayal of secrets; light/dark. Balances and adjustments must be accomplished socially as well as individually. Thus, adjustments between groups through marriage or the sharing of totems are parallel to and dependent upon self-control and equanimity among the individuals who comprise those groups. Similarly, reciprocity in marriage and gift-giving has its counterpart in empathic understanding—the reciprocity of viewpoints. The most condensed symbol of these reciprocities and balances is the pair of terms town/bush, the ramifications of which we have traced out in many narratives.

Most of the themes and formal procedures reviewed above are evi-

dent in the narratives collected in this chapter. Thus, the opposition in
the hunger narratives and in the hare-hyena narratives between an unjust elder and a clever youngster who redresses injustices appears here
as an opposition between a scheming senior wife and a virtuous junior
wife. The connection between these two kinds of elder-younger relationships is made clearer when we recall that a junior wife (*gberinya*)
addresses her elder co-wife as *n'koro* ("elder sister"), while a senior wife
(*bare* or *baramusu*) addresses her junior co-wife as *n'doge* ("my younger
sister"). These usages reflect the frequency of sororal polygyny among
the Kuranko, but it is also the case that a man explicitly compares the
relationships among his wives with the relationships among his children.
Conflicts and jealousies among co-wives reflect the biased or preferen-
tial behavior of a husband toward one wife, but they may also arise out
of the status inequalities of co-wives, their different temperaments and
backgrounds, and the different fortunes of their children. In everyday
life all such inequalities tend to be explained in terms of the wife's
behavior toward her husband. Even if a husband is indifferent to his
wife, she is told to "bear up for the sake of the children." However, in
the co-wife narratives problems of inequality and bias in domestic life
are subject to slightly different interpretations.

The connection between the narratives which deal with tensions
among co-wives and those which are concerned with the plight of orphans can be best understood by considering the link which the
Kuranko make between the fate of children and the behavior of
mothers. Just as a woman should treat her co-wife like a sister, so a
mother should treat her co-wife's child as if it were her own. The identifications which are formally established in terminology—co-wife =
sister, co-wife's child = own child—are, however, not always realized
in practice. It is recognized that a mother will love and care for her own
child (*den gbere*) with a devotion which it is difficult to extend to other
children, even though she may perform all the duties expected of a
surrogate mother. Similarly, a child refers to its mother's co-wife not as
mother (*na*) but as *na kura* ("new mother"). Problems in the control
over and extension of emotional ties are central to many narratives. It is
as if the goals of fosterage, co-parenthood, and the classificatory kinship
system cannot be realized, and so give rise to fictional images such as
the benevolent spirit of the bush who can bestow all favors, grant all
wishes, and care for a stranger's child as well as for its own. Such images
invert the ordinary view which associates love and care with *close* relationships (genealogically and geographically).

These contrasts between close and distant kin (which reflect distinctions between uterine and nonuterine relationships) are discussed in depth in the narratives in chapter 6. They are also touched upon in N.33 where the name of Soresawa's first braid of hair was "Your brother's child is your child but not your real child." Soresawa tells the chief that one's own child would not place the value of a shirt over the value of a person's life, and in this way he brings attention to the discrepancy between formal affiliations and emotional attachments. In the narratives in this chapter the same contradictions occur, but the problem of abolishing discriminations between real child/child by name, uterine/nonuterine sibling, or kinsman/stranger becomes one of making good the discrepancy between private feelings and social prescriptions. The resolution of these problems clearly involves the search for a transcendent morality.

Finally we should note the manner in which the opposition between the wife-mother and the seductress-buffalo in the Mande Fabori narratives now becomes an opposition between the good wife and the bad wife in the co-wife stories, and is further transformed into an opposition between the good mother and the bad mother in the orphan stories. The ambiguity of love is thus shown to be closely connected to the ambivalence of primary bonds. The contradictions between appearance and reality are also crucial, since the good is often masked and evil exaggerated in order to increase the dramatic effect of the stories. The way in which this contradiction is overcome draws us back to the theme of "pureheartedness" and the notion of harmony between inner states and social actions.

It is perhaps apposite that the narratives before us contain some of the most beautiful and engaging songs in the entire corpus. The unison and harmony achieved in the storytelling session by singing together exemplify the resolutions and reconciliations which are sought within the stories themselves.

N.35: *Why the Senior Wife Should Not Abuse Her Junior Co-Wives*

Narrated by Kenya Fina Marah. Recorded at Kondembaia, March 1970.

This narrative is about a chief and his *baramuse* [senior wife]. When a person is favored by life, he or she should not look down on other people or annoy them. If you are the *baramuse* you should not blame your co-wives for everything that goes wrong in the household.

The women plotted against her. They met to conspire against their co-wife. They said, "Companions, why don't we plot the downfall of our co-wife?" So they went to an old woman and told her that whenever something went wrong in the household the chief's *baramuse* would blame them and disgrace them. They said, "We are fed up with being disgraced, so, grandmother, help us." The old woman told them to fetch some raffia and two blades of cuttygrass. They brought these things to her and the old woman made them into something [a fetish].* The old woman said, "Tell me the name of the *baramuse*." They gave her name. As the old woman made that fetish she called out the name of the *baramuse*. When it was made, the old woman told them that one of them should take it and put it under a stone in the chief's washing yard so that when the chief bathed the next day the thing would talk to him as a human being talks. Then when the chief asked who put it there it would point out the person and name no one else but the *baramuse,* since her name had been put in the fetish. The women said, "All right." They took it and one of them put it in the chief's washing yard.

The next morning the *baramuse* heated water for the chief. She took the water to the washyard. The chief went to have his bath. He took off his clothes. He took the pan and dipped it in the water. As he splashed the water over himself the fetish began to sing:

> *N'ko i le Birisi Konde, n'to gbe de*
> *I le Birisi Konde, n'to gbe de*
> *N'ko ini m'bolo kone ke ma fele*
> *Ini na tafe kela ke ma fele*
> *I le Birisi Konde, 'ko n'de le nara i la*
> *Nnnnn na, ko i le ma na na de, fe fe fe fe fe*

> (I say you, Birisi Konde, look at me clearly
> You, Birisi Konde, look at me clearly
> I say you, look at my bracelet
> May you look at my lapa
> You, Birisi Konde, [they] say I brought you
> "Mother," I say that you did not bring me,
>   at all at all at all at all at all)

---

*In this narrative the fetish is given a human name: Birisi Konde.

The chief said, "Eh!" He could not even take his bath. He took his clothes quickly and went away. He ordered that the big men of the town beat the drum. He said, "There is something in my washing yard." They sounded the drum. Everyone went to the chief's washing yard. They said to the chief, "Well, you will have to call all your wives. This thing can talk, so it will point out the person who put it here." They searched for it, searched for it, searched for it, but they could not find it. At last a policeman lifted up a stone and they saw it lying there. The man said, "Chief, perhaps this is it." They said, "Put it down, then, and let us see it." He put it down. They said, "Perhaps it will talk." Then the fetish became angry. They said, "Let everyone stand still and listen to it. It will point out the person who brought it here. Whoever did not bring it here, the fetish will not point her out."

The women who had gone to the old woman went first. They whispered, "If this thing points us out we are finished." They whispered this. As each one stood before the fetish, it sang:

Nnnn na, ko i le ma na na de, fe fe fe fe fe

("Mother," I say that you did not bring me,
   at all at all at all at all at all)

All the women came, one after another, and the thing exonerated them. All the women who had brought it there were exonerated. Then the *baramuse*'s lady-in-waiting came and stood there. She sang:

I le Birisi Konde, n'to gbe wa
N'ko ini n'de bolo la wodi felen de
Ini n'kun-na-yala ke be ma fele
I le Birisi Konde, ko n'de le nara i la

(You, Birisi Konde, look at me clearly
I say you, look at this, my own bracelet of white coins
May you all look at my head tie
You, Birisi Konde, [they] say I brought you)

The fetish sang:

Nnnn na, n'ko i le ma na na de, fe fe fe fe fe

("Mother," I say that you did not bring me,
   at all at all at all at all at all)

So the thing exonerated her. The people said, "*Baramuse, this matter is almost settled now. Everyone has come and the thing has said that they did not put it here. Those that are from other houses and from other *luiye* have come. The thing has said that they did not put it here. Now chief, your *baramuse* should come and justify herself." The chief said, "All right."

(Before then the chief had sworn that he would burn the person who had brought that living thing and put it in his washing yard. But no one should treat love lightly. If someone you love is guilty of some crime you will not carry out the promised punishment).*

The *baramuse* came and stood there. She wore her finest shoes. She did not think that the thing would point her out. She put on her white coin bracelets, her gold earrings, and gold necklaces. She dressed in all the fine clothes that her co-wives had never had. As she sang she took them off, piece by piece.

> *I le Birisi Konde, n'to gbe de*
> *Ini n'kana-kone ke be ma felen de*
> *Ini n'tolo-la-sene ke be ma felen de*
> *I le Birisi Konde, ko n'de le nara i la*

> (You, Birisi Konde, look at me clearly
> May you look at all my neck beads
> May you look at all my gold earrings
> You, Birisi Konde, [they] say I brought you)

The fetish sang:

> *Ehhhh na, n'ko i le le nara n'de la, yeri te te te*

> (Ehhhh, "mother," I say it was you who brought me,
>   yeri te te te)

She said, "Eh!" She tore the necklace from around her neck and went and took one of the other wives' necklaces. She said, "Well, perhaps it has pointed me out because I am dressed differently from my co-wives." So she put on some different clothes. She went back and stood in front of the fetish. She said, "Well, I really must prove my innocence now. This is a false accusation. I did not bring this thing." The people said, "You must try now. Many people have come and the thing has said that you brought it. Try again now."

---

*This implies that the chief's love for his *baramuse* will make him go back on his word.

The woman sang [as before, except that one new line is added: *Ini n'sen-do-sambara ke be ma felen de* (May you look at my shoes)].

She sang this about four times but the thing still said that she had brought it. She sang it ten times but the thing still said that she had brought it. Then the people said, "Chief, this thing was not brought from afar. When you favor someone they will often do something that you did not expect of them." They sounded the drum once more. They said to the chief, "Well, those who you thought were responsible, did they do it? They did not do it. The person who is closest to you did it." The chief bowed his head and said, "Mmmm, I did not think this would happen."

He got up and went straight to the woman. He took the gold earring from her right ear. He took the other earring from her left ear. He took the gold necklace from her neck and the bracelets from her wrists. He said, "Well, from today she is my *baramuse* no more." He sent her from the *luiye* and made another wife his *baramuse*. The house was filled with people, and the chief and his new *baramuse* loved each other. Everything went smoothly from that time on. Therefore, if you are the *baramuse* never look down on your co-wives. That woman became despised by the chief.

N.36 *Silemani and His Dog*

Narrated by Noah Bokari Marah. Recorded (in English), March 1970.

There was once a man who had two wives. One wife bore a son. The other wife was childless. The little boy's mother died, so the boy was looked after by his mother's co-wife. The woman did not like the boy and she decided to poison him.

The boy had a dog. The dog did not go out with the boy; it stayed around the house to watch the woman. Whenever the woman prepared food for the boy she put poison in it. The dog would run to the boy and sing:

> *Sileman di Sileman, Sileman di Sileman*
> *I la wulu wa koro ye*
> *Kinne minala i ka wo don yo*
> *Yi kalne minala i ni wo mi yo*
> *Ni m'fagara n san na Silemani ta i ye dugu ro*
> *Silemani, i la wulu wa koro ye*

(Sileman, oh Sileman . . .
Your dog has observed something
The little portion of cooked rice that is coming for you, you
must not eat it. All right?
The cooking water that is coming, you drink that. All right?*
When I am dead, in that year, Sileman, go to some other place
Sileman, your dog has observed something)

This went on until Silemani was old enough to make a farm.
When Silemani went to clear his farm, his mother's co-wife prepared two lots of food. She put poison in one lot; the other lot she
left unpoisoned. She figured that when Silemani ate the poisoned
food and died, she would be able to eat the unpoisoned portion
and so clear herself of blame.

Silemani's dog observed all this. When the woman took Silemani
his food, the dog would run on ahead of her and arrive at the farm
first. It would tell Silemani which food was poisoned and which was
not.

The woman became increasingly envious of Silemani because he
was liked by both old and young. When Silemani's dog died he left
that place and went to another part of the country. He was much
loved there and he became very prosperous. He founded a village
that he named Nyawulia, "village of the useful dog." He named the
village Nyawulia because of the help his dog had given him and
because he did not want to forget the faithfulness and kindness of
dogs.

N.37: *The Orphan Child and the Stirring Spoon*

Narrated by Sara Mantene Marah. Recorded at Firawa, Christmas Day,
1969.

There was once an orphan child.† The child's mother was dead
and the child had been left in her mother's co-wife's care.

---

*One day the woman poisoned the rice, the next day the cooking water. In this way she
hoped to trick Silemani into eating or drinking the poisoned food. The third and fourth
lines of the song change according to which food has been poisoned.
†*kelne* = "one little"; all-alone; orphan child. In this narrative the child's father and
mother are both dead; she is in the care of her mother's co-wife and her father's younger
brother (who inherited the child and the child's mother's co-wife when the child's father
died).

One day the child dropped the woman's stirring spoon in the dirt. The woman said, "Eh, you have dropped my spoon in the dirt. You must wash it, but wash it nowhere else but in the river called Kulfagayi." The child said, "Eh, mother, don't make me go there to wash the spoon. My mother is dead and I have been left in your care. Don't make me go there to wash it. There are crocodiles in that river and wild animals on the way. Don't make me go there. My mother left me in your care." The woman said, "Well, you know me, my word is final. You must go and wash the spoon in no other river but the river called Kulfagayi." She gave the spoon to the child. The child started off. She walked as far as from here to Kabala, but passed through no towns on the way. When she had gone as far as from here to the Seli River,* she sang this song:

> My mother's co-wife's stirring spoon fell in the dirt, my
>   mother's co-wife's stirring spoon fell in the dirt
> She says that I must not wash it in any river but the river
>   Kulfagayi
> Kulfagayi is a long way away, and the way there is full of
>   dangers
> Oh, oh, such is the lot of an orphan child

The child was now a long way from home. She said (to herself), "The leopards are growling, and the lions are roaring. What am I to do? I am all alone here. Let me look up to God and go on. He will look after me." Then she said (thinking of her mother's co-wife), "Eh, do you not realize that my mother left me in your care? You sent no one but me to wash your spoon in Kulfagayi, to wash it in no other river but Kulfagayi. O God, save me." Then she continued on her way. She reached a place where the leopards were growling. She sang once more [as before].

She said, "Oh, these leopards are going to devour me today. I will not survive these dangers." But the child did not know that when her mother had died the woman had gone to Kulfagayi and been changed into a crocodile. When the child reached the river

---

*Kabala is about 35 miles from Firawa; the Seli River is about 10 miles from Firawa. The fictional river Kulfagayi is not identified, by the narrator, with any actual river. The meaning of *kulfagayi* is obscure, but includes the words *faga* ("to die," "to kill") and *yi* ("water").

Kulfagayi, the leopards were growling along its banks. The child sang once more [as before].

Then she dipped the stirring spoon in the water and began to wash it. The girl's mother looked up and saw that it was her daughter. The mother came and caught the child and carried her down into the river to her hole. The mother said to her, "Why are you here? You did not know that when I died I became a crocodile. Here I have everything I want, thanks to God. I can do anything for you if you need help." The child said, "Well, mother, you have seen how filthy I am. And, just because the stirring spoon slipped from my hands and fell in the dirt, your co-wife told me to go and wash it, but in no other river but Kulfagayi. I did not know that you were in the river." The child went on, "Mother, even if you do everything you can to help me, I must take this spoon back to your co-wife just to show her that God is all-powerful and that He has watched over me as I came here to wash the spoon. Whatever one does in this world, one should believe in God. That is why I should go and let your co-wife see me." So her mother gave the child seven trunks filled with dresses; she sent a trunk for her co-wife, one for her daughter's father's sister, and one for her daughter's "father." All these trunks were filled with dresses. Then she filled several boxes with other things and gave the girl £9,000. She said to the girl, "Now go, greet your father and give him these things. To my co-wife, who thought that you would die on your way here, give one trunk of dresses." She then sent seven strong men to carry the seven trunks for her daughter.

They traveled through the night and reached the town in the dark. The girl went and knocked at her father's door. Her father said, "Who is it?" She called her name. She said, "Open up, it is Fatamata. I don't want anyone to know that I am here, so please open the door quickly." Her father opened the door and said, "Have you come, my child?" The girl said, "Yes." Her father said, "La ila ila la, there is no God but Ala." The child said, "I have come from my mother's." Her father said, "Is your mother in Kulfagayi?" The girl said, "Yes, she is there. God alone is my chief. My mother did not die, she went to Kulfagayi. She asked to be remembered to you. She said that she will never again come here, and she gave me these trunks to bring to you. Open these trunks. Whatever you find inside them is yours. My mother gave me this trunk filled with dresses, together with this gold stirring spoon, for her co-wife. She gave me this other trunk to give to her co-wife's daughter; this other trunk is for your sisters and for my sisters."

In the morning they summoned everyone and gave them the gifts. Three days later, that co-wife called her own daughter to her. She said, "You will never prosper. Look at your companion. She has gone and brought all these things for her father and for all of us, but you idle the time away here. If you stay like that you will never prosper." She went on, "Now, you are not going to eat here today. Look here, look at this golden stirring spoon that your companion has brought to replace the one that fell in the dirt. Now, get ready to go." That girl dropped her stirring spoon in the dirt, then picked it up and went off. When she reached a far-away place, she began to sing:

> My mother's stirring spoon fell in the dirt, my mother's stir-
> ring spoon fell in the dirt.
> She says that I must not wash it in any river but the river
> Kulfagayi
> Kulfagayi is a long way away, and the way there is full of
> dangers
> Oh, oh, such is the lot of a child

The child went on until she reached Kulfagayi. The mother of the other girl looked up and saw her. She came quickly to the surface, caught the child and carried her down into the river to her hole. She took a trunk filled with pythons, another trunk filled with vipers (which we all know are poisonous; if one bites you, you will die; if you are bitten, there is no cure, you will go to *lakira*), and another trunk filled with scorpions. She gave all these to the girl, these seven trunks filled with all the evil things you can think of. She filled the trunks with all these horrible things. Then she said to the girl, "Now, you must take these seven trunks to your mother. They are all for your mother. Don't let anyone else see you. Go straight to your mother's room, lock the door, and open the trunks there."

When the child returned to town, she went straight to her mother's room. She knocked at the door. "Mother, mother, I have come." Her mother said, "Speak quietly and slowly so that your

father doesn't overhear us." The girl said (quietly), "I have come."
Her mother said, "Be quiet! Don't let anyone hear you! Come in
quietly."

When the girl was inside, the woman said, "Open one so that we
can see what is in it, but don't make a noise lest your father know
that you have come back. Lock the door so that no one will disturb
us. Your companion was silly enough to show everything to your
father." So they locked the door. Then they opened the first trunk,
but only a little. They opened the second trunk, but again only a
little. They opened the seven trunks. Then the girl told her mother
to open them all properly. She opened this one, this one, this one,
this one, this one, this one, this one. The snakes and scorpions
came out and beat them to death.

Therefore, it is not good to be covetous. Therefore, it is not
good to be envious. If someone has done something and you do
not know how he did it, but are envious and want to do the same
thing, then that envy will bring trouble. It is through envy that we
have snakes and scorpions in the world today. It is because when
that orphan went to the river called Kulfagayi and got all those
things, her mother's co-wife became envious and told her own
daughter to go to the same place and get those things as well. She
brought the snakes into the world.

Co-Wives and the Ambiguity of Beauty

The prevalence and incidence of the theme of co-wife conflict in narratives from throughout the African continent attest to the difficulties
of solving effectively the many problems associated with polygyny. The
following remarks by Francis Mading Deng on the Dinka could apply
equally to the Kuranko.

> Polygyny and the way it stratifies people on the basis of sex and age
> is fertile soil for jealousies, tensions, and conflicts. The intensity with
> which the stories dramatize the themes of co-wife jealousies indicates
> how obsessively concerned with them the Dinka are. . . . The Dinka
> practice polygyny with an awareness of its negative complications and
> implications. (Deng, 1974:173)

It has been argued that polygyny, because of its uneven sex ratio,
tends to encourage adultery because if a wife were to insist on remaining faithful to her husband she might run the risk of going childless; she

may seek a lover in order to have a child by him (Paulme, 1963a:9). Other writers have noted that polygyny causes competition among co-wives for sexual, material, and emotional advantages (Faladé, 1963:225–226; Dupire, 1963:82–83; Lamphere, 1974:107). Quite often, the husband fails to maintain the elementary rules of justice and equity so essential to polygyny, and this leads to jealousy among wives (Dupire, 1963:67).

Most of these problems occur in Kuranko society.[2] But they tend to be discussed in terms of their effect upon the fate of children. Unequal privileges in the household cause tensions and rivalries among co-wives, not just because some wives want certain advantages for themselves, but because a mother who has been hard done by will feel that her own child's prospects are thereby harmed. Yet to seek to secure advantages for one's own child is often regarded as a form of self-seeking since those advantages, so the Kuranko argue, can only be got by taking them from another person's child. The fortunes and misfortunes of different children in the family are thus interrelated and reflect the conduct of mothers. A mother should endure her lot and suffer the disadvantages which her children may suffer. The same passivity should obtain when a woman's children prosper, for she must never boast of her own or her children's fortunes. In my view, witchcraft fantasies and confessions among Kuranko women reflect the profound contradiction between a view which holds that women are responsible for the fate of their children and a view which stresses that women must be passive and forebearing. In confessing to witchcraft a woman assumes active control over the guilt and self-incrimination which her culture visits upon her; she bravely embodies and expunges the worst fears of men, namely that women may actively intervene in the processes of destiny.

A woman's conduct as a forebearing and dutiful wife and as a devoted mother is thought to ensure the prosperity of her children. Any deviation from this passive norm is considered to have disastrous consequences. For example, in several narratives discussed in chapter 5 (N.19, for example) inversions of the status positions of a ruler's wives lead to drastic changes in the fortunes of their children. The fate of the true heir depends upon the behavior of his mother. Yet, in restoring her son's birthright, the woman is made responsible for her husband's death. Perhaps the most difficult choices which Kuranko women have to make are those between doing what is necessary for the welfare of their children and doing what is necessary for personal happiness. In the narratives these choices are discussed in terms of the opposition between maternal love and sexual love, the latter being inimical to the former. The typical image of the mother is one of a devoted, stoical, dutiful woman who serves the interests of her husband and therefore of her children. By contrast, the seductress is usually depicted as a shape-shifter, half-person, half-animal, inconstant, deceitful, and self-willed.

Kuranko women refer to several sources of discontent in domestic life: a large age gap between husband and wife, status inequality between senior and junior wife, a senior wife's misuse of her authority by interfering with the rota system which theoretically ensures a just allocation of tasks and set times for each wife to share her husband's bed, competition for the husband's approval or favors, anxieties over the health and welfare of children, anxiety accompanying temporary barrenness, problems in rationalizing the unequal fortunes or endowments of children in the polygynous household, and personal incompatibilities among co-wives (see Jackson, 1977b:137–147, 177–178). If wronged or miserable, a woman may appeal to her brothers for help. Or she may ask her *numorgo* (husband's younger brother), with whom she has a joking relationship, to intercede for her. But Kuranko women are quick to point out that such appeals are seldom efficacious. Moreover, husbands dislike their wives spending too much time with natal kin or age-mates, and a woman's co-wives, a potential source of comfort and support in adversity, are often the causes of her unhappiness. That this is not always so is indicated by the way in which wives sometimes conspire to outwit or mock their husband, a pattern of behavior which is evident in several narratives.

In the narratives with which we are immediately concerned, problems arising from the senior wife's misuse of her authority are central. This may be because no redress at all is possible in such cases, because the senior wife's authority is granted by the husband much as an elder brother's authority is granted by the father. For reasons already given, a woman may not approach her husband directly. It can be suggested, therefore, that the figure of the malevolent or unjust *baramusu* (beloved/favored wife) assists the displacement of aggression from the real source of a woman's grievances—an indifferent, unjust, or inaccessible husband. The fact that polygyny seems to give rise to problems of age and status inequality may reflect the functional relationship between polygyny and social stratification (Clignet, 1970:21). But these problems do not center upon the husband-wife relationship, at least not in the narratives; rather, they are worked out in terms of fictionalized conflicts between an unjust senior wife and a virtuous junior wife.

The concern for the correct use of authority, which underlies the co-wife narratives, is equally apparent in the narratives collected in chapters 3 and 4. We saw there how injustices are redressed by the wronged person employing the same tricks against the wrongdoer. Deceit is always turned against the deceiver. Furthermore, we noted how the wrongdoer is generally someone who choses to use his authority or magical powers for selfish rather than social ends. He is at last displaced by his erstwhile victim or by an underling who, by choosing to use the same powers properly, deserves to gain the social position which his persecutor must forfeit. Through this fictional pattern, positive attributes such as cleverness, strength, magnanimity, and self-control are brought into alignment with responsible social positions. There is thus the appearance of a determinate relationship between social and psychophysical dimensions of reality.

From a purely formal point of view, each narrative is characterized by a number of simple switching operations which accomplish various transitions and transformations within a given set of elements. These elements include the stock figures, events, situations, objects, and attributes which are typical of folktales everywhere. What differs from society to society are the kinds of formal operations and transformations which are carried out, and these are decided by the problems which people choose to bring the folktale to bear upon. The sense that a problem has been solved and an ambiguity reduced derives from the fact that the same elements are present at the close of the narrative that were given at the start. In cybernetic language we might say that the transformations create no new element, and that "the set of operands is *closed* under the transformation" (Ashby, 1964:II). The same point is made by Lévi-Strauss in his account of the similarity between mythical thought and the activity of the *bricoleur*.

> His universe of instruments is closed and the rules of the game are always to make do with "whatever is at hand," that is to say with a set of tools and materials which is always finite and is also heterogenous because what it contains bears no relation to the current project, or indeed to any particular project, but is the contingent result of all the occasions there have been to renew or enrich the stock or to maintain it with the remains of previous constructions or destructions. (Lévi-Strauss, 1966:17)

Recombining and reshuffling the stock elements by using such schemes as chiasmus has the effect of altering our way of experiencing the problems which those elements are made to signify. This in turn assists us in breaking free from habitual ways of looking at these problems. Suspense occurs when we are confronted by issues, albeit in allegorical guise, which we ordinarily take for granted or prefer to leave undiscussed. Surprise occurs when we find ourselves sharing in the resolution of a problem which we thought to be insoluble, or participating in the construction of moral meanings which we thought were already made. It goes without saying that these new modes of awareness are inefficacious. Folktales and myths change nothing while they remain rigorously bracketed apart from reality and while people manipulate only homologues or simulacra of the real world. But folktales are neither futile nor pathetic. The active engagement of individuals in a project which involves a search for appropriate ethical interpretations and responses to actual situations must be regarded as an exercise in seizing advantage over fortuity and over all that at first glance appears to lie outside the scope of personal determination.[3]

Let us now turn to a more detailed study of co-wife narratives. Most are concerned with jealous attachments which prevent cooperation and sharing. In one narrative a married woman rubs a witch ointment on her body which kills other women whom her husband marries and brings home. Fortunately, the ointment has one fault: it should not be allowed to dry on the skin. One new wife, knowing this, delays coming to live with her husband so that the ointment will dry on the senior wife's body and kill her. In another tale, a young wife who has not borne any children for her husband is pleased when her senior co-wife dies. She sings in celebration of the things which she now has to herself: her husband's children, his granaries, his sacks of groundnuts, and his sexual favors. But her shamelessly outspoken sentiments bring about her own death, and the narrator concludes the tale with the advice: "Don't celebrate another person's misfortune."

In these and other comparable narratives the wives who do not want their husbands to marry other women are like the women who refuse to marry (see the narratives summarized on pp. 148–49), or like the widow who refuses to remarry. In every case, selfish compulsions prevent the realization of social goals. The figure of the woman who wants to keep her husband to herself (and employs deceit to this end) is also reminiscent of the corrupt, gluttonous, or covetous status superiors in the hunger narratives and in the hare-hyena narratives. Selfishness always implies uncontrolled appetites or emotional fixations. And it is usually a clever and virtuous status inferior who plays the active role in redressing the injustices which occur. In one narrative (told by Denka Marah), a senior wife kills her junior co-wife by means of witchcraft, but the dead woman's spirit is able to inform the husband of what really occurred and he kills the senior wife. Once more, the person who is at first the victim becomes the active agency whereby the wrongdoer is punished. The countering of evil strategies is then usually accompanied by an exchange of roles, so that the corrupt senior wife is either banished or dies and the junior wife takes her place.

The problem of corruption in the use of authority is clearly related to the problem of controlling appetites and emotions. And problems of self-restraint are greatest when there is a scarcity or unequal distribution of resources such as foodstuffs, blessings, talents, physical abilities, and natural endowments. Jealousy and envy are likely to arise in such situations, and justice and equity must be created by compensating for these unfair apportionments. In N.35 inequalities are both social and behavioral. Indeed, there is a polarization in these narratives, as in others, of socially determined attributes on the one hand (status and authority) and psychophysical attributes on the other (behavior, appearance, natural abilities). Ambiguities occur when a person in a high status position behaves badly by misusing his or her authority, or by using another person's trust as a means of deceit. In N.35 the senior wife is loved and trusted by her husband, but she uses this trust as a means of exploiting and ill-treating her co-wives. Deceptive appearances are signified by the senior wife's finery, but this does not fool the fetish, which embodies clarity of vision and a sense of justice which cannot be perverted. In a parallel tale the marginal and incorruptible powers of an old woman are the means by which deceit is found out and justice done. A man marries a woman for her great beauty, but she is a monkey in disguise. Her tail, which remains unchanged (much to the disgust of her co-wives), betrays her true nature. The man's senior wife exploits her husband's trust in her, by recounting a fake dream in which it is allegedly foretold that all the wives will daub the walls of the new house undressed. The new wife seeks the help of an old woman and, to cut a long story short, the tail is taken from the new wife and attached to the senior wife. The following day the wives appear naked to daub the house walls and the senior wife is shamed when her tail is discovered, just as she sought to shame her junior co-wives.

In these narratives affections and appearances are shown to be misleading. Stripping off clothes signals the stripping away of false appearances, while the disgrace of the senior wife signifies the end of love. Each narrative concludes by emphasizing the nature of correct behavior and the proper use of authority. Correct behavior implies a consonance between intentions and actions (appearances do not belie reality), while the proper use of authority involves a balance between command over subordinates and concern for their welfare (desires do not pervert duty). In Kuranko thought, the stripping away of clothes also signifies a transfer of status. Thus, the senior wife loses her position and a junior wife assumes it. In the process, positive behavioral traits come to be associated with responsible social positions.

The way in which the sweet words of love and false appearances distract people and pervert the course of justice is a theme which recurs throughout the corpus of Kuranko narratives. And, as we have seen many times already, these same deceptions are turned against the deceiver in order to redress injustices. In an unpublished narrative related by Sumayila Kargbo of Firawa, a chief has two wives. He promises to send people to work for his junior wife, but his senior wife tells him that if he does not send the people to work for her instead, this will signify that he does not love her. The chief then decrees that the senior wife's work should be done first. The junior wife forthwith changes herself into a beautiful bird and distracts the people with her singing. Everyone, including the chief, is so spellbound by the bird's song that no work is done at all. In this narrative the symmetry of the senior wife's sweet words and the junior wife's sweet song reinforces the sense of closure which occurs when the perversion of secular justice is countered by a kind of poetic justice.

It is important to note that misrepresentations and deceitful ruses are only justified when they are means of redressing an injustice which has already been done. If we recall the fate of the hare in N.18 when he chooses to use deceit for purely selfish ends, we will appreciate the parallel situation in another co-wife narrative where the junior wife kills her senior co-wife simply because she is jealous of her and lazy. The junior wife is finally found out and killed, the transitional episode centering upon a song overheard by an old woman by a lakeside. Such liminal markers provide breaks between the initial situation in which injustices are done and the denouement in which the injustices are redressed.

Two themes emerge from the foregoing discussion. First, the power of love tends to work against the disinterested use of authority. Second, superficial appearances tend to prevent good judgments of behavior. Much of the force of these narratives depends upon ambiguities present in the term *baramusu*, and in the concept of beauty (*kin*). English-speaking Kuranko often translate the term *baramusu* as "working wife/woman," or as "beloved wife," or as "senior wife." These translations indicate that the term connotes economic, emotional, and status privileges. In the context of the narratives, however, it is the supposedly close emotional bond between the *baramusu* and her husband which is played up. It is because she is her husband's best-beloved and most trusted wife that she is able to deceive him and to abuse her junior co-wives without his knowledge. This contrast between manifest behavior and subjective character is also a source of ambiguity in the concept *kin*.

In one tale Denka Marah refers to the 56 wives of the chief as being each "as short and ugly as a horn in the armpit of a tortoise." It must be understood, however, that the contrasted terms *kin* (beautiful/good) and *yugu* (ugly/bad) may be used to describe both aesthetic qualities and behavioral traits. Thus, a person whose behavior is considered antisocial may be called "ugly" or "unbeautiful" (*ma kin*) since, as one informant expressed it, "if a person's ways are not good, then he is not good, and whatever is not good is ugly." I once asked a group of young unmarried men to tell me what traits they found admirable in a woman. One man answered, "If a wife could prepare good food and bear children for her husband, then she would be admirable (*kin*)." Another man commented, "If a woman is beautiful then it is because she is faithful to her husband." A third man noted that "Even if a woman has a long graceful neck and fine features, if she behaves badly then she could not be called beautiful." Others concurred with this view, and it was clear that good or fine behavior was more highly valued than good looks, although the same term, *kin*, was used of both behavior and appearance. On another occasion I was sitting with a group of men when a young man whom I did not know joined us. One of my companions observed that the young man was "beautiful," and when I expressed surprise (for his looks seemed to me to be unremarkable), he pointed out that the young man had a fine presence (*miran*). Behavior, comportment, and fluency or prowess in speaking are all considered to be more important than mere appearances, posturings, and vainglory. Yet the concept of *kin* has a wide range of connotations. It may be compared with the classical

Greek term *kalos*, which meant beautiful, handsome, attractive in appearance, as well as praiseworthy, honorable, admirable, and good in action, behavior, and achievement (Dover, 1974:69–73).[4]

In the narratives, key contrasts are drawn between apparent and real goodness, and between senior and junior social positions. The fact that the senior wife in N.35 is only apparently good means that a reshuffling of elements must occur so that virtue comes to be associated with the senior position and deceit extirpated. The junior wife often exemplifies real goodness, although her role is marginal and her qualities are at first hidden from sight. The marginal status of the junior wife reflects her lack of real authority within the household, as well as the fact that she is less fully assimilated into her husband's household than the longer-established senior wife (Clignet, 1970:47). For these reasons, junior wives are in real life likely to be more dissatisfied and more refractory than senior wives; certainly most divorces occur within the first two years of marriage (Jackson, 1977b:99). But in the narratives, the social and psychological marginality of the junior wife makes it appropriate that she should signify the extrasocial powers which can perceive error and redress injustices. Her identity tends to merge, however, with other liminal figures, such as the old woman fetish-maker who appears in N.35 and comparable narratives. Through these marginal agencies, each of which signifies a disinterested and incorruptible justice, deceits are discovered and goodness transferred to the position of authority where it should, ideally, be concentrated. The transition of junior wife to senior position is at the same time a transformation of marginal powers into secular authority.

The Plight of Orphans

I collected eleven narratives whose main theme was the plight of orphan children; two are published here. This particular theme appears more frequently than the theme of co-wife conflict because the Kuranko are mainly concerned with the ways in which conflicts between co-wives affect the fate of children. Thus, the orphan narratives must be studied as extensions or transformations of the co-wife narratives.

The Kuranko word which I have translated as "orphan" is *kelne*. It means literally "one little," but can be used of a child who has been orphaned, abandoned, or even neglected. Strictly speaking, an orphan in Kuranko society is a child whose real mother is dead. The child is thus "all alone" in the world. I refer to the foster mother (who is customarily the child's mother's co-wife) as a "stepmother" since the Kuranko word *na kura* ("new mother") has similar connotations to the English term.[5] The Kuranko say that an orphaned child may be neglected or mistreated by its stepmother. Because a father plays a negligible role in child care, he will be blind to these injustices. It is also said that a man has many wives and children; he will accordingly have to disperse his affections and attentions among many individuals. A mother, by contrast, can devote a great deal of time and attention to her own children.

It is important to establish the extent to which the fictional image of the neglected orphan child is an accurate reflection of real situations. Sinkari Yegbe once told me that the saddest of all stories are those which deal with unrequited love and with the plight of orphans. When I asked her whether orphans actually suffer the kinds of disadvantages attributed to them in the narratives, she said, "Yes, in the old days they really did suffer. After preparing food, the orphan's *na kura* would tell the child it could take the leavings. That is why the first people [the ancestors] told stories about children whose real mothers were dead." In another account of the ill-treatment of orphans, Morowa Marah's wife also stressed the way in which some women share food unequally in order to deprive the orphan of nourishment. She noted too that the luckless child's father will remain ignorant of the injustice because he accepts his wife's word in matters concerning the welfare of his children (Jackson, 1977b:143).

In the narratives, as in everyday discourse, food deprivation is a recurring metaphor for emotional neglect and social injustice. The metaphor of being without clothes is also common. It is not surprising, therefore, that the fantasized compensations for the misfortunes of orphans are gifts of fine raiment, food, and wealth. Of all these, food is primary. In N.36 the child's stepmother gives the child an impossible task to perform: washing a cooking spoon in a far-off river in the wilderness. In another tale it is famine which makes the woman abandon her twin children in the bush so that she can carry some wild yams back to the village.

In yet another unpublished narrative, told by Yanku Pore Kargbo of Firawa, two boys, one of whom is an orphan, are sent to scare birds from the rice farm. The mother of the first boy brings food to the farm, but she tells her son not to share it with the orphan. A bush spirit called *kukuwe* then comes to the farm carrying a deer which he has caught. Using the deer as bait, the bush spirit tries to entice the orphan child to descend from the bird-scaring platform. But the child sees through the *kukuwe's* sweet words and cleverly counters the busy spirit's stratagems. Finally the *kukuwe* goes away and leaves the deer, singing as he goes, "Child, you have a golden tongue." Later, the stepmother persuades her own son to try to get a deer from the *kukuwe*, using the same ruse. But the child descends from the bird-scaring platform after singing only one line of the song, and he is devoured by the bush spirit.

In another narrative, which I collected in two versions (one related by Minata Konde of Kamadugu Sukurela, the other told by Balansama Marah of Firawa), a stepmother refuses to give food to the orphan child in her care. Soon after this, the *ture* logs over the child's mother's grave begin to take root and grow. The tree bears abundant fruit. Whenever the orphan is hungry he sings to the tree, which then lowers its branches and offers its fruit. The song is worth citing.

> Where an orphan child eats, a child with a mother may not eat;
> Where a child whose mother is alive eats, a child whose mother is
>   dead may not eat;
> So come down, *ture,* come down, my mother's *ture* . . .

The stepmother discovers that the orphan has access to the "sweet fruit" of the *ture* tree, and she sends her own son to pick some of the fruit. The boy cannot stop eating, and he refuses to climb down from the tree. The orphan makes the tree lift up its branches, so stranding his half brother. The villagers then promise the orphan bridewealth and a bride if he will make the tree lower its branches. So the orphan is abundantly compensated for his initial misfortune, while the step-mother and her own child are disgraced.

In these two unpublished narratives a contrast is drawn between the orphan child who is able to control his appetites, and his half brother who is unable to delay immediate gratification. The half brother follows his mother's advice without question, but the orphan child shows a de-tached and independent attitude of mind which enables him to turn apparent adversity to his advantage. His control over the raising and lowering of the limbs of the *ture* tree signifies a control over his emo-tional attachment to his mother. The half brother's overweaning at-tachment to his own mother entails a dependency and foolishness which bring about his downfall. The narratives thus establish a link between the absence of a mother and the presence of an independent attitude. What seems to be a disadvantage is shown to be an advantage, just as in N.6, *The Woman Who Tricked the Nyenne into Telling Their Names*, Keti Ferenke showed that hunger often makes people wise and resourceful.

These examples indicate that kinship bonds are often spoken of in terms of nurturance and food-sharing. Yet, dependence upon such bonds is not altogether desirable, and may have the same socially negative consequences as uncontrolled appetites or emotional obsessions. The strongest of all kinship bonds is undoubtedly the primary bond between mother and child. This bond signifies dependency, emotionality, and nurture. Outgrowing or severing this bond, and learning to bring appetites and emotions under systematic control, are the main purposes of initiation. Thus, the source of nurturance is often regarded ambivalently because dependency upon early kinship attachments can prevent a person from growing up and assuming full responsibility for the world in which he lives. As we saw in the prevented-successions narratives, social continuity is threatened if the young resist growing up or the old prevent the young from growing up. In the narratives brought together in chapter 7 we saw how the fate of children is endangered if mothers cannot control their own emotional impulses. The ambivalence of primary bonds thus springs from an existential conflict between the tendency to want to abnegate control to another and the drive to assume responsibility for the world in which one lives.[6]

The narratives establish two important contrasts. The first is between the independent orphan and the dependent half brother. The solitary and detached social status of the orphan serves to dramatize his independence and self-restraint. Conversely, the half brother's overweening attachment to his mother is, in the narrative context, a metaphor for dependency, unrestrained emotionality, and lack of insight and judgment. The second contrast is between the bad "mother" and a good caretaker figure. While the stepmother attempts to poison, kill, starve, or steal from the orphan, the surrogate parent helps foster the orphan's independence. The acts of attempted murder or poisoning, of starving or stealing, must be understood metaphorically. This is because such acts do not occur typically in real life, but, as fictional images, they convey real fears, particularly the fear that the mother, who is a source of solace and succor, will prevent the development of the child's independence. There is, of course, a functional relationship between the mother/stepmother contrast and the orphan/half sibling contrast because conflicts among *fadennu* (half siblings) are thought to derive from conflicts among their mothers. Even when only one of these contrasts occurs in a narrative, the other is implied. The ambivalence of the mother-child bond occurs in the relationship between half siblings and in both cases gives rise to the problems whose solutions are sought in these narratives.

Negative and positive elements of this ambivalence are polarized in the contrasts between malevolent and benevolent figures. By killing or driving off the malevolent figure (usually the stepmother), an artificial solution is offered to the problem of "the simultaneous presence in kinship bonds of love and hate" (Freeman, 1973:117). The creation of a state of unequivocal amity depends upon the timely intervention of a caretaker figure from *outside* the kinship universe: a *nyenne* or God. In other words, bonds of communitas are established in lieu of kinship bonds. This way of managing the ambivalence of kinship bonds by eclipsing them altogether is equally evident in Kuranko rites of initiation and of sacrifice (Jackson, 1977a, 1977b).

The absence of fathers in these narratives can now be explained. First, the father's role in child care is, in real life, negligible. Second, the narratives imply that true moral worth, including amity, is won by deliberate choice and through purposeful action; it should not be regarded as a product of external or fortuitous factors. Kinship bonds are externally given and immutable, and, because they cannot be chosen or changed, they cannot serve to epitomize moral worth. This is why narratives which deal with problems of moral judgment and responsibility tend to employ a nonkinship idiom, while narratives concerned with justice in the allocation and performance or rights and duties remain within the universe of kinship. In the totemic narratives, for example, acts of altruism and magnanimity are performed by nonkinsmen, strangers, and animals. And in the group of narratives which deal with reciprocity (N.27–N.31), friendship or relationships between individuals and bush spirits are the predominant means of discussing problems of choice, judgment, and responsibility. In the narratives about orphans the crucial problem is one of eclipsing kinship ties altogether so that the child becomes a responsible, self-governing person. This is very much the "problem" which is worked out in initiation rites, and in both instances the greater emotional pull of maternal attachments means that breaking free from the father is only a secondary theme. Thus the father's role is minimal. The father does not appear at all in N.36 and N.37. In two other similar narratives the father lays down an absurd rule or blindly follows bad advice, and is finally made to regret his stupidity. But in no narrative is he a central figure. Nor does he ever actively or effectively compensate for the injustices suffered by the orphan child. His ineffectual and peripheral role is, however, contrasted with the powerful extrasocial agencies and figures which help the orphan and punish his persecutor. I collected three versions of N.36; in each version the supernatural helper is a dog. In N.37 and in the story of the *ture* tree, the dead mother's spirit is the orphan's help. In all other narratives, the benevolent helper is a bush spirit.

The problem of having no mother alive reflects the fact that co-wives do not ordinarily share in the raising of each other's children. There is an intensely dyadic relationship between mother and child, and this is evident in the oft-repeated Kuranko phrase "The child's destiny is in its mother's hands." It is also true that the unequal fortunes or endowments of children in the household are causes of dissatisfaction and latent hostility among co-wives. The situation is directly comparable to that found among the Bété (Clignet, 1970:177–179). Despite these realities, Kuranko men assert that a mother should and can behave in a motherly way to all the children nominally in her care, both real and classificatory. In the case of sororal marriages this may be true, and the term for a sororal marriage, *sole bambane*, means "small raffia basket on the back," implying that the younger sister will help the older sister with child care and domestic work. But in many cases there is a disparity between the dogma of cooperation among co-wives and actual domestic practice. Repressed guilt, springing from hostility felt toward a co-wife or a co-wife's child, may find an outlet in witchcraft confession (Jackson, 1975). And the narratives about quarrelsome co-wives and deprived orphan children are further evidence of unresolved conflicts in domestic life. In conversation, informants tend to avoid coming to terms with these issues, and use offhand remarks such as "God will take care of the orphan child." In the narratives, similar evasions are evident. It is always through the agency of an extrakinship figure that injustices are corrected and the discrepancy made good between what is and what should be. Let us now examine more closely the character of these marginal figures.

In most of the narratives, the disadvantaged child is cared for and helped by a *nyenne*, a creature of the wild. But the *nyenne*'s role is complementary to the role of an old woman herbalist or fetish-maker who makes possible the child's return to the town. The old woman, who supplies crucial information in exchange for a surfeit of food, is the central mediator in N.8 and in three unpublished orphan stories. In one she facilitates the return to life and to the town of a murdered good wife. In another she tells the chief what she has seen at the lakeside, and as a result the "beautiful" girl and her mother are brought back to the town. The same events occur in another tale, except that the chief is deposed by a merman, and the girl and her mother become rulers in his stead.

From a purely formal standpoint, the narrative events imply transformations in which good moral qualities, which are initially disguised or associated with marginal individuals, are coalesced with high status positions. That kindness, magnanimity, justice, moral and physical beauty are attributed to marginal figures indicates the degree to which social harmony is sought through powers and agencies which are ordinarily beyond and even inimical to the social order. Movements between the town and the wilderness signify a dialectic between givenness and choice, community and individuality. The old woman's gift of knowledge in exchange for food reminds us too of a recurring contrast between want and plenty. But material concerns do not determine the narrative themes. The scarcity or unequal apportionments of food afford a metaphorical means of bringing into discussion problems of inequality and lack of all resources, physical, intellectual, and emotional.

Similarly, the contrast between town and wilderness is closely related to other contrasts such as belly/back (of a house), seed/husk[7] (of words), male/female (semen = seed; womb = husk), and elder/younger. While the sustenance of individual life and the maintenance of the social system depend upon the seed or town, we find that the wilderness or the "back yard" (*sundu kunye ma*) is the source, in ritual and in narratives alike, of the compensatory powers which can be tapped to redress injustices, protect life, and restore harmony. The narratives explore, through several allegorical dimensions simultaneously, the ethical imperatives of this feedback between the town and the wilderness. Drawn from a society whose strangeness and remoteness make it a kind of wilderness for us, the narratives present the means of bringing to life a new awareness of our common humanity.

9 *Directions*

For me, one of the most arresting aspects of everyday life in a Kuranko village is the great amount of time people devote to the intense discussion of matters which to a stranger often seem trivial, time-consuming, and even pointless. Every anthropologist encounters something in his adopted society which produces anxiety and irritation. In my case it was this disputatious element in Kuranko life. Heated debates would arise and end unpredictably, often taking precedence over matters which seemed to me more pressing. A domestic argument would attract a crowd and be thrown open spontaneously to the comments of all and sundry. A simple misdemeanor would become the subject of the most complicated discussion, and minor points of local history, etymology, or genealogy would soon engage the interest of passersby, all eager to advance their views until general agreement was reached.

The delight with which people initiated argument and the volubility of their discourse seemed quite baffling to me until I realized that speech was one of the keys to understanding the tenor and purpose of Kuranko social life. My own research project was, of necessity, like a prolonged interior monologue. Highly personalized and addressed to issues in an intellectual community far from the village world where I was living, my research work distorted my perception of Kuranko activity. Whereas my work often demanded an intellectual separation from village life, Kuranko activity entailed the subversion of personal goals in the interests of creating a viable moral community. As we have seen in so many of the narratives, openness and directness in speaking are crucial to this project. I was thus brought round to the view that Kuranko activity had to be understood in terms which were different from those I was accustomed to, and that I would have to overcome the contradiction between my own sense of individual project and the strongly communal character of Kuranko life. In addressing this book, a synthesis of African and Western ideas, both to the Kuranko and to the world of scholarship I hope to compensate in some measure for the divisions that literacy and anthropology impose upon us.

Kuranko narratives must be seen as part of the continual interplay of viewpoints referred to above. As Keti Ferenke Koroma stressed, the *tilei* are a form of critical scrutiny, a way of looking closely at matters of central concern to the whole community. I have taken the view, moreover, that the narratives facilitate discussion of pressing ethical issues in everyday life. Like ordinary discussion (*kiraboi*) and dialectic (*sosole,* lit. "denial"), the narratives rehearse the values upon which communitas is built: mutuality, reciprocity, equity, openness. And in both domains of discourse each person declares his own view and discovers his own meaning. I have emphasized, however, that agreement is arrived at, not imposed. The narratives suspend orthodox solutions and reach out for resolutions that cover and highlight problems met in real life. Dramatic inversion and ethical obscurity are apparent everywhere, not only because such devices encourage the critical participation of an audience but because they inspire people to decide upon values which are ordinarily left undiscussed. In narratives and discourse alike the Kuranko thus express the conventional wisdom of the collectivity through their own individual perspectives. A balance between personal autonomy and collective interdependence is achieved. Indeed, it can be suggested that one criterion of efficient social organization is the extent to which idiosyncratic and collective imperatives find expression in the same activity at the same time.

Kuranko narratives are not mere fables that present ready-made moral conclusions. They suggest rather than impose answers to existential dilemmas and anxieties. Such a view also informs Bruno Bettelheim's study of European fairy tales, *The Uses of Enchantment* (1978). Bettelheim argues that the tales provide a child with the vicarious means of resolving problems of growing up, of discovering his or her own identity. Unlike myths, whose solutions are "definite," the fairy tale "is suggestive; its messages may imply solutions, but it never spells them out. Fairy tales leave to the child's fantasizing whether and how to apply to himself what the story reveals about life and human nature" (1978:45). Elsewhere Bettelheim notes that the tale is therapeutic *because* the reader is free to find his own solutions through it (1978:25). Expurgation undermines the psychological usefulness of the tales and reduces the number of meanings which may be found in them. Such expurgation may be considered a form of adult tyranny over the imaginative freedom of the child. Certainly the common notion that folktales are naive children's fables beneath the dignity of mature attention is often a result of the ways adults have censored and trivialized the tales both in relating and in publishing them.

Kuranko narratives epitomize the folktale in its pristine form. They are related and enjoyed as much by adults as by children. Indeed, many of the narratives have greater appeal to adults and so must be accorded the same critical attention usually reserved for the novel or play in Western societies. The Kuranko *tilei* is a sophisticated form of spoken art. But in order to appreciate it fully we must consider it within a wider context of storytelling events, interpretative discourse, cognitive style, ethical concern, and praxis. Individual texts are to a large extent products of a collector's work, and such texts, isolated from the site of their genesis and reproduction, often seem naive and whimsical. The very meaning of the tales is altered and distorted by the method of collecting them. It is thus important that analysis of texts should involve returning them to their social context rather than furthering their detachment from it. In this way we may avoid the simplistic views that folktales exemplify an infantile phase of animistic thought or express mythopoeic faculties of the primitive imagination.

Folktales cannot be written off as atrophied myths or children's fables. The minor place which folktales occupy in literate societies should not blind us to their importance in tribal societies with tightly knit communities and comparatively simple technologies of communication. We must emphasize the didactic role of the folktale in socialization, and the way in which the folktale mediates ethical discussion. We must also recognize the allegorical character of the folktale. It is not enough to reduce the meaning of a tale to the laws underlying its composition, or to show that it reveals innate properties of the human mind. Nor is it sufficient to apply unreservedly the standard interpretations of symbols from the unconscious of literate Westerners to the narratives of preliterate peoples. Kuranko narratives are ways in which people create community and interpret the world which they work in together. The narratives are not merely means of personal catharsis, vicarious self-fulfillment, or psychological defense.

The Sociology of the Folktale

I want to turn now from questions relating to the interpretation of tales in specific ethnographical contexts to some of the problems of studying the folktale as a genre. Here we enter a domain of discourse in which "unintentional inevitabilities" and hidden impersonal factors are paramount, and we address ourselves to understanding the relationships between literary genres, social history, and cultural transformations.

The first point that needs to be made clear is that the relationship between literary genre and subject matter is indeterminate. For instance, direct parallels can be found, at the level of subject matter, when we compare the Cinderella folktale (which has a worldwide distribution), Richardson's novel *Pamela,* and numerous teleplays and soap operas which deal with the triumph of the socially disadvantaged heroine. Again, there are parallels to be drawn between Defoe's *Robinson Crusoe* (perhaps the first novel) and the Kuranko narrative *The Origin of the Yimbe Drum* (N.27). Both are allegories of the wilderness[1] in which the heroes, isolated from the social order, must create a world from hitherto untapped resources. While the young hero in the Kuranko narrative braves the hazards of the wilderness to acquire a drum which will prevent the disintegration of the community, Robinson Crusoe uses his resourcefulness for personal gain. The Kuranko hero makes initiation, the ritual means of shaping and reshaping the moral community, possible. Robinson Crusoe is, by contrast, the triumphant individualist, a "monitory image of the ultimate consequences of absolute individualism" (Watt, 1972:102). Whereas Defoe's hero saves his soul by overcoming the world, the hero of the *yimbe* drum narrative saves the community by overcoming his own individual inclinations. But the different moralities depicted in these allegories are not determined by differences between the structure of folktales and the structure of novels. Rather, they reflect differences in the social and moral milieux from which the allegories emerge. It seems to me that we have to account independently for the appearance and disappearance of genres and the appearance and disappearance of subject matters. Here my main concern is with the latter.

It has been possible to show that the Kuranko *tilei* is integrated with a particular form of social organization, a particular conception of the person, and a particular configuration of ethical postulates. The basis of Kuranko social life is the local community. I have shown elsewhere (Jackson, 1977b) that the community is a product of concerted ritual practice and that it transcends kinship, religious, and secular political distinctions. The concept of personhood (*morgoye*) suggests a style of personal activity. It connotes a spirit of mutuality issuing from acts of individual magnanimity within the community.[2]

The community is not some epiphenomenon. It *is* the unit of production, consumption, ownership, and exchange. The link which I have emphasized between Kuranko narratives and initiation rites is a crucial one because these are the principal contexts in which the values of community are rehearsed and thrown into relief. Indeed, these are the theaters in which the production and reproduction of the community take place. But the social order would never be made and maintained unless at the same time every person found in that enterprise some personal meaning. Narratives and initiation rites are milieux in which each person realizes his or her potential to interpret and decide upon the world. As Raymond Williams points out, literary production is creative in the sense of being a specific practice of self-making, of self-composition, *as well as* one of the most "distinctive, durable, and total forms" of social process (1977:210–212). In the Kuranko case, this process of self-making is masked, because the holistic emphasis on community necessitates playing down the autonomy of the individuals who produce it. Both in the narratives and in rituals the sense of self gives way to what Louis Dumont calls "sociological apperception" (1972:39). But this eclipsing and depersonalizing of the individual in art should not be taken to mean that the individual as an empirical agent does not exist. The "particular man"—the empirical subject of speech, thought, and will—exists in all societies, though the independent, autonomous, and essentially nonsocial conception of moral personhood is typical only of modern societies (Dumont, 1965:15).

In Kuranko narratives the notion of the person reflects the ontological priority of the collectivity. But the Kuranko universe is a personalistic one, and this collectivity includes bush spirits, ancestors, fetishes, a divine creator, as well as man. As we have seen, these are not thought of as separate entities but as various aspects of being.[3] Thus an animal may epitomize the essence of personhood (in the totemic myths), a fetish may possess will and discernment (N.27), injustices may be redressed by God (N.28), by a fetish (N.35), or by a clever animal like the hare (N.13–N.17), and bush spirits may act as responsible human beings, aiding the disadvantaged and supporting the just. Naturally, these personalized forms can easily exchange guises. God turns into a woman in N.28, a buffalo turns into a woman in N.34, and in many narratives parts of the body are removed and replaced, destroyed and restored, as if the body and life were impermanent states. I take the view that metamorphosis and shape-shifting cannot be understood in terms of the idea of one *entity* changing into another. These transformations involve relocations of consciousness and reapportionments of moral and intellectual properties. The transformation of the incestuous brother and sister into crocodile and turtle in N.26 is comparable to the situation in which an unjust elder is displaced by a wise youngster. In both cases there is an ethical redistribution in which outward form or social role is made to be consistent with inner qualities or personal ability. In Kuranko narratives personhood is thus spoken of without necessary reference to *a* particular person or to any intrinsically moral entity.

In Kuranko thought the emphasis is thus upon the collectivity as a field of interdependent elements. As in Gestalt theory, the "self" is "the system of contacts at any moment," and as such "the self is flexibly various"; it is "the contact-boundary at work; its activity is forming figures and grounds" (Perls, Hefferline, and Goodman, 1951:235). The person is a governor in the cybernetic sense, an agent and adjudicator, but not an innovator. Like the Ojibwa, who make no cardinal use of any concept of impersonal forces as major determinants of events, the Kuranko see persons as "*loci* of causality in the dynamics of the universe" (Hallowell, 1969:73).

Because the Kuranko emphasize that persons are agents of action rather than fixed entities, they do not think of the individual as a repository of private memories or possessed of an idiosyncratic unconscious. In the narratives we find no evidence of memory mixing with desire, or private compulsions reflecting unique biographies. Whereas the European fairy tale is, as Bettelheim observes, a vehicle for the discovery of personal identity, the Kuranko *tilei* is concerned wholly with the creation of community. The fantasies entrained by European tales — winning riches, becoming renowned, marrying into the aristocracy — contrast dramatically with the emphases in Kuranko narratives on creating an equitable distribution of scarce resources, on ensuring that exceptional gifts are used for the good of all, on ensuring that people are equal to the offices they hold, on redressing injustices, righting wrongs, and reconciling divergent interests. This emphasis on equilibrium is also evident in the connection which the Kuranko draw between illness and disturbed interpersonal relationships (see pp. 28–29).[4] A balanced complementarity is sought between men and women, elder and younger, chief and commoner, community and wilderness. But the transformations in the narratives which bring about this harmony are not consequences of heroic ambition. Nor are individual emotions such as greed, lust, and revenge the motivating forces behind narrative action. By Western standards Kuranko narrative figures seem passionless and flat, and if they set the world to right they do so not because of personal reasons or visions but because they are the active agencies through which such changes take place. In other words they do not make a new world; they alter the balance of the world that already exists.

This dispassionate quality may obtain for the listeners as well. When a child hears a story about an injust chief deposed by a resourceful youngster, he is probably less likely to fantasize becoming a chief himself than to perceive the need for chiefs to be just. The emphasis is thus not upon realizing some personal goal, either in the narrative action or in the listener's imagination. The emphasis is upon making specific attributes such as intelligence, bravery, strength, and moral worth coincide with the appropriate social roles.

European tales often work toward the triumph of a personal quest or unfold the story of an individual's fate. Magical mediators abound in both African and European narratives (as well as in advertising), and the bush spirits, fetishes, old women herbalists, and verbal charms in Kuranko tales are structurally equivalent to the magical foods, cosmetics, drinks, tobaccos, clothes, physical regimes, books, tours, and marvelous gadgets which hold out the promise of changes in fortune and identity in European and American media. But while the Western media conjure up images of movement across class lines, the Kuranko narratives seek to stabilize the boundaries between men and women, elders and youngsters, chiefs and commoners, Muslims and pagans. In European tales the relationships between feudal estates or social classes are central, but in tribal societies relationships between sex, age, and generational categories are the most critical issues. Different social formations, moreover, are linked to different conceptions of the person. Whereas the hero in European tales strives to rise above his social lot, the figures in Kuranko tales are less self-motivated. They create a new balance between established social categories, and effect a new integration of given abilities and offices. In the Kuranko *tilei* there is no quest for a personal truth beyond preexisting realities. The folktale addresses itself to problems of equity, justice, mutuality, and complementarity — that is, to problems of creating a moral community. The novel, by contrast, centers on the "journeying self," to use Maurice Natanson's phrase. It is about the "problematic hero" (Lukács, 1971). Lucien Goldmann points out that Lukács employs this term to highlight the manner in which the novel deals with a radical split between the hero's ideals and the reality of the world. Unlike the accidental breakdowns of social order which we find in the folktale, the degradation of the world depicted in the novel reflects a historical inevitability.

> Writing fiction is essentially a matter of trying to reconcile actual social relationships, which are determined by the infrastructure of production, with the ideals or values which the individual hopes to realize in his own life and which are already inscribed in myths. This reconciliation is impossible. It is in this impossibility that *Don Quixote,* or *Anna Karenina* find their origin and their achievement. (Zéraffa, 1976:44)

If the hero in the novel does transcend his or her situation, then it is through the artifice of writing. Fictional resolutions remain abstract and ethical (Goldmann, 1975:5). Like the resolutions in Kuranko narratives, they are mediated by formal transformations whose magical and total efficacy would be impossible in real life.

Every Kuranko narrative rehearses essentially the same values in different ways. Every novel offers a different ethical view. The novel is thus open to history, the folktale is closed to it. By this I mean that for the Kuranko, as for most tribal peoples, the moral community is not something which has to be brought into being: it has already been created by the "first people" in ancestral times. As I have noted elsewhere, the moral community is therefore something to be *recapitulated* through human praxis (Jackson, 1977b:17–18). In such a society, where history is annulled and narrative characters are deprived of any biography, no permanent split exists between givenness and possibility. Authentic values are recreated; they do not have to be invented. It is clear that the novel emerges in a highly individualistic society characterized by an awareness of irreversible time and inconstant space.

As Louis Dumont observes, "the individualist revolution" is "economically characterised by a displacement of the main value stress from society as a whole (holism) to the human individual taken as an embodiment of humanity at large (individualism)" (Dumont, 1971:32). There are many ways of understanding the rise of individualism. Durkheim related it to increasing division of labor and differentiation of social roles. Marx argued that the "private individual," as opposed to the "social individual," emerges with capitalism. The person becomes a private proprietor, an owner of the means of production and of labor power (Nicolaus, 1973:51). Alan Macfarlane (1978) takes the view that individualism arises with the decline of the peasantry, as personal interests override group interests in the land market. C. B. MacPherson concentrates his attention on the seventeenth-century split between a world view which stressed the moral value of community and one which played up the moral worth of the individual. MacPherson calls the latter view "possessive individualism." It is characterized by the assumptions "that man is free and human by virtue of his sole proprietorship of his own person, and that human society is essentially a series of market relations" (MacPherson, 1962:270).

Dumont rejects the materialist view (1971:36–37), and like many other writers who have treated the subject, he emphasizes the total configuration of ideas, of which individualism is a part, and eschews inquiry into the conditions under which these ideas are produced. We would thus have to consider, without wanting to reduce one factor to another, the emphasis which Descartes placed on the individual mind as the locus of thought processes and truth, the themes of moral introspection and exalted individuality in the English Renaissance, the growth of privacy and of the closely bonded nuclear family, and the fragmentation of rural communities as urbanization increased. And we would have to consider the revolution in technologies of communication which, by the end of the eighteenth century, had made literacy and the printed word mediators of enormous changes in Europe (Goody, 1977:26). Not only did widespread literacy have a great impact on cognitive style. Control of the means of the production and reproduction of knowledge became a significant aspect of economic and political domination.

It is outside the scope of this book to try to pinpoint in space and time the rise of individualism or account for the underlying causes of this ethic. I am convinced, however, that an individualistic *attitude* can be prompted by a variety of factors equally, including the rise of a market economy, the emergence of widespread literacy, increased geographical mobility, social upheavals, and accidents of fortune. But these individual *attitudes* may not always conform to the "official" *ethic*. This is why one finds truly creative individuals masked in tribal societies, and authentic communities often driven to the margins of modern societies. It is because the pronounced ethic never determines entirely the thought and action of real persons that we must avoid using sweeping we/they distinctions when comparing various societies (Goody, 1977:chapter 1). Indeed, it is the interplay between the pronounced ethic and contrary attitudes which is the very subject matter of Kuranko ₍arratives.[5]

There is no doubt that the rise of the novel coincides with the rise of individualism. While some writers argue that the very structure of the novel is homologous with the structure of exchange in a liberal economy (Goldmann, 1975:1), we need only note here the impact of individualism on the subject matter of the novel. As Michel Zéraffa points out, "It is always the individual who provides, and reflects, the novel's social dimension" (1976:27). In fact, the individual actually stands out *against* a social background. Unlike the figures in folktales, the hero in a novel is a true character. He represents the individual person, possessing a personal identity, a personal memory and name (Zéraffa, 1976:82; Watt, 1972:19–23). This emergence of the individual character in the novel is clearly related to the rise of individualism.

> By weakening communal and traditional relationships, it fostered not only the kind·of private and egocentric mental life we find in Defoe's heroes, but also the later stress on the importance of personal relationships which is so characteristic both of modern society and of the novel. . . . (Watt, 1972:200)

Insights into the unique character of the fictional hero or heroine were afforded by the private letter, and Richardson in particular paid careful attention to private experience and the domain of individual consciousness. Truth becomes a private matter, and this individualistic attitude is reflected equally in the importance given to originality in the actual composition of literary work. Hence the appositeness of the term "novel."

By contrast, the figures in folktales are depersonalized and detemporalized. The figures in Kuranko *tileinu* have stereotypical names like Tamba and Sira, or their names are allegorical like Gbeyekan Momori and Gbentoworo. These figures lack biographical depth. Personal memories or visions do not explain their actions. Nor are there personal futures or fortunes to reward their good deeds. Moreover, the space and time contexts of narrative events are often vague, switching to and fro between make-believe settings and real locations but never becoming really specific. In the novel, place and period are described with increasing verisimilitude so that the principle of realism obtains equally for both character and context (Watt, 1972:28–29). In myths and folktales, reality is always treated obliquely and analogically.

In turning now to consider ethical aspects of the novel and the folktale, it is important first to reiterate a point made earlier. For the Kuranko, the ethical postulates upon which community is founded were decided by the "first people" long long ago. Man's lot is to continually rehearse the ancestral values, thus bringing ancestral time and contemporary time into alignment. In this process "history" is annulled. However, we must contrast the unquestioned authority of ancestral decrees with the absence of any prescriptive rules about how these decrees are to be realized. Kuranko morality is, moreover, distributive, and moral obligations are contingent upon the sex, age, residence, and role of the individual. Therefore, although ancestral words are never questioned, the matter of realizing ethical ideals or of forming ethical judgments in such a relativistic universe is always problematical. Kuranko narratives call into question not the truth of ancestral values but the modes of attributing responsibility, evaluating alternative courses of action, and apportioning resources fairly. Even the growing impact of Islam in Kuranko villages does not seem to be altering this emphasis. Among many Kuranko, conversion to Islam rarely involves doctrinal conformity. As in other predominantly nonliterate societies where ethical prescriptions are enshrined in sacred books, the problem always exists of interpreting and realizing the truth in social practice. In such societies the homiletic tradition is strong. Sacred books tend to be associated with oral fables, parables, and homely anecdotes which bridge but do not necessarily close the gap between ideology and practice.

The novel emerges in a social and ethical context which differs markedly from that of the Kuranko. The Reformation in the sixteenth century challenged the social homogeneity of medieval Christendom, and by the late seventeenth century, with the rise of commercial and industrial classes, an individualistic order prevailed (Watt, 1972:67). The tradition of the novel begins with Defoe's *Robinson Crusoe*, a work that "annihilated the relationships of the traditional social order." Ian Watt notes that the old order of moral and social relationships "was shipwrecked, with Robinson Crusoe, by the rising tide of individualism" (1972:103). The novel's openness to new values contrasts with the folktale, which is concerned with the balance between complementary and contradictory elements within a *given* universe. The folktale engenders a search for equilibrium; the novel entails a struggle for authentic values. While the novel is constructed lineally in terms of chains of cause and effect,[6] the folktale reflects a world of causal circuits in which any element is continually subject to reciprocal modification by any other element. For the Kuranko, correct behavior is not a matter of unthinking compliance 'to ancestral decrees or aspiring to emulate a divine ideal. It is a matter of discernment and of self-governance, of the mutual adjustment of various forces within a universe that is *not* divided into essentially opposed categories (animate/inanimate, natural/supernatural) but is unitary. As we have seen, each person's behavior is linked to the fortunes of the group and vice versa. Each person affects and is affected by the balance of forces between human, ancestral, divine, and magical spheres. This conception of human being, which is so characteristic of many nonliterate peoples, "confers a cosmic dimension to the individual's responsibility" (Godelier, 1977:198). Each person is responsible to society and to nature. The successful initiation of a neophyte accomplishes the rebirth of an entire community. Reciprocity between a narrative figure and a bush spirit (in N.27) assists the reintegration of an entire moral order. The ethical world of the novel is unlike this, for the hero is usually in quest of a personal goal. Thwarted by his social circumstances, his responsibility is to realize a moral value which he personally embodies.

Modern consciousness disparages the folktale and the social order it represents. The decline of the folktale can be related directly to a shift in values from the moral primacy of communitas to the moral imperatives of individual freedom, individual autonomy, and individual rights. As Peter Berger puts it, "modern man has suffered from a deepening condition of 'homelessness'" (Berger, Berger, and Kellner, 1974:77). A profound nostalgia for lost community underlies my own fascination for societies like the Kuranko, but each time I return to Sierra Leone I am made more aware that my own search runs counter to the modernistic pursuits of Kuranko villagers. It is only a matter of time before involvement in the market economy, migration, urbanization, wage labor, and schooling all contribute to the emergence of an individualistic attitude in even the most inaccessible villages. Although the folktale as a genre will survive such changes, as it has in Europe, it may be in an impoverished form. Certainly its subject matter will change. When I collected tales from Kuranko secondary school pupils in 1970, I was surprised to find the written texts so spare and simplistic. Without the oral context of narration, performance, and discussion around a family hearth or in a village setting the tales become trivialized. They end up as merely individual mementos of a village childhood. Such texts give an anthropologist little idea of the real meaning of oral narratives.

The decline of the folktale coincides with a movement toward individualism, as well as an interest in rationalism and realism. Once the individual is regarded as separable from the community it is likely that he will separate other things too and contemplate them, as he might contemplate himself, as having intrinsic properties which can be isolated, reflected upon, named, and even experimented with. T. S. Eliot called this "the dissociation of sensibility." Maurice Godelier has shown that this transformation involves a breakup of the personalistic universe, where nature is invested with human attributes such as consciousness and will. It also entails a movement away from thinking by analogy (Godelier, 1977:176–177). Godelier argues that this personalistic conception of the universe, in which analogies are continually drawn between human and extrahuman events, leads to illusory representations of man and his world and inexact explanations of the order of things (1977:207). This is comparable to the process which Marx called the fetishization of commodities. In producing either mythical images or material commodities, the thing produced is made to appear external to and indifferent to the nature of the producer. Marx challenged this ontological division between person and thing, and insisted that the product is always human activity though in an objectified or frozen form. How then can we understand the Kuranko tendency to regard *tileinu* as given elements of tradition and not products of individual creative work?

In the first place, most *tileinu* are undoubtedly very old and their authors are anonymous. Sinkari Yegbe once told me that the narratives are set in the past because they were made in the past, by the first people. In the second place, the *tileinu* are not merely told in a family or community setting; this setting actually determines the way in which the tale is told and the ethical viewpoint it will convey. In the third place, the tales are made out to be external to the creator or narrator in order to distance them from individual biographies and so make them available to everyone. Metaphor, analogy, and allegory lift people from the plane of immediate and personal concerns. These figurative techniques create an "objective correlative" of the subjective world, and on this plane shared meanings may be discovered or feigned.[7]

Disclaiming the veracity and individual authorship of a work may thus serve a moral purpose. It may be a conscious literary device, and not a form of alienated consciousness. Indeed, false attribution is characteristic of both oral and written traditions, and examples can be found for every epoch.[8]

The Kuranko disclaim individual authorship for the same reason that the narrative figures lack depth of character. The person is not an autonomous moral entity, and creative practice cannot be separated from the total social situation in which the individual locates himself. For the Kuranko, this total situation includes bush spirits, mankind, ancestors, animals, a high God, trees, rocks, rivers, and man-made objects. Though Keti Ferenke makes a distinction between stories he puts together himself and traditional stories, he always insists that the stories "belong to everyone" and are received rather than invented. Like Arthur Rimbaud, who hit upon the false significance of the ego and declared "I is some one else," Keti Ferenke gives us a world view not pervaded by the spirit of possessive individualism. It is intriguing that societies in which oral traditions are privately owned and inherited are characterized by the same competitive, materialistic, and individuating elements which have ineluctably come to dominate the field of artistic production in Western societies.

Metaphor, metonomy, analogy, and allegory do not necessarily imply a false view of the universe. Indeed, such fictional devices may be the only means by which we discover shared meanings in the world. Literature is a humanizing influence. It unsettles our habitual ways of looking at the world. Founded upon illusions about the working of the world, it cannot of course mediate changes in it. But literature can transform our experience and bring into discussion things which we ordinarily take for granted. In this way, literature opens up to us the possibility of choosing and varying points of view, "not under the pressure of a *de facto* situation, but for a virtual use," of orienting ourselves "in relation to the possible . . . , and not in relation to a limited milieu" (Merleau-Ponty, 1965:175–176). Merleau-Ponty also notes that this human dialectic is ambiguous, since the activity which brings about the appearance of social and cultural structures also has "as its meaning to reject them and to surpass them" (1965:176). If this existential ambiguity is especially apparent in creative activity it is because this activity is precisely where man makes himself out of the situations that make him. I have emphasized the ways in which Kuranko narratives contradict hierarchy, throw open the village world to the influence of bush spirits, accommodate anomalous elements and marginal beings, and assign to peripheral figures such as youngsters, women, *jeli*s, *fina*s, and totemic animals the powers of redressing injustices, apportioning resources, and recreating the moral community. In the parenthetic domains which literature allows us we discern the nature of human freedom: "the small movement which makes of a totally conditioned social being someone who does not render back completely what his conditioning has given him" (Sartre, 1969:45).

Appendix

N.38: *The Calabash and the Country Pot*

Narrated by Keti Ferenke Koroma. Recorded at Kabala, February
1979.

Kuranko text with word-for-word English interlinear

Ke kele n de taranta
man one there lived

woliya musu kele furu
that did woman one marry

nar muse ke furu an be muse ke ar to ha san woronfila
if woman this married he and woman this were there for years seven

muse ke ma dan soron
woman this did not child get

a ko so ni muse do furu fana fose wo si dan soron
he said let me woman some marry again perhaps that will child get

a muse do fana nyini
he woman some again found

muse mara a bolo morgo fila
woman made his handperson two

awa lun kele al musu kina wo wolta
now day one his wife elder that got up

a tara bola al morgon' bare
she went visit her people's home

a nana taran al morgon' bara fi keri
she before went her people had calabash picked

an bel tila
they were splitting

a ko wa fi koli do de ma
she said let you calabash seed some give me

an ya fi koli fila bi
they then calabash seed two took

an ya a di a ma
they then her gave it to

a nara fi koli kela a bolo
she came calabash seed this her hand

a che an bare
she reached their home

ai ya fi ki
she then calabash planted

a ferenta
it germinated

koni a kine sundu kunye ma kanto sisin' bi
but it planted backyard where fowls were

fi koli wo nyansana
calabash seed they unearthing

awa a doge muse min nyini san al ke bolo
now her younger sister who found recently her husband

bonku dage wo bolo koni a kure ar tege a la
clay pot that hand but it's bottom was cut off

ai ya a fo a doge wo ma
she then said her younger that to

kali gbe a ko n'dogo i nyandi
now then she said my younger your pardon

i la bonku dage kore wo di ma
your clay pot broken that give me

na a burun na fi koli kona
let it cover my calabash seed over

sisenu bi a nyensana
fowls are it scattering

a ko na burun a kona sisen' ka na al bo
she said me cover it over fowls will not it get out

a doge wo ya fo kali gbe a ko a bi
her younger that then said now then she said it take

a tara bonku dage kore wo bi
she went clay pot broken that take

ka nala ka burun fi fera wo kona
to bring to cover calabash plant that over

fi yelta wo wei la
calabash climbed that hole through

fi wo tol' yela
calabash that continued climbing

gbe e tola namfala [repeated four times]
then it continued flourishing

a doge wo ya buiye bi
he younger that then belly take

wo bilakore soron
that male child get

a le fana na fi ke ara gbo ara gbo
her also her calabash this had borne fruit borne fruit

kelna kadau morgo be fi ke sana
at once every person all calabash this buying

morgon' bi bola Freetown
people are coming from Freetown

morgon' bi bola Makeni
people are coming from Makeni

an bi nala fi ke sana
they are coming calabash this buying

fi ke gbola tun
calabash this bearing continuously

muse ke gbe ar banaiya
woman this then she wealthy

ar nunfule ba soron al fi ke ro
she wealth big got her calabash this in

ninki nani
cows four

ar sage sang saga nani
she sheep bought sheep four

ar seni fore nani sang
she gold ring four bought

ar kure sang kura segi
she clothes bought clothes eight

wo bel marne a bolo
that all kept her hand

wo be bonne fi sonke kel to
that all got out calabash prize this in

lun keli muse ke ya a dogo musu ke keli
day one woman this then her younger wife this called

n doge le la a ko
my younger is you she said

oh ala ma dan dang n de ye
oh God did not child make myself for

koni ala ar dan dang i le ye
but God has child made you for

ba bi mai tore mi kela ma a kela i le li ye
because today we labor what doing we are doing you for

i ma ninki nani ke ye
you not cow four this see

i nal mara yo
you let keep all right

me nal kel mala al furu fan la
we are going to this make his bridewealth

awa i mal kura segan ke ye
now you not clothes eight this see

kura nani ke i le teli wo la
clothes four this you own that

kura nani ke n de teli wo la
clothes four this mine is that

m bi fenfen soron na bi ala ara dang i le li ye
whatever thing get me today God has made for you

ba ala ya dan di i le li ma
because God has child given you to

awa i ma saga nani ke ye
now you not sheep four this see

saga file ke i ni wo la mara
sheep two this you let that to keep

wo ni yiri ba ka wo ma i la dan la furu fan la
that let prosper much to that make your child his bridewealth

saga file ke hon i te kela n de kela
sheep two this here yours this one mine this one

i ma seni fore nani ke ye
you got gold ring four this see

m bi fenfen nyina i le li tan
whatever thing find yours it is very own

ba ala ya dan dang i le li ye
because God has child made your own

seni fore fila ke i te fore fila ke n de
gold ring two this yours ring two this mine

koni wo be ro fi wo gbola de
but that all in calabash that bearing yet

m ba lun keli kel dimera a doge wo la
but day one this pained her younger that her

a ko n koro ar nunfule ba soron fi ke ro
she said my elder has wealth great got calabash this in

a tara a ko n koro na bonku dage do m bolo
she went she said my elder my clay pot give my hand

na bonku dage kore i don ya a lon ka fo
my clay pot broken you do know to say

bonku dage kore ni ya a burun fi fera kona
clay pot broken if then you covered calabash plant over

ai bola a wei la le nye
it came out it hole through didn't it

an ta namfala gbe kude
and went on flourishing then continuously

a ko n koro na bonku dage do m bolo
she said my elder my clay pot give my hand

bonku dage dune fi kona wo si bo nyo kama
clay pot entwining calabash cover that how come off there how

a koro tara bonku dage san loli
her elder went clay pot bought five

a nara
she came

wo la a ko i la bonku dage nyorgo le
that one she said your clay pot sort is

wo la a ko n sa a fe n ko na bonku dage
that one she said I not want I say my clay pot

ka ta che morgo ban' ma ka na dine ke madia
to go reach people big to come young one this beg

a ko fo na bonku dage
she said except my clay pot

a koro ko tana ma ta i la bonku dage bi
her elder said wrong not go your clay pot take

a tara kali gbe ka bonku dage sagan
she went there then to clay pot pull off

fi woronta wurtu
calabash uprooted *wurtu*

a tara al bonku dage kore la
she went her clay pot broken with

a tara a sigi
she went she sat

wo tinyane feu
that spoiled completely

tele wo ro gbe fi fagara
sun that in then calabash died

al gbalta
it dried up

ai ya ba mi di a ma wo
she then goat which gave her to that

ai ya kure mi di a ma wo
she then clothes which gave her to that

ai ya seni mi di a ma wo
she then gold which gave her to that

ai ya ninki min di a ma wo
she then cow which gave her to that

ai ya a dama la segi a koro ma
she then it all returned her elder to

a ko i ke dama mala na den kelan kel la ko ke don
she said you this all did my child one this because of this one

i ti ke tone don n kela li a don na
you will this benefit eat me alone it is it eat

a ko n del den kela ke fisa i la nunfule ke dama do
she said my child one this better your wealth this all than

eh wo ko tana ma
eh that said bad not

n de ma fo koni ni i le li ara fo i de la ma to ala ma
I did not say but if you it have said your mouth with let leave God to

a ko m bara dinye
she said I have endured

musu kina wo sigira a la moniye la a bolo
woman elder that sat down her painfulness with her hand

lun keli al dan wo gbe ar tama ar tama san kure
day one her child that then has walked has walked recent

musu kina ke gbe ar to sigi ni al dandakoro
woman elder this then she left sitting her porch

a ko a ni al kone dun
she said let him bead wear

koni musu kina ke a ma a yigi tege dan kela di
but woman elder this did not her hope cut child this one oh

awa fan do soron a na a di dine
when thing some get she will it give child

wo ma a bole sigine a koro
that one her hand sitting it under

musu kina sigine gbe al koni dunna
woman elder sitting then is bead wearing

dan wo nara kali gbe ka a bole dun kone wo ro wunya
child that came there then and his hand put bead that in *wunya*

a kone sagan
he bead pulled off

musu kina wo bolo kone wo tegera
woman elder that hand bead that cut

kone donu bora a bole wei la
bead some got out his hand hole through

kelan mi tora a bolo ai ya wo la dun a da ro
one that left his hand he then that put his mouth in

ai ya a la kunu
he then it swallowed

nyane yal so eh
woman got up eh

a tara a na ware
she went his mother place

na i la dan ar na kone koli kunu
mother your child has come bead seed swallowed

musu dine wo tara kone dosini nani sang
woman younger that went bead dozen four bought

a nara wo la
she brought that

wo ko m bi nyena na kone le ma
that said I want my bead it is

ka ta dosini tan sang ka bamba morgo bannu koma
to go dozen ten bought to back people big behind

ka na wo la
to bring that one

a ko ade na kone
she said no my bead

ka kina madia ka koe be ke
to elder beg to thing all do

musu kina fo kona kone
woman elder said except bead

ko m ba i la kone koli al bo
said well your bead seed it take out

ai ya dine bira
she then child held

ai ya kana tege
she then throat cut

ai ya a buiye fara
she then its belly split open

ai ya an nuge fara
she then its intestines opened up

ai ya a la kone koli la bo
she then her bead seed took out

a ko n yuse ar kime
she said my heart it cool

min ya fi kure woron woliya ko yugumel damba
one who calabash stem uprooted that one thing bad made

ka min ya dan kana tege
or one that child throat cut

wo la tu ni morge ya ko nyume ke a sare le ko nyume la
that is why if person thing good does his reward is thing good

koni ni morge ya ko nyume ke ye ni ya a sara a yugu me la
but if person thing good does for you if you him pay with bad

a si segi i le li ma
it will return you on

al ban le wo la
it is finished that one

English translation

There was once a man. He got married, but after seven years his wife had not borne him a child. The man decided to take another wife, hoping that she would bear him a child. He married again. So he had two wives.

One day his first wife decided to visit her parents. When she arrived at her parent's place she found them splitting open a calabash. She said, "Will you give me some calabash seeds?" They took two seeds and gave them to her. When she returned home she planted the seeds. But no sooner had they begun to germinate in the backyard than the fowls unearthed them. Now her younger co-wife had a clay pot with a broken bottom. The elder co-wife said to her, "Pardon me, but will you give me your broken clay pot so that I can cover my calabash seeds with it. The fowls are unearthing the seeds, and the clay pot will protect them." Her younger co-wife said, "Take it." So the elder co-wife took the broken clay pot and covered the calabash seeds with it. The calabash grew up through the hole in the bottom of the upturned pot. It climbed high and flourished.

The younger co-wife then became pregnant. She bore a male child. At the same time, the elder co-wife's calabash had borne abundantly. Everyone came to buy calabashes. People came from Freetown. People came from Makeni. And the calabash continued to bear in abundance. The woman became wealthy from selling calabashes. She bought four cows, four sheep, four gold rings, and eight articles of clothing. She kept all these things in her possession. They were the rewards of having such a fruitful calabash.

One day the woman called her younger co-wife. She said, "You are my junior. God did not give me a child, but he gave you a child. Let also my labor benefit you. Do you see these four cows? Keep them as bridewealth for your son. Do you see these eight articles of clothing? Four are for you, and four for me. Whatever I have got, God has made for you as well. God has given you a child.* Now then, you see these four sheep? Two are for you. May they prosper and increase so that your son will have bridewealth to give. Do you see these four gold rings? Whatever I get is yours, because God has given you a child. These two gold rings are for you, and these two are for me. And the calabash will bring us even more wealth."

But one day the younger co-wife became envious of her elder co-wife's good fortune. She said to herself, "My elder co-wife has got a

---

*The woman is implying that she and her co-wife should be like sisters: they should share the wealth from the calabash and share in the raising of the child.

great amount of wealth from this calabash." She went to her elder co-wife and said, "Give me back my clay pot, the broken old clay pot you know that I gave you, the clay pot that you covered your calabash plant with, the clay pot with the hole through which the calabash grew, the calabash plant that flourished and bore so abundantly. Give me back my clay pot."

(Now then, how could one remove the clay pot from the calabash plant without destroying it?) The elder co-wife brought five other clay pots. She came with them and said, "These are the same sort of pots as yours." But the younger co-wife said, "I do not want those; I said that I wanted my clay pot." The elder co-wife fetched the elders and in front of them she begged her younger co-wife to accept the replacement pots. "No," she said, "I want only my pot." The elder co-wife said, "All right then, go and take it." The woman pulled it off the calabash plant. The plant was uprooted, *wurtu*. She went away with her broken clay pot. The plant was completely ruined. It soon died in the hot sun, and dried up.

The younger co-wife then gave back everything she had been given: the goat, the clothes, the gold, the cow. She returned everything to her elder co-wife. She said, "You gave me all these things because of my child. But I am going to be the only person to benefit from him. My child is better than all your wealth." The other woman said, "Eh, that is all right. I did not say that, but since you have said it may God not forget."* She said, "I have endured enough." And she sat down with her head in her hands.

One day, not long after the child had begun to walk, the elder co-wife got up from her porch and said, "Let him wear some beads." (She had not given up all hope.†) Then she took some beads to thread for the child, who had been left in her care. The child came up and pulled at the bead string, *wunya*. He pulled some beads off. The woman let him take them. Some of the beads fell through his fingers, but the bead that he held onto he put in his mouth. He swallowed it. The woman got up and went to the child's mother's place. She said, "Mother, your child has swallowed a bead seed." The younger co-wife went and bought four

---

*The elder co-wife did not make the comparison *explicit* between the child and the wealth. Now that the child is equated unambiguously with the calabash seed, the elder co-wife is entitled to behave in the same manner as her junior co-wife.
†The narrator tells us that the woman had not let herself become discouraged (*yigi tege*, lit. "hope cut"). It is also implied that she did not bear any grudge against the child.

dozen new beads. She brought them to her elder co-wife. But the elder co-wife said, "I want my bead." The other woman bought ten dozen beads and asked the elders to plead for her.* Still the elder co-wife said, "No, I want my bead." The younger co-wife said, "Well then, take it." The other woman grabbed the child, cut his throat, slit open his belly and his intestines, and found her bead. She said, "I am satisfied."

Who did wrong, the woman that uprooted the calabash plant or the woman that cut the child's throat?†

That is why good is the reward of good deeds, and why if you repay kindness with evil you will suffer evil in turn. That is the end.

*ka bamba a kome, lit. "to carry on the back behind," i.e. to ask a person to stand up for you, to plead on your behalf (you stand behind him as he speaks).
†The answer to the dilemma is that the younger wife was in the wrong, since the tragic end to the story was the inevitable outcome of that initial malice. The ambiguity in the story reflects the way in which the contrast between child and calabash is played up and the distinction between the two wives played down. Subtle symmetries and repetitions occur: broken pot (barren womb)/fruitful calabash (fruitful womb); splitting calabash to get seed (koli)/splitting child's belly to get bead seed (koli); wealth borne by calabash plant/child borne by woman, etc.

Notes

Chapter 1

1. Ambiguity is cognate with what Arthur Koestler calls "bisociation." Koestler coined this term in order to distinguish between the routine skills of thinking along given lines, and creative thought, which always involves unexpected switchings among several possible lines of thought.

> When two independent matrices of perception or reasoning interact with each other the result . . . is either a *collision* ending in laughter, or their *fusion* in a new intellectual synthesis, or their *confrontation* in an aesthetic experience. The bisociative patterns found in any domain of creative activity are trivalent: that is to say, the same pair of matrices can produce comic, tragic, or intellectually challenging effects. (Koestler, 1964:45)

2. The term *luiye* or *lu* is used to designate slightly different groupings among other Mande peoples. Among the Mandinka of western Mali the terms *lu* and *lutigi* designate "household" and "household head" respectively (Hopkins, 1971:101–2), while the Gambia Mandinka use the term *kabilo* for both the extended family and the compound it occupies in the village (Gamble, n.d., p.1). Among the Malinke of the Upper Niger, *lu (lou)* usually designates the "concession" of an extended family or *kabila*, though *kabila* can also refer to a quarter within the village (Leynaud, 1966:44; Bernus, 1956:240; Montrat, 1935:109).

3. In their account of the comparable notion of *hake* among the Mende, Harris and Sawyerr (1969) suggest that the word is related to the Arabic *haqyqun* ("consequence").

Chapter 2

1. Phylogenetically, human thought and communication display increasing ambiguity:

> Compared to that of lower animals, human "thought" is characterised by the generation of more alternatives. More meanings can be attributed to objects and a greater number of connections (relations) between these meanings arise. In this way, human thought is less stimulus bound; action can be delayed; a given stimulus gives rise to a greater number of outcomes, creating more uncertainty and ambiguity. (Schroder, Driver, and Streufert, quoted in Laughlin and D'Aquili, 1974:92)

Sir Peter Medawar notes that this increasing ambiguity is a consequence of the fact that while cultural patterns and individual actions are built up out of genetically evolved systems, they are not determined by them. Human evolution is typically "exogenetic" and cultural patterns as well as individual actions always remain matters to be decided (Medawar, 1976:506). For this reason ethical problems are an inherent aspect of human culture.

2. Because human culture demands and depends upon the existence of language and other forms of conceptual communication, alternative possibilities of thought and action are first entertained and represented semantically. But words and concepts are arbitrary conventions, not necessarily bound to particular visual images and objects. As Edmund Leach points out, this means that an ambiguity surrounds the sense-images and conceptualizations which certain things may evoke, and sound-images can be used metaphorically in relationship to all kinds of objects. "A choice is thus implied in the inherent arbitrariness of the linguistic sign" (Leach, 1976:21).

3. I collected about ten dilemma tales among the Kuranko, but Bascom reports that no true dilemma tales have been collected or published among the neighboring Malinke (Bascom, 1975:9–10). In several studies of stages of moral judgment and moral development, dilemma tales have been used to elicit data (Kohlbert, 1969; Piaget, 1932). In his research on polygyny in Africa, Clignet used indigenous dilemma tales to establish comparative attitudes to moral problems in the field of kinship relations (Clignet, 1970:176).

4. Burridge's study of Tangu narratives is informed by a similar view:

> Tangu traditions run a course in experience, pose problems and suggest solutions. And though both problems and solutions tend to be oracular, forcing men in community to formulate and make moral decisions for themselves, the process of narration marshals experience, conjures an awareness of what is involved and so generates further comprehension. (Burridge, 1969:410)

5. All these disruptions of ordinary classifications and understanding are examples of what Caillois calls *paidia* (1961:27). *Paidia* is negative play: "an essentially destructice act, violating the order imposed upon experience by our cognitive categories" (Davis, 1977:16). *Paidia* creates ambiguity, which we then seek to reduce. The relation between intolerance of ambiguity and anxiety defenses has been treated in several notable studies (Perls, Hefferline, and Goodman, 1951; O'Connor, 1952; Smock, 1957; Davis, 1974).

6. As Pasquier notes in his study of a Mossi narrative (1975), this opposition is probably crucial in understanding any African narrative. The contrast between town and bush is, of course, an ecological given, but the allegorical meanings which attach to it in various societies are fascinating in their variety. The dialectic between "moral" and "divine" which Burridge shows to underpin Tangu narratives has its physical corollary in the contrast between town and bush. This contrast suggests differences between reciprocity and nonreciprocity, self-restraint and self-willedness, and so on. (Burridge, 1969:xviii-xix). In his study of western Enga stories, Meggitt also notes that "one obvious function of stories about demons and great snakes is to stress a fundamental opposition between the demons-in-the-forest and the humans-in-the-settlement. This, in turn, may perhaps be an expression of a more general view of a dichotomy between nature and culture (thus demon : human :: forest : cultivation :: nature : culture) . . ." (Meggitt, 1976:68). Richard Davis has traced the significance of the same dichotomy in northern Thai myth (1974:13–14), and in Africa the contrast is pervasive. In their research among the Kpelle of Liberia, Cole, Gay,

and their colleagues discovered that a "basic and pervasive distinction" existed between "forest things" and "town things" (Cole et al., 1971:63–66). Jeanne Bisilliat has shown that Songhay healers work in terms of a distinction between "village diseases" and "bush diseases"; medical treatment involves subtle discernments and careful action to bring about a correct balance between human and extrahuman domains (Bisilliat, 1976). Legends of the BaMbuti of the Ituri forest of northeast Zaire are pervaded by the contrast between Bantu villagers and Pygmy forest-dwellers (Turnbull, 1959:48). Among the Mende of Sierra Leone, the contrast between the village (*ta*, lit. "a container"), signifying order and control, and the forest (*ndo*), signifying diversity and unpredictable powers, is expressed at all cultural levels (Jędrej, 1976:41–44). This theme also appears in Fulani thought: the bush is a metaphor for solitude, and signifies "separation from men or the absence of human community" (Riesman, 1977:254).

7. Geneviève Calame-Griaule has noted that variations among texts often seem due "to the fact that the teller had forgotten the story or had got the themes mixed up." The restoration of "the authentic version" is established by the audience, "because everybody knows the whole repertoire" (Calame-Griaule, 1963:199).

8. This difficulty was, in my case, compounded by my difficulties with the language. But lexical ambiguity (puns, homonyms, homophones) and amphiboly are important elements in Kuranko narrative art.

9. The following metamorphoses occur in the narratives: woman → tsetse fly (N.1); woman → white chicken; woman → goat; girl → knife → stone; female hyena → seductive woman (N.27); female buffalo ⟷ seductive woman (N.34); monkey → beautiful woman; God → beautiful woman (N.28); *nyenne* → person; man → crocodile (N.24); dead → living (N.25, N.32). The frequency with which the animal ⇆ woman transformation occurs is discussed in chapter 8.

10. The Kuranko have a fund of stories which tell how the monkeys, chimpanzees, and baboons once lived in towns with people. Because the monkeys and apes were incorrigible gluttons, thieves, and troublemakers, they were driven into the bush. In several narratives there are references to monkeys as deceitful, gluttonous, prone to lie and cheat. Similar references occur in tales from other areas in Sierra Leone. According to a Krio tale recorded by Mudge-Paris (1930:317), the monkeys are in the bush because they once stole from people, and a similar story is told among the Temne, who say that the monkeys are *misim* ("taboo") because they were human beings metamorphosed by the prophet for violating Friday prayer (Trimingham, 1959:67). It is intriguing that the opposite transformation occurs in Gogo myth. Cattle used to be numerous, and were once wild animals. Cattle sought refuge from lions in the homesteads of men, and thus ceased to be "wild" buffalo and became "domesticated" cattle (Rigby, 1971:262).

11. The *nyenne* are directly comparable to the fairies of English folk literature, which were believed to be "beings of a middle order between men and angels, or . . . 'spiritual animals'" (Briggs, 1967:11). In some African societies the beings of the wild first gave mankind such cultural techniques as cooking, cultivation, iron-making, and shooting with bows and arrows (Goody, 1972:8).

12. "A fetish consists of one or more objects to which supernatural personality and power are attributed. The spirit thus associated with a fetish is not a distant god nor a still sentient human ancestor but a vaguely personalised in-

dwelling power believed to be influenced by appropriate offerings." (Forde, 1958:9).

13. This point is made by Innes in his study of songs in Mende folktales (1965:60–61). In his account of the Xhosa *ntsomi*, Scheub notes that the "most potent use" of songs "is at the height of crises, when the artist seems to have no recourse but to express herself in song." Scheub also points out that chants occur at "critical moments in *ntsomi* performances, providing a motivation for action or an insight into character without the necessity for analytical statement" (Scheub, 1975:50,53).

14. Meyer uses a Gestalt approach to show that ambiguity is important "because it gives rise to particularly strong tensions and powerful expectations. For the human mind, ever searching for the certainty and control which comes with the ability to envisage and predict, avoids and abhors such doubtful and confused states and expects subsequent clarification" (Meyer, 1965:51).

15. This is often the case among the Mende (Innes, 1965:54), the Limba (Finnegan, 1970:385), and other African peoples.

16. See also Lévi-Strauss, 1966:93.

> The mythical system and the modes of representation it employs serve to establish homologies between natural and social conditions or, more accurately, it makes it possible to equate significant contrasts found on different planes: the geographical, metereological, zoological, botanical, technical, economic, social, ritual, religious and philosophical.

17. Every action, idea, or word is thus like a "figure" whose definition depends upon its "ground." The background embodies numerous associations, negations, and possibilities which are momentarily latent or suppressed. One of the "hidden" or suppressed backgrounds in all human action is the mind of the individual person. Cultural codifications do not normally make reference to the unique configuration of motives, experiences, memories, and abilities which together define an individual. Steiner notes that "no two human beings share an identical associative context," and he emphasizes the importance of recognizing that all speech forms and notations "entail a latent or realized element of individual specificity" (1975:170).

18. *Sosogoma tilei* are so called because they are stories to which the listeners must respond by "pointing out" an appropriate answer or resolution. *Sosogoma* is from the verb *ka sogo*, "to point out."

19. Similar functions attach to art objects in other societies. For example, among the Lega, art objects used in the *bwami* association have a variety of meanings and functions. They serve as means of moral instruction, but they mediate rather than designate meanings.

> . . . the objects themselves *demand interpretation since their forms do not reveal what they are and what they mean*. From one point of view sculptures and other initiation objects are reminders (*kalolesia*) of things to be done or not to be done and mnemonic devices (*kakengelezio*) that facilitate the enormous amount of memorizing, of aphorisms and of actions, required by the initiations. (Biebuyck, 1973:170, my emphasis)

20. C.f. Jaspers's and Heidegger's views that "all Knowledge is interpretation," and that "the procedure in understanding texts is a simile for all comprehension of Being" (Kaufmann, 1956:34). For lucid accounts of the hermeneutic tradition in sociology see Ricoeur, 1963.

21. The manner in which narratives remodel the given world rather than invent new structures of action is suggested by Lévi-Strauss's concept of *bricolage* (1966), and by Hymes's essays in the ethnography of speaking (1971:1975).

22. In some societies, fire is associated with ordered society. For example, among the Kaguru the words "custom" (*umoto*, lit, "of fire") and "fire" (*moto*) have the same derivation. The hearth is central to the social order, and cooking is the dominant symbol of enculturation (Beidelman, 1970:92).

23. Eliade has observed that the folktale "in the last analysis . . . is reducible to an initiatory ordeal" and to the arduous sequence of events marking the passage, by way of a symbolic death and resurrection, "from ignorance and immaturity to the spiritual age of the adult." He also notes that "the tale takes up and continues 'initiation' on the level of the imaginary," thereby suggesting a functional equivalence between myth and rite (Eliade, 1964:201–202).

Burridge has also made extensive reference to the connection between Tangu narratives and enculturation. He writes: "Again and again the narratives take up the theme of how boys may be made into responsible men, moral beings in the fullest sense" (1969:241).

24. In his comments on Dinka folktales, Deng makes a similar observation. He notes that the "mysteriousness of the night and the circumstances of the delivery give stories a quality which approximates a dream. Furthermore, they in fact make people sleep, and so form a bridge between reality and dream world" (1974:30).

25. This belief may be explained by the fact that night and bush signify the temporal and spatial dimensions of human freedom from social constraint. These terms suggest a suspension of community life as well as a realization of personal independence. This independence may be sinister and clandestine, as in witchcraft, but it has positive connotations as well. Bush and night imply the severance of dependency upon parents, and since stories are associated with night and bush it is reasonable that the belief should arise that stories told in the daytime would precipitate this severance, i.e. that one's parents would die.

26. *Serawayili* = praise-singer of the hunters (from *seraima* or *serama*, a six-stringed harp-lute). Among the Malinke, the hunters' harp is known as *dozo konu*, while the six-stringed harp-lute is called *burunuba*. The praise-singer of the hunters is known as the *dozo serawa* (G. Rouget: Notes to musique Malinké, Collection Musée de l'Homme, LDM 30113).

27. Hunter stories comprise a special category of narratives in Herskovits's collection of Dahomean narratives. Herskovits explains the central place of the hunter-hero by noting that hunting "traditionally extends the frontiers" of the world; the hunter is military scout in time of war, importer of herbs and cures, mediator between his people and people of distant settlements, and colonizer of new lands (Herskovits and Herskovits, 1958:28–29).

28. This principle applies to both folktales and proverbs. Alan Dundes notes that:

> Like other forms of folklore, proverbs may serve as impersonal vehicles for personal communication. A parent may well use a proverb to direct a child's action or thought, but by using a proverb, the parental imperative is externalized and removed somewhat from the individual parent. The guilt or responsibility for directing the child is projected on to the anonymous past, the anonymous folk. A child knows that the proverb used by the scolding parent was not made up by that parent. It is a proverb from the cultural past whose voice speaks truth in traditional terms. It is the "One", the "Elders", or the "They" in "They

say", who direct. The parent is but the instrument through which the proverb speaks to the audience. (1975:35)

29. Lévi-Strauss speaks of this process in a famous passage:

> . . . it is in the last resort immaterial whether . . . the thought processes of the South American Indians take shape through the medium of my thought, or whether mine take place through the medium of theirs. What matters is that the human mind, regardless of the identity of those who happen to be giving it expression, should display an increasingly intelligible structure as a result of the doubly reflexive forward movement of two thought processes acting one upon the other, either of which can in turn provide the spark or tinder whose conjunction will shed light on both. (1970:13–14)

30. *ka korsi*: to scrutinize, look closely at, discern.

31. This view is probably a reflection of a universal experience. "The source of our experience seems to be outside ourselves. In the creative experience, we experience the source of the created images, patterns, sounds, to be within ourselves but still beyond ourselves" (Laing, 1967:33).

32. C.f. Bauman (1975), who analyzes the ways in which narrative performances set up or represent "interpretative frames" within which the messages being communicated are to be understood. Bauman mentions insinuation, joking, imitation, translation, and quotation as examples of interpretative framing (pp. 292–293).

33. Rattray notes that this period of license depends upon a variety of techniques for disengaging the tales from everyday life: the tales are only permitted to be told after dark; the narrator disguises his voice with nasal accents (when speaking the spider's part); the names of animals and of the sky-god are substituted for the names of real individuals' personal names, and individuating features are avoided; the narrator invariably prefaces his tale with a statement to the effect that what he is about to say is not true (he will say, "We don't really mean to say so; we don't really mean to say so") (Rattray, 1928; 1930:vi, x–xiii). Rattray draws analogies between the parenthetical situation of the tales and the Ashanti customs of *bo akutia* ("vituperation by proxy") and the interregnum when, for a brief period during the enstoolment of a new chief, people could abuse members of the ruling family (1930:xi–xii).

34. Although there is no Kuranko theater, theater among the Malinke and Bambara shows that the same topics treated in the narratives provide scenarios in plays, masques, and satires (Labouret and Travélé, 1928).

Chapter 3

1. As Trivers points out, the rise of reciprocal altruism in hominid evolution is accompanied by a relaxation of linear dominance hierarchies (Trivers, 1971:45). It is as if the Kuranko clan narratives were rehearsing an evolutionary process as a moral imperative.

2. This may be phrased as a categorical imperative: "Act only on that maxim through which you can at the same time will that it should become a universal law" (Kant, 1965:88).

3. The dominant allegorical motif may be compared to old European customs such as those of the Lord of Misrule or the Feast of Fools, which signalled a temporary inversion and parodying of ordinary roles and offices, or the Roman Liberties of December (Saturnalia), when winter gloom was lightened

by the restoration of the golden reign of Saturn, and for a short while laws lost their force and a mocking ruled over a topsy-turvy world (Welsford, 1968:198–199).

4. The narratives are less concerned with mere precepts than with problems inherent in the exercise of authority. Individual responsibility (internal authority, self-mastery) for maintaining justice and equity is crucial. The narratives are thus concerned with a "morality of association" and they examine intentions rather than physical consequences in judging actions (c.f. Rawls, 1971:468–472; Kohlberg, 1969:398).

5. In Sierra Leone, "country-pot," "country-cloth," etc. signify articles of local or native manufacture, in contrast to imported articles.

6. Since the Kuranko concept of the person (*morgoye*) is a *social* concept, entailing a community of persons who acknowledge each other's interests as reasons for actions, self-interest is not strictly speaking inconsistent with the interests of others or with the good. As Abelson has noted, there is a tendency for many writers to regard self-interest as necessarily inimical to group-interest and to morality (1977:117). When I use the term "self-interest" I mean behavior that happens to be, *according to Kuranko standards*, antisocial and wrong, i.e. behavior that undermines community.

Chapter 4

1. Animals, birds, and insects occur in about 30 percent of the narratives I collected, and of these about 30 percent are hare-hyena stories. Of the seventeen hare-hyena stories which I recorded, more than half were given by two narrators: Nonkowa Kargbo of Benekoro (four narratives during one session, 3 March 1970), and Keti Ferenke Koroma of Kondembaia (five narratives from three sessions). Seven of the seventeen hare-hyena narratives were recorded during a single storytelling session at Benekoro (3 March 1970). The low proportion of animal tales may reflect that such tales tend to be told more frequently by children or young men (five of the seventeen tales); most of the narratives in my collection were, however, given by adults. Of thirteen stories written for me on request (the subject matter was not prespecified) by Kuranko secondary school students at Kabala, eight were animal tales, and of these, five had the hare as trickster.

2. In his account of fables from the West Sudan, Monteil notes that the hare epitomizes hypocrisy and cunning, and is the nephew of the hyena. Monteil regards this kinship identification as a reflection of the bad tricks the sister's son plays upon his mother's brother in real life (Monteil, 1905:7). It is not clear whether the term *neveu* is used in the Latin sense, as meaning "grandson" or "descendant" (the sense it has in La Fontaine's fables), or whether it is used in the modern sense. Among the Kuranko the hare is never designated "nephew" (*berinne*).

3. For a general account of the main animal characters in different African societies (and different societies in Sierra Leone) see Innes, 1964:9. The animal tricksters among the Mende, Limba, and Temne—the spider and the royal antelope—seldom appear in Kuranko tales.

4. Of *Sulwe*, the hare, the Ba-Ila of Zambia say: "He is extremely wary . . . , it is most difficult to entrap him. He has the power, more than most animals, of lying low and saying nothing. You may step over him in the veld and never know he is there" (Smith and Dale, 1968, II:340–341).

5. Odysseus was "doomed to cleverness at his birth." His grandfather, Au-

tolycus, a wily, law-avoiding rogue, gave Odysseus the name "man of Odium" to commemorate his own experiences of life (Hermes, patron of the trickster, had conferred the dubious talents of deceit and guile upon Autolycus). But while Odysseus derives his trickster character from his mother's side, he traces his descent to only respectable distinguished people through his father, Laertes (Stanford, 1968:12).

6. This problem arises from what Gluckman (1956:27–53) has called "the frailty in authority": when a chief's personal abilities are not commensurate with the attributes and capabilities associated with the office. In the past, Kuranko chiefs wielded considerable power; their word, ideally embodying the ancestral code, was absolute. Although certain cult associations such as *kome* may have checked the abuse of chiefly power, the Kuranko acknowledge that if a chief was unjust or excessively brutal then people "would be able to do nothing but grumble in the corners and pray for his demise." One chief is rather mockingly remembered by the nickname *kinan kiri* ("old tie-up"), because of his habit of ordering people bound as a punishment for minor offenses.

7. The Dogon, Bozo, and Bambara also exaggerate the stooped gait (*démarche penchée*) of the hyena, as well as its foul smell, hairy body, nasal voice, and red teeth and eyes (Calame-Griaule and Ligers, 1961:114). In twelfth-century Europe, the inflexible attitude of the hyena was explained in rather similar ways. According to the Latin Bestiary, the hyena "is unable to turn around, except by a complete reversal of its body, because its spine is rigid and is all in one piece" (White, 1954:31). White also remarks a belief held in parts of Ethiopia: the hyena is said "not to be able to turn its eyes backward, owing to its rigid backbone, and to be blind in that direction unless it turns round" (1954:32).

8. Of Dogon, Bozo, and Bambara narratives, Calame-Griaule and Ligers note: "The hyena defecating, a sign of panic, is a comic element which recurs often in the tales" (1961:45). Among the Ugogo and Kaguru of East Africa the hyena is regarded as evil and sexually hermaphrodite (Rigby, 1971:264; Beidelman, 1961, 1963). In European tradition, both the hare and the hyena are often regarded as hermaphrodite and able to change their sex (Rowland, 1973:91, 112; White, 1954:31). This fallacy, which supports the view that these animals are fickle, may arise from the fact that it is actually difficult to distinguish the sex of the young of these creatures (Van Lawick and Van Lawick-Goodall, 1970:158).

9. Lambo (Nigeria; 1961:61), Evans-Pritchard (Azande; 1967:29), Johnston (Hausa; 1966:xliv), Rattray (Akan-Ashanti; 1930:xii), Mbiti (Akamba; 1966:23).

10. The same problems of reciprocity and justice pervade the Legba narratives of Dahomey and the Zande trickster tales. The Ture narratives of the Azande demonstrate the necessity of breaking unjust rules and correcting inflexible attitudes. All trickster tales seem to imply that immersion in the given, established values and conventions of the social order must be offset by free play, experimentation, and detachment. Inasmuch as the Kuranko trickster, Fasan, "plays with" possibility and invents ways of "getting round" impossible situations, he epitomizes the spirit of play. And play, to use Jerome Bruner's phrase, is a "special form of violating fixity" (1976:31). The playful hare is, of course, characterized as a younger brother; youth *is* play.

11. The ecstatic character of the younger/smaller or culturally alienated person is widely known in societies throughout the world. I have discussed this connection at length elsewhere (Jackson, 1978c).

12. In exactly the same way, mutual play-encounters among primates occur within a context of nonmutuality and rank-differentiation (Reynolds, 1976:623–624).

13. Peter Reynolds notes that "The simulative mode of action is paradoxical: the system's operations should have their normal consequences, yet those consequences must at the same time be rendered inconsequential" (1976:621). The reason is that in the simulative mode of action there is less energy expenditure and less danger to the participants. The buffering of play behavior from consequences is thus paralleled by an analogous phenomenon in social interactions: play fighting does not lead to injury, nor play sex to offspring (Reynolds, 1976).

14. The motif of the deceiver/trickster outsmarting a powerful partner or foe and riding him in public is fully examined by Denise Paulme (1975b).

15. Such a view is also developed in Ba-Ila tales, particularly explanatory tales:

> As for these explanations, it will be seen that none of them is assigned to any natural cause, but all to personal volition. And not always, indeed but rarely, to that of higher powers.
>
> . . . whether it springs from good or evil, it is always a person that affects the destiny. This, one may say, is typical of the higher native thought, that explains things not by mere self-acting dynamism but by the activity of the will. (Smith and Dale, 1968, 2:337, 338)

These views are also echoed in the Igbo notion that a man chooses his fortune:

> Hence the saying *Obu etu nya na chie si kwu*, which we often hear when a man's misfortune is somehow beyond comprehension and so can only be attributable to an agreement he himself must have entered into, at the beginning, along with his *chi*, for there is a fundamental justice in the universe and nothing so terrible can happen to a person for which he is not somehow responsible. (Achebe, 1975:97)

16. Among the neighboring Limba, however, it is usually an unscrupulous and greedy *husband* (spider) who attempts to keep food from his *wife* (Finnegan, 1967:291–296). Although a different relationship, the same structural distinction between superordinate and subordinate obtains in both societies (Husband : wife :: elder : younger).

17. Quintilian summarized this mode as

> one whereby we wish by exciting a suspicion to be understood differently from what we actually say, not in a contrary sense (as in ειρωνεία) but in a hidden sense that is left for the hearer to discover. . . . It has three uses: one when it is unsafe to speak openly; the second when it is indecent to speak openly; and the third for the sake only of more elegance and greater novelty and variety than if expressed in straightforward language. (quoted by Stanford, 1939:18–19; translation by H.E. Butler, Loeb series)

18. It is noteworthy that Ben-Amos entitles his study of storytelling events in Benin "Sweet Words," an appellation which presumably reflects an Edo usage as well as the fact that Edo narratives are accompanied by instrumental music (Ben-Amos, 1975).

19. It is of course well recognized in psychoanalytic theory that sweets are symbols of sexual pleasure (see Carvalho-Neto, 1972:66).

20. The Kuranko distinguish "raw" (*kuran*), "cooked" (*tei*), "rotten" (*tuli*), and "roasted" (*mintane*). "Smoked" foods are "dry" (*gbala*). There is no term for

boiled, probably because cooking is usually synonymous with boiling. The term *yi gbusana* ("bubbling water") is the closest one can get to describing boiling as a process of cooking.

Chapter 5

1. A few randomly selected examples will indicate the character of these myths. Among the Hottentot death came into the world when the hare garbled a message which the moon had entrusted to an insect to pass on to mankind (Radim, 1952:63). In a myth which the Swazi share with other southeast Bantu peoples, death is imposed upon man "by the arbitrary and fickle nature of *Umkhulumcandi* or *Umvelamcandi*" (The First Being) and the laziness and greed of an animal. The First Being sent the chameleon to tell man that he would live forever, but the lizard, who had been given the opposite message, passed the chameleon (who had stopped to eat some tasty berries) and so delivered his message to man first (Kuper, 1947:177). A Kono narrative from Sierra Leone illustrates a theme which is widespread in South America (Lévi-Strauss, 1970:156) and Melanesia (Wagner, 1972). In the Kono myth man was meant to share with the snakes the ability to renew life periodically by sloughing off the old skin; through trickery or theft the snakes stole the gift from man (Parsons, 1964:110).

2. These reversals and exchanges correspond on the formal plane to chiasmus, but there is some evidence that they reflect actual intrigues and machinations in Kuranko dynasties in the past. Sayers records an account of Saramba's birth which is of interest in this respect (see also N.3).

> Furumuru Kaini had ten sons, amongst whom (Marankali) Mankalia and Saramba. Really Mankali was the elder of the two, but Saramba, afterwards the great leader of the Korankos, was given seniority. It was done by a trick of the old women, because they liked Saramba's mother, who was kinder to them than was Mankali's. So they announced Saramba's birth first and concealed that of Mankali, though he was born a little earlier, though on the same day. (Sayers, 1927:82)

This "plot" is identical to one which occurs in several Kuranko narratives on the changeling theme (see Jackson 1979) and crops up again in a folk rumor which circulated among the Mossi after the succession of Mogho Naba Sagha II (Skinner, 1964:45).

Similar folk rumors also surround European dynastic successions. The theme of the substituted bride is found in thirteenth-century poems dealing with Charlemagne, and the changeling motif is well known in connection with James II's heir. The theme of the "disguised man" has been fully explored in the African context by Denise Paulme (1963b).

3. For example, in the Mande case, Sundiata's mother was the *second* of Maghan Kon Fatta's three wives (Niane, 1965), and in other African states where the principle of primogeniture was asserted there is abundant evidence that the most capable person often acceded whether he was the eldest son or not (Goody, 1966; Southwold, 1966). Like the Mossi and the Swazi, the Kuranko place considerable ideological emphasis on the importance of rank in determining succession, but in practice manipulations of both vertical and lateral possibilities and the "good character" of the contender are of greatest importance (Skinner, 1964; Kuper, 1947).

4. Onians (1973) also cites traditions of generation from the legs. The Afri-

can examples are fascinating. A Masai narrative, recorded by Hollis, tells of an old man who has no wife and lives alone; his knee becomes swollen, and six months later, thinking it to be an abscess, he lances it and two children emerge: a boy and a girl (Hollis, 1905:153). Among the Moi clan of the Nandi there is a similar tradition that one of the first men (the Dorobo) gave birth to a boy and a girl. His leg became swollen, and when it at last burst open a boy emerged from the inner side of the calf and a girl from the outer side; these two are the ancestors of everyone on earth (Hollis, 1909:98). The Wakulwe (who live in the region between Lakes Nyasa and Tanganyika) believe that Ngulwe (God) "caused a child, known as Kanga Masala, to come out of the (first) woman's knee" (Melland and Cholmeley, 1912:21). Alice Werner notes that this idea reappears in a Hottentot myth where the name of the supreme being is "Wounded Knee" or "Sore Knee," a being capable of repeated rebirths and resurrections (Werner, 1925:157). The same author cites a similar example from Junod's collection of Baronga narratives, in which the mother of Bokenyane, the culture hero, was afflicted with a boil on her shinbone; the hero emerged from the boil when it finally burst (Werner, 1925:222) A Sonjo myth relates how the culture hero, Khambageu, was born from his father's swollen leg (he had no mother) (Gray, 1965:56).

The motif occurs in contemporary writing from Africa. In *The Palm-Wine Drinkard* (1952), Amos Tutuola's hero spends three years with his father-in-law in the latter's town. When he has passed three years there he notices that his wife's left-hand thumb has become swollen. One day, punctured on a palm-tree thorn, the thumb bursts open and a child emerges, able to talk "as if he was ten years of age." Within an hour the child has grown to a height of three feet, and he asks his mother, "Do you know my name?"

5. Bunker and Lewis have traced out the philological and "unconscious" connections among such words as "knee," "know," "generate," "generation," and they suggest that the leg (particularly the knee) is a kind of male womb of the "second birth" (1965:364). Onians has made an intensive study of similar connections in Roman and Greek thought, and he shows that suppleness and fluidity in the legs connoted potency and strength (1973: chapters 4 and 5). It is also noteworthy that the Presocratic terms for the sense organs ("the body") were *melea* and *quia*, i.e. "limbs" (Popper, 1969:410). The symbolic equation leg = genitals is widely recognized in psychoanalytic research (see Freeman, 1968:383–384 for a review of some of the relevant literature).

6. Among the Yoruba, for example, the *ese* (leg) is the vital part of a person in both a physical and a spiritual sense, a symbol of power and of activity. *Ese* is complementary to *ori* (inner head, "destiny"), and the realization of one's destiny depends upon the way one comports oneself (Abimbola, 1973:77).

7. Alliances between lineages through marriage also depend upon the same unimpeded movement. In a narrative not included here a man marries a woman who feigns lameness and refuses to get up off the ground and walk. Her husband is obliged to carry her home after the marriage, but later succeeds in making her walk by pretending to be dead. Her curiosity aroused, the woman gets up. The man leaps back into life and shows up the woman's sham.

Difficulties in walking (lameness or stiffness in the legs) are recurring images in the various versions of the Sunjata epic and connote a psychological "block," namely the heir's reluctance to grow up and displace his father (Jackson, 1979:122).

In other narratives, self-immobilization is a noble sacrifice which ensures the survival of a dependent or ally. One Kuranko clan myth relates how a nonruler once saved the life of a ruler (stranded and famished in a wilderness) by giving him some of the flesh from the calf of his leg to eat (Jackson, 1974:408). In a version of the Sunjata epic from the Gambia the hero severs some flesh from the calf of his leg, cooks it, and gives it to a *griot* to eat. The *griot*, whose knowledge of traditions underwrites the social order, is thus given life, although Sunjata himself must limp in pain to their destination (Innes, 1974:59-61).

8. *Gbele* can also mean expensive, i.e. hard to buy, as in the phrase *ke de gbele ke ko* ("this is more expensive than that").

> 9. Ritual practice, which always aims to facilitate *passages* and/or to authorize encounters between opposed orders, never defines beings or things otherwise than in and through the relationship it establishes practically between them, and makes the fullest possible use of the polysemy of the fundamental actions, mythic "roots" whose polysemy is partially reproduced by linguistic roots. . . . But, being broader and vaguer than the linguistic root, the mythical root lends itself to richer and more varied interplay. . . . (Bourdieu, 1977:120-121)

A similar point is made by Rappaport, who points out that rituals reduce ambiguity and provide occasions for the "transduction of information" between different systems: the psychophysiological and the social (1971:26-27).

10. This polarization of attributes which refer respectively to rank and to appearance occurs in Indo-European tales and is well illustrated by the Cinderella story, which, though chiasmus, produces an identification of beauty and high estate, ugliness and low estate. The magical transformers in the story are, as in the Kuranko case, drawn from the world of the organic (e.g. the pumpkin coach).

Chapter 6

1. Burridge arrives at a similar conclusion in his study of Tangu narratives. He writes: "It cannot be too often emphasized that within the narrative idiom neither men nor women nor children are indivisible entities, persons. Nor are they necessarily categories in a direct and formal sense. They are *puoker*, beings revealing elements or aspects or axioms or refractions of meaning" (1969:250).

2. Paul Riesman has noted the same significance of the bush in Fulani thought:

> . . . it is from the bush that man obtains his necessary subsistence, and to do this he must bow to its demands. This necessity has a double consequence: it makes man aware of his weakness in relation to it: it gives each person the possibility of individualizing himself insofar as he takes the responsibility of providing for his own needs. One may express the same idea another way: whatever the actual capabilities of the individual, when he puts himself into direct relation with the bush he thereby separates himself . . . from the rest of the community. If, on the contrary, his relation with the bush is mediated—as, for instance, with the young child who has not yet mastered his own "bush"—the individual is then in a state of dependence upon the person or persons who intervene between him and the bush. (1977:254)

3. This sequence of events and the flight of the hero is identical to an episode in the Sunjata epic which Pageard has published (1961:55-56).

4. It is not explicit in the narrative, but Keti Ferenke assured me that the brothers were nonuterine brothers, i.e. *fadennu*.

5. Gbeyekan Momori epitomizes the Kuranko ideal of goodwill and magnanimity, i.e. *morgoye* (personhood). By contrast, the other Momori is "not a person."

Chapter 7

1. This particular division of loyalties is the key issue in one of the most widely told West African dilemma tales. There is a Bura story in which a man finds seven eyes. He keeps two for himself and two for his wife. Since he has three eyes left to distribute, his problem is to decide whether he should give two to his own mother, in which case he will feel ashamed toward his wife and *her* mother, or whether he should give two to his mother-in-law, in which case he does not express his true inclinations (Clignet, 1970:150). In a comparable Bété narrative, a man is crossing a river in a boat with his wife, his mother, his wife's mother, and his sisters. If he is the only one who knows how to swim, and if the boat overturns, whom does he save? (Paulme, 1973a:526). These tales bear a remarkable resemblance to what is possibly the first recorded dilemma tale, posed by the Greek philosopher Carneades. If a man is in a shipwreck, and on the ship are his mother-in-law and his grandmother and he can only save one of the two, whom should he save, his mother-in-law or his grandmother?

2. This situation is exactly comparable to that described by Marilyn Strathern among the Mt. Hagen peoples of Papua New Guinea: "Choices presented in a woman's intermediary role . . . lead to the fear that they will exercise choice entirely for their own ends" (1972:308).

3. The situation is reminiscent of a Kofyar (Nigeria) narrative which plays up the sexual ambiguity of God's tenth wife, who, according to rumor, has a penis. Netting's commentary upon the narrative is apposite:

> When Kofyar men are confronted with the very real weapons of women, as they must be daily in the domestic round, their elaborate shields of institutionalized symbols prove to be a poor defence. The male can only fall back on his physical difference, the seat of what is known in Nigeria simply as his "power." At least he has what no woman can hope to possess, his manhood, his penis. But behind this brave assertion whispers the psyche of his society, the mythic presentiment, that perhaps she has that, too. (Netting, 1969:1045)

4. This narrative is very similar to a Gbande story from Liberia called *The man with three plaits of hair* (Dennis, 1972:233).

5. In a Kuranko narrative concerning the origins of Mande Fabori (told by Karifa Mansare of Firawa), it is said that Mande Fabori "was a *nyenne*, but a *nyenne* from the town." A strong wind carried a daughter of a chief into the bush. She conceived a child by a bush spirit. The child is born after a forty-year gestation period, and has prodigious strength and skill. But he dies if he goes to the town (washing and shaving kill him), which is why his effigy is now the way people mediate communications with him. The effigy, or Mande Fabori "house," stands on the edge of every Kuranko village, midway between the community and the wilderness.

6. Edmund Leach's comments on the ambiguous status of women are pertinent here:

Every married woman first joins the lineage group as an alien. She is intrinsically evil; a foreign object, a sexual object, dirty. But in due course she becomes the mother of new members of the lineage. In this second capacity she is intrinsically good, the very criterion of virtue and cleanliness, the antithesis of a sexual object. The moral polarity thus involves the following equivalents

wife		sexual		dirty		sinful
:		:		:		
mother		asexual		clean		sinless

(Leach, 1976:74–75)

Pasquier makes a comparable point in his analysis of ambiguity of women among the Mossi (1975:695–696).

Chapter 8

1. In Kabylia (Algeria) social conformity is a matter of respecting rhythms, keeping pace, not falling out of line. "Respect for collective rhythms implies respect for *the* rhythm that is appropriate to each action—neither excessive haste nor sluggishness. . . . A man must walk with a measured pace (*ikthal uqudmis*) neither lagging behind nor running like a dancer, a shallow, frivolous way to behave, unworthy of a man of honour" (Bourdieu, 1977:162).

2. For polygyny rates among the Kuranko see Jackson (1977b:140).

3. "Mythical thought for its part is imprisoned in the events and experiences which it never tires of ordering and re-ordering in its search to find them a meaning. But it also acts as a liberator by its protest against the idea that anything can be meaningless . . ." (Lévi-Strauss, 1966:22).

4. Within Africa an exact parallel is found in the Lega (Zaire) notion of *busoga,* "which expresses a combination of social, moral, and physical distinction" including poise, equity, moderation, and generosity of spirit in the exercise of authority (Biebuyck, 1973:128–132).

5. Like the LoDagaa, Ashanti, and Tallensi of Ghana, the Kuranko have no one word for stepparent (see Goody, 1976:52). In his study of a Hausa tale, William Bascom refers to the bereaved girl's mother's co-wife as "stepmother," and he explicitly compares this tale to the Indo-European story of Cinderella (Bascom, 1972). As Goody points out, Cinderella is largely a European tale and it is "plain Cinderella could not have been invented in a society without stepmothers or hypergamous marriage" (Goody, 1976:55). Although, like Bascom, I use the term "stepmother," it should be understood that the choice of the word reflects my wish to avoid the more accurate but cumbersome "mother's co-wife."

6. This ambivalence is powerfully and metaphorically conveyed in the references to succoring and killing in the Lozi song:

He who kills me, who will it be but my kinsman,
He who succors me, who will it be but my kinsman

(Gluckman, quoted in Freeman, 1973:115).

7. "Seed" (*kole*) in Kuranko implies the essence of a thing, its substance, its intrinsic quality. Thus *saan kole* (lit. "seed/bone of the sky") means "the empyrean" and *dugu kole* (lit. "seed/bone of the ground") means "the bare ground."

Chapter 9

1. In his preface to *Robinson Crusoe,* Defoe suggests that the story is both allegorical and historical (Watt, 1972:100).

2. In his study of Akan ethics, J.B. Danquah outlines a similar set of ideas. "What the Akan take to be the good is the family. . . ." This maxim summarizes entirely the Akan notion of the good. The family, i.e. the interests of the community, is the supreme good. The ideal is beneficence (*yiyeyo*)—"doing good, active love and prosperity" and not merely impersonal love or passive benevolence (Danquah, 1944:ix-x).

3. Such a view is not uncommon among preliterate peoples. A. Irving Hallowell has shown that in Ojibwa thought and myth the category of being is "by no means limited to *human* being"; it can include ancestors, supernatural beings, and both animate and inanimate things (Hallowell, 1969:51–52). In his study of Chumash (California) oral narratives, Thomas Blackburn outlines a personalistic worldview in which plants, animals, birds, celestial bodies, and natural forces are all part of the social universe to which man belongs (1975:66). Writing of New Guinea, Peter Lawrence shows that it would be impertinent to distinguish between the sphere of the supernatural and that of the natural since gods and spirits are just as much a part of the order of nature as are birds, animals, and totems (Lawrence, 1967:12).

4. This is reminiscent of Navaho thought, where a balance between good and evil is achieved through ritual action; illness is a result of disharmony, and curing rites not only affect the sick person but restore harmony to the universe (Kluckholn, 1949:362–364).

5. Each culture contains also the negation of its manifest pattern and nuclear values, through a tacit affirmation of contrary latent patterns and marginal values. *The complete real pattern of a culture is a product of a functional interplay between officially affirmed and officially negated patterns possessing mass"* (Devereux, 1967:212, author's emphasis).

6. Lawrence Durrell's *Alexandria Quartet* is a notable exception and marks the beginning of a new phase in the development of the novel.

7. The first stanza of Robert Henryson's *Morall Fabillis of Esope the Phrygian* is an eloquent comment upon this principle of artifice (my translation).

> Thocht feinyeit fabils of ald poetre
> Be not al grunded upon truth, yit than
> Thair polite termes of sweit rhetore
> Richt pleasand ar unto the eir of man;
> And als the caus that thay first began
> Was to repreif the haill misleving
> Off man be figure of ane uther thing.

> (Though feigned fables of old poetry
> Are not all grounded upon truth, yet
> Their polished expressions of sweet rhetoric
> Are extremely pleasing to our ear;
> Also the cause why they first began:
> To reprove man's entire wrong-living
> By analogy with some other thing).

8. In the author's preface to *Moll Flanders* (the first English novel), Defoe pretends that Moll is a real person, and that his novel is based upon her autobiography, shoddy and uncouth in style, which came into his hands.

Sterne employs another device: when questioned about the design of his strange book, Tristram Shandy says "Ask my pen; it governs me; I govern not it." In a series of comments which follow his novel *Moravagine*, Blaise Cendrars discusses how he wrote the work. He reports on an experience which many fiction writers have, of being taken over by the characters and becoming the tool of a "mysterious other" (Cendrars, 1956:222–223). Malcolm Lowry confesses a similar feeling in a letter to Conrad Aiken on the writing of *Under the Volcano*: "I do not so much feel as if I am writing this book as that *I am myself being written*" (cited in Costa, 1972:23, emphasis in text). The use of personae is another way of disengaging a work from subjectivity, as are various rhetorical devices such as passive voice and feigned objectivity. The manner in which the Kuranko attribute their narratives to divine or ancestral inspiration has its counterpart in the tendency of many European writers and scholars to father ideas onto false sources. In Wolfram's *Parzifal,* for instance, the chief source was Chrétien's romance *Li Contes del Graal.* But six times in the course of his work, Wolfram refers to Kyot as his source in addition to Chrétien. He even refers to Kyot's sources. However, "No such scholar-poet is known to history" and it is probable that Kyot is Wolfram's invention (Mustard and Passage, 1961:xxiv). In the Middle Ages there was a strong tendency to argue from a text or proverb. Individuals did not hazard moral sentences of their own, and authority was always sought in external sources such as proverbs, maxims, texts, and biblical examples (Huizinga, 1972:218–221).

Glossary of Kuranko Words

Kuranko Terms Frequently Referred to in the Text

Ala, also Altala	Allah; supreme being; creator god
baraka	blessedness, good fortune
baramuse, also *baramusu, bare*	senior wife; "beloved wife," "preferred wife"
bese (pl. *besenu*)	magical medicine
bilakore	uninitiated boy
bimba kumenu	ancestral words (*kuma* = word)
biran	affine
biranke	male affine (*ke* = male)
biranye	affinity
biriye	the rite of initiation
bontigi	household head; "house owner" (*tigi* = master, owner)
dan gbere, also *den gbere*	real child; own child
danka	curse
dan yeli, also *halale dan*	blood child
dege	rice flour, used in sacrifices
den fole	first child
den ke sare	firstborn male child
den na ban	lastborn
di	sweet
dienaye	friendship
dimusu sire	firstborn female child
dinyon	husband's sister; brother's wife
dogoma, also *doge, dogo, dogone*	junior, younger, smaller; younger sibling; *also* Hare (the trickster)
don, dondon	quiet; silence
due	men's cult
fa	father; sir
fadan(pl. *fadennu*)	father's son; half brother; ortho-cousin
fadenye	relationship between half brothers; rivalry

fafei	initiation lodge; "bush house"
fa keli meenu	"father one persons"; nonuterine siblings
fanke	power; strong, powerful ("having authority")
faragbaran	"dividing rock"; a flat, exposed expanse of rock, usually granite
Fasan	Hare, the trickster
Fasuluku	Hyena
fele	a fetish
ferensola	"town of twins"; the Kuranko area as a whole; nation
fina, also *finaba*	bard; genealogist; orator
fira	bush, wilderness
fira morgo	bush person
fisa mantiye	relative superiority/inferiority in status
fol' morgonu ko dane	the first people; ancestors
fona	millet
fuguriye	misfortune, cursedness
gbe	white; pure; clear; true
gbele	enduring; hard; strong
gbeleye	strength
gberinya	junior wife
gberinya musu	junior co-wife
gbeyekan	"pureness of language"; pure-hearted, honest, straightforward, open
hake	retributive justice; "guilt"
hankili, also *hankilimaiye*	cleverness; understanding; gumption; common sense
hankili ma	stupid (often applied to Hyena)
jeli, also *jeliba*	xylophonist; praise-singer
kafiri	infidel, unbeliever
ke	male
kebile	subclan or lineage; "family"
ke dugu	male domain
ke koe	action
kelne	"one little"; all-alone; orphan
kemine	young initiated man
kemine gbana	unmarried man; idler, drifter
kende	healthy; well-behaved
kendeye	health; propriety
kene	love; friendship
kere (pl. *kerenu*)	cooperative work group; a system of production, distribution, and exchange
kile (pl. *kilenu*)	path
kin	goodness, beauty; good, beautiful
kine (cf. *kore*)	cooked rice
kinenu	elders
kiraiye	sickness, illness
kore (cf. *kine*)	uncooked rice; "elder," "senior"
koro	elder, senior, bigger; *also* elder sibling; Hyena

koroya	elderhood
kuma	word
kuma kore	"venerable speech"; traditions; words of wisdom; "old talk"
lakira	abode of ancestral spirits (cf. Arabic *al-akhira*)
lankona	a unit of value in barter exchange
latelan	straightforward; true
luiye	courtyard, compound
lutigi	luiye headman
m'berin	my mother's brother; sometimes used as a term of address by a wife of her husband, particularly if the marriage is avuncular
m'biran	my in-law
m'bo	my companion
m'fa	my father; "sir"
m'fannu	sirs
miran	presence; self-possession, dignity, confidence, bearing; charisma
mirannu	personal belongings; personal property; containers
miria koe	thought
miriye yugume	bad thought (*yugu* = ugly, bad)
morgo	person
morgo ba	"big men"; elders
morgo di keye	"sweet person"; a sociable person
morgo dugune	devious person
morgo fiennu	enemies, aliens
morgo ma kela	"not a person"; an unsociable person
morgo telne	"straight up-and-down" person
morgoye	personhood; mindfulness of others; magnanimity
musu	woman, female
musu ba	"big woman"; initiated woman
musu dugu	female domain
musu korone	old woman
na	mother
na keliye	motherhood; "mother oneness"
na keli meenu	uterine siblings; "mother one persons"
nakelinyorgoye	kinship; "mother one partnership"
na kura	"new mother"; mother's co-wife
n'dogo, also *n'doge*	my younger sibling; my junior
n'koro	my elder sibling; my elder
nie	life energy, life-force
ninne	a person's shadow; "little life"
noe	secular power, force
numorgo	husband's (wife's) younger brother; joking partner
numorgoya tolan	joking relationship
nyenne	bush spirit(s); djinn
nyere	self
nyere morgoye	selfhood
nyemakale	lowest ranked estate, comprising *fina*s and *jeli*s

sabu	moral agency; cause, reason
sanaku	joking partner
sanakuiye tolon	interclan joking alliance, partnership
sarane	parable, proverb, adage
sawura	destiny, fate
segere	women's cult (perhaps derived from French-speaking Guinea: *segere* = secret)
sue	town; domain of man
suma	grain; germ of anything, e.g. *sumafan* = "secret thing," cult association or secret society
sumburi	divorce; *also* elopement
sundan	stranger, guest; suitor
sundanye	strangerhood
sundu kunye ma	backyard; rubbish heap; marginal domestic area
sunkuron	young, newly initiated woman
tene	father's sister; aunt
tersan (pl. *tersannu*)	sister (if man speaking); more generally sibling of the opposite sex
tersan koe	brother-sister incest
tersanye	relationship between brother and sister
tianye	weakness, lassitude; irresponsibility, indifference
tigi	master, owner (cf. *bontigi, lutigi*)
tilei (pl. *tileinu*)	story, folktale, narrative
til'sale	storyteller
ture	a species of tree, branches of which are placed over the lower part of a grave
yelemakoe	laughter act, joke, jest
yiri	steadiness of mind and body
yiriyara	imbalance
yugu	ugly; bad
yuse	heart; temperament
yuse gbele	strong heart

References

Abelson, R. 1977. *Persons: A Study in Philosophical Psychology.* Macmillan, London.

Abimbola, W. 1973. "The Yoruba concept of personality." In G. Dieterlen (ed.), *La notion de personne in Afrique noire* (pp. 72–89). Centre National de la Recherche Scientifique, Paris.

Abrahamsson, H. 1951. *The Origin of Death.* Studia Ethnographica Upsaliensia, no.3, Upsala.

Achebe, C. 1975. *Morning Yet on Creation Day: Essays.* Heinemann, London.

Ames, D. (recorder) 1950. "Lion of Manding: A Wolof epic." In H. Courlander, *A Treasury of African Folklore* (pp. 71–78). Crown, New York.

Ashby, W. R. 1964. *An Introduction to Cybernetics.* Chapman and Hall, London.

Auerbach, E. 1959. "Figura" (translated by R. Manheim). In *Scenes from the Drama of European Literature* (pp. 11–76). Meridian Books, New York.

Barnes, H. 1961. *The Literature of Possibility.* Tavistock, London.

Barthes, R. 1967. *Elements of Semiology.* Cape, London.

Bascom, W. R. 1972. "Cinderella in Africa." *Journal of the Folklore Institute*, 9:54–70.

———. 1975. *African Dilemma Tales.* Mouton, The Hague.

Bateson, G. 1958. *Naven.* Stanford University Press, Stanford.

———. 1973. *Steps to an Ecology of Mind.* Paladin, London.

Bauman, R. 1975. "Verbal art as performance." *American Anthropologist*, 77(2):290–311.

Beidelman, T. O. 1961. "Hyena and rabbit: A Kaguru representation of matrilineal relations." *Africa*, 31:61–74.

———. 1963. "Further adventures of hyena and rabbit: The folktale as a sociological model." *Africa*, 33:54–69.

———. 1970. "Myth, legend and oral history: A Kaguru traditional text." *Anthropos*, 65:74–97.

Ben-Amos, D. 1975. *Sweet Words: Storytelling Events in Benin.* Institute for the Study of Human Values, Philadelphia.

Benjamin, W. 1970. *Illuminations* (edited and with an introduction by Hannah Arendt; translated by H. Zohn). Cape, London.

Berger, P.L., Berger, B., and Kellner, H. 1974. *The Homeless Mind.* Penguin Books, Harmondsworth.

Bergson, H. 1911. *Laughter: An Essay on the Meaning of the Comic.* Macmillan, London.

Bernstein, B. 1973. *Class, Codes and Control* (v.I: "Theoretical studies towards a sociology of language"). Paladin, London.

Bernus, E. 1956. "Kobané: un village malinké du Haut Niger." *Cahiers d'Outre-Mer*, 9:239–262.

Berry, J. 1961. *Spoken Art in West Africa*. Oxford University Press, London.

Bettelheim, B. 1978. *The Uses of Enchantment: The Meaning and Importance of Fairy Tales*. Penguin Books, Harmondsworth.

Biebuyck, D. 1973. *Lega Culture: Art, Initiation, and Moral Philosophy among a Central African People*. University of California Press, Berkeley.

Bird, C. 1971. "Oral art of the Mande." In C. T. Hodge (ed.), *Papers on the Manding* (pp. 15–25). Mouton, The Hague.

Bisilliat, J. 1976. "Village diseases and bush diseases in Songhay: An essay in description and classification with a view to a typology" (translated by J.B. Loudon). In A.S.A. monograph 13, J.B. Loudon (ed)., *Social Anthropology and Medicine*. Academic Press, London.

Blackburn, T. 1975. *December's Child: A Book of Chumash Oral Narratives*. University of California Press, Berkeley.

Booth A. H. 1960. *Small Mammals of West Africa*. Longmans, London.

Bourdieu, P. 1977. *Outline of a Theory of Practice* (translated by R. Nice). Cambridge University Press, Cambridge.

Brain, R. 1977. *Friends and Lovers*. Paladin, London.

Briggs, K. M. 1967. *The Fairies in Tradition and Literature*. Routledge and Kegan Paul, London.

Bruner, J. 1976. "Nature and uses of immaturity." In J. S. Bruner, A. Jolly, and K. Sylva (eds.), *Play: Its Role in Development and Evolution* (pp. 28–64). Penguin Books, Harmondsworth.

Bunker, H. A., and Lewis, B. D. 1965. "A psychoanalytic notation on the root GN, KN, CN." In G. B. Wilbur and W. Muensterberger (eds.), *Psychoanalysis and Culture*. International Universities Press, New York.

Burridge, K. 1969. *Tangu Traditions*. Clarendon Press, Oxford.

Caillois, R. 1961. *Man, Play, and Games* (translated by M. Barash). Free Press, New York.

Calame-Griaule, G. 1963. "The oral tradition as an art form in African culture." *Présence Africaine*, 47:197–214.

Calame-Griaule, G., and Ligers, Z. 1961. "L'homme-hyène dans la tradition soudanaise." *L'Homme*, 1(2):89–118.

Camara, S. 1972. "Introduction à l'étude des 'tali Mandenka'." Summary of a paper delivered at the Conference on the Manding, School of Oriental and African Studies, London, 1972.

Carvalho-Neto, P. de. 1972. *Folklore and Psychoanalysis* (translated by J. M. P. Wilson). University of Miami Press, Coral Gables, Florida.

Cendrars, B. 1956. *Moravagine*. Grasset, Paris.

Clignet, R. 1970. *Many Wives, Many Powers: Authority and Power in Polygynous Families*. Northwestern University Press, Evanston.

Cole, M., Gay, J., Glick, J. A., and Sharp, D. W. (in association with T. Ciborowski, F. Frankel, J. Kellemu, and D. F. Lancy). 1971. *The Cultural Context of Learning and Thinking: Exploration in Experimental Anthropology*. Basic Books, New York.

Costa, R. H. 1972. *Malcolm Lowry*. Twayne, New York.

Courlander, H. 1975. *A Treasury of African Folklore*. Crown, New York.

Cronise, F. M., and Ward, H. M. 1903. *Cunnie Rabbit, Mr. Spider, and the Other Beef: West African Folktales*. Swan and Sonnenschein; Dutton, New York.

Cullen, J. M. 1966. "Reduction of ambiguity through ritualization." In J. Huxley (ed.), *A Discussion of Ritualization of Behaviour in Animals and Man* (pp. 363–374). Philosophical Transactions of the Royal Society, series B, v.251, London.

Danquah, J. B. 1944. *The Akan Doctrine of God, a Fragment of Gold Coast Ethics and Religion.* Lutterworth Press, London.

Davis, R. 1974. "Tolerance and intolerance of ambiguity in Northern Thai myth and ritual." *Ethnology,* 13(1):1–24.

———. 1977. "Myth, play, and alchemy." *Canberra Anthropology,* 1(1):15–23.

Dawood, N. J. 1968. "Introduction" to *The Koran.* Penguin Books, Harmondsworth.

Defoe, D. 1840. *The Fortunes and Misfortunes of the Famous Moll Flanders.* Thomas Tegg, London.

Deng, F. M. 1974. *Dinka Folktales: African Stories from the Sudan.* Holmes and Meier, New York.

Dennis, B. G. 1972. *The Gbandes: A People of the Liberian Hinterland.* Nelson-Hall, Chicago.

Devereux, G. 1948. "Mohave coyote tales." *Journal of American Folklore,* 61:233–255.

———. 1961. "Art and mythology, part 1: A general theory." In B. Kaplan (ed.), *Studying Personality Cross-culturally.* Harper and Row, New York.

———. 1967. *From Anxiety to Method in the Behavioural Sciences.* Mouton, The Hague.

———. 1969. "Normal and abnormal: The key concepts of ethnopsychiatry." In W. Muensterberger (ed.), *Man and His Culture: Psychoanalytic Anthropology after Totem and Taboo* (pp. 113–136). Tapling, New York.

Diamond, S. 1972. "Introduction" to P. Radin, *The Trickster: A Study in American Indian Mythology.* Schocken Books, New York.

Douglas, M. 1968. "The social control of cognition: Some factors in joke perception." *Man* (new series), 3(3):361–376.

Dover, K. J. 1974. *Greek Popular Morality in the Time of Plato and Aristotle.* Blackwell, Oxford.

Dumont, L. 1965. "The modern conception of the individual." *Contributions to Indian Sociology* 8:13–61.

———. 1971. "Religion, politics, and society in the individualistic universe." The Henry Myers lecture 1970, *Proceedings of the Royal Anthropological Institute for 1970,* R.A.I., London 1971:31–41.

———. 1972. *Homo hierarchicus.* Paladin, London.

Dundes, A. 1971. "The making and breaking of friendship as a structural frame in African folk tales." In P. Maranda and E. Köngäs Maranda (eds.), *Structural Analysis of Oral Tradition* (pp. 171–185). University of Pennsylvania Press, Philadelphia.

———. 1975. *Analytical Essays in Folklore.* Mouton, The Hague.

Dupire, M. 1963. "The position of women in a pastoral society (the Fulani WoDaaBe nomads of the Niger)." In D. Paulme (ed.), *Women of Tropical Africa.* University of California Press, Berkeley.

Duvignaud, J. 1972. *The Sociology of Art* (translated by T. Wilson). Paladin, London.

Eliade, M. 1964. *Myth and Reality.* Allen and Unwin, London.

Eliot, T. S. 1951. *Selected Essays*. Faber and Faber, London.

Empson, W. 1953. (3rd ed.) *Seven Types of Ambiguity*. Chatto and Windus, London.

Erikson, E. H. 1966. "Ontogeny of ritualization in man." In J. Huxley (ed.), *A Discussion of Ritualization of Behaviour in Animals and Man* (pp. 337–349). Philosophical Transactions of the Royal Society, series B, v.251, London.

——. 1972. "Play and actuality." In M. W. Piers (ed.), *Play and Development*. W. W. Norton, New York.

Evans-Pritchard, E. E. 1967. *The Zande Trickster*. Clarendon Press, Oxford.

Faladé, S. 1963. "Women of Dakar and the surrounding urban area." In D. Paulme (ed.), *Women of Tropical Africa* (translated by H.W. Wright) (pp. 217–229). University of California Press, Berkeley.

Fernandez, J. W. 1971. "Persuasions and performances: of the beast in every body . . . and the metaphors of everyman." In C. Geertz (ed.) *Myth, Symbol, and Culture* (pp. 39–60). W. W. Norton, New York.

Finnegan, R. 1967. *Limba Stories and Story-telling*. Clarendon Press, Oxford.

——. 1970. *Oral Literature in Africa*. Clarendon Press, Oxford.

Fletcher, A. 1964. *Allegory: The Theory of a Symbolic Mode*. Cornell University Press, Ithaca.

Forde, D. 1958. *The Context of Belief: A Consideration of Fetishism among the Yakö*. Liverpool University Press, Liverpool.

Freeman, J. D. 1968. "Thunder, blood, and the nicknaming of God's creatures." *Psychoanalytic Quarterly*, 37:353–399.

——. 1973. "Kinship, attachment, behaviour and the primary bond." In J. Goody (ed.), *The Character of Kinship* (pp. 109–119). Cambridge University Press, Cambridge.

Frye, N. 1963. *Fables of Identity: Studies in Poetic Mythology*. Harcourt, Brace and World, New York.

——. 1966. *Anatomy of Criticism*. Atheneum, New York.

Gamble, D. P. n.d. Economic conditions in two Mandinka villages: Kerewan and Keneba. Report to the Government of the Gambia, Colonial Office, London.

Gluckman, M. 1955. *The Judicial Process among the Barotse*. Manchester University Press, Manchester.

——. 1956. *Custom and Conflict in Africa*. Blackwell, Oxford.

Godelier, M. 1977. *Perspectives in Marxist Anthropology* (translated by R. Brain). Cambridge University Press, Cambridge.

Goldmann, L. 1975. *Towards a Sociology of the Novel* (translated by A. Sheridan). Tavistock, London.

Goody, J. 1966. "Introduction" to J. Goody (ed.), *Succession to High Office*. Cambridge University Press, Cambridge.

——. 1972. *The Myth of the Bagre*. Clarendon Press, Oxford.

——. 1976. *Production and Reproduction: A Comparative Study of the Domestic Domain*. Cambridge University Press, Cambridge.

——. 1977. *The Domestication of the Savage Mind*. Cambridge University Press, Cambridge.

Gray, R. F. 1965. "Some parallels in Sonjo and Christian mythology." In M. Fortes and G. Dieterlen (eds.), *African Systems of Thought*. Oxford University Press, London.

Hallowell, A. I. 1969. "Ojibwa ontology, behavior, and world view." In S. Diamond (ed.), *Primitive Views of the World*. Columbia University Press, New York.

Harris, W. T. and Sawyerr, H. 1969. *The Springs of Mende Belief and Conduct*. Sierra Leone University Press, Freetown.

Henryson, R. 1974. *Poems* (selected and edited by C. Elliott). Clarendon Press, Oxford.

Herskovits, M. J. and Herskovits, F. S. 1958. *Dahomean Narrative: A Cross-cultural Analysis*. Northwestern University Press, Evanston.

Hollis, A. C. 1905. *The Masai, Their Language and Folklore*. Clarendon Press, Oxford.

——. 1909. *The Nandi, Their Language and Folklore*. Clarendon Press, Oxford.

Hopkins, N. S. 1971. "Mandinka social organization." In C. T. Hodge, (ed.), *Papers on the Manding*. Indiana University Publications, Research Center for the Language Sciences, Bloomington, Indiana.

Horner, G. R. 1966. "A Bulu folktale." In M. Jacobs (compiler) and J. Greenway (ed.), *The Anthropologist Looks at Myth* (pp. 145–156). University of Texas Press, Austin.

Huet, M. 1978. *The Dance, Art and Ritual of Africa* (photographs by M. Huet; text by Jean-Louis Paudrat). Collins, London.

Huizinga, J. 1972. *The Waning of the Middle Ages* (translated by F. Hopman). Penguin Books, Harmondsworth.

Hymes, D. 1971. "The contribution of folklore to sociolinguistic research." In A. Paredes and R. Bauman (eds.), *Towards New Perspectives in Folklore* (pp. 42–50). University of Texas Press, Austin.

——. 1975. "Breakthrough into performance." In D. Ben-Amos and K. S. Goldstein (eds.), *Folklore: Performance and Communication* (pp. 11–74). Mouton, The Hague.

Innes, G. 1964. "Some features of theme and style in Mende folktales." *Sierra Leone Language Review*, 3:6–19.

——. 1965. "The function of song in Mende folktales." *Sierra Leone Language Review*, 4:54–63.

——. 1974. *Sunjata: Three Mandinka Versions*. School of Oriental and African Studies, London.

Jackson, M. 1974. "The structure and significance of Kuranko clanship." *Africa*, 44(4):397–415.

——. 1975. "Structure and event: Witchcraft confession among the Kuranko." *Man* (new series), 10:387–403.

——. 1977a. "Sacrifice and social structure among the Kuranko." *Africa*, 47(1):41–49 (parts 1 and 2), and 47(2):123–139 (part 3).

——. 1977b. *The Kuranko: Dimensions of Social Reality in a West African Society*. Hurst, London.

——. 1978a. "An approach to Kuranko divination." *Human Relations*, 31(2):117–138.

——.1978b. "The identity of the dead: Aspects of mortuary ritual in a West African society." *Cahiers d'études Africaines*, 66–67 (2–3):271–297.

——. 1978c. "Ambivalence and the last-born: Birth order position in convention and myth." *Man* (new series), 13:341–361.

———. 1979. "Prevented successions: A commentary upon a Kuranko narrative." In R. Hook (ed.), *Fantasy and Symbol: Studies in Anthropological Interpretation*. Academic Press, London.

Jędrej, M. C. 1976. "Medicine, fetish, and secret society in a West African culture." *Africa*, 46(3):247–257.

Johnston, H. A. S. 1966. *A Selection of Hausa Stories*. Clarendon Press, Oxford.

Kant, I. 1956. *Groundwork of the Metaphysic of Morals*, (translated by H.J. Paton). Hutchinson, London.

Kaufmann, W. 1956. "Introduction" to W. Kaufmann (ed.), *Existentialism from Dostoevsky to Sartre* (pp. 11–51). Meridian Books, New York.

Kilson, M. D. de B. 1961. "Social relationships in Mende Domeisia." *Sierra Leone Studies* (new series), 15:168–172.

Kluckholn, C. 1949. "The philosophy of the Navaho Indians." In F. S. C. Northrop (ed.), *Ideological Differences and World Order: Studies in the Philosophy and Science of the World's Cultures* (pp. 356–384). Yale University Press, New Haven.

Koestler, A. 1964. *The Act of Creation*. Hutchinson, London.

Kohlberg, L. 1969. "Stage and sequence: The cognitive-developmental approach to socialization." In D. A. Goslin (ed.) *Handbook of Socialization Theory and Research* (pp. 347–480). Rand McNally, Chicago.

Kuper, H. 1947. *An African Aristocracy: Rank among the Swazi*. Oxford University Press, London.

Labouret, H. and Travélé, M. 1928. "Le Theâtre Mandingue." *Africa*, 1:73–97.

Laing, R. D. 1967. *The Politics of Experience and the Bird of Paradise*. Penguin Books, Harmondsworth.

Lambo, T. A. 1961. "Growth of African children (psychological aspects)." In T. A. Lambo (ed.) *First Pan-African Psychiatric Conference*, Abeokuta, Nigeria, 12–18 Nov, 1961.

Lamphere, L. 1974. "Strategies, cooperation, and conflict among women in domestic groups." In M. Z. Rosaldo and L. Lamphere (eds.), *Women, Culture, and Society* (pp. 97–112). Stanford University Press, Stanford.

Laughlin, C. D. and d'Aquili, E. G. 1974. *Biogenetic Structuralism*. Columbia University Press, New York.

Lawrence, P. 1967. *Road Belong Cargo*. Melbourne University Press, Melbourne.

Leach, E. R. 1969. *Genesis as Myth and Other Essays*. Cape, London.

———. 1976. *Culture and Communication: The Logic by which Symbols Are Connected*. Cambridge University Press, Cambridge.

Lévi-Strauss, C. 1963. *Structural Anthropology v.1* (translated by C. Jacobsen and B. Grundfest-Schoepf). Basic Books, New York.

———. 1966. *The Savage Mind (La Pensée sauvage)*. Weidenfeld and Nicolson, London.

———. 1967. *The Scope of Anthropology*. Cape, London.

———. 1968. "Le triangle culinaire." *L'Arc*, 26(1):19–29.

———. 1969. *The Elementary Structures of Kinship* (translated by J. H. Bell, J. R. von Sturmer, and R. Needham). Eyre and Spottiswoode, London.

———. 1970. *The Raw and the Cooked: Introduction to a Science of Mythology 1* (translated by J. and D. Weightman). Cape, London.

———. 1973. *From Honey to Ashes: Introduction to a Science of Mythology 2* (translated by J. and D. Weightman). Cape, London.

————. 1977. *Structural Anthropology v.2* (translated by M. Layton). Allen Lane, London.

————. 1978. *The Origin of Table Manners, Introduction to a Science of Mythology 3* (translated by J. and D. Weightman). Cape, London.

Leynaud, E. 1966. "Fraternités d'âge et sociétés de culture dans la Haute-Vallée du Niger." *Cahiers d'études Africaines*, 6:41–68.

Lukács, G. 1971. *The Theory of the Novel* (translated by A. Bostock). Merlin Press, London.

Lundin, R. W. 1953. *An Objective Psychology of Music*. Ronald Press, New York.

Macfarlane, A. 1978. *The Origins of English Individualism: The Family, Property and Social Transition*. Cambridge University Press, Cambridge.

MacPherson, C. B. 1962. *The Political Theory of Possessive Individualism, Hobbes to Locke*. Clarendon Press, Oxford.

Malinowski, B. 1963. *Sex, Culture, and Myth*. Hart-Davis, London.

————. 1974. *Magic, Science, and Religion and other Essays*. Souvenir Press, London.

Mbiti, J. S. 1966. *Akamba Stories*. Clarendon Press, Oxford.

Medawar, P. B. 1976. "Does ethology throw any light on human behaviour?" In P. P. G. Bateson and R. A. Hinde (eds.), *Growing Points in Ethology* (pp. 497–506). Cambridge University Press, Cambridge.

Meggitt, M. J. 1976. "A duplicity of demons: Sexual and familial roles expressed in Western Enga stories." In P. Brown and G. Buchbinder (eds.), *Man and Woman in the New Guinea Highlands*. A special publication of the American Anthropological Association, n.8:63–85.

Melland, F. H., and Cholmeley, E. H. 1912. *Through the Heart of Africa*. London.

Merleau-Ponty, M. 1962. *Phenomenology of Perception* (translated by C. Smith). Routledge and Kegan Paul, London.

————. 1965. *The Structure of Behaviour* (translated by A.L. Fisher). Methuen, London.

Meyer, L. B. 1956. *Emotion and Meaning in Music*. University of Chicago Press, Chicago.

Monteil, C. 1905. *Contes Soudanais*. G. Leroux, Paris.

Montrat, M. 1935. "Notes sur les Malinkés du Sankaran." *Outre-Mer*, 1935, pp.107–127.

Mudge-Paris, D. B. 1930. "Tales and riddles from Freetown, Sierra Leone." *Journal of American Folklore*, 43:317–321.

Mustard, H. M., and Passage, C. E. 1961. "Introduction" to *Parzifal*, by Wolfram von Eschenbach. Vintage, New York.

Nadel, S. F. 1964. "Morality and language among the Nupe." In D. Hymes (ed.), *Language in Culture and Society: A Reader in Linguistics and Anthropology* (pp. 264–266). Harper and Row, New York.

Netting, R. McC. 1969. "Women's weapons: The politics of domesticity among the Kofyar." *American Anthropologist*, 71:1037–1046.

Niane, D. T. 1965. *Sundiata: An Epic of Old Mali* (translated by G. D. Pickett). Longmans, London.

Nicolaus, M. 1973. "Foreword" to K. Marx, *Grundrisse* (translated by M. Nicolaus). Penguin Books, London.

O'Connor, P. 1952. "Ethnocentrism, 'intolerance of ambiguity,' and abstract reasoning ability." *Journal of Abnormal Psychology*, 47:526–530.

Onians, R. B. 1973. *The Origins of European Thought*. Arno Press, New York.

Pageard, R. 1961. "Soundiata Keita and the oral tradition." *Présence Africaine*, 8:53–72.

Parsons, R. T. 1964. *Religion in an African Society: A Study of the Religion of the Kono People of Sierra Leone*. E. J. Brill, Leiden.

Pasquier, A. 1975. "Interpretation symbolique d'un conte Mosi." *Cahiers d'études Africaines*, 15:669–698.

Paulme, D. 1961. "Litterature orale et comportements sociaux en Afrique noire." *L'Homme*, 1:37–49).

———. 1963a. "Introduction" to D. Paulme (ed.), *Women of Tropical Africa* (translated by H.W. Wright). University of California Press, Berkeley.

———. 1963b. "Un conte de fées Africain: Le garçon travesti ou Joseph en Afrique." *L'Homme*, 3(2):5–21.

———. 1964. *Les gens du riz*. Plon, Paris.

———. 1973a. "Oral literature and social behaviour in Black Africa" (a translation of D. Paulme, 1961). In E. Skinner (ed.), *Peoples and Cultures of Africa* (pp. 525–542). Natural History Press, Garden City, New York.

———. 1973b. "Blood pacts, age classes, and castes in Black Africa." In P. Alexandre (ed.), *French Perspectives in African Studies*. Oxford University Press, London.

———. 1975a. "Typologie des contes Africaines du decepteur." *Cahiers d'études Africaines*, 15:569–600.

———. 1975b. "Hyene, monture de lievre (vingt versions d'un conte Africain)". *Cahiers d'études Africaines*, 15:619–633).

Perls, F. S., Hefferline, R. F., and Goodman, P. 1951. *Gestalt Therapy*. The Julian Press, New York.

Piaget, J. 1932. *The Moral Judgment of the Child*. The Free Press, Glencoe.

Popper, K. 1969. *Conjectures and Refutation*. Routledge and Kegan Paul, London.

Popper, K., and Eccles, J. 1974. "Falsifiability and freedom." In F. Elders (compiler and interviewer), *Reflexive Waters*. Souvenir Press, London.

Propp, V. 1968. *Morphology of the Folktale*. University of Texas Press, Austin.

Radin, P. 1952. *African Folktales and Sculpture*. Folktales selected and edited by P. Radin with the collaboration of E. Marvel. Bollingen series 32, Pantheon, New York.

Rank, O. 1959. *The Myth of the Birth of the Hero*. Vintage, New York.

Rappaport, R. A. 1971. "The sacred in human evolution." *Annual Review of Ecology and Systematics*, 2:23–44.

Rattray, Capt. R. S. 1928. "Some aspects of West African folk-lore." *Journal of the African Society*, 28:1–11.

———. 1930. *Akan-Ashanti Folk-tales*. Clarendon Press, Oxford.

Rawls, J. 1971. *A Theory of Justice*. Belknap Press of Harvard University Press, Cambridge, Mass.

Read, K. E. 1955. "Morality and the concept of the person among the Gahuku-Gama." *Oceania*, 25(4):233–282.

Reynolds, P. C. 1976. "Play, language, and human evolution." In J. S. Bruner, A. Jolly, and K. Sylva (eds.), *Play: Its Role in Development and Evolution* (pp. 621–635). Penguin Books, Harmondsworth.

Richards, A. 1969. "Characteristics of ethical systems in primitive human society." In F. J. Ebling (ed.), *Biology and Ethics* (pp. 23–32). Academic Press, New York.

Ricoeur, P. 1963. "Structure et herméneutique." *L'Esprit* (nouvelle série), 11:596–627.

Riesman, P. 1977. *Freedom in Fulani Social Life, an Introspective Ethnography* (translated by M. Fuller). University of Chicago Press, Chicago.

Rigby, P. 1968. "Some Gogo rituals of purification." In E. R. Leach (ed.), *Dialectic in Practical Religion* (pp. 153–178). Cambridge University Press, Cambridge.

———. 1971. "The symbolic role of cattle in Gogo ritual." In T. O. Beidelman (ed.), *The Interpretation of Culture: Essays to E. E. Evans-Pritchard* (pp. 257–291). Tavistock, London.

Rimbaud, A. 1957. *Illuminations* (translated by L. Varese). New Directions, New York.

Rouget, G. 1970. "Transcrire ou décrire? Chant Soudanais et chant fuégien" (avec collaboration avec Jean Schwarz). In J. Pouillon and P. Maranda (eds.), *Échanges et Communications*, v.1 (pp. 677–706). Mouton, The Hague.

Rowland, B. 1973. *Animals with Human Faces: A Guide to Animal Symbolism*. University of Tennessee Press, Knoxville.

Sartre, J-P. 1949. *What Is Literature?* (translated by B. Frechtman). Philosophical Library, New York.

———. 1969. "Itinerary of a thought." *New Left Review*, 58:43–66.

Sayers, E. F. 1927. "Notes on the clan or family names common in the area inhabited by Temne-speaking people." *Sierra Leone Studies* (old series), 12:14–108.

Scheub, H. 1975. *The Xhosa Ntsomi*. Clarendon Press, Oxford.

Schwab, G. 1914. "Bulu folk-tales." *Journal of American Folk-lore*, 27:266–288.

Simmel, G. 1959. "The adventure." In K. H. Wolff (ed.), *A Collection of Essays*. Ohio State University Press, Columbus.

Skinner, E. P. 1964. *The Mossi of the Upper Volta*. Stanford University Press, Stanford.

Smith, E. W., and Dale, A.M. 1968. *The Ila-speaking Peoples of Northern Rhodesia* (2 vols.). University Books, New York.

Smock, C. D. 1957. "The relationship between 'intolerance of ambiguity,' generalization, and speed of perceptual closure." *Child Development*, 28(1):27–36.

Southwold, M. 1966. "Succession to the throne in Buganda." In J. Goody (ed.), *Succession to High Office*. Cambridge University Press, Cambridge.

Stanford, W. B. 1939. *Ambiguity in Greek Literature: Studies in Theory and Practice*. Blackwell, Oxford.

———. 1968. *The Ulysses Theme: A Study in the Adaptability of a Traditional Hero* (2nd revised edition). Blackwell, Oxford.

Stanley, M. 1973. "The structures of doubt: Reflections on moral intelligibility as a problem in the sociology of knowledge." In G. W. Remmling (ed), *Towards the Sociology of Knowledge: Origin and Development of a Sociological Thought Style* (pp. 397–452). Routledge and Kegan Paul, London.

Steiner, G. 1975. *After Babel*. Oxford University Press, London.

Strathern, M. 1972. *Women in Between: Female Roles in a Male World: Mount Hagen, New Guinea*. Seminar Press, London.

Thompson, S. 1955–58. *Motif-Index of Folk Literature* (6 vols.). Indiana University Press, Bloomington.

Todorov, T. 1970. "De l'ambiguïté narrative." In J. Pouillon and P. Maranda (eds.), *Échanges et Communications*, v. 2 (pp. 913–918). Mouton, The Hague.

Trimingham, J. S. 1959. *Islam in West Africa*. Clarendon Press, Oxford.

Trivers, R. L. 1971. "The evolution of reciprocal altruism." *The Quarterly Review of Biology*, 46(1):35–57.

Turnbull, C. M. 1959. "Legends of the BaMbuti." *Journal of the Royal Anthropological Institute*, 89:45–60.

Turner, V. W. 1970 (first published 1967). *The Forest of Symbols*. Cornell University Press, Ithaca.

Tutuola, A. 1952. *The Palm-Wine Drinkard*. Faber and Faber, London.

van Lawick, H., and van Lawick-Goodall, J. 1970. *Innocent Killers*. Collins, London.

Wagner, R. 1972. *Habu: The Innovation of Meaning in Daribi Religion*. University of Chicago Press.

Watt, I. 1972. *The Rise of the Novel*. Penguin Books (in association with Chatto and Windus), Harmondsworth.

Welsford, E. 1968. *The Fool: His Social and Literary History*. Faber and Faber, London.

Werner, A. 1925. *The Mythology of All Races, v.7: Armenian and African*. Marshall Jones, Boston.

White, T. H. (translator and editor). 1954. *The Book of Beasts* (Being a translation from a Latin Bestiary of the 12th century, made and edited by T. H. White). Cape, London.

Williams, R. 1977. *Marxism and Literature*. Oxford University Press, Oxford.

Willis, R. G. 1967. "The head and the loins: Lévi-Strauss and beyond." *Man* (new series), 2:519–534.

Winnicott, D. W. 1974. *Playing and Reality*. Penguin Books. Harmondsworth.

Wober, M. 1974. "Towards an understanding of the Kiganda concept of intelligence." In J. W. Berry and P. R. Dasen (eds.), *Culture and Cognition: Readings in Cross-Cultural Psychology* (pp. 261–280). Methuen, London.

Zéraffa, M. 1976. *Fictions; The Novel and Social Reality* (translated by C. and T. Burns). Penguin Books, Harmondsworth.

List of Narratives

Index